BLACK'S NEW TESTAMENT COMMENTARIES

GENERAL EDITOR: HENRY CHADWICK, D.D.

THE GOSPEL ACCORDING TO ST. MATTHEW

A COMMENTARY ON
THE GOSPEL ACCORDING TO
ST. MATTHEW

FLOYD V. FILSON, Th.D.

DEAN EMERITUS, AND PROFESSOR EMERITUS
OF NEW TESTAMENT
McCORMICK THEOLOGICAL SEMINARY, CHICAGO

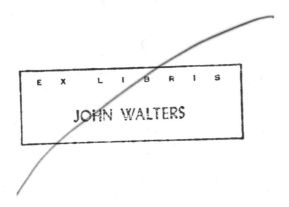
ADAM & CHARLES BLACK
LONDON

FIRST PUBLISHED 1960
REPRINTED 1967
SECOND EDITION 1971
REPRINTED 1975, 1977
A. AND C. BLACK LIMITED
35 BEDFORD ROW, LONDON WC1
© 1960, 1971 FLOYD VIVIAN FILSON
ISBN 0 7136 1231 2

PRINTED AND BOUND IN GREAT BRITAIN BY
MORRISON AND GIBB LTD, LONDON AND EDINBURGH

FOREWORD

THIS book is a commentary on the Gospel of Matthew. In its preparation I have given continual attention to the Synoptic Problem and to the author's use of Mk., Q, and probably other written sources. Such source study is indispensable. So is study of the (at best conjectural) conditions under which the gospel tradition was remembered, used, and shaped in the earliest days of the Church. As a result of such conditions the writer of Matt. was under some limitations of knowledge concerning just what Jesus did and said. But whatever limitations of knowledge and understanding hampered him in his writing, it is his Gospel that we possess, and in some important respects it has a priority and superiority over any of the varied and even conflicting source reconstructions that deserve study. So my primary attempt has not been to reconstruct sources but to grasp and state the meaning of the Gospel author. My main concern has been to make clear how he understood the gospel story and what he wanted the Church to get from his book.

Such a commentary continually raises questions as to what Jesus really did and said. It could not be written without attention to the historical Jesus, and it frequently tries to throw light on his career and teaching. But this book is not a life of Jesus. Its primary and essential task is to help the reader of the Gospel to enter into its author's faith, understanding, and purpose. We must ask first of all what he thought Jesus did and said, and what he thought this meant for the Church.

My method has been to discuss in a rather extended Introduction the literary questions and some important themes of the Gospel. Then, section by section, I give a fairly literal translation and a commentary which offers as much discussion of exegetical, historical, and theological questions as space limitation permits. I have listed in a selected Bibliography some of the books important for the study of Matt.

I write the name Matthew (without quotation marks) to refer to the Apostle. 'Matthew' (with quotation marks) refers to the

v

author of the Gospel. The abbreviation Matt. refers to the Gospel itself. In referring to the other Gospels, I use the unabbreviated name for the traditional author and the abbreviation (Mk., Lk., Jn.) for the Gospel.

FLOYD V. FILSON

*McCormick Theological
Seminary, Chicago*

CONTENTS

INTRODUCTION

I. IMPORTANCE IN THE CHURCH

RENAN called the Gospel of Matthew the most important book ever written. So sweeping a statement, though difficult to prove, calls attention to the persistent influence of this Gospel in the Church. From the second century on, it is the most quoted of the Gospels, and the vaguer patristic reminiscences of gospel material most often resemble Matt. It is true that our earliest gospel manuscripts include many copies of the Gospel of John, and this could suggest that its early influence equalled or surpassed that of Matt., but the early (papyrus) manuscripts come from Egypt, and show the extensive influence of Jn. there, while the evidence for the influence of Matt. comes from all areas of the Church.

It thus is not surprising that when the fourfold Gospel canon was formed, and when later the list of authoritative N.T. writings was made, Matt. was regularly placed first. This position was fitting, for Matt. is the Gospel which persistently emphasizes the deep dependence of the N.T. on the O.T., and yet asserts also that there is in the N.T. a plus, a new element, so that the gospel is no mere continuation or improvement of the O.T. but rather a decisive new word of God. Matt. links the N.T. with the O.T. and at the same time insists that God's central act in Jesus Christ brings the new age.

From the early second century to the present day the Gospel of Matthew has received continuous recognition. It has proved a fruitful resource in preaching, teaching, and theological discussion. In recent years the Gospel of Mark has won new attention by reason of its vital narrative movement, its vigorous Christian witness, and its generally acknowledged early date. The Gospel of Luke has appealed to the humanitarian concern and literary interest of many Christians. The Gospel of John has long been to multitudes of Christians the key witness to the gospel. But the Gospel of Matthew continues to exercise

I

a steady, widespread, and deep-going influence on the entire Church. Its strength is not in narrative power, literary appeal, or mystical depth, but in its proved and persistent capacity to shape Christian thought and church life. What features have given it this early, continued, and widespread influence?

II. Leading Features of the Gospel

1. The Gospel is the work of a real author. He worked with traditional material. His aim was not to imagine or invent episodes or sayings, but to present the common message of his Church. He was the voice of the Church rather than an imaginative individualist. But he gave distinctive form to the common church tradition. His personal character and Christian purpose have left their imprint on the inherited teaching. Intensive study to discern his sources is necessary and instructive, but it must not obscure the thoroughness with which he put his personal stamp on the entire Gospel.

2. The Gospel is a unity. Because it is the work of a real author, his style, spirit, and purpose are reflected throughout. Attention to his use of sources may create the impression that this Gospel is a loose compilation, uneven in style and varying in tone, but precisely where we are convinced that the author has used sources, his deft changes have imposed on the material the marks of his own interests and style and so have shaped it to serve his own purpose.

3. The Gospel maintains throughout a clear focus on Jesus Christ. He is the central figure of the entire Gospel. The author does not mar his presentation by personal parade or by detours undertaken to indulge secondary interests. Jesus of Nazareth, the Christ, the rightful King of the Jews, the Lord and final Judge of all men, is the constant object of loyal attention. Because this concern is common to all four Gospels and to our own church worship and teaching, we are likely to underestimate it. But it is prominent and determinative; the author never departs from this Christocentric focus.

4. The Gospel is notable for its completeness. This feature does much to explain its wide use in the Church. It is true (cf.

Jn. xx. 30; xxi. 25) that a Gospel of such limited length as Matt. or Jn. is but a meagre selection of all that might have been remembered and recorded. Matt. is not diffuse; in fact, it is amazingly compact. But it contains in adequate form the essentials of the Christian story. It begins with the birth of Jesus and continues to his resurrection appearance and final commission to his disciples. It not only includes the essential outline of Jesus' ministry, but builds into its account of his movements and doings a remarkably comprehensive report of the chief themes of his teaching. It does not lose from view the actual situation of the historical Jesus, with its definite Jewish background and setting; but it faithfully includes both the insight of faith into the meaning of that historical career and a forecast of wider outreach in the coming world mission of the Church. Thus Matt. is not a fragment or a sketch but a complete Gospel. It leaves the impression not of flashing brilliance but of balanced completeness.

5. The Gospel is orderly and well arranged. Interest in geography and chronology, though present, plays a minor role. The writer's primary concern is to present his content effectively. To this end he groups material; he knows that orderly topical presentation of material will help others more than would a day-by-day chronicle of what Jesus did and said. So he constructs five large discourses: The Sermon on the Mount (v-vii), The Charge to the Twelve Disciples (x), The Parables of the Kingdom (xiii), Relations between Disciples (xviii), and The End of this Age (xxiv-xxv). Numerical patterns appear throughout the Gospel. Five great discourses (see above), three examples of piety (vi. 1-18), seven Woes against the scribes and Pharisees (xxiii)—such familiar examples show the author's concern to arrange his material in a clear, orderly, usable, and easily remembered form. But his basic interest was not in literary patterns. He knew such patterns; he inherited some of them. At times he broke them to make them serve his purposes. For example, back of vi. 1-18 was a neat literary structure: first a general warning against performing characteristic acts of piety to impress other people (vs. 1), and then three examples: almsgiving (vss. 2-4), prayer (vss. 5 f.), and fasting (vss. 16-18). Into this pattern 'Matthew' inserts other sayings on prayer, including the Lord's Prayer (vss. 7-15); he inserts them here because

topical grouping, rather than neat literary pattern, is his real concern. In ch. xxiii the seven Woes (vss. 13-36) do not provide the structure of the entire discourse, in which topically related material precedes and follows the Woes. In fact, the Woes themselves have no neat uniformity of pattern; numerical pattern rather than literary symmetry marks their structure. The order of the Gospel results from the author's concern to arrange material in the form most effective and practical for use in the Church.

6. The Gospel is the work of a Christian churchman who writes to serve the needs of the Church and especially of its leaders. This is not to deny that he had an evangelistic and missionary interest. But the author knew that it is only one of the essential and prominent interests of the Church. The Church worships; it learns its heritage; it teaches its converts, its children, and inquirers; it lives together; and it gives its witness to the world. For all of this common life it needs a clear, usable, complete, trustworthy record of its basic story and testimony. As it spreads and grows, its leaders in particular need such a solid basis for their teaching and witness to Christ. 'Matthew' was a churchman who wrote such a Gospel for the worship, teaching, common life, and active witness of the Church. He was a Christian teacher, who wrote what he had been teaching, and arranged it to enable others to share effectively in this continual teaching task.

The Church, which emerged within Judaism and yet soon spread beyond the bounds of Judaism, needed an interpretation of the O.T. which would be faithful to its historical roots and yet would give Christians a vivid sense of the miraculous new work of God in Jesus Christ. It needed clues to the deep meaning of God's work in this historical figure. It needed to hear the gospel message of the Kingdom with its assurance both of present divine action and of the certain future triumph of God's cause. It needed to know the acts and teachings of Jesus that would spur the faith, direct the worship, and guide the varied daily life of his followers. It needed some clues as to how grace and discipline are to be combined in the community life of disciples. It needed to sense the urgent evangelistic and missionary obligation of the Church. It needed a document which

4

leaders of limited ability and understanding could use in guiding
the worship, teaching, life, and witness of the Church.

The Gospel of Matthew met that need and continued to meet
it in subsequent generations. Its author was a Christian teacher
who has proved the teacher of centuries of Christian leaders and
worshippers. The Church honoured and cherished his work because he had given it a powerful and useful tool for its common
life and mission. He was great precisely because he made it
his concern to serve Christ and to further the work of Christ
through the Church. He was outstanding not because he tried to
do the unusual but because by dedicated ability he presented
faithfully the common message of the Church in a way well
suited to meet the needs of the Church and its leaders. He wrote
in one place; he represented a particular background; but he rose
above the provincial and the petty; he wrote for the Church and
expressed its common heritage.

III. Sources Used by the Author

The unity of this Gospel is a unity imposed on material derived from various sources. As the above reference to broken
patterns indicates, the author inherited gospel tradition and
used it to serve his own purposes. He was not an eyewitness
reporting what he himself had seen and heard. His aim was to
give a trustworthy and useful presentation of the gospel story
which he had received from a number of sources. He both
respected his sources and shaped them to serve the practical
purposes he had in mind.

Were these sources oral or written? If written, were they
written in Aramaic, the prevailing spoken language of Jesus'
environment, or in Greek? Can any of them be identified? Our
answers to these questions can only be tentative.

Jesus taught by word of mouth and sent his disciples out to
do the same. The Gospels never hint that he wrote out his
teaching or that his disciples wrote it down as he gave it. The
finding of the Dead Sea Scrolls increases the evidence that
Palestinian Jews wrote religious documents in the days of Jesus,
but nothing suggests that Jesus or his first disciples hastened

to record in writing his sayings or actions. He was a Johnson without a Boswell. So the first reports about his acts and teachings were oral reports, and mainly, we may assume, in Aramaic.

It has been claimed that the first disciples soon gave the gospel tradition a fixed oral Aramaic form, either by constant repetition or by official control. This would not explain the frequent verbal agreements between our Synoptic Gospels unless we could assume an equally fixed oral Greek translation of that Aramaic tradition, for the agreements that prompt the theory are found in our Greek Gospels. This theory of a verbally fixed and officially controlled oral tradition rests on no evidence and does not explain the facts.

The tradition certainly was translated from Aramaic into Greek. Some scholars have placed this transition many years after the death of Jesus and in some country other than Palestine. We cannot assume such delay. Palestine had a considerable though not numerically dominant Greek-speaking population. A Greek-speaking synagogue in Jerusalem is attested by the Theodotus inscription, and the Greek inscription in the temple, warning Gentile visitors not to enter the inner courts, shows that Greek-speaking Gentiles also visited Jerusalem (see Wright-Filson, *Westminster Historical Atlas to the Bible*, pp. 95, 106). Palestine was more widely bilingual than is often supposed, and it is not surprising that even in the earliest days there were Greek-speaking Jewish Christians in the Jerusalem church (Acts vi). Thus while Jesus regularly taught in Aramaic, and the dominant language of the earliest Church was Aramaic, a Greek tradition of the sayings and acts of Jesus must have existed from those earliest days, and it was in fact the Greek-speaking Christians who, scattered by persecution (Acts viii. 1; xi. 19), spearheaded the expanding evangelistic outreach of the Church. The original Aramaic tradition has left its mark on our Gospels, but the first Greek form of the tradition was Palestinian, Jewish, and very early.

For a time, then, the gospel tradition was handed on in fluid oral form, both in Aramaic and Greek. How long it was before written documents gave it more definite form is hard to say. The view that during and immediately after Jesus' ministry his hearers wrote down his sayings if not his deeds is extremely unlikely.

The most vigorous attempt to trace the process that shaped the tradition has been made by Form Criticism. It assumes, and rightly, a period of oral tradition during which the Church used the gospel material in its worship, teaching, and controversy. It assumes, with somewhat less basis, that during that period each item of tradition—each saying, parable, or incident—was transmitted as a separate item and was freely shaped and altered to meet the needs of church use. It is generally silent or sceptical about any real historical interest or accuracy in the transmission of this material. In its extreme form, Form Criticism tends to ascribe to the Church not only the selection and literary shaping of the material but also its creation. This extreme scepticism overlooks the presence of eyewitnesses in the first-century Church; it wrongly gives to pious but uncontrolled inventiveness complete dominance over historical memory. Such extreme views are unfounded. But the method has made clear two important facts: (1) The Church did remember, use, and even shape the gospel tradition to meet the needs of its ongoing life. (2) The Gospels are therefore sources for the life of the early Church as well as for the life of Jesus. They are documents of faith and give evidence of those early years of the Church for which we have no adequate direct historical description. These facts, however, do not warrant disregard of the Church's real historical interest; it had a real historical tradition with which to work.

How the tradition first took written form is not clear. On one view, the first written document assembled O.T. passages regarded as fulfilled in the life and work of Jesus. The finding among the Dead Sea Scrolls of a document which combines several prophetic passages gives some support to such a theory (J. M. Allegro, *JBL*, lxxv, pp. 182-187). 'Matthew' has an obvious interest in such prophetic passages. Did he find them already gathered into a document for the convenience of teachers in the Church? One view is that the 'Logia' which Papias says that Matthew composed were really 'oracles' or O.T. passages which Matthew had assembled in one useful document. Since Jesus and early Christian teachers regarded his work as the fulfilment of Scripture, it is possible that some Christian listed in a very early document the passages which Christian teachers saw fulfilled in the work of Jesus. But this cannot be proved; such a document cannot be found or reconstructed. The solid truth in the theory is that the earliest Church made constant use of the O.T. and used it to show that the coming and work of Jesus fulfilled prophecy.

A second possibility is that the first written gospel source was a collection of sayings of Jesus. To the earliest Church Jesus was the Prophet, the Christ, the Son of God, the Lord, the coming Judge of all men, His followers must have been concerned to know and observe what he had taught. Such teachings would show what the exalted Lord wanted his disciples to do; they would indicate by what standard he would judge men at the end. The Church attached immense importance to the teaching of Jesus, and that teaching, first in oral and then in written form, was preserved, used, applied, and at times adapted to the needs of the Church. But how soon it was written down we cannot say.

Still a third view is that the earliest written gospel source was the story of Jesus' passion and resurrection. Each Gospel gives a detailed passion and resurrection narrative. That one week occupies eight chapters in Matt., six in Mk., over five in Lk., and nine (or ten) in Jn. For no other period do the Gospels give so detailed and connected a narrative (minor sequences appear in Mk. i and Jn. i). Obviously the Church greatly needed such connected narrative to show Jesus' innocence, his final rejection by Jewish leaders, and the central significance of the cross and resurrection.

We cannot determine the date or content of the first written form of the gospel tradition. We must assume that clusters of material began to be formed—relevant Scripture passages, sayings and parables, incidents with a common theme, and a connected passion and resurrection story. This grouping could have occurred first in oral or in written form. It could have occurred in Aramaic, in Greek, or independently in both; but any early Aramaic form was evidently soon translated into Greek, for we know only the Greek form of the tradition.

What sources did the author of Matt. know and use? In the

ancient Church Matt. was considered the earliest of our Gospels. This is the official position of the Roman Catholic Church, and a few Protestants hold it. But it is church tradition which explains the appeal of this view. The close agreements between Matt. and Mk. are more naturally explained by saying that the author of Matt. used Mk. as his basic narrative source. In most parallel sections Mk. is more detailed than Matt.; Mk. seems to be the fresh, vigorous original work and Matt. the compressed and later writing.

But Mk. has relatively few sayings of Jesus, while Matt. has many. In these sayings Matt. is often closely parallel with Lk. Some scholars hold that Luke knew and used Matt. as a written source; it is more widely held that both 'Matthew' and Luke used a third (earlier) document (no longer extant), which consisted mainly or entirely of sayings. The writing of our longer and more adequate Gospels presumably made that earlier source obsolete, so that it fell into disuse and disappeared. This elusive source is usually called Q (a symbol generally explained as the initial letter of the German word *Quelle*, 'source'). It seems more reasonable to assume that 'Matthew' and Luke used such a source than to say that Luke used Matt.; Lk. is so different from Matt. and so independent of Matt.'s viewpoint that it is hard to believe that its author systematically used Matt. as a written source.

To assume the use of Q by no means solves all the problems about the origin of Matt. In some passages Matt. and Lk. agree almost word for word; in others the two Gospels show somewhat less agreement; in still others they differ in wording much more than they agree. It is impossible to determine how much material should be assigned to the hypothetical source Q. A further complicating fact is that many sayings in Matt. (and in Lk.) are found only in this one Gospel. Did any of them come from Q? That is, did 'Matthew' use Q sayings which Luke found no reason to use, and did Luke use Q sayings which 'Matthew' did not include? And it would be pushing the Q hypothesis too far to say that all of the sayings peculiar to Matt. were taken from Q. Matt. must rest on still other sources, oral or written. B. H. Streeter (*The Four Gospels*, ch. 9) held that back of Matt. lies a third document; the gospel writer used not only Mk. and Q but

2   9

also M. We may be confident that back of Matt. lay sources of information not available to the authors of Mk. and Lk.; such material, so far as written, may have been recorded in one document (M) or in several; but the exact form and limits of such a document or documents elude us. To a limited extent Matt. rests also upon items of oral tradition current in the area where it was written. And in its present form Matt. owes much to the editorial activity of the author who shaped his source material into a unified Gospel.

IV. Setting and Date of the Gospel

The Gospel does not say where or when it was written, and no clear clue leads to a certain answer to these questions. We must begin by reconstructing as accurately as possible the situation which the Gospel reflects. If the author used the Gospel of Mark as a basic source, we must look for a situation and date where Mk. would be available, known, and respected.

1. The prominent use of the O.T., and particularly the repeated emphasis on fulfilment of O.T. prophecies, reveals a deep concern of the author. The use of O.T. words and ideas is common N.T. practice, and the emphasis on fulfilment of prophecy is by no means peculiar to Matt., but this theme is more prominent in Matt. than in any other N.T. writer. Thirteen times Matt. contains the formula, 'that the word might be fulfilled which was spoken by the Lord through the prophet' (e.g. i. 22). The author considered this fulfilment theme of crucial importance for himself and his readers.

But it was not the Levitical laws, the ceremonial rules, which had this importance for him. On the contrary, he alone cites Hosea vi. 6, and he cites it twice (ix. 13; xii. 7). He is concerned with events in Jesus' life which fulfil O.T. promises, and with O.T. teaching which finds full expression in what Jesus taught. This latter point, that Jesus gave a perfect expression to what the O.T. Law had set forth in limited form, would have particular point for those who recognized authority in that Law. This reflects the background not only of the writer but also of the readers he had especially in mind.

2. This indicates that the writer and first readers of Matt. were Christians of Jewish origin. We do not mean that every Gospel which shows Jewish background and interest must have been written by a Jewish Christian for Jewish Christians. John Mark presumably wrote the Gospel of Mark; he was a Jewish Christian; but it is generally agreed that he wrote for the largely Gentile Roman Church. Luke, the author of the Third Gospel, had a strong interest in Judaism, and began and ended his gospel story in the temple; but he was a Gentile Christian, and wrote for Gentile Christians. Our point, therefore, must be carefully stated to be convincing. There is in Matt. an unequalled interest in the promise and fulfilment theme, in the full statement of God's will on matters which the Law had treated only in imperfect form, and in the intensity of the clash between Jesus and other Jewish leaders. The atmosphere of this Gospel is such as to have special point for those who had come from Judaism and needed assurance that the Christian gospel not only fulfilled the O.T. promises but also gave the full statement of the will of God on points where the O.T. Law was inadequate.

3. This Jewish Christian note is clearly expressed without surrender to narrow nationalist tendencies in the early Church. The lack of emphasis on Jewish ceremonial Law and the clear statements of Jesus which point to a world mission show that the author did not belong to or write for a narrowly exclusive Jewish-Christian group. He was not a 'Judaizer', and the Church in which he lived was not made up of 'Judaizers'.

4. The writer gives no hint that he was closely allied with any sectarian Jewish group. He may be suspected of legalistic tendencies because he codified the teaching of Jesus, but he clearly sees in the gospel message a radical break with the position of the scribes and Pharisees. He had just as little sense of kinship with the Sadducees or with Jewish zealot tendencies. Were his chief ties with the Essenes? The Dead Sea Scrolls found at Qumran show parallels to Matt., and it has been asserted that John the Baptist, Jesus, and 'Matthew' show indebtedness to the Essenes and acquaintance with Essene writings and regulations. The existence of such parallels must not be denied. But the differences should not be ignored and they are more impressive than the parallels. One great difficulty

in assuming direct Essene influence on such a Jewish Christian as 'Matthew' is that the Qumran sect was a monastic type of sect. There is no evidence that its members broadcast their teaching and circulated their writings in any general way. Nevertheless, the Dead Sea Scrolls give direct first-century evidence concerning the life and thought of one Jewish sect, and this provides extensive clues to the theological and social atmosphere in which first-century Jewish Christians lived. Common indebtedness to the O.T. will explain many parallels between Matt. and the Scrolls. Some points of teaching in Matt. have parallels in first-century Pharisaism, whose better features find little recognition in our Gospels. But other phases of the thought and general outlook of Matt. find parallels in the Dead Sea Scrolls, and rather than assume that these Scrolls circulated freely in Palestine, that Christian leaders were in vital and constant touch with their thought, and that (as some scholars tend to claim) most other inter-testamental literature is Essene in origin, it would seem preferable to assume that in many aspects the Scrolls reflect a first-century atmosphere which was current in wider circles of Palestine and Syria than merely the monastic Essene communities.

This conclusion offers a viewpoint from which to consider the so-called 'Gnostic' strain of Matthew. The origin of Gnosticism is a moot question. One widely held view—based on documents much later than the Apostolic Age—is that Gnosticism was definitely developed and clearly crystallized before Christianity appeared; it was, on this view, a syncretistic movement of basically Gentile origin, and as soon as Christianity appeared, this Gnostic movement promptly exercised a strong influence on Christians and injected important features of theology into the gospel. But some such 'Gnostic' features appear in Hellenistic Judaism and in Essene and other Palestinian sects of first-century Judaism. Moreover, the clearly developed Gnostic position, with its radical dualism, its hostility to the O.T., and its rejection of the Jewish doctrine of God as Creator of the material world, first appears in the second century A.D. as a reaction to the basic Christian gospel; as far as it appears in N.T. writings, it is only in a partial development which falls short of such rejection of God as Creator; such first-century Gnostic tendencies are essentially rejected by the Apostles, and any N.T. emphasis on knowledge, discipline, and the dramatic descent of a heavenly Redeemer roots in first-century Judaism and shows no such form as Gnosticism later took when fully crystallized. The Dead Sea Scrolls show a deep interest in knowledge and in discipline, and provide evidence that the background of so-called 'Gnostic' tendencies in Matt. is in Judaism, in aspects of its life which the Qumran sect shared with other Jews. The intertestamental literature of Judaism needs re-study in the light of the Scrolls. One point that such re-study may be expected to confirm is that while the Gospel of Matthew, with its emphasis on knowledge and discipline and redemption, rests solidly on the words and work of Jesus and his disciples, it has its basic larger background in the first-century Judaism reflected in part in the Scrolls. The author of Matt. was not an Essene; there is no evidence that Jesus ever was; it cannot be proved that John the Baptist was; but we may well be grateful for the light which the Scrolls now throw on the first-century Judaism which was the secondary background of this Gospel.

5. The primary setting of this Gospel is in the Christian Church. The author was a Jewish Christian, and we must emphasize the word 'Christian'. He was a convinced churchman, and wrote as a working leader, an active and effective teacher, in the Church. Matt. alone of the four canonical gospels uses the word 'Church'. Even Matt. has this word in only two verses. xviii. 17 refers to a local group of disciples, and says nothing concerning the organization of the Church. xvi. 18 gives a foundation role to Peter, but shows no concern for details of organization and says nothing about successors of Peter. Indeed, the authority given to Peter in xvi. 19 is given to the entire Church acting together in xviii. 18. This Gospel clearly was not concerned primarily with details of church organization; considered as a whole, it shows no deep interest in such questions. But the fact that Matt. is the only Gospel which makes any explicit reference to the Church is significant. It reflects the author's consciousness that his Church is a clearly separate fellowship. He is of course as conscious as any first-century Christian of the ties of the Christian group with Judaism. But he is equally aware that the rejection of Christ by the Jewish

leaders leaves the Christian group clearly separate from the official Jewish fellowship, and he is convinced that Jesus clearly anticipated this. Official Jewish rejection of Jesus has forced the movement that represents true Judaism to live separate from current Judaism. This rejected group has the true gospel; it has the responsibility to spread this gospel. Each Christian must see in this church fellowship the primary tie of human life, the tie that takes priority even over family ties (xii. 49 f.). The Church may include unworthy members (xviii. 17) and may even have false prophets among its leaders (vii. 22), but it is to the author a definitely separate religious fellowship.

This Church can exercise discipline (xviii. 17). It has its own manner of prayer (vi. 9). As the role of the Twelve and the importance of Peter show (x. 1-4; xvi. 18 f.), specific leaders have a rightful place in its life. Ch. x in its entirety implies that the Church has recognized leaders, and they are to carry on their witness and work in spite of all opposition. The possibility of false prophets (vii. 22 f.) shows plainly that faithful prophets have a place in the Church's life. Moreover, the very writing and form of Matt. indicate the important role of Christian teachers. This Gospel was written not so much for private reading as for the guidance of Christian teachers in their work. This teaching, however, was not merely the work of educating those already added to the Church. The teaching work also had a vital role in the evangelistic witness which for 'Matthew' was an inherent part of the Church's task.

6. The setting of this Gospel was not in some exclusive and narrow group of Jewish Christians, but rather in some place and group which had contacts with the wider Church. The Gospel was known early in the second century. It was the Gospel most widely accepted during that early period. It had no difficulty in finding acceptance in the Gentile Church. So it could not have come from a group out of touch with the wider Church. The Gospel circulated in the wider Church so promptly and widely that it must have come from a Jewish-Christian circle friendly to neighbouring Gentile Christians.

If the Gospel could be dated before the Jerusalem church fled to Pella about A.D. 66 (Eusebius, *Ch. Hist.* iii. 5. 3) we could consider Jerusalem as the place of writing. Even so, the concern of the Jerusalem church for the ceremonial Law would raise a question, and Antioch in Syria might be a better setting for a Gospel which shows no interest in Levitical regulations. If, however, this Gospel depends on Mk. as its basic source, and we date Mk., in accordance with the earliest tradition, after the death of Peter, we must date Matt. later than A.D. 66. The earliest possible date would be in the seventies, and a date in the eighties or even in the nineties would be preferable. (Since we have no series of exactly dated specific Christian events in the seventies and eighties, we cannot attempt an exact dating.) At this later time the place of writing is hard to determine. The Christians who fled from Jerusalem about A.D. 66 went northeast across the Jordan to Pella. Their later history is obscure. It is doubtful whether there was a strong Jewish-Christian Church in Jerusalem during the eighties and nineties. We do not know what ties Christians of Pella or Jerusalem had with the wider Church after Jerusalem fell in A.D. 70. The place of writing of Matt. must remain uncertain, but origin in Syria, whether at Antioch or elsewhere, or in Phoenicia, as Kilpatrick suggests (*Origins of the Gospel According to St. Matthew*, ch. 7), seems more likely than origin in Jerusalem, and would explain better how the Gospel found its way so promptly and easily into the life of the entire Church. For this Gospel writer was in touch with the wider Church and his Gospel circulated in it promptly and freely, with no suspicion such as would have attached to a writing from a suspect separatist group of Christians.

The Gospel's interest in Peter would go well with origin in Antioch in Syria or in some neighbouring city of Syria. The ancient tradition that Peter was the first bishop of Antioch (see, e.g., Eusebius, *Ch. Hist.* iii. 36. 2) reflects a definite interest in Peter in that Syrian region. It was there rather than in Jerusalem that a Gospel which gives great prominence to Peter could most easily have been written. James the Lord's brother held a position of pre-eminence in Jerusalem and Palestine, according to the testimony of Acts (xii. 17; xv, 13-21; xxi. 18) and of later Jewish tradition. Origin of Matt. in a Jewish-Christian circle of Syria (or Phoenicia) in the eighties or nineties is the most satisfactory answer to the question of setting and date.

V. Authorship

1. The Tradition. Ancient tradition is unanimous in naming the Apostle Matthew as the author of this Gospel. This tradition appears early; it was found by Eusebius (*Ch. Hist.* iii. 39. 16) in the writings of Papias, who wrote about A.D. 130. It finds repeated and explicit statement in important ancient writers: Irenaeus (*Against Heresies*, iii. 1. 1), Pantaenus (quoted by Eusebius, *Ch. Hist.* v. 10. 3), Tertullian (*Against Marcion*, iv. 2), Origen (quoted by Eusebius, *Ch. Hist.* vi. 25. 4), Eusebius (*Ch. Hist.* vi. 25. 3), and many others. The same testimony comes from gospel manuscripts which give this Gospel the heading: 'According to Matthew'. Did these words originally mean: 'The Gospel according to the teaching known to have been given by Matthew'? The long line of ancient witnesses clearly meant more than this. They meant that the Apostle Matthew wrote this Gospel.

The patristic tradition is equally explicit and unanimous in asserting that Matthew wrote this Gospel *in Hebrew* (cf. Papias: Ἑβραΐδι διαλέκτῳ). The word Hebrew may refer here, as elsewhere in ancient usage, to Aramaic. It is usually thought that Aramaic was the common Semitic language in the first Christian centuries; Hebrew was known to the scholars and could even be used in the synagogue services, but Aramaic was the spoken language of the common people in Semitic circles of Palestine and Syria. This seems probable (though H. Birkeland, *The Language of Jesus*, argues that Hebrew was spoken in Palestine in Jesus' time); on this view, the ancient Christian writers meant that Matthew wrote his Gospel in Aramaic (of which our Greek Matt. could be a translation).

This tradition, early, unanimous, and explicit, is impressive. But note this: Papias is the key witness. Irenaeus, for example, obviously knows and uses Papias as an authority. No tradition demonstrably independent of Papias exists. What did he say?

Unfortunately Papias' five-volume *Exposition of the Oracles of the Lord* has not survived. Meagre quotations appear in later Christian writings, but of its discussion of Matt. only the following brief sentence has been preserved (Eusebius, *Ch. Hist.* iii. 39. 16): 'Matthew therefore compiled the oracles in the Hebrew

16

language, and each one translated them as he was able' (Ματ-
θαῖος μὲν οὖν Ἑβραΐδι διαλέκτῳ τὰ λόγια συνετάξατο, ἡρμήνευσεν
δ' αὐτὰ ὡς ἦν δυνατὸς ἕκαστος).

Concerning this statement, so crucial for all later church
tradition on Matt., note the following points: (1) The sentence
is only part of the complete statement Papias wrote. (2) Papias,
bishop of Hierapolis in Asia Minor, wrote in Greek. (3) He no
doubt knew and used the Gospel of Matthew in Greek. (4)
Eusebius, who knew the entire work of Papias, understood
Papias to be speaking of our Greek Matt., and we have no reason
to think that he misunderstood Papias on this point. (5) Papias,
then, thought that our Matt. had been written in Hebrew
(Aramaic), and so evidently regarded the Greek Matt. he used
as a translation. (6) When Papias spoke of 'the oracles' (τὰ
λόγια), he probably meant not merely the sayings of Jesus, but
the Gospel containing both sayings and deeds of Jesus. This
seems clear from what Papias says about Mark: as Eusebius
reports (*Ch. Hist.* iii. 39. 15), Papias first says that Mark recalled
'the things said or done by the Lord', and then, a little later,
referring to Mark's record of this same material, calls it a compilation of 'the oracles of the Lord'. Thus 'oracles' here includes both sayings and deeds. Similarly, when Papias says that
'Matthew composed the oracles', he probably means a Gospel
account such as our Greek Matt. contains. (7) The quotation
from Papias given by Eusebius does not recommend our Greek
Matt. as an adequate or authoritative translation of the Hebrew
(Aramaic) original. It says nothing on that issue. This point has
been strangely ignored. Papias says that 'each one translated
them as he was able'. If this refers to oral translations of the
original Hebrew (Aramaic) Matt., made by Christian leaders and
teachers as they used the Gospel in their work, it says nothing
about any written Greek translation or translations. If, however,
it refers to written translations, it indicates that several or many
honest attempts at translation had been made and they were of
varying adequacy, but none is recommended as fully adequate
and authoritative. In either case, the surviving words of Papias
do not stamp our Greek Matt. as an authoritative translation of
the Hebrew (Aramaic) original. No doubt Papias said more concerning Matt. than Eusebius quotes, and to Eusebius Papias was

evidently a strong supporter of the authenticity of our Greek Matt., but what Eusebius quotes suggests doubt rather than assurance on this point.

The Papias tradition is open to serious question. Matt. comes to us in Greek; no Hebrew or Aramaic original exists; our Greek Matt. bears convincing signs of having been written in Greek; Greek sources, including our Greek Mk. and one or more other written sources, were used in writing it. Thus internal evidence and source dependence argue that the Papias tradition is misleading or untrustworthy. The Greek Matt. we know is not the direct translation of a Hebrew (Aramaic) original.

For this reason other explanations of the Papias statement have been offered. (1) Since 'the oracles' could mean the O.T. Scriptures, perhaps Papias meant a collection of O.T. passages, made by Matthew in the original Hebrew, and presenting prophecies which the Church saw had been fulfilled in the career of Jesus. The prominent interest of Matt. in fulfilment of prophecy gives some support to this idea. (2) 'The oracles' may mean only the sayings of Jesus; Matthew then compiled the sayings of Jesus in a document which the authors of Matt. and Lk. used as a written source. The use of this document, commonly referred to as 'Q', could explain how the name of Matthew became attached to our Matt.; he did not write it, but he wrote a document which, translated into Greek, was one of its sources. (3) 'The oracles' may mean a source document used by 'Matthew' alone. It then would be something like the 'M' source proposed by B. H. Streeter—a Jewish-Christian source used only by the author of Matt. The name of Matthew, connected with the source first in its Hebrew (Aramaic) form and then in Greek, could have been transferred to the complete Gospel of Matthew, which thus took its name not from the name of its actual author but from the Matthean material it included.

Each of these three conjectures is an honest attempt to explain both the tradition, the fact that our Matt. is a Greek composition, and the evidence that one or more sources used by 'Matthew' may have been translated from Hebrew or Aramaic. But none of these theories is fully convincing. Eusebius certainly, and Papias in all probability, spoke of our Matt. They thought its origin was in a Hebrew (Aramaic) form. This does not seem true of our Greek Matt. The way is open for alternate hypotheses (after all, the ancient Church had some reason or pretext for connecting this Gospel with Matthew), but none of them is capable of proof. They point to types of source material used in Matt., but no real evidence connects any particular body of such source material with the Apostle Matthew.

2. Matthew the Tax Collector. The N.T. offers little help in assessing the possible connection of the Apostle Matthew with the Gospel that bears his name. He is mentioned in all four N.T. lists of the Twelve. In Matt. x. 3 and Acts i. 13 he is eighth in the list; in Mk. iii. 18 and Lk. vi. 15 he is seventh. Only Matt., however, says he was a tax collector, and his name does not occur in the N.T. outside of Matt. ix. 9 and the lists of the Twelve.

The call of Matthew to be a disciple is reported in Matt. ix. 9 (the festive meal which, according to ix. 10, Jesus and his disciples shared with 'many tax collectors and sinners' may have been served in Matthew's house). But the parallel accounts in Mk. and Lk. speak not of Matthew but of Levi, whom Mk. further identifies as son of Alphaeus. Were Matthew and Levi different men, or are these two names of the same man? For a Greek-speaking Jew to have both a Jewish and a Greek name was nothing unusual. The difficulty here is that both Matthew and Levi are Jewish names and that no Gospel clearly uses both of the same man. Was Matthew the Apostle called a tax collector only because he was wrongly identified with Levi the son of Alphaeus?

If Matthew was a tax collector, he undoubtedly could read and write, and so could record what Jesus had said and done. As a tax collector in bilingual (trilingual) Galilee, he would have known Greek as well as Hebrew and Aramaic. This is the significance of his occupation for our inquiry into the authorship of Matt.

3. Internal Evidence. Since the Papias tradition is not perfectly clear, since our Gospel is not a translation of a Hebrew (Aramaic) original such as Papias ascribes to Matthew, and since the N.T. references to Matthew tell us nothing decisive for our study of authorship, we must depend on internal evidence. The use of Greek sources (including Mk.) argues that

Matt. was written in Greek rather than in Hebrew or Aramaic. If Hebrew or Aramaic sources lie back of it, those sources were translated into Greek before being used by the author of Matt. (a possible exception: he may have translated from the Hebrew some of his O.T. quotations). The use of such written sources, and especially the use of Mk., which was not written by an eyewitness Apostle, argues that the author of Matt. was not himself an Apostle, and so was not Matthew. His intense concern for the relation between the Jewish Law and the Christian gospel, and the note of controversy with Jewish sects, indicate that he was a Jewish Christian. But he was not a narrow nationalist or Judaizer; he was alive to the world mission of the Church, and was evidently in vital touch with the wider Church, so that his Gospel could move out into the various provinces of the Roman Empire and quickly appeal to Gentile Christians. His deep Jewish roots and loyalty are combined with catholic contacts and outlook. The skilful organization and grouping of material mark him as a Christian teacher with decades of experience. His name we do not know, and do not need to know. He has written a masterly and usable Gospel, which has played a commanding role in all succeeding generations of the Church.

VI. PURPOSE AND OUTLINE

1. Purpose of the Writer. The basic aim of the author is not artistic desire for creative literary expression, or intellectual curiosity to determine the actual course of historical events, or biographical interest in the development of an intriguing personality. He is an earnest and dedicated Christian, and the writing of the Gospel is for him an act of obedience to the risen Christ, who is his Lord (xxviii. 16-20). He seeks to honour and serve Christ. In full agreement with this aim, he wants to further the work of the Church. He is loyal to the Church and writes to serve its needs.

His immediate aim is to provide the Church's teachers with a basic tool for their work. He writes after the eyewitnesses have all but disappeared. Others must carry the Christian leadership and witness, and their growing number presents an increasing need for trustworthy guidance in their work. In the conditions of that time, few individual Christians would possess written copies of gospel material. Most Christians would hear the Christian story told or read to them by their leaders. This author has provided a work suitable for these leaders to use both in leading worship and in their teaching task.

His aim is not directly and primarily evangelistic. He seeks chiefly to support the work of faithful teaching rather than the stirring appeal for initial repentance and faith. This means that he anticipates a twofold use of his Gospel. First of all, as we have said, he thinks of the continual worship and teaching within the Church, where a constant teaching ministry is necessary to instruct and guide those who believe in Jesus Christ. The use of the Gospel through the centuries has proved how well he was able to serve this need. But the Church has a continuous evangelistic task; even though the writer is not primarily an evangelist, he cannot forget the great commission to evangelize all nations. He knows what the brevity of the sermon summaries in Acts sometimes makes us forget, that evangelistic appeal must be based on information and explanation; it inherently contains an element of teaching. When it has attracted inquirers, and even after it has reached its mark and won converts, it must be confirmed by more detailed teaching. So this great Christian teacher aims not only to inform and direct the lives of those already members of the Church, but also to give the teaching material to accompany and confirm the evangelistic witness of missionary preachers. The Church must win and baptize converts; then, as the risen Christ instructed his disciples, it must always be 'teaching them to observe all that I have commanded you' (xxviii. 20).

Scholars in recent years have often spoken of the liturgical purpose and use of this Gospel. Such use in the common worship certainly was one aspect of the author's objective. But unless we unreasonably expand the term liturgical, we find our best statement of the writer's aim in his purpose to serve the teaching work of the Church. His central concern was not liturgical worship or evangelistic appeal but the varied and unceasing task of Christian teaching.

2. Outline of the Gospel. No single outline fully states the

Gospel's scope and the writer's purpose. It may help if we note three methods of outlining the book, show the limitation of each, and point out how the writer's aim permits no simple outline.

(a) As B. W. Bacon has emphasized (in *Studies in Matthew*), this Gospel gives prominence to five large collections of teaching. Each of the five is clearly the author's literary construction; each ends with a unique transitional formula: 'And it happened when Jesus had finished, etc.' (vii. 28; xi. 1; xiii. 53; xix. 1; xxvi. 1). The fact that these discourses are obviously the author's compilation emphasizes the importance he attached to them. Indeed, Bacon and others think that in constructing his Gospel around these five discourses 'Matthew' intended the readers to understand that his Gospel supersedes the five books of Moses. If we take these five discourses as our guide, we may use Bacon's outline:

i, ii. Preamble.
iii. 1-vii. 29. Concerning Discipleship.
viii. 1-xi. 1. Concerning Apostleship.
xi. 2-xiii. 53. Concerning the Hiding of the Revelation.
xiii. 54-xix. 1a. Concerning Church Administration.
xix. 1b-xxvi. 2. Concerning the Judgment.
xxvi. 3-xxviii. 20. The Epilogue.

This outline does not fully satisfy. It is doubtful whether the author's basic aim was to surpass or replace the five books of Moses. Emphasis on the five great discourses gives insufficient attention to the narrative content of the Gospel. And the words 'preamble' and 'epilogue' are inadequate to express what the birth, death, and resurrection of Jesus meant for the author.

(b) Numerous scholars, of whom we may take A. H. McNeile as representative (*Gospel According to St. Matthew*, p. xii), point out that the general outline of Matt. follows that of Mk. If we take this fact as decisive, we may construct an outline which follows a chronological and geographical pattern:

i. 1-ii. 23. The Genealogy, Birth, and Infancy of Jesus.
iii. 1-iv. 11. The Immediate Preparation for the Ministry.
iv. 12-xiii. 58. The Galilean Ministry.
xiv. 1-xviii. 35. The Period of Wandering and Retirement from Galilee.

xix. 1-xx. 34. The Journey to Jerusalem.
xxi. 1-xxv. 46. The Ministry in Jerusalem.
xxvi. 1-xxviii. 20. The Passion and Resurrection Story.

It is true that Matt. contains a general chronological and geographical pattern. This does justice to the Gospel as the story of an actual human life. But the author's topical grouping of material shows that detailed chronology and geography were not decisive for his purpose. The teaching of Jesus, the mystery of his purpose, and the theological meaning of his work find limited expression in this outline.

(c) This Gospel emphasizes the confession of Peter (xvi. 13-20), and specific teaching concerning the Cross immediately follows this key event. To reflect the full purpose of the author an outline must give that confession a key role. Who was Jesus? What did he come to do? How did the divine purpose and method emerge during his ministry? The following outline gives some attention to these questions:

i. 1-ii. 23. The Birth and Infancy of the Divine Son of David.
iii. 1-iv. 11. The Immediate Preparation for the Ministry of the Son of God.
iv. 12-xvi. 20. The Public Ministry and First Clear Recognition of the Christ the Son of God.
xvi. 21-xx. 34. The Christ Goes to Jerusalem to Die as the Suffering Servant.
xxi. 1-xxv. 46. The King of Israel is Rejected by the Jews but Will Yet Establish His Kingdom.
xxvi. 1-xxviii. 20. The Crucified and Risen Christ Receives Lordship Over All Creation and Commands a World Mission.

Such an outline centres attention on the person of Christ and on the divine plan working out in the gospel story. Its weakness is that the Gospel shows no clear advance in Christology from section to section, and makes no clear distinction between the main titles used of Jesus. The outline fails to give any prominence to the five great discourses, and takes little notice of the emergence of the church idea in the Gospel.

Thus a perfectly satisfactory outline is hard to construct. The outlines given above or suggested by others focus attention on important features of the Gospel, but the teaching interest in topical grouping of material and the desire to present early and often the Church's witness to Jesus prevent a clear and steadily advancing development of either a chronological, a geographical, or a theological outline. This sacrifices literary neatness, but the experience of the Church attests the practical value of the way the author adapted his material to the teacher's work in the Church.

VII. The Text of the Gospel

The numerous textual variations in Greek manuscripts and ancient versions of Matt. create at first sight an appearance of confusion in the text of the Gospel. But this impression is misleading. It is clear that the dominant mediaeval type of text, which prevails from the fourth century on, is secondary and untrustworthy. Westcott and Hort built a critical text which relied mainly on Codex Vaticanus (B) and to a considerable extent on Codex Sinaiticus (‭א‬). They called this text 'Neutral', thus implying that the forces which had corrupted other types of text had had no notable influence on this B‭א‬ text. Scholars generally reject this extreme claim for the B‭א‬ type of text; in the Old Latin, the Old Syriac, the early papyri, Codex Bezae (D), and other manuscripts they find readings that deserve serious consideration in our search for the original wording. However, this has not led to general rejection of the Westcott and Hort text; in details it may need correction, but on the whole it is dependable. Almost all modern textual scholars, after they have rejected a blind adherence to Westcott and Hort's so-called 'Neutral' text, nevertheless agree with Westcott and Hort in the great majority of readings. The Nestle text, and the text of Huck's *Synopsis of the First Three Gospels*, do not differ radically from it. The present commentary usually follows the Nestle text.

No final critical text of Matt. is available or can be constructed. But the variations still in question are of minor importance for the interpretation of the Gospel. They are noteworthy for study of style and for the meaning of details; scholarship means unceasing attention to details and construction of general views on the basis of such patient study. But the uncertainty in the text of Matt. must not be exaggerated. The available critical Greek text of Matt. is substantially dependable.

VIII. Prominent Themes

1. THE PERSON OF JESUS

The Gospel does not present a clearly formulated Christology. The figure of Jesus Christ is central throughout, and the entire Gospel helps the reader to understand who Jesus was (and is), but it gives no systematic teaching on this subject. The numerous titles used of Jesus must not be sharply distinguished. They overlap in meaning; each borrows added meaning from the others.

Indifferent and hostile attitudes towards Jesus are frankly reported. Some hearers are impervious to his message; some give it no sustained attention; others let competing interests crowd it out (xiii. 3-23). They see his mighty works but find in them no compelling call to faith (xi. 20-24). Jewish leaders deny that God sent Jesus; his healing works they ascribe to the working of Satan (xii. 24); they call him 'that impostor' (xxvii. 63).

'Matthew' develops his portrait of Jesus against this background of indifference and hostility. Jesus was a real human being; he was tempted (iv. 1-11; xvi. 23), he prayed (xxvi. 39), he was ignorant on some subjects (xxiv. 36), he felt forsaken on the cross (xxvii. 46). His human limitations are not so frankly presented in Matt. as in Mk., but they still appear. He was a man of humble origin. While his birthplace hinted at his royal connection (ii. 5 f.), his home in Nazareth made him a Galilean (xxvi. 69) and so something of a provincial; he came from an obscure town, unmentioned in the O.T. or in any first-century source outside the N.T. 'Matthew' seems to see in the name Nazareth a reference to Isa. xi. 1; he connects the word Nazorean, taken as a reference to Nazareth, with the *nētzer*, 'shoot', of that verse. But the obscurity of Nazareth remains a fact. Even in such an unimportant town Jesus takes a humble role; his boyhood neighbours are sceptical about his ability to play a prominent role in the wider world (xiii. 54-58). The humble, homeless, insecure lot of Jesus during his ministry continues this unimpressive aspect of his life.

But this humble aspect is always coupled with a transcendent dimension. The very name Jesus held memory and promise. It was the Greek form of the O.T. name Joshua, which meant that 'Yah(weh) saves' (or, is salvation), and though it was a common name in first-century Jewish communities, Jesus was the one person truly entitled to bear it, 'for he will *save* his people from their sins' (i. 21). He was a member of God's special people, 'the son of Abraham' (i. 1), and so heir of all the promises and fitted to carry the gospel of promise to others. We must note later his climactic position in the royal Davidic line.

A number of current titles of honour are used of Jesus. He was a 'teacher', and in three passages used this title of himself (x. 24 f.; xxiii. 8; xxvi. 18). We may consider 'rabbi' the equivalent of 'teacher', but Matt. has no favourable use of 'rabbi'; the disciples are not to accept this title (xxiii. 7 f.), and it is applied to Jesus only in two addresses by Judas (xxvi. 25, 49). The title teacher, however, clearly implies outstanding honour. Jesus was known for the note of authority in his teaching; his vigorous, independent 'I say to you' led 'Matthew' to comment on this note (v. 22, 28, 32, 34, 39, 44; vii. 29).

Another title of honour, 'prophet', was applied to Jesus both by others (xvi. 14; xxi. 11, 46) and by himself (x. 41; xiii. 57). He spoke with direct authority from God. He claimed an authority even greater than that of the O.T. prophets. Whether any thought of him, or whether he thought of himself, as the great prophet promised in Deut. xviii. 15, 18 is not clear, but some saw in him the fulfilment of the expectation that Elijah would return at the end of the age (Mal. iv. 5), and all of the popular identifications reported to him in xvi. 14 classify him as a prophet.

A title which one might have expected to play a prominent role in the Matthean portrait of Jesus is that of the Suffering Servant. In content the Servant portrait is present, but only xii. 18 actually quotes the title, and while viii. 17 cites Isa. liii. 4, 'Matthew' makes little explicit use of this title and pattern of thought.

Some of the content of the Suffering Servant figure appears

in the use of the title 'Son of Man'. The author of Matt., like
the authors of the other three Gospels, never uses this title in
his own remarks or in narrative. It always occurs in a saying of
Jesus himself; it is Jesus' favourite self-designation. The title has
O.T. roots in the Psalms (viii. 4), in Ezekiel (ii. 1; etc.), and in
Daniel (vii. 13 f.), and also seems to echo the usage of the Book
of Enoch. For Jesus the title describes well his humble earthly
life (viii. 20: 'nowhere to lay his head'), the necessity of his
suffering (xvii. 22; xx. 18), and his exalted role as Lord and final
Judge (xxv. 31). The title is characteristic of the Gospel in that
it combines both the humble and the exalted aspects of the
career and person of Jesus.

Prominent among the titles which 'Matthew' uses of Jesus are
those which point to his royal, Messianic dignity. Chief of these
is 'Christ'; Jesus fulfils the Jewish expectation that God will
send an anointed leader to deliver and lead Israel. Also used with
proud emphasis (except for xxii. 41-46, where Jesus, to avoid
current nationalist and political expectations, rejects the title)
is the title 'Son of David', which appears from the genealogy
(i. 1) to the last days in Jerusalem (xxi. 15). Charged with the
same note of royal Messianic position are the titles 'King of the
Jews' (ii. 2; xxvii. 11, 29, 37), 'King of Israel' (xxvii. 42), 'your
king' (xxi. 5), and 'the king' (xxv. 34, 40); 'his kingdom' in xvi.
28 carries the same reference, with eschatological focus. More
general terms which point to climactic realization of the hopes of
Israel are 'the capstone' or 'the head of the corner' (xxi. 42) and
the indication that in Jesus 'something greater' than the temple,
Jonah, or Solomon is present (xii. 6, 41 f.). The temptation
narrative (iv. 1-11) shows that Jesus put aside unworthy political, military, and nationalistic aspects of his people's Messianic
hope, but this Gospel never forgets that Jesus fulfilled the real
meaning and promise of that hope.

The Messiah was usually conceived by Israel as a human
leader of unique goodness and power. 'Matthew' means more
than this by the term; Jesus is 'the Son of God' (iv. 3, 6; viii.
29), or 'the Son of the living God' (xvi. 16), or, at the baptism
and transfiguration, 'my beloved Son' (iii. 17; xvii. 5), or, in the
words of Scripture, 'my Son' (ii. 15; Hos. xi. 1). Such titles
never deny or obscure the humanity of Jesus; they mean at least

in part that Jesus is the expected Messiah of Israel. But they suggest a leader who is more than a good and great man, and the outraged protest of Jewish leaders that Jesus was claiming and exercising divine functions (ix. 3; xxvi. 65) receives supporting content from xi. 25-30, where an intimate relation with the Father and an ability to give divine blessings imply a Christology that goes far beyond the idea of a human king. The trinitarian baptismal formula in xxviii. 19 is not paralleled elsewhere in this Gospel (or in the N.T.), but like xi. 25-30 it uses the filial relation to express the fullest meaning of the person of Jesus in relation to God. The Messianic title has taken on a fuller meaning than it usually had in Jewish Messianic thought.

This divine rank and function is clearly expressed in the title 'Lord'. This title κύριος does not occur in xxviii. 18, where the substance of the title is clearly present in the claim to exaltation and world dominion, but 'Lord' is used of Jesus, if we include passages in parables and other teaching where the reference to him seems clear, a total of about forty-nine times. There could be dispute about the meaning of a few of these passages, but the astonishing number of references shows that for 'Matthew' Jesus had unique power and authority during his ministry, and is now the exalted risen Lord of the Church.

The exalted Christ, given Lordship over all things in heaven and on earth, promises that 'I am with you always' (xxviii. 20). This recalls an earlier promise that 'where two or three are gathered in my name, there am I in the midst of them' (xviii. 20); he will give his Church constant, powerful guidance and support. And while 'Matthew' does not give in clear form the later doctrine of incarnation, he does see in the birth and presence of Jesus the realization of an Old Testament promise; 'they will name him Emmanuel, which means, God with us' (i. 23); in him God is present to 'save his people from their sins' and to be in their midst 'to the end of the age' (i. 21; xxviii. 20).

2. MOSES AND THE LAW

Moses is mentioned in the N.T. nearly eighty times, more than any other O.T. figure. The references utilize both O.T. data and current Jewish traditions. Our present concern is with

Matt. Behind the Herod story in ch. ii lies the Moses legend; Pharaoh was warned of the birth of Israel's redeemer, and after Pharaoh's death Moses was told that the way was clear to return to Egypt (cf. Ex. iv. 19). Matt. does not refer to the expectation of a prophet like Moses (Deut. xviii. 15, 18), and there is no real evidence that he had this expectation in mind when he told of John's ministry in the wilderness (ch. iii) and reported that Jesus was a prophet (xvi. 14). Whether the idea of the second Moses as Messiah was current in Jesus' day is not entirely clear; if so, it could have influenced the Matthean theme of the Christ who was the great teacher of his people. For certainly the parallel is striking between Moses receiving the Law on the mount and Jesus giving the new revelation of God's will on the mount (v. 1). We need not go so far as B. W. Bacon, who held that in Matt. the five great discourses are the new Law which supersedes the five books of Moses. This hardly does justice to the passages in Matt. which affirm the continuing validity of the Mosaic Law (v. 17 f.). But the Sermon on the Mount does present the teaching of Jesus as a superior revelation of God's will, and this suggests that Matthew was comparing and contrasting Jesus with Moses. However, this parallel and contrast were not the Gospel's central concern. In fact, Matt. contains fewer references to Moses than does any of the other three Gospels.

What does 'Matthew' present as the attitude of Jesus towards the Mosaic Law? To a great extent that attitude was positive. When Jesus denied the divine origin of the oral tradition, which to the Pharisees constituted part of the revealed law of God (xv. 3, 6), he did so in part to prevent the Jews from obscuring the claims of the Law. xxiii. 3, 'do and observe whatever they tell you', seems to accept the entire position of the Pharisees, but the real point in this verse is to warn the crowds not to follow the *practice* of the scribes and Pharisees; their teaching, Jesus says, is better than their practice; in so far as they teach the Law, they deserve respect. xxiii. 23 indicates that Jesus accepted a scribal expansion of the tithing law to cover even small plants. But whatever concessions these verses may imply, the main drive of Jesus' teaching in Matt. is clear; he rejects the oral tradition, and does so to protect the importance and authority of the Law contained in Scripture.

Jesus in Matt. clearly affirms the importance of this Law. He tells the healed leper to show himself to the priest and offer the gift Moses commanded (viii. 4). When the rich young man wants to know what to do to enter into life, Jesus tells him to keep the commandments given in the Law (xix. 17-19). He tells his followers to keep the Scriptural teaching of even unworthy leaders (xxiii. 2 f.), since they 'sit on Moses' seat'; he speaks as though disaster on the Sabbath has special terror (xxiv. 20); he himself keeps the Passover (xxvi. 18). Most important of all, he declares that his purpose is not to tear down the Law but to fulfil it (v. 17 f.). It is often claimed that Jesus could not have spoken v. 18: 'Not one iota or one part of a letter will pass away from the law until all things take place'. The objection is valid if this verse is taken with rigid literalness, for Jesus did not hesitate to challenge the literal form of precepts of the Law. But in a deep sense the verse represents the attitude not only of 'Matthew' but also of Jesus. For him the Law revealed the will of God; his purpose was not to fight that revelation but to affirm it, clarify it, and give it fuller expression. He did not think his work hostile to the Law of God as given in the O.T. That Law was a real divine revelation and it carried authority.

At times a more critical attitude is expressed. Though Moses gave permission to divorce one's wife, that was only 'because of your hardness of heart' (xix. 8), and though Matt. v. 32; xix. 9 recognize one ground for divorce which Mk., Lk., and Paul do not allow, even in Matt. Jesus intends to exclude at least part of the permission he found in Deut. xxiv. 1. When challenged for eating with tax collectors and sinners, or for letting his disciples do what was considered work on the Sabbath, Jesus stoutly asserts his freedom not only from oral tradition but even from all legal bonds by quoting Hosea vi. 6, 'I desire mercy and not sacrifice' (ix. 13; xii. 7). Most astounding of all is his declaration that not only is oral tradition not binding, but even food laws do not define what defiles a man (xv. 10-20); consistently developed, this would eliminate the entire 'kosher' system.

Why does Jesus speak in this critical way? In part it comes from putting the important things first when there is a clash of interests. He points out that priests do manual labour on the Sabbath without guilt, since they have a higher duty to carry on the acts of worship in the temple (xii. 5). Just so Jesus' concern for tax collectors and sinners cannot yield to laws of ritual cleanness; this concern for needy people warrants disregard for the usual laws of ceremonial purity.

Thus this criticism of current legal practices does not spring from an antinomian desire to be free for selfish indulgence. Quite the contrary. Jesus considers the obedience which he teaches to be more demanding than the usual legal standards of his day (v. 20). The entire teaching of v. 21-48 shows that he has a deep respect for the Law and a penetrating discernment of its spiritual objective, and is concerned to state that objective fully and express it in life. In his emphasis on treating others with respect and helpfulness (vii. 12), and with love which follows from and expresses love for God (xxii. 34-40), he does not discard the Law; as both passages say, this is what 'the law and the prophets' are concerned to achieve, a life of human kindness and love, in which loyalty to God and love for neighbour fulfils the Law's demand. His message of repentance and forgiveness removes all idea of earning and deserving God's gifts; it makes life a willing obedience which surpasses legal uprightness.

Yet though Jesus accepted the Law as Scripture, found in it the revelation of God's will, and fought all lax indifference to its demands, he was no legalist and the Law was not the centre of his teaching. His own teaching takes pre-eminence over the literal prescriptions of the Law; it is by study and interpretation of the Law that he comes to the deeper truth he teaches, but his own teaching carries an independent note of authority. 'You have heard that it was said to the men of ancient times' by God through Moses, 'but I say to you' (v. 21 f.; etc.). The eternal welfare or ruin of men will be determined by whether they obey or disregard his teaching (vii. 24-27). And he himself, the Lord of the Sabbath (xii. 8), the authoritative teacher, the Christ of God's people, is the personal centre of loyalty. The Law is not the focus of the life of the disciple; the disciple follows Jesus, who not only has supreme authority now but also will speak the decisive word at the end and so will determine the eternal lot of man (xxv. 34, 41). He holds this position not as the supreme lawgiver, greater even than Moses, but as the preacher of repentance and forgiveness, the active bringer of God's healing and redeeming mercy, who does not cancel the demand of the Law, but enables his followers to do more than the scribes and Pharisees and yet to find that his 'yoke is easy' and his 'burden is light' (xi. 30).

'Matthew' is often called a legalist, and his practice of codifying the teaching of Jesus raises a strong suspicion that he had a legalistic tendency. But his portrait of Jesus far transcends legalism, and with a very few possible exceptions such as v. 18 and xxiii. 3 it reflects the essential attitude of Jesus himself.

3. THE KINGDOM

The central theme of Jesus' preaching in Matt. is the Kingdom. The usual phrase, 'kingdom of heaven' (32 times), is never found in any other N.T. book. Four times we find 'kingdom of God', a phrase found in the other Gospels and in other N.T. writings. Similar phrases are 'thy kingdom', 'the kingdom of their Father', and 'my Father's kingdom' (vi. 10; xiii. 43; xxvi. 29). The kingdom can also be called the kingdom of Jesus, the Son of Man (xiii. 41; xx. 21); it is also called 'the kingdom', without further description. There is no real difference between these varied expressions. The word 'heaven' is used in ancient Jewish writings as a surrogate for 'God', and a study of parallel passages shows that Matt. repeatedly has 'kingdom of heaven' where Mk. or Lk. or both have 'kingdom of God'.

The essential meaning of 'kingdom' ($\beta\alpha\sigma\iota\lambda\epsilon\iota\alpha$) is the active kingship and effective rule of God, established by the work of Jesus Christ. This for 'Matthew' and the early Church was not a timeless reality; no verse occurs which refers to the kingdom as a past fact. It is rather a remarkable new, decisive, and final work of God. John the Baptist announced its imminence (iii. 2), and Jesus began his public ministry with the same stirring proclamation (iv. 17). Ps. cxlv. 13 may speak of God's everlasting kingdom, and no doubt Jesus and his disciples would have found meaning in this verse, but his references to the kingdom are limited to the note of newness and expectancy.

Why is this? The opening announcements (iii. 2; iv. 17) point to the answer. The sin of man means that God's effective rule has not yet been established. Jesus comes to establish that

effective rule. His forerunner John the Baptist and he himself
therefore summon men to repent and believe the good news that
God is now acting with power to defeat the forces of evil and
establish his effective rule over his people. To establish it calls
for more than repentance and faith; it calls for obedience to
Jesus' teaching concerning the will of the Father (vii. 21).
Descent from the patriarchs, membership in the people of Israel,
will not guarantee membership in the kingdom; the unbelieving
and disobedient in Israel will lose their offered privilege and men
of other peoples will receive it (viii. 11 f.; xxi. 43). The poor in
spirit, the persecuted, will possess it (v. 3, 10); the humane and
kind will be welcomed into the kingdom by the Son of Man, the
King who acts for his Father (xxv. 34).

Did 'Matthew' consider this kingdom present or future? In
other words, did he think that Jesus had regarded it as present
or future? The Gospel clearly indicates that the kingdom in its
full form is future. The reign of God is not yet fully effective.
It will be finally and completely established at the end of the
age, and the Son of Man will act for the Father in establishing
it (xvi. 28; xx. 21; etc.). Every evil power will be crushed; all
men will be judged; the perfect eternal order will be established.

Is the kingdom entirely future or is it already present in its
beginnings? Some passages give no clear answer. They could
refer to already present stages of the kingdom, or to future
developments which will come in the course of historical events,
or to the full reign of God after the end of history. However,
even though the term kingdom always points on to the end of
history for its full realization, some passages indicate that the
kingdom is already partially present.

The petition in the Lord's Prayer, 'Thy kingdom come' (vi.
10), has this meaning. It follows a petition that the Father's
name may be hallowed, and precedes a petition that the Father's
will may be done on earth as in heaven; these are prayers that
God may be reverenced and his will done *now*; this hallowing,
this coming of the kingdom, this doing of God's will, refer to
partial realization even now of the divine order which will be
perfectly established at the end of history. If these three petitions pray only for the coming of the perfect final kingdom, the
worshipper's daily prayer receives no answer in his daily life.

33

Note also vi. 33: 'Seek first the kingdom and his righteousness, and all these things will be given you in addition'. He who rightly seeks the kingdom and makes it his first concern will receive food and clothing 'in addition'. 'In addition' indicates that the quest for the kingdom will be answered at least in part in this present life, where food, drink, and clothing are real needs.

The obscure saying of Jesus that violent men have been taking the kingdom (xi. 11 f.) since the days of John the Baptist indicates that a new day has come in Jesus' ministry; something not available before is now there to enter; the kingdom is more than a promise and a hope; in some degree it is a present reality. Clearer still is xii. 28; the divine power by which Jesus expels the demons demonstrates that 'the kingdom of God has just come to you'.

The only natural explanation of the parables of growth in ch. xiii is that they present the kingdom as a present reality whose greater final form is sure to come. This sense of the present beginning of a radically new day and order comes out also in the reference to the privilege of the disciples, who now see and hear what the forward-looking prophets and righteous men of earlier days had longed to see and hear (xiii. 17). The natural explanation of the binding and loosing on earth by Peter (xvi. 19) is that the keys of the kingdom have to do with his work in this present age, before the final judgment; and xviii. 18 f. refers to the same active exercise of divinely given power in the present age. xxi. 31 may be thought to refer to the future entrance of the tax collectors and sinners into the kingdom, but the present tense of the verb suggests that the kingdom privilege of these people begins in their relation to Jesus during his ministry. Similar is xxiii. 13; the scribes and Pharisees are not entering the kingdom, and they are doing all they can to keep others from entering. Only a present kingdom, existing in a world where evil surrounds the disciples and constantly tries to infiltrate and defeat their cause, fits the parables of ch. xiii, especially those of the darnel and the net (xiii. 24-30; 47-50). Many interpreters deny that Jesus could have spoken such parables, which indicate a temporary presence of unworthy elements in the kingdom. However, 'Matthew' saw in the kingdom a present struggle between members loyal to Jesus and opposing evil forces. Moreover, Judas was one of the Twelve; obviously the present power of the kingdom (xii. 28) did not prevent the struggle between God's rule and the Satanic powers from reaching into the select circle of the leading followers of Jesus. The kingdom was to 'Matthew' and to Jesus a present fact, though only in its limited beginnings; the full and unchallenged rule of God was yet to come.

When? Soon. Very soon. x. 23 is puzzling. To us it may seem to promise the Twelve something which was not fulfilled before they returned to Jesus. 'Matthew' found in it a clear indication that the victory of Christ's cause, the coming of the Son of Man in power and glory, was not far off when he wrote. xvi. 28 supports this sense of imminence and expectancy; the end was considered near. Jesus did not know the exact time, and his disciples could not know it (xxiv. 36). The end might delay a bit and men become careless (xxiv. 48). But the end was near (xxiv. 34). God has already begun to act with power; the kingdom is already present in its beginnings; it will come soon in full force and in final form. Both the absolute claim of God upon his people and the urgent necessity to repent, believe, and obey find telling expression in this vivid sense of imminence. The writer of Matt. is sustained in this vivid confidence by the knowledge that the risen Christ, the Lord of the Church, has been given all authority in heaven and on earth (xxviii. 18), and so his rule is present, his power is real, and his victory is certain.

4. THE MIRACLES

It is axiomatic to 'Matthew' that Jesus exercised remarkable power. The Pharisees could not deny it (xii. 24). Even Herod Antipas had heard of these mighty acts (xiv. 2). 'Matthew' does not claim to report them all; Chorazin, Bethsaida, and Capernaum were the cities in which the greatest number of miracles had been done (xi. 20-24), yet the Gospel tells no specific miracle done at Chorazin or Bethsaida; 'Matthew' thus knows of more mighty deeds than he describes. Matt., the other Gospels, and Acts all testify that Jesus performed many miracles, striking acts of power in which the eye of faith saw the special and purposeful working of the living God to further his divine purpose.

We must not overstress the uniqueness of this aspect of Jesus' ministry. He himself noted that others who did not follow him could do striking deeds. False prophets did them (vii. 22); so did disciples of the Pharisees (xii. 27); even demonic powers could perform them. This may help us to understand why, when Jesus performed miracles, he did not win immediate and universal support from those who knew of them. While Jesus became indignant when opponents ascribed his exorcisms to the working of Beelzebul (xii. 24), he did not attempt to win people by such remarkable acts. One meaning of the Temptation (iv. 1-11) is that Jesus refused to use his power to pressure people into accepting his claims. He refused to give a sign, that is, a miracle done just to prove his claims and compel faith in him (xii. 39; xvi. 4); the apparent exception, the sign of Jonah, is taken as a reference to the resurrection, and so to a future event which only faith can see. Jesus tried to avoid publicity for his healings (ix. 30); he obviously wanted to direct central attention to his gospel of the kingdom.

The gospel narrative repeatedly indicates that compassion led Jesus to heal and help people. He responded in active sympathy to human need. At times 'Matthew' indicates that Jesus could and did heal every sick person brought to him (iv. 23 f.; xii. 15; xiv. 35 f.; xv. 30). But more than once he notes the need of faith in the sick persons or at least in their friends, and at Nazareth lack of faith keeps Jesus from doing many mighty works (xiii. 58). The importance of faith is connected with the manner in which he healed. Usually he did so with a word (in the case of Gentiles, as viii. 13 and xv. 28 show, he spoke while at a distance). When he touched a person (viii. 3, 15), or people touched the tassel of his garment (xiv. 36), his touch expressed sympathy and inspired confidence, and the touching of his garments, while probably indicating a tinge of superstition in the needy persons, also showed faith that he could help them.

These mighty acts were not a human achievement but the work of God, whose nature is power as well as wisdom and love; indeed, 'Power' can be used as a designation for 'God' (xxvi. 64). The Gospel indicates that this divine power worked in Jesus through the gift of the Spirit; he casts out demons by the Spirit of God (xii. 28). His opponents likewise assumed that a super-human power explained his miracles of exorcism (xii. 24); what aroused his indignation, however, was that they were so per-verted in spiritual understanding that they could see his beneficent Spirit-caused acts and call them the work of the devil (Beelzebul).

These mighty acts were essential to his God-given mission. The Messiah, 'Matthew' knew, was expected to possess and exercise such striking power; Isa. xxxv. 5 ff. and rabbinic sources indicate that such an expectation existed (cf. xi. 5). The mighty works of Jesus showed that the eschatological drama had begun. As xii. 28 clearly indicates, his exorcisms, his defeat of the powers of evil and his reclaiming of men to mental and physical health by the power of the Spirit of God, are for Jesus and for 'Matthew' clear evidence that the Kingdom has begun to come. The eschatological time has dawned. Evil is being defeated and the rule of God is advancing.

This may help us to see what it means when Jesus raises the dead and does the so-called nature miracles. To us these stories raise problems, but to 'Matthew' they show that the divine power is beginning to transform this present imperfect world, damaged by sin and sickness; now begin new days of life and health and blessing. It was common N.T. expectation that a new heaven and a new earth would be established. The mighty acts of Jesus showed the compassion of God and of his Servant the Christ; they showed the power of faith; they showed believers the divine approval of Jesus; but above all they showed the rule of God being established and they gave promise of the full and final triumph of God's will in a perfect order certain to bless and protect God's loyal children.

5. THE CROSS AND RESURRECTION

The cross is first of all a historical fact. Jesus was cruci-fied. He was innocent of any wrong that could have justified the crucifixion (xxvii. 4), but his enemies did bring it about, though the story makes clear that neither the Jewish leaders, nor the manipulated Jewish mob, nor Pilate, nor Judas, nor the frightened disciples acted with honour and courage. 'Matthew' placed heavy emphasis on the guilt of the Jewish leaders, but he hardly accepted Pilate's plea that in condemning Jesus he himself was innocent and upright (xxvii. 24). Pilate knew that Jesus was not guilty (xxvii. 18), and the real aim in giving Pilate's words is to attest Jesus' innocence, which the message from Pilate's wife also underlines (xxvii. 19).

Jesus foresaw that he would be put to death. There is no clear evidence in Matt. that he foresaw the cross from the time of the baptism; only after the confession of Peter at Caesarea Philippi does he speak of it to his disciples. This need not mean that he had not suspected earlier what was coming, but the lack of emphasis on the cross before Caesarea Philippi and the repeated emphasis after that event indicate that it was towards the end of his public ministry, after the clear rejection of his message and leadership by the Jewish leaders, that he definitely accepted the cross as a certainty. Then he presented the cross as inevitable. Because Jesus was determined to persist in his appeal to his people to prepare for and enter the dawning kingdom, he could see no escape from seizure, condemnation, and death; his painful struggle in Gethsemane was the final facing and acceptance of what he had foreseen for months.

But this inevitable event did not mean for Jesus the defeat of his work. The cross was consistent with the nature and spirit of his ministry. From the time of the temptation he had turned from self-promotion, from nationalist and military aims, from the use of spectacular force or external compulsion. He taught; he went to people in friendship; he helped those in need and brought sympathy to those who suffered. This life of unselfish love and helpfulness, described in Isa. xlii. 1-4 as that of God's true servant (xii. 18-21), meant readiness to pay a personal cost to bring God's help to men. The cross as the way of costly love and faithful obedience was the final act in doing what Jesus had been doing all through his ministry; he 'came not to be served but to serve, and to give his life as a ransom for many' (xx. 28); in this verse the consistency between the death and the ministry is clearly expressed. And this lets us see how Jesus could ask others to take up their crosses; the spirit of his life and death must be reflected by his followers in active, costly love.

This means that Jesus accepted the cross as the will of God. When he said that he 'must . . . suffer' (xvi. 21), he did not mean merely that men would surely bring him to death, but that this was God's plan, which he in loyalty accepted. Because he would not reject the divine plan, it was true of him, as the taunting hostile cry ironically said, 'Others he saved; himself he cannot save' (xxvii. 42).

Another indication that the cross was God's will for him is his statement that his death fulfils Scripture. 'The Son of Man goes as it is written concerning him', 'that the Scriptures of the prophets might be fulfilled' (xxvi. 24, 54, 56). The work of God in the O.T. period looked forward to the full realization of God's redemptive plan in the cross; here deep continuity with the history of Israel is combined with advance beyond that earlier divine working.

At the Last Supper Jesus used the broken bread and the wine to symbolize his death, and he called the wine 'my blood of the covenant, shed for many for forgiveness of sins' (xxvi. 28). The Gospels differ in the wording of Jesus' reference to the wine, but in each case it symbolizes his impending death and indicates that his death will not mean hopeless defeat but will rather prove the decisive factor in achieving the divine redemptive purpose. His suffering will fulfil God's plan and give the needed help to his followers. These references to his suffering are never spoken in despair; they couple with prediction of death the promise of the resurrection (xvi. 21; xvii. 23; xx. 19). It has been argued that Jesus did not foresee his death and that his disciples later ascribed to him these words of hope. 'Matthew' and the other evangelists considered them authentic. And why not? The signs of rejection and hostility were unmistakable and the danger of death became increasingly acute. Jesus thought clearly enough to see this. It posed a crucial question: How could he, who was doing God's will, ignore the signs of rejection or accept death as the last word? Could he have gone on in a tortured bewilderment or naïve unconcern that sought no explanation of his approaching death? The disciples never thought that they were his equal in intellectual alertness and insight; they were certain that he had first grasped what was coming and had related the cross to the divine purpose. No one has ever suggested a convincing alternative to this gospel tradition. Jesus foresaw his death, and accepted it as a decisive act in furthering the work of God. He looked beyond death to the resurrection.

There is another way to say what Jesus did. The O.T. figure of the Suffering Servant deeply influenced his thinking and his understanding of what the O.T. anticipated. 'Matthew' rarely quotes the Isaiah Servant passages. iii. 17 seems to include a reminiscence of Isa. xlii. 1; viii. 17 quotes Isa. liii. 4; xii. 18-21 quotes Isa xlii. 1-4; and 'many' in xxvi. 28 seems to recall Isa. liii. 11 f. But the spirit of the Suffering Servant is prominent in the Matthean picture of Jesus; he rejects current nationalistic or militaristic ideas of the expected Jewish leader, and while he includes the note of glory and mighty triumph in his thought of the Son of Man, his accent on humble life, suffering, and death shows his kinship with the Suffering Servant figure. This combining of the Messianic, Son of Man, and Suffering Servant figures in a way that gives the latter a dominant role cannot be shown to have existed in Israel before Jesus. Matt. and the other Gospels testify that it was Jesus who fused these expectations in this form. This is the only convincing explanation of how Jesus understood his work.

In Matt. and in the N.T. generally the resurrection is the interpreting clue by which to understand the cross. Jesus himself did more than predict the cross; he spoke of his resurrection, his further role in God's plan, and his final triumph. And it was in fact the resurrection which rallied the disciples to continue their witness.

Like the cross, the resurrection has a congenial background in the ministry of Jesus. One meaning of the gospel stories of raising persons from the dead (ix. 25) is that Jesus is lord over death; he had this power and could give it to his disciples (x. 8). He taught that there would be a resurrection (xxii. 23-33) and that he would rise from the dead (xvi. 21; xvii. 23; xx. 19; xxvi. 32). The clear witness of the Gospel, and indeed of the entire early Church, is that Jesus did rise from the dead, meet his disciples, and assure them that as the risen Lord he would be with them and at the end of the age would achieve the final victory of God's purpose. No one produced his body to discredit this claim. There exists no better explanation of the renewed

faith and courageous witness of his disciples than their assurance
that he had risen and rallied them. This confident faith lies back
of all that 'Matthew' writes.

6. THE CHURCH

Matt. is justly called the ecclesiastical Gospel, not merely
because only this Gospel contains the word 'church' (xvi. 18;
xviii. 17), but also because of its vital role in the Church's life
and work. 'Matthew' wrote not to establish himself as a literary
figure but to serve the needs of the Church in which he was an
active leader.

The Greek word for Church, ἐκκλησία, refers to a called
assembly and so to those united in such an assembly. But to
'Matthew' the Church was not chiefly or solely a human
assembly. The N.T. reflects the background of the LXX, and
the O.T. usage refers to the assembly of the people of God, the
congregation of those whom God has called. To understand the
word Church requires constant attention to this idea of God's
chosen people.

This people may be said to have its centre in God, but for
'Matthew' and his fellow-Christians it was equally true to say
that it has its centre in Jesus Christ. Men know the Father and
receive his benefits through the Son (xi. 25-30). Jesus calls the
Church 'my Church' (xvi. 18) and it is his action and death that
found it (xxvi. 28). He is with any two or three of his people
who gather in earnest prayer, and he will be with his chosen
leaders in their mission (xviii. 20; xxviii. 20).

The continuity between the O.T. people of God and the
Church which Jesus Christ established goes much deeper than
word usage. The life and worship of Christ's followers has a
framework taken from Judaism (vi. 1-18). Jesus went to the
Jews; rarely and only at urgent request did he minister to Gentiles (and then he healed at a distance); at first he told his disciples to limit their ministry to Israel (x. 5 f.; xv. 24). His own
life and message were markedly Jewish in character and showed
deep indebtedness to the O.T.

Yet certain aspects of this Jewishness set Jesus and his group
apart from the usual Judaism of his day. He knew himself to be

sent 'to the *lost* sheep of the house of Israel' (xv. 24). Mercy rather than sacrifice (ix. 13; xii. 7), compassion rather than formal keeping of Sabbath rules (xii. 11 f.), were central for him. What moved him was the pure and single motive of doing the will of God with a willing spirit. He was concerned not for the divisive aspects of Judaism but for those concerns deep in the O.T. and the Jewish heritage which could open the door to the wider reach of God's purpose.

This wider outlook is clearly present in Matt. This Gospel may be called the Jewish-Christian Gospel; its Jewish-Christian writer was deeply aware of the Jewishness of Jesus and was deeply loyal to his own people. But he kept lifting his eyes to look beyond Judaism. The visit of the Magi is an early assertion of the divine purpose to reach the Gentiles through the new-born child (ii. 1-12). The Galilee where Jesus began and centred his ministry was 'Galilee of the Gentiles', a region with Gentile contacts, and his fame drew people from Syria and the Deca-polis—a hint that his work must reach beyond the borders of Judaism (iv. 15, 24 f.). viii. 11 f. speaks of the Kingdom rather than of the Church, but its prediction that many Gentiles will enter the Kingdom, while many Jews are rejected, transcends a merely Jewish outlook (cf. xxi. 43; xxiii. 38). God's servant Jesus will 'proclaim judgment to the Gentiles', 'and Gentiles will put their hope in his name' (xii. 18, 21). 'The field is the world' (xiii. 38). The gospel will be 'preached in the whole world'; the disciples are to 'go therefore and make disciples of all nations' (xxvi. 13; xxviii. 19). The absence of emphasis on rigid conformity to Jewish ceremonial law, and the repeated hints of the world outreach of the Gospel, show active sympathy with the expanding missionary Church. The author of Matt. is no narrow die-hard Judaizer who cannot see beyond the bounds and practices of Judaism.

For 'Matthew' the Church was not a leaderless democracy. Jesus chose the Twelve and gave them special responsibility (x. 2-4) not only for a mission during his ministry, but for future years, and even at the judgment (xix. 28). They are promised special knowledge of the mysteries of his teaching concerning the Kingdom (xiii. 11). Peter is given special prominence and responsibility (xvi. 17-19). He is clearly presented as the most prominent and dynamic of the Twelve. Luke confirms that Jesus counted on Peter for special leadership (Lk. xxii. 32). Because 'Matthew' continually groups sayings by topic, it may be that xvi. 17-19 was not all spoken at one time and on the occasion of xvi. 13-16. But the testimony that Jesus gave Peter a unique place in his movement is credible, and Peter's active role in the crucial early years of the Church supports this conclusion. The passage says nothing about successors; it is not a legal and rigid enactment of ecclesiastical law; but it must not be trimmed down to a warm praise of Peter's faith. Jesus praises Peter, gives him a place of leadership, and promises him that his acts and decisions will have divine support. This does not mean that false decisions will have to be approved by God; Jesus himself, four verses later, calls Peter 'Satan' when he makes a wrong decision. But Peter's leadership will be basic, and God will give power and effect to his right actions and decisions. Peter the believing disciple and apostle will be the rock on which the Church will be built.

This prominence is not hierarchical and legal. What Jesus promises to Peter he promises also to the entire group of disciples (xviii. 18). Note that he even gives the same promise to any two or three sincere disciples who agree in their prayer (xviii. 19 f.). No reader expects God to give to these two or three anything contrary to the divine wisdom and will. But the promise to them is as unconditional as the one to Peter. Actually both promises have an unspoken spiritual condition; actions, decisions, and requests must accord with God's will or he will not approve them. This should be clear from the rebuke Jesus gives to Peter in xvi. 23. The Gospel is not giving legalistic, unconditional promises. Once this is recognized, the outstanding role of Peter can be acknowledged and seen in proper perspective.

How is the Church related to the Kingdom? If the Kingdom were entirely future, there would be no problem. But only by deleting passages can any of the Gospels be forced to witness to a purely future Kingdom. Jesus knew that the Kingdom was beginning in his own work, and so the Church and the early stages of the Kingdom overlap. In Matt. the Kingdom is present in an initial stage, and it is not free from involvement in the imperfections of this age. The word of the Kingdom may fail to take root; it may establish only shallow and temporary roots in some lives; it may become choked by worldly forces; but in spite of all this it does yield a rich harvest (xiii. 3-23). The enemy may sow hostile seed; a clear separation between the righteous and the wicked may not be possible until the last judgment; but the message and power of the Kingdom are already effective (xiii. 24-30). The parable of the catch of both good and bad fish carries the same point (xiii. 47-50). This apparently compromising mixture of good and evil troubles many interpreters. Surely, they think, God acts with perfect effectiveness; his rule, if present at all, exists in unclouded purity. As for 'Matthew', this clearly was not his view. As for Jesus, he chose twelve disciples, and one was Judas Iscariot. The Gospels paint a picture of real beginnings; truly divine power moves forward in a situation full of hostility. Perhaps 'Matthew' has developed allegorically what Jesus taught in parables. Perhaps the compromises 'Matthew' saw in the Church coloured his picture of Jesus' career. But for Jesus as for 'Matthew' the Kingdom has begun and yet meets hostility from without and disloyalty from within.

In two respects 'Matthew' distinguishes the Church and the Kingdom: (1) The Church is temporary, and will give way to the perfect and full rule of God in his eternal Kingdom. (2) The Church is thought of in terms of its mission. It must evangelize and teach in order to bring men to faith and train them in obedience to God's will. This mission of the Church—not its formal government—is the real concern of 'Matthew'. In that active work he took his place, and to further that work he wrote his Gospel.

SELECTED BIBLIOGRAPHY

Aland, Kurt, *Synopsis Quattuor Evangeliorum*. Stuttgart, 1964.

Allen, W. C., *A Critical and Exegetical Commentary on the Gospel According to S. Matthew*. Edinburgh, 1907.

Arndt, W. F., and Gingrich, F. W., *A Greek-English Lexicon of the N.T. and Other Early Christian Literature*. Chicago, 1957.

Bacon, B. W., *Studies in Matthew*. London and New York, 1930.

Benoit, P., *L'Evangile selon saint Matthieu*. Paris, 1950.

Birkeland, H., *The Language of Jesus*. Oslo and London, 1954.

Black, M., *The Dead Sea Scrolls and Christian Doctrine*. London, 1966.

Black, M., *An Aramaic Approach to the Gospels and Acts*. 2nd ed., Oxford, 1954.

Brownlee, W. H., *The Dead Sea Manual of Discipline* (BASOR). New Haven, 1951.

Bornkamm, G., *Jesus of Nazareth*. New York, 1960.

Bornkamm, G., Barth, G., and Held, H. J., *Tradition and Interpretation in Matthew*. Philadelphia, 1963.

Bultmann, R., *Die Geschichte der synoptischen Tradition*. 5th ed., Göttingen, 1961. Eng. Tr., *The History of the Synoptic Tradition*. Oxford, 1963.

Butler, B. C., *The Originality of St. Matthew*. Cambridge, 1951.

Cross, F. M., Jr., *The Ancient Library of Qumran and Modern Biblical Studies*. New York, 1958.

Cullmann, O., *Peter: Disciple, Apostle, Martyr*. London and Philadelphia, 1953.

Dalman, G. H., *The Words of Jesus*. Edinburgh, 1909.

Davies, W. D., 'Knowledge in the Dead Sea Scrolls and Mt. 11:25-30'. *HTR*, xlvi (1953), pp. 113-129.

Davies, W. D., *The Sermon on the Mount*. New York, 1966.

Dibelius, M., *From Tradition to Gospel*. New York, 1935.

Dobschütz, E. von, 'Matthäus als Rabbi und Katechet'. *ZNW*, xxvii (1928), pp. 338-348.

Dodd, C. H., *Parables of the Kingdom*. London and New York, 1936.

Dodd, C. H., *According to the Scriptures*. London, 1952.

Gaster, T. H., *The Dead Sea Scriptures in English Translation*. Rev. ed., Garden City, New York, 1964.

Gerhardsson, B., *Memory and Manuscript: Oral Tradition and Written Transmission in Rabbinic Judaism and Early Christianity*. Lund, 1961.

GOSPEL ACCORDING TO ST. MATTHEW

Goodspeed, E. J., *Matthew: Apostle and Evangelist*. Philadelphia, 1959.

Harris, J. R., *Testimonies I-II*. Cambridge, 1916-1920.

Hawkins, J. C., *Horae Synopticae*. 2nd ed. Oxford, 1909.

Heuschen, J. (ed.), *La Formation des Evangiles*. Bruges, 1957.

Huck, A., and Lietzmann, H., *Synopsis of the First Three Gospels*. 9th ed. Tübingen, 1936. Eng. Ed. by F. L. Cross, 1954.

Hunt, B. P. W. Stather, *Primitive Gospel Sources*. London, 1951.

Jeremias, J., *The Eucharistic Words of Jesus*. Oxford, 1955. Rev. ed. 1966.

Jeremias, J., *The Parables of Jesus*. London, 1954. Eng. Tr., Rev. ed. 1963.

The Jerusalem Bible. Garden City, N.Y., 1966.

Johnson, S. E., *The Gospel According to St. Matthew* (Interpreter's Bible, vol. vii). New York, 1951.

Kilpatrick, G. D., *The Origins of the Gospel According to St. Matthew*. Oxford, 1946.

Kittel, G. (ed.), *Theologisches Wörterbuch zum Neuen Testament*. Vols. 1-8 have appeared; Vol. 9 is in process. An English Translation in eight volumes is well over half completed.

Klostermann, E., *Das Matthäusevangelium*. 2nd ed. Tübingen, 1927.

Knox, W. L., *The Sources of the Synoptic Gospels*. 2 vols. Cambridge, 1953-1957.

Kümmel, W. G., *Einleitung in das N.T.* 14th ed. 1965. Eng. Tr. *Introduction to the New Testament*. Nashville, 1966.

Lohmeyer, E. (and W. Schmauch), *Das Evangelium des Matthäus*. Göttingen, 1956.

Manson, T. W., *The Teaching of Jesus*, 2nd ed. Cambridge, 1935.

Massaux, T., *Influence de l'Evangile de saint Matthieu sur la litterature chrétienne avant saint Irénée*. Louvain, 1950.

McArthur, H. K., *Understanding the Sermon on the Mount*. Harper, 1960.

McNeile, A. H., *The Gospel According to St. Matthew*. London, 1915.

Micklem, P. A., *St. Matthew*. London, 1917.

Montefiore, C. G., *The Synoptic Gospels*, 2 vols. 2nd ed. London, 1927.

Moore, G. F., *Judaism in the First Centuries of the Christian Era*. 3 vols. Cambridge, Mass., 1927-1930, Oxford, 1930.

Nestle-Aland ed. of the Gk.N.T. 1963.

Nineham, D. E. (ed.), *Studies in the Gospels*. Oxford, 1955.

Parker, P., *The Gospel Before Mark*. Chicago, 1953.

46

SELECTED BIBLIOGRAPHY

Peake's Commentary on the Bible. Rev. ed. by M. Black and H. H. Rowley. Nelson, 1962.

Plummer, A., *An Exegetical Commentary on the Gospel According to St. Matthew.* 2nd ed. London, 1910.

Reumann, J., *Jesus in the Church's Gospels.* Philadelphia, 1968.

Robinson, T. H., *The Gospel of Matthew.* London, 1928.

Schlatter, A., *Der Evangelist Matthäus.* Stuttgart, 1929.

Schniewind, J., *Das Evangelium nach Matthäus.* 8th printing. Göttingen, 1956.

Stanton, V. H., *The Gospels as Historical Documents.* 3 vols. Cambridge, 1903-1920.

Stendahl, K., *The School of St. Matthew.* Uppsala, 1954.

Stendahl, K. (ed.), *The Scrolls and the N.T.* New York, 1957, London, 1958.

Strack, H. L., and Billerbeck, P., *Kommentar zum N.T. aus Midrasch und Talmud.* 4 vols. München, 1922-1928.

Streeter, B. H., *The Four Gospels.* 4th ed. London, 1930.

Studia Evangelica, edited by Aland, K., Cross, F. L., Danielson, J., Riesenfeld, H., and Van Unnik, W. C. Berlin, 1959.

Taylor, V., *The Formation of the Gospel Tradition.* London, 1933.

Torrey, C. C., *The Four Gospels.* New York, 1933, London, 1934.

Torrey, C. C., *Documents of the Primitive Church.* New York, 1941.

Vaganay, L., *La Question synoptique.* Tournai, 1952.

Wright, G. E., and Filson, F. V., *Westminster Historical Atlas to the Bible.* 2nd ed. London and Philadelphia, 1956.

TRANSLATION AND COMMENTARY

THE GOSPEL ACCORDING
TO ST. MATTHEW

i. 1-17. THE GENEALOGY OF JESUS CHRIST

The genealogy of Jesus Christ, the son of David, the son of 1
Abraham. Abraham was the father of Isaac, Isaac the 2
father of Jacob, Jacob the father of Judah and his brothers,
Judah the father of Perez and Zerah by Tamar, Perez the 3
father of Hezron, Hezron the father of Ram, Ram the 4
father of Amminadab, Amminadab the father of Nahshon,
Nahshon the father of Salmon, Salmon the father of Boaz 5
by Rahab, Boaz the father of Obed by Ruth, Obed the father
of Jesse, and Jesse the father of David the king. 6
  David was the father of Solomon by the wife of Uriah,
Solomon the father of Rehoboam, Rehoboam the father 7
of Abijah, Abijah the father of Asa, Asa the father of 8
Jehoshaphat, Jehoshaphat the father of Joram, Joram the
father of Uzziah, Uzziah the father of Jotham, Jotham 9
the father of Ahaz, Ahaz the father of Hezekiah, Heze- 10
kiah the father of Manasseh, Manasseh the father of
Amos, Amos the father of Josiah, and Josiah the father of 11
Jechoniah and his brothers at the time of the deportation
to Babylon.
  After the deportation to Babylon, Jechoniah was the 12
father of Shealtiel, Shealtiel the father of Zerubbabel,
Zerubbabel the father of Abiud, Abiud the father of Elia- 13
kim, Eliakim the father of Azor, Azor the father of Zadok, 14
Zadok the father of Achim, Achim the father of Eliud,
Eliud the father of Eleazar, Eleazar the father of Matthan, 15
Matthan the father of Jacob, and Jacob the father of 16
Joseph the husband of Mary, of whom was born Jesus
who is called Christ.

17 So all the generations from Abraham to David were fourteen generations, and from David to the deportation to Babylon were fourteen generations, and from the deportation to Babylon to the Christ were fourteen generations.

It is not surprising that the first verse of Matt. refers to **Jesus.** He is the subject of the entire Gospel. Even when others are mentioned, they appear only because of their relation to him. This is true even of the genealogy. Jesus is the **Christ,** the fulfilment of God's promise that he would send to his people an anointed King (Christ in Greek and Messiah in Hebrew mean 'anointed'); the genealogy promptly expresses his connection with Israel, with that promise, and with the O.T. God's special promises to Israel had begun with **Abraham** (Gen. xii), so it was important to carry the genealogy back to him (cf. Ruth iv. 18-22; 1 Chron. i. 34; ii. 1-15). The promise that David's descendant would rule over his people (2 Sam. vii. 12-16) explains why Jesus is at once called **Christ** and **son of David** (vs. 1), why David is called **the king** (vs. 6), and why the genealogy is traced through the line of kings (vss. 6-11) rather than through Nathan as Lk. iii. 31 does. The **deportation to Babylon** is mentioned not out of general historical interest but because it marked a sad new stage in God's dealings with Israel; from the deportation to the coming of Jesus there was no son of David ruling over Israel; God's people must wait for the promised 'King of the Jews' (ii. 2) to appear. This Gospel will end with a world outlook (xxviii. 19); it begins with firm anchor in Israel's national heritage and hopes, which find their fulfilment in Jesus Christ.

Four problems deserve mention: (1) The genealogy refers to four O.T. women: **Tamar** (in spite of her ruse 'more righteous than' Judah; Gen. xxxviii. 26), **Rahab** (the harlot of Josh. ii, assumed in Matt. to be the mother of Boaz), **Ruth** (a Moabitess, but loyal to Israel's God; Ruth i. 16), and Bathsheba **(wife of Uriah;** David sinfully took her; 2 Sam. xi. 4). They are mentioned not in idle gossip or to reflect on Mary's purity, but to imply that just as these women in unexpected ways had a place in the Messianic genealogy, so Mary by God's unusual

working became the mother of the Christ. (2) Three kings
(Ahaziah, Joash, Amaziah) are omitted after **Joram** in vs. 8,
and one (Jehoiakim) after **Josiah** in vs. 11. This is hardly accidental; royal descent of Jesus according to promise is the point
of the genealogy; the omissions make the list of kings fit the
14-14-14 pattern, which is important to 'Matthew' not simply
because he likes threefold groupings, or because of his sense of
symmetry, but because it makes the importance of Abraham,
David, the Captivity, and Jesus stand out, and perhaps to recall
that the numerical value of the Hebrew letters in the name
David totals 14. (3) The actual number of new names in vss.
12-16 is not 14 but 13. Either there has been an error in count-
ing, or an early omission of a name, or Mary is included in the
series (which otherwise in normal Jewish manner reckons
descent through the father), because of her unusual role as the
virgin mother of Jesus. (4) The text of vs. 16 is not entirely
certain; other readings appear in ancient manuscripts and versions; the best attested variant reads: 'And Jacob was the father
of Joseph, to whom the virgin Mary was betrothed; he was the
father of Jesus who is called the Christ'. But the usual text is far
better attested and is probably original.

i. 18-25. THE BIRTH OF JESUS CHRIST

**Now the birth of Jesus Christ occurred as follows. After 18
his mother Mary had been betrothed to Joseph, before
they came together, she was found to have conceived by
the Holy Spirit. Joseph her husband, because he was 19
righteous and did not want to expose her, decided to
divorce her secretly. But when he had reached this de- 20
cision, behold, an angel of the Lord appeared to him in a
dream, saying, 'Joseph, son of David, do not be afraid to
take Mary your wife, for she has been made to conceive
by the Holy Spirit. She will bear a son, and you shall name 21
him Jesus, for he will save his people from their sins.'
All this took place that the word might be fulfilled which 22
had been spoken by the Lord through the prophet, who
said:**

23   'Behold, the virgin will conceive and bear a son,
          And they will name him Emmanuel',
      which means 'God with us'.

24   When Joseph awoke from sleep he did as the angel of
25   the Lord had commanded him; he took his wife, but he
      had no marriage relations with her until she had borne
      a son; and he named him Jesus.

In Matt. the birth of Jesus fulfils God's promises to Israel; it fulfils specific prophecy (vs. 22). It establishes the royal line of Jesus' ancestry; as the son of David, he is the Christ (vss. 1, 16, 17, 18; some manuscripts in vs. 18 read not **Jesus Christ** but simply **the Christ**). His birth is the miraculous coming of God into human life to dwell with men (cf. John i. 14) and save them from their sins (vs. 21).

Since betrothal was legally binding, Joseph is called **her husband** (vs. 19) and Mary **your wife** and **his wife** (vss. 20, 24). To break the bond Joseph would have to divorce her. He thought that Mary had violated the marriage tie by sinful relations with another man. In his uprightness he thought divorce necessary, but with a kindly concern to cause Mary a minimum of shame and public disgrace he **decided to divorce her secretly,** with the minimum number of legal witnesses (two, in rabbinical sources). **Son of David:** These words of the guiding **angel** (cf. ii. 13, 19) indicate Joseph's essential role; Jesus' legal descent from David passes through Joseph. **Jesus** is the Greek form of the Hebrew name Joshua. The interest here is not in Joshua's career but in the root meaning of his name: 'Yah(weh) saves' or 'Yah(weh) is salvation'. The child will fulfil the promise in the name; he will act for God or as 'God with us' to **save his people** Israel **from their sins.** The genealogy might suggest a political, nationalistic leader; this name points to a ministry of spiritual redemption.

The link with the O.T. and with God's promises to Israel is shown in Matt. not only by the genealogy (and specific teaching of Jesus, e.g. v. 17), but also by citation of specific prophecies fulfilled in Jesus' life. The entire history of God's working has unity. These prophetic passages were **spoken by the Lord through the** ancient **prophet;** their fulfilment is likewise God's

working; **the Holy Spirit** has caused Mary to have a son, and
an angel, speaking for God, explains the situation to Joseph.
This central event, **God with us,** does not happen by chance or
by natural causes or human planning. The gospel is the story of
what God has done for man's salvation.

Isa. vii. 14 is quoted from the LXX, which however reads
'you shall name' instead of **they will name.** The Hebrew
speaks of a 'maiden', a young woman ready for marriage, but
the LXX and Matt. use the word **virgin.** The Isaiah passage
speaks of a 'sign'; it may well mean a supernatural though
hardly a virgin birth; it refers to a child soon to be born, in
whose early childhood the international situation will change
radically and the danger to God's people will be removed; it
promises God's coming and intervention to help his people;
'Matthew' sees a parallel in God's coming in Jesus to redeem
his people; he knows the virgin birth story, though it was not
part of the common preaching message of the Church, and he
finds a forecast of it in the LXX form of the Isaiah passage;
even though the Hebrew of Isaiah does not contain the literal
virgin birth idea, the specific redemptive action of God is
present even there, just as it is in the birth of Jesus Christ.
'Matthew' (like the LXX in Isa. viii. 8, 10 but not in vii. 14)
explains what **Emmanuel** means, to emphasize that God
comes redemptively to men in the person and saving ministry
of Jesus.

Took: Into his home, thus publicly accepting Mary as his
wife, but without normal **marriage relations. Until she had
borne a son:** Implies that such relations were later established;
see on xiii. 55-56. **He named:** The Greek could also mean that
she, Mary, named Jesus. But the ancestry is traced through
Joseph; in vs. 21 Joseph is instructed to name the son; Joseph
therefore gave the name.

The Virgin Birth was not part of the basic preaching message
of the Apostolic Age, which began with the ministry of John the
Baptist and the baptism of Jesus. The story came to 'Matthew'
and Luke through more private channels of tradition. The two
evangelists agree on main points: the virgin's conception by the
power of the Holy Spirit; the conception during the period of
betrothal to Joseph; the divine guidance in the choice of the

name Jesus; the birth in Bethlehem of Judea; the childhood in Nazareth. Their story is rooted in Jewish life and linguistic usage; it did not originate in Gentile circles. They speak of a physical miracle, the birth of a son to a woman who had had no sexual intercourse with a man. But the basic theological truth that they express is that God sent Jesus; he was more than a human Davidic king; as the Son of the living God (xvi. 16) he is indeed the Christ, the expected Jewish Messiah, but in his life and work he is linked with God in a deeper way, so that his coming means **God with us;** his coming had long been purposed and was a specific powerful act of God to save men.

This theological affirmation of the unique, purposeful work of God in sending Jesus Christ into the world is essential to the gospel story. Whoever takes the birth story as poetic and figurative must take care not to drain away the vigour and firmness of that affirmation. On the other hand, those who, to protect the divine initiative and to centre God's historical working in Christ, accept literally the story that Jesus had no earthly father must preserve the New Testament conviction that Jesus was born as a real human being and lived a truly human life.

CHAPTER II

---

ii. 1-12. THE MAGI WORSHIP THE NEWBORN KING

1 **Now when Jesus was born in Bethlehem of Judea, in the days of Herod the King, behold, Magi from the East came**
2 **to Jerusalem, saying, 'Where is the newly born King of the Jews? For we saw his star when it rose, and have come**
3 **to worship him.' When King Herod heard this he was**
4 **troubled, and all Jerusalem with him, and he called together all the chief priests and scribes of the people and**
5 **inquired of them where the Christ was to be born. They said to him, 'In Bethlehem of Judea'; for this is what**

stands written through the prophet:

> "And thou, Bethlehem, land of Judah,   6
>   art by no means least among the princes of Judah.
> For from thee will go forth a ruler,
>   who will shepherd my people Israel."'

Then Herod secretly summoned the Magi and learned 7
from them exactly when the star appeared. And he sent 8
them to Bethlehem and said, 'Go and make careful inquiry concerning the child; and when you have found
him, report to me, so that I too may go and worship him'.
After listening to the king, they departed; and behold, the 9
star which they had seen when it rose went before them
until it came and stood above where the child lay. And 10
when they saw the star they rejoiced with extremely
great joy. And when they entered the house they saw the 11
child with Mary his mother, and they fell down and worshipped him; and they opened their treasure chests and
offered to him gifts of gold and frankincense and myrrh.
Then, since they were divinely instructed in a dream not 12
to return to Herod, they departed to their own country by
another road.

This section illustrates important aspects of this Gospel.
Jesus was born among the Jews. But they were not alive to their
privilege; the political powers did not understand or tolerate
him; a representative group of Gentiles offered the worship due
him. In his ministry his own people, and especially their leaders,
were mostly indifferent or hostile; Herod Antipas suspected him
and Pilate failed to protect him; he ministered almost entirely
to his own people, but a few Gentiles who had the boldness and
faith to gain his help were forerunners of the many others who
were to be won for Christ (xxviii. 19-20).

In this birth story, however, the Jewish leaders play no active
part. They know where the Christ is to be born. But they do not
sense what is happening, or inquire into the report the Magi
bring. They fail by being passive. **Herod** the Great, puppet
king of Palestine under Roman control (40–4 B.C.), is Jesus'
active opponent. This dates the birth of Jesus at least some
weeks or months before Herod's death in the spring of 4 B.C.

Herod is explicitly called **king** to contrast his false, unworthy rule with the rightful claim of the child just born. To Herod the Christ is essentially a political and military figure. As i. 21 shows, this is not the main idea in Matt., but the Christ rightly claims full loyalty from his people and in the end will doom unworthy human rulers such as Herod. Jesus is the true **King of the Jews** (vs. 2), **the Christ** (vs. 4), the promised **ruler of Israel** (vs. 6); he rightly receives more homage than is due the usual human ruler (vss. 2, 8, 11).

The mention of the Magi cannot obscure the strongly Jewish interest of the story. Jesus is the **King of the Jews.** He is born in **Bethlehem of Judea,** in the **land of Judah;** this birthplace of David was the fitting place for the Son of David (i. 1) to be born. His birth there is found anticipated in prophecy, but the quotation of Micah v. 1, 3 (with a reminiscence of 2 Sam. v. 2) agrees with neither the Hebrew nor the LXX text. It freely blends O.T. materials in a way which the Essene commentaries of the Dead Sea Scrolls show was current in first-century Judaism, and gives the material a Messianic interpretation: At Bethlehem will be born a royal **ruler** from the tribe of **Judah,** and as the Son of David he will **shepherd Israel** as God had called David to do.

Neither Herod nor the Jews nor their leaders sense what is happening. **Herod** and **all Jerusalem** are **troubled** by a rumour they do not understand or welcome, but they do not 'go over to Bethlehem and see this thing that has happened' (Luke ii. 15). One small representative group sees a sign and journeys far to respond to the hint of God's action in history. The **Magi,** not crafty magicians, as the word implies in other N.T. passages, but teachable and wise men from the East (Persia?), point Gentile readers of the Gospel to the right attitude to Christ. We are not told how they deduced that a new King of the Jews had been born, nor why they should worship him, nor how many they were. The traditional number of three probably is deduced from the three gifts mentioned (vs. 11); that they were kings may have been inferred from Isa. lx. 3 (cf. Rev. xxi. 24). Their gifts were costly, worthy of the King to whom they were brought.

The story does not say that **the star** guided the Magi on their trip westward to Jerusalem. But since it is said to go **before them** from Jerusalem southwestward **to Bethlehem**, it seems implied that on earlier stages of their journey the star had led them. Herod told the Magi to go to Bethlehem; the star's guidance was not needed for this last stage of the journey; but its reappearance was an encouragement and an assurance of success in the search. How long before the Magi reached Jerusalem the star had attracted their attention we are not told, but since Herod had the soldiers kill all children two years old and younger (vs. 16), a fairly long journey from the East seems implied.

The Magi by their coming had pointed to the unique and royal role of the newborn child. 'Not even in Israel' was there 'found such faith' (viii. 10) when the Christ was born. And the cunning plan of Herod to kill a potential rival failed when they did not return to lead him to the King of the Jews.

ii. 13-23. JESUS KEPT FROM THE HERODS

When they had departed, behold, an angel of the Lord 13
**appeared to Joseph in a dream and said, Rise, take the
child and his mother, and flee to Egypt, and stay there
until I tell you, for Herod is about to search for the child
to kill it. So he arose and while it was night took the child** 14
and his mother and departed to Egypt, and stayed there 15
**until the death of Herod, that the word might be fulfilled
which had been spoken by the Lord through the prophet,
who said, 'Out of Egypt I called my son'.**

Then Herod, when he saw that he had been deceived 16
**by the Magi, was greatly angered, and he sent and put to
death all the male children two years old and younger in
Bethlehem and in the entire surrounding region, according to the exact time he had learned from the Magi. Then** 17
was fulfilled the word spoken through Jeremiah the prophet, who said,
　'A voice was heard in Ramah,　　　　　　　　　　18
　　weeping and great lamentation;
　Rachel bewailing her children,
　　and she refused to be comforted, for they are dead'.

19 After Herod died, behold, an angel of the Lord ap-
20 peared to Joseph in a dream in Egypt and said, 'Rise, take
the child and his mother, and go to the land of Israel, for
those who were seeking the life of the child are dead'.
21 So he arose, took the child and his mother, and went into
22 the land of Israel. But when he heard that Archelaus was
king of Judea in place of his father Herod, he was afraid
to go there; and being divinely instructed in a dream he
23 departed to the district of Galilee, and he went and settled
in a city called Nazareth, that the word spoken through
the prophets might be fulfilled, 'He will be called a
Nazorean'.

God protects his Son. Through **an angel** he speaks to
Joseph **in a dream** (this is the usual pattern in Matt. i, ii).
The Son will meet opposition continually until finally he
accepts the Cross. That opposition begins as soon as he is born.
Herod will not give up his kingship over the Jews to a rival; he
will act with ruthless cruelty; God knows this and acts to thwart
him. Instant flight, covered by darkness, as soon as Joseph
awakes from the sleep in which he is instructed, shows Joseph's
diligent care for Jesus and Mary. Nothing indicates how long
before Herod died the flight occurred, or how long the stay in
Egypt lasted. If the flight occurred much before Herod died in
4 B.C., this would place Jesus' birth many months or even a few
years earlier.

The thought of the return from Egypt to Palestine leads
'Matthew' to quote Hos. xi. 1. This (cf. also Num. xxiv. 8)
recalls the bringing of Israel out of bondage in Egypt in the
time of Moses. But 'Matthew' is not interested merely in that
historic deliverance. He rather sees in the Hosea verse a divine
action which points forward to the calling of Jesus out of
Egypt. The quotation agrees with the Hebrew rather than the
LXX; either 'Matthew' translated directly from the Hebrew or,
perhaps more likely, used a Greek version other than the LXX.

In Matt. **Herod** and his sons are enemies of the true King,
the Christ. Herod attempts to kill Jesus; his son Archelaus is a
threat to Jesus' safety (ii. 22); his son Herod Antipas executes
John the Baptist and is suspicious of Jesus (xiv. 2). Herod's

brutal act here may recall Pharaoh's hostility to Moses and the children of Israel (Exodus i, 11). Cf. also the hostility of the political power to God's Son in Rev. xii, where the dragon seeks to devour the newborn child 'who is to rule all the nations'. Herod, like the dragon, was **angered.** Having failed by cunning to identify and kill the newborn King of the Jews, he kills all boy babies **two years old and younger** in the entire Bethlehem region. This implies that Jesus had been born some months before, but not two years before; Herod is leaving a margin of error. From the way Herod killed members of his own family, including even his own sons, it is clear that his character is accurately depicted here.

For 'Matthew' this wholesale massacre fulfils Jeremiah's prophecy (xxxi. 15), which laments the captivity of Rachel's descendants. In Matt. God, speaking through Jeremiah, refers to the massacre of Rachel's descendants by Herod's soldiers. **Ramah:** About six miles north of Jerusalem, on the road the conqueror would take in leading captives from Jerusalem to Babylon (cf. 1 Sam. x. 2). But Gen. xxxv. 19; xlviii. 7 speak of Rachel as buried 'on the way to Ephrath, this is, Bethlehem', and 'Matthew' thinks of Rachel as connected with Bethlehem, suffering inconsolable grief over the cruel slaughter of her helpless children.

The narrative in Matt. i, ii is told from the point of view of Joseph, who now acts once more to carry out the divine purpose. Herod is dead; **those who were seeking the life of the child** refers mainly to Herod, but also to those he had commanded to find and kill the newborn King of the Jews. The command to return **to the land of Israel** recalls vs. 15 (Hosea xi. 1) and Jesus' rightful place among the chosen people in the promised land. **Israel** is a large enough geographical designation to include **Galilee,** which was not the original destination of Joseph; in Matt. he had lived at Bethlehem and intended to return there, and only turned aside to Galilee when a new danger threatened. **Archelaus** became ruler of Judea (not **king,** for the Romans refused to honour Herod the Great's will which named Archelaus king of Judea and Samaria) on Herod the Great's death. Josephus tells that he quickly crushed with brutal force a Jewish protest against his rule. Joseph feared that this brutal ruler would continue his father's attempt to find and kill Jesus. Matt. does not say explicitly that Joseph was directed to settle in **Nazareth,** but since vs. 23 sees God's promise and purpose fulfilled in the residence there, the divine instruction probably is thought to include settling at Nazareth. There Archelaus could not harm Jesus; Herod Antipas, another son of Herod the Great, ruled Galilee and Perea; he evidently was not considered such a threat to Jesus' safety as was Archelaus.

The prophecy said to be fulfilled by residence at Nazareth is not found in the O.T. Yet the reference is obviously to the O.T. **prophets.** Only here in Matt. is a quotation ascribed to the prophets as a group; does this plural imply a general reference to more than one O.T. passage? Some think that the puzzling reference points to Num. vi, and implies that Jesus took a nazirite vow (Num. vi) and encouraged or required his followers to do so. Others with more point connect vs. 23 with Isa. xi. 1, which says that a branch (*nētzer*) will grow out of the roots of Jesse. Certainly no O.T. passage refers to Nazareth, which is first mentioned in the N.T. Indeed, it is a question whether the Greek word **Nazorean** (Ναζωραῖος) originally referred to Nazareth. 'Matthew' clearly thought it did, and the early Church agreed with him. But the word is hard to derive from the name Nazareth. So some have thought that it refers to Jesus as an 'observant' of a special Jewish way of life or as a member of some Jewish sect, which he later left to assume independent leadership. No explanation is fully satisfactory; to 'Matthew' the point is that the Nazareth residence, like every stage of the coming and work of Jesus, was directed by God and fulfilled his purpose and promise.

CHAPTER III

iii. 1-12. THE MINISTRY OF JOHN THE BAPTIST

1 In those days came John the Baptist, preaching in the
2 wilderness of Judea, saying, 'Repent, for the Kingdom of
3 Heaven has drawn near'. For this is the one spoken of

62

through Isaiah the prophet, who said:
> 'A voice of one shouting in the wilderness:
> "Prepare the way of the Lord;
> Make straight his paths"'.

Now this John was dressed in clothing made of camel's 4 hair and wore a leather belt around his waist, and his food was locusts and honey from wild bees. Then went 5 out to him Jerusalem and all Judea and all the region near the Jordan, and they were baptized by him in the Jordan 6 River, openly confessing their sins.

But when he saw many of the Pharisees and Sadducees 7 coming to the baptism, he said to them, 'You brood of vipers, who warned you to flee from the impending wrath? Produce fruit then that befits repentance, and do 8, 9 not suppose that you may say to yourselves, "We have Abraham as father", for I tell you that God can raise up from these stones children to Abraham. Even now the axe 10 lies at the root of the trees; every tree therefore that does not produce good fruit is cut down and thrown into the fire.

'I baptize you with water for repentance; but he who 11 comes after me is stronger than I am; his sandals I am not worthy to remove; he will baptize you with the Holy Spirit and fire. His winnowing fork is in his hand, and he 12 will clear off his threshing floor and gather his wheat into the granary, but will burn up the chaff with inextinguishable fire.'

Up to this point Matt. has an independent narrative, with only an occasional content parallel with Luke i-ii. Now begins the common Synoptic material; 'Matthew' seems to use as sources Mk. and at least one other document (Q) which Luke also knows and uses. With vss. 1-6 cf. Mk. i. 1-6; Lk. iii. 1-6. In Matt. no sharp break is intended here; **in those days** indicates that **John the Baptist** appeared while Jesus was still living at Nazareth (ii. 23). Nothing is told of John's ancestry, home, or earlier life; his importance for the Gospel story is that he preached and baptized. He is called **the Baptist** for two reasons; his baptism had unusual importance as preparation for the

imminent **Kingdom,** and his baptism of Jews was an innova-
tion, though Jews probably were already practising proselyte
baptism (the repeated washings of the syncretistic Qumran sect
were not a real parallel). All four Gospels agree that John
preached **in the wilderness,** a phrase from Isa. xl. 3; only Matt.
adds **of Judea,** which indicates strictly the barren region west
of the Dead Sea (including the region of the Qumran sect), and
more broadly extends northward up the western part of the
Jordan Valley, where John worked if (vs. 6) he baptized repentant Jews in the Jordan River. Since, however, as the Synoptic Gospels agree, Herod Antipas arrested and executed John,
the Baptist must later have worked on the eastern side of the
Jordan, for this Herod, tetrarch of Galilee and Perea, had no
jurisdiction over the western side except further north where
Galilee touched the Jordan.

John's message is summarized in the very words with which
Jesus opens his ministry (iv. 17). **Repent** ($\mu\epsilon\tau\alpha\nu o\epsilon\hat{\iota}\tau\epsilon$) means
in Greek to change one's mind in a radical way; the correspond-
ing Hebrew שׁוּב and Aramaic תוּב mean 'to turn', to reverse
completely one's life direction. **Kingdom of Heaven** occurs in
the N.T. only in Matt. (32 times); Matt. also has (4 times) 'Kingdom of God', the phrase used elsewhere in the N.T.; both
phrases mean the active, effective rule of God over his people.
In a sense God has never lost his Lordship, but sin and dis-
obedience have prevented its realization in his world. Now, John
says, God is about to establish his effective rule; those who
repent and welcome God's Lordship will be blessed and secure;
judgment will strike those who reject God's will.

Isa. xl. 3 speaks of preparations for God to lead the exiles
home from Babylonia to Palestine on a specially prepared
straight highway. To 'Matthew' this passage describes John's
work, preparing **the way of the Lord,** i.e. of Jesus, who to
every Christian of the Apostolic Age was the living Lord. The
Hebrew and LXX of Isa. xl. 3 say 'the paths of our God'. But
all three Synoptists read **his paths,** the paths of Jesus, for whom
John prepares the way.

Elijah was expected to return to prepare the way for God's
final work (cf. Mal. iv. 5). Vs. 4 (cf. xvii. 12 f.) identifies John
as the expected Elijah (cf. Mk. i. 6; contrast John i. 21); John,

like Elijah (2 Kings i. 8), 'wore a garment of haircloth, with a girdle of leather about his loins', and ate food available in the wilderness. His message had the authentic prophetic ring; it attracted an immense crowd, though it is hyperbole to say that all residents of **Jerusalem, Judea,** and the **Jordan** Valley flocked out, heard John, confessed their sins, and were baptized; this steady stream (the tense of the verbs is imperfect) indicates a remarkably large and obedient response to his preaching.

With vss. 7-10 cf. Lk. iii. 7-9, which gives John's blast in almost identical wording. But in Lk. John addresses 'the crowds', while in Matt. he warns Jewish leaders. **Pharisees:** This group worked especially through the synagogue; they promoted earnest study of the Mosaic Law and careful obedience to it and to the oral tradition which interpreted it. **Sadducees:** The priestly party; their leadership centred in the temple at Jerusalem. 'Matthew' says that **many** of these two outstanding groups came to **the baptism;** he does not say that John refused to baptize them, though what John says here and Jesus says in xxi. 32; xxiii. 13 would imply that they did not meet God's demand.

Formal outward response without deeds that express repentance is worse than futile; it brands the pretenders as a **brood of vipers,** low and poisonous creatures who flee in haste before the onrushing fire that sweeps across the wilderness. Just as merely formal response is futile, so is good ancestry; physical descent from **Abraham,** the father of Israel, counts for nothing where repentance and obedience to God is lacking; God can reject such physical descendants and by his miraculous power **raise up** to Abraham other **children** who will yield the required obedience (note the fleeting glimpse of God's power to bring Gentiles into the kingdom). Cf. Jn. viii. 30-44. The barren fruit **tree** is cut down (cf. Lk. xiii. 6-9); Jesus later uses this same illustration (vii. 19), as he repeats in iv. 17 what John preaches in iii. 2. Divine judgment is ready to be executed on the barren, unprofitable tree; Jewish leaders who do not repent and yield prompt obedience to God will be struck by sharp, irrevocable judgment; only quick repentance can save them. Does John seem too stern? Jesus spoke with similar sternness; no gospel is needed if there is no judgment; and John promised to those who **repented** forgiveness and a place in the Kingdom soon to come.

With vss. 11 f. cf. Mk. i. 7 f.; Lk. iii. 15-18. In Matt. John is still addressing Pharisees and Sadducees; he frankly tells them that his role is limited; he announces the imminent coming of one who can fully execute God's purpose. John can baptize **with water;** this external rite symbolizes the repentance which the person baptized has expressed. But John cannot give the spiritual power that forgiven men need, nor can he execute the judgment that must strike unrepentant lives. A **Stronger** One is coming to do these things. John feels his own limitations and the Coming One's greatness so strongly that he confesses himself unworthy to **remove** (βαστάσαι may also mean 'carry') the **sandals** of his successor for whom he is preparing the way.

The Stronger One will execute a double ministry. To those who respond in repentance and, it is implied, in faith, he will give **the Holy Spirit.** All four Gospels contain this promise (cf. Jn. i. 33 and the fulfilment in Jn. xx. 22 and Acts ii. 33). But to those who do not repent he will bring the **fire** of judgment; **fire** cannot mean here, as in Acts ii. 3, the fire of the Holy Spirit's kindly presence and power, for vs. 12 plainly speaks of the consuming fire of divine judgment. The threshing of grain on the flat open-air **threshing floor** was well known in Palestine. Using this as illustration, John describes the sifting process by which the good grain, the repentant and obedient people of God, will be gathered into **the granary** of the Kingdom of Heaven, while **the chaff,** the sinful and unrepentant members, will be consumed with the fire of judgment against which the stubbornly wicked can find no protection. Here as later 'Matthew' warns that everlasting ruin will strike the unrepentant life. And the judgment is near at hand; the Stronger One has already taken up the **winnowing fork,** and is ready to carry out the judgment, to separate the sheep from the goats (xxv. 31-46). Thus John stresses the stern side of the imminent ministry of the Stronger One.

iii. 13-iv. 11. THE BAPTISM AND TEMPTATION OF JESUS

13 **Then Jesus came from Galilee to the Jordan, to John, to**
14 **be baptized by him. But he tried to forbid him, saying, 'I**

need to be baptized by you, and do you come to me?'
Jesus answered and said to him, 'Permit it now; for it is 15
fitting that we thus fulfil all righteousness'. Then he permitted him. And when Jesus was baptized, he at once 16
went up from the water; and behold, the heavens were
opened, and he saw the Spirit of God descending as a
dove, coming upon him; and behold, a voice came from 17
the heavens, saying, 'This is my beloved Son, in whom I
was well pleased'.

Then Jesus was led up into the wilderness by the Spirit, iv.
to be tempted by the devil. And when he had fasted forty 2
days and forty nights, he afterward grew hungry. And the 3
tempter approached and said to him, 'If you are the Son
of God, command these stones to turn into loaves of
bread'. But he answered and said, 'It is written, "Not by 4
bread alone shall man live, but by every word that comes
from the mouth of God"'. Then the devil took him into 5
the holy city, and placed him on the pinnacle of the
temple, and said to him, 'If you are the Son of God, throw 6
yourself down; for it is written, "He will give his angels
orders concerning you", and "upon their hands they will
carry you, lest you strike your foot against a stone"'.
Jesus said to him, 'Again it is written, "You shall not put 7
the Lord your God to the test"'. Again, the devil took him 8
to the top of a very high mountain and showed him all the
kingdoms of the world and their splendour, and said to 9
him, 'All this I will give you if you fall down and worship
me'. Then Jesus said to him, 'Depart, Satan; for it is 10
written, "The Lord your God you shall worship, and him
only you shall serve"'. Then the devil left him, and 11
behold, angels came and ministered to him.

With vss. 13-17 cf. Mk. i. 9-11; Lk. iii. 21 f. 'Matthew' has
not mentioned Galilean interest in John the Baptist. But obviously he thinks that John's work was widely known in Galilee,
for his statement that Jesus **came from Galilee** to be baptized
implies that Jesus had heard of John and reached this decision
while still in Galilee.

Only 'Matthew' has vss. 14 f. John discerned, he implies, that

Jesus was the Stronger One, superior in nature and able to baptize with the Holy Spirit and fire. John assumed that the greater one should not be baptized by the lesser one. **Tried to forbid:** The Greek imperfect (διεκώλυεν) indicates an action attempted but then given up. All four Gospels, partially for apologetic reasons, stress John's feeling of inferiority; John is amazed at the very idea that he should baptize Jesus: **And do you come to me?** The word **now** (ἄρτι) concedes that this reversal of positions is temporary—another apologetic touch. His supreme rank does not release Jesus from the obligation **to fulfil all righteousness;** he is one with his people and must join with them in the acts which express response to God's spokesman and dedication to God's will. His coming to baptism expresses his sense that John is right, divine judgment is impending, Israel must repent and be baptized and by obedience prepare for the coming Kingdom; all of Israel, including the Stronger One, must share in this preparation. 'Matthew' did not think of Jesus as personally sinful; he inserts vss. 14 f. partly to exclude this idea.

At the baptism Jesus stood in the Jordan River and probably submerged himself at John's consent and direction. As he **went up from the water** the decisive event of his baptism occurred: the Holy **Spirit** descended on him. This is described as a more objective occurrence than the vision Jesus had in Mk. That the heavens opened and the Spirit descended gently, as a dove would descend and light on a person, means that the Spirit was sent from God and given to Jesus. Had not Jesus possessed the Spirit before? The Spirit is not thought of here as a passive presence, but as an active power which comes upon the person to rouse him to action and give him power and guidance for his work. Jesus at baptism is equipped for his task; he is made to know that he must at once begin his ministry, and he is given the power and direction for it.

The **voice** from heaven is the voice of God (just as the Kingdom of Heaven is really the Kingdom of God). It says three things: (1) It openly acknowledged Jesus as God's **Son** (cf. xi. 25-27). He has a unique relation to the Father. (2) He is the **Beloved.** This word expresses not merely favoured position with the Father, but also God's choice of him for a ministry to

God's people. (3) The Father approves his coming to baptism and joining with his people in preparing for the coming crisis. The Greek aorist in εὐδόκησα has sometimes been understood as timeless approval of the Son by the Father ('am always well pleased') but it probably expresses approval of the submission to baptism which has just occurred **(was well pleased)**. This expression of approval is another answer to the objection faced in vss. 14 f.

The words of the heavenly voice are not an exact quotation, but they recall Psalm ii. 7 and Isa. xlii. 1 and reflect the identification of Jesus with the Messianic King of Psalm ii and the Servant of Isa. xlii; Jesus knows when his ministry opens that he is the expected Messianic leader of Israel, and that he must act in the spirit of the Servant of Second Isaiah. Whether Jesus already foresaw the suffering of that Servant as his inescapable role is not stated; perhaps he did. One thing is clear; Jesus, like 'Matthew', worshipped, thought, and lived in the atmosphere of O.T. expectations. He inevitably understood his mission in the light of them; whatever new aspects of truth came to him, he began with the O.T. and never discarded it.

With iv. 1-11 cf. Mk. i. 12 f.; Lk. iv. 1-13. A testing period inevitably followed the baptismal experience. Jesus had responded to John's preaching, dedicated himself to God's cause, received the Spirit, and realized that he was the expected Messianic King of Psalm ii and the Servant of Isa. xlii. 1. How was he to use his power? How far was he to conform to popular expectations concerning the coming leader of God's people? To live is to choose, to decide between good and evil alternatives. **The Spirit** leads him apart for a time of decision, but **the devil** is present to urge selfish, sceptical, ambitious, compromising procedures. **Led up:** Westward from the Jordan River, here below sea level, to the **wilderness** heights. **Forty days:** A round number, used of Moses (Ex. xxiv. 18) and Elijah (I Kings xix. 8); cf. the wilderness wandering of Israel, forty years (Num. xiv. 33 f.). In Mk. Jesus was tempted, thinking and making decisions, through the entire period; Matthew places all of this conflict at the end of the period. Jesus concentrated on three issues that faced him. 'Matthew' (and Luke in different order) gives the three in pictorial form (cf. vs. 8; from no mountain could one literally see **all the kingdoms).**

The tempter appeals to selfish instincts of self-preservation and tries to stir up doubt. God's **Son,** the Beloved, given the Spirit, should not suffer hunger and insecurity. Lonely, hungering, unacclaimed by man, is he really God's Son? Here as in the other two temptations, Jesus answers with words from Deuteronomy (each quotation in Matt. follows the LXX rather closely); what was spoken there to Israel Jesus takes to heart as a member and now leader of Israel. He here cites Deut. viii. 3. **It is written:** He accepts the words as inspired by God and authoritative for his people. Man's real life depends on more than **bread;** it comes from obedience to what God speaks. He does not affirm or deny that he can work a miracle to meet his own needs. But he faces the real issue: Will he doubt his Sonship, resent his present need, and use his power for his own benefit, or will he wait for God to guide him in the use of his power and position? He determines to live in faith, demand nothing for himself, wait for God to direct him. Throughout his ministry he refused to use his power for his own benefit.

The scene of the second temptation is Jerusalem, **the holy city,** so called in the N.T. only in Matt. and Rev. Cf. Neh. xi. 1, 18; Isa. lii. 1; Dan. ix. 24. At **the temple** God's power might be expected to be at its maximum. **Pinnacle:** Literally a 'little wing'; some lofty projection or pinnacle from which a deadly fall was possible. Again the devil challenges Jesus to test his Sonship; surely God will protect his **Son** from injury or death. Scripture, the devil says ('the devil can cite Scripture for his purpose'), justifies the test; Psalm xci. 11a, 12 promises God's care to those who 'have made the Lord your refuge'. A pious-sounding misuse of Scripture! **Carry you:** Catch you, hold you up, keep you from serious injury or death. Jesus refuses to test God; Deut. vi. 16 warns against doing that; it would show lack of faith. He accepts the assurance of Sonship and refuses to doubt God or to work a miracle to satisfy doubt in anyone else.

The third temptation hardly refers to any **mountain** Jesus knew; from no mountain could he survey **all the kingdoms of the world.** In his mind's eye Jesus sees the world, which all lies within the Kingdom God's Son is to win. How can he win it?

The devil has an easy answer: Serve the devil and rule the world. In modern terms, be practical, realistic, ready to compromise; 'the end justifies the means'. To help people you must get position and power; the good you can do will justify the necessary compromises that promise quick results. But this calls for divided loyalty; the devil gets the leading role with God a poor second. Deut. vi. 13 gives Jesus his answer. 'No man can serve two masters' (vi. 24). The essential thing is not temporal power, quick superficial outward results, hasty seizure of Messianic role and authority; it is full, undivided service of God alone. **Depart, Satan**: Cf. xvi. 23.

The devil left him: Jesus faced temptation again (xvi. 23 and xxvi. 36-46 show this), but he here put aside unworthy appeals and chose clearly to work in ways that were loyal to God in both aim and method. The ministry of **angels** probably includes both spiritual support and provision in some way of needed food for the body.

CHAPTER IV

iv. 12-25. THE OPENING MINISTRY IN GALILEE

When he heard that John had been imprisoned, he de- 12
parted into Galilee, and leaving Nazareth he went and 13
settled in Capernaum-by-the-sea, in the region of Zebulon
and Naphthali, that the word might be fulfilled which was 14
spoken through Isaiah the prophet, who said, 'Land of 15
Zebulon and land of Naphthali, way of the sea, beyond the
Jordan, Galilee of the Gentiles, the people that sat in dark- 16
ness have seen a great light, and on those who sat in the
land and shadow of death light has dawned'.

From that time Jesus began to preach and to say, 'Re- 17
pent, for the Kingdom of Heaven has drawn near'.

As he walked along by the Sea of Galilee, he saw two 18
brothers, Simon called Peter and Andrew his brother,
casting a net into the sea, for they were fishermen. And 19

he said to them, 'Come, follow me, and I will make you
20 fishers who catch men'. They at once left the nets and
21 followed him. And going on from there he saw another
pair of brothers, James the son of Zebedee and John his
brother; they were in the boat with Zebedee their father,
22 putting their nets in order. And he called them. They at
once left the boat and their father and followed him.
23   And he travelled about in all Galilee, teaching in their
synagogues and preaching the gospel of the Kingdom and
healing every disease and every sickness among the
24 people. And the report about him went out into all Syria,
and they brought to him all those who were seriously ill
with various diseases and were tormented by severe
pains—demoniacs and lunatics and paralytics; and he
25 healed them. And large crowds from Galilee and the
Decapolis and Jerusalem and Judea and Transjordan
followed him.

With vss. 12-17 cf. Mk. i. 14 f.; Lk. iv. 14 f. The Synoptics
report no ministry of Jesus before John was imprisoned; cf. Jn.
i. 29-iv. 43. 'Matthew' clearly implies that John's arrest led
Jesus to go to **Galilee**. This move was not a flight from danger,
as some have thought. Herod Antipas, tetrarch of Galilee and
Perea, had arrested John in Perea, on the east side of the Jordan.
When Jesus went to Galilee, his move was an answer to Herod;
he took up in Herod's territory the work which Herod had tried
to stop by arresting John; he began his ministry with a challenge
rather than with a retreat.

On his return to Galilee Jesus visited **Nazareth,** but soon
centred his Galilean ministry in busy **Capernaum** (modern
Tell Hum), on the north-west shore of the Sea of Galilee. It lay
in the old tribal district of Naphthali, here grouped with the
district of Zebulon as the scene of Jesus' Galilean ministry. In
Jesus' coming to this region 'Matthew' sees the fulfilment of
Isa. ix. 1-2, quoted in a form agreeing with neither the Hebrew
nor the LXX, though reflecting features of both. Isaiah recalls
the invasion of Northern Israel by Tiglath-Pileser in 733–
732 B.C. and promises new glory for this region under a great
(perhaps Messianic) king. To 'Matthew' these words promise

Jesus' coming to bring **light** to those in the **shadow** not of Assyrian invasion but of human sin (vs. 17). **Way of the sea:** Here of the road from Damascus past the Sea of Galilee to the Mediterranean. **Beyond the Jordan:** The region of Israel east of Jordan; cf. iv. 25; xix. 1. **Galilee of the Gentiles:** Galilee was always more open to Gentile attack and contacts than Judea. In Matt. meaning is seen in this fact; while Jesus ministers almost entirely to the Jews, several such fleeting suggestions forecast that the gospel will reach the Gentiles.

From that time and **began** emphasize that a new stage now opens; cf. xvi. 21; xxvi. 16. Jesus opens his ministry; 'Matthew' mentions no preaching before this proclamation at Capernaum, which takes up the message of John (iii. 2). Jesus calls for a radical change of the entire direction and attitude of men's lives, in view of the impending decisive action of God to establish his full and effective rule over his people. **Has drawn near** ($\dot{\eta}\gamma\gamma\iota\kappa\epsilon\nu$): Cannot mean 'has come'; the same word occurs in iii. 2, where John cannot have meant 'has come'.

With vss. 18-22 cf. Mk. i. 16-20 (Lk. v. 1-11 is quite different). Vs. 13 implies that it was on the beach at Capernaum that Jesus called his first disciples. In Matt. he had not seen them before (cf. John i. 40 ff.); this emphasizes the note of authority inherent in Jesus' summons to follow him. The two pairs of brothers were the first and foremost of the Twelve; from their number came the inner trio, **Peter, James,** and **John;** Peter was the most prominent of the Twelve; Peter and John were a prominent pair of leaders (cf. Acts iii. 1); and James must have been vigorous, for he was the first of the Twelve to be martyred (Acts xii. 2).

When Jesus gave **Simon** the name Peter is not certain; Mark iii. 16 implies it was before Peter's confession (see on xvi. 18), but it probably was not so early as this first call (yet cf. Jn. i. 42). Peter and **Andrew** were wading out, throwing out a casting-net, and encircling the fish. At Jesus' call, they **left their nets,** business, and means of livelihood, and began to go with Jesus wherever he went, to learn his message and help in any way they could. The other two **brothers,** with their father **Zebedee,** had pulled their boat up on the beach, and were mending or arranging **their nets** for the next fishing trip. Jesus **called them** and they too responded **at once**. The cause of the Kingdom came first and commanded complete dedication.

With vss. 23-25 cf. Mk. i. 39 (iii. 7 f.); Lk. iv. 44 (vi. 17). Note a similar summary in ix. 35. These summaries indicate that Jesus travelled about Galilee to reach the people, that the Gospel tradition contained many more significant events than the Gospel recounts, and that wide, enthusiastic response is the background for the teaching of chs. v-vii and for the sending out of the Twelve in ch. x. The itinerant ministry had three aspects: Jesus taught in the **synagogues**, no doubt explaining how the Scriptures regularly read there pointed to the impending coming of the Kingdom; he preached in the open, announcing with urgent appeal the coming of **the Kingdom** and the need of repentance; he healed **every** kind of illness (three striking kinds are named). News of this spread north throughout non-Jewish **Syria**; to all parts of **Galilee**; east to Transjordan, including the **Decapolis**, a league of Hellenistic cities, originally ten, and all but one located east of the Sea of Galilee and the Jordan River; and south to **Jerusalem** and **Judea**. What chiefly stirred the hearers was the power of God at work in Jesus to heal the sick. The power he would not use for selfish benefit (iv. 4) he was glad to use to help suffering people.

This passage is the immediate background of the Sermon on the Mount. Enthusiasm over the healings dominates vss. 23-25. Though Jesus was sympathetic to every human need, his urgent concern was to prepare people for the coming Kingdom, of which his healings, if people would only see it, were a first expression (cf. xii. 28). They must listen to his preaching and feel its urgency.

CHAPTER V

---

v. 1-12. THE BEATITUDES

1 **When Jesus saw the crowds, he went up into the mountain; and when he sat down his disciples came to him,**
2 **and he opened his mouth and taught them, saying,**

'Blessed are the poor in spirit,   3
    for theirs is the Kingdom of Heaven.
Blessed are those who mourn,   4
    for they will be comforted.
Blessed are the meek,   5
    for they will inherit the earth.
Blessed are those who hunger and thirst for   6
    righteousness,
    for they will be filled.
Blessed are the merciful,   7
    for they will receive mercy.
Blessed are the pure in heart,   8
    for they will see God.
Blessed are the peacemakers,   9
    for they will be called sons of God.
Blessed are those who have been persecuted on   10
    account of righteousness,
    for theirs is the Kingdom of Heaven.
Blessed are you when men reproach and perse-   11
    cute you and say every evil thing against
    you—falsely—on account of me.
Rejoice and exult, for your reward is great in   12
    heaven;
    for so did they persecute the prophets who
    preceded you.'

With vss. 1-2 cf. Lk. vi. 12, 20. **The mountain**: Not a snow-capped peak; an accessible height where many could see and hear him. Four times Matt. refers to a mountain at a key point in the narrative: the climactic temptation (iv. 8); the Sermon on the Mount (v. 1); the Transfiguration (xvii. 1); and the meeting of the risen Christ with his disciples (xxviii. 16). Jewish teachers gave formal teaching while seated. Matt. mentions only **his disciples** as hearers, but **the crowds** are near (cf. iv. 23-25), and vii. 28 says they heard the Sermon; this implies that Jesus taught them with his disciples standing near him. **Opened his mouth**: Suggests formal, important teaching.

'Matthew' has collected material and organized it in a topical manner. To much of the Sermon Luke has parallels, scattered through six chapters; this indicates the form in which 'Matthew' found this material. No doubt one available source gave a sermon summary which served as the nucleus of the present Sermon; but we cannot reconstruct that core sermon with certainty, and most of the present Sermon has been added to the original nucleus.

What sermon theme did 'Matthew' have in mind for the expanded Sermon? Was it the New Law which replaces the Law of Moses? 'Matthew', like Jesus, did not discard the Law of Moses; but only v. 17-48 deals with the relation of the Gospel to the Law. Was it a charter for a new, separate Church? Hardly; it prescribes no organization, and 'Matthew', like Jesus, regarded the Christian group as the true Israel, faithful to Israel's heritage. Was it a Christian ethic? The word ethic is sadly inadequate, for the Sermon makes the relation to God basic. The Sermon describes to Jewish hearers the life of the true disciple; 'Matthew' presents it to Christian readers to show how the true Christian lives.

The Beatitudes (cf. Lk. vi. 20-23) are a well-known form of Biblical speech, particularly prominent in Matt., Lk., and Rev. (where seven occur). **Blessed**: An ejaculation: 'O the happiness of'. The blessedness, approval, and well-being is God's gift and working. How many beatitudes are there? **Blessed** occurs nine times. Are the words **Rejoice and exult** (vs. 12) in effect a tenth beatitude? Since vs. 11 largely repeats vs. 10, are the two verses one beatitude, and the total eight? Then, since ancient manuscripts differ in the order of vss. 4 and 5 and such uncertainty often indicates an insertion, is vs. 5, derived from Ps. xxxvii. 11, a later scribal addition, leaving seven beatitudes? Probably 'Matthew' has collected nine beatitudes, the last two quite similar but different in literary pattern. The nine do not describe nine different classes of persons; the true disciple will possess most or all of these characteristics. Similarly, the promised blessings are not divided among separate classes of disciples, but are all aspects of the blessing God gives now and later to loyal disciples.

Poor in spirit: Cf. Isa. xi. 4; lvii. 15; lxi. 1. Lk. vi. 20 says simply 'poor', and the tone of his beatitudes and woes implies 'poor in material goods'. But Luke assumed that the poor had an attitude not of cynicism or rebellion but of faith in God. This

necessity of right inward attitude 'Matthew' has protected by
the correct interpretative addition, **in spirit.** However, this
expresses no sympathy for the needy; Luke thus preserves an
authentic note of Jesus' teaching. 'Matthew' reflects truly the
spiritual condition of God's blessing; those who accept the
hardships and limitations of life without bitterness towards man
or God, and thus place their lives in God's hands, will be
blessed. They will enter and find joy in **the Kingdom of
Heaven.** When will this Kingdom come? The word **is** suggests
present possession of the privilege. But all the beatitudes except
vss. 3, 11 speak of the blessedness as future. Since Aramaic,
which Jesus spoke, had no 'is' in the saying, a dominant future
reference is probable. Jesus spoke with strong emphasis on the
gifts of God which his humble, faithful people will receive when
the perfect eternal Kingdom is established. Yet he certainly did
not mean that their present life is devoid of meaning and blessing. In his ministry and mighty works the Kingdom began to
come; something of its blessing was open to God's people; the
full blessing was to come in the fully established Kingdom.

Mourn: Cf. Isa. lxi. 1, which this beatitude echoes. Not
merely those who mourn the loss of loved ones, or sorrow over
sin, but all who undergo life's hard experiences, crushing dis-
appointments, and bitter losses, and yet in conscious or mute
faith turn to God for help. **Comforted:** By God's comforting,
renewing, strengthening presence and help.

Meek: This verse echoes Ps. xxxvii. 11. **Meek:** More than
'gentle'; humble and trustful towards God even though outward conditions of life are not easy. It is the opposite of the self-
centred, brazen attempt to be independent of God. It accepts
life under God without complaint or inner bitterness. **Inherit
the earth:** The Psalm meant inherit the promised Land,
Canaan, though the setting of faith and worship of God were
not absent. In Matt. the phrase is figurative; the meek will enter
the Kingdom and as God's people know all the privileges of
fellowship with God.

Righteousness: A life fully conformed to the will of God in
thought, word, worship, and act. **Hunger and thirst:** Just as
the body hungers and thirsts for the food and drink without
which life cannot continue, these people desire to know and do

God's will; their need of active obedience to God is so basic that without it they cannot live. This way of describing a life completely dedicated to God has large agreement with what Paul means by faith. **Be filled:** Their lives will know the privilege and joy of loyal response to God.

Merciful: Here and in vs. 9 Jesus speaks of relations with others. Those who are understanding, gentle, forgiving, and quick to relieve the suffering and need of others will **receive mercy.** People tend to treat kindly those who show them kindness, but the meaning here is that God will deal mercifully with those who have shown mercy to their fellow-men; cf. vi. 14 f.; xviii. 21-35; Jas. ii. 13. God's people fail; they need God's kindly mercy; they will receive it if they have been kindly and merciful.

Pure in heart (cf. Ps. xxiv. 4): Not merely free from lust and evil desire; single-minded in complete loyalty to God and his purposes; the opposite of 'a double-minded man, unstable in all his ways' (Jas. i. 7 f.). **See God:** Not merely in some rare fleeting vision, but in a life lived in full fellowship with God and in full accord with his will.

Peacemakers: Those whose attitudes, words, and actions preserve friendship and understanding where it exists and restore it where it has been destroyed by human friction and strife. **Sons of God:** 'Sons of' often means 'having the nature and showing the spirit of' someone. These peacemakers show the spirit of the forgiving, seeking Father, who wants all to be at peace with him and with one another. By bringing good-will, understanding, and reconciliation into damaged human relations they do God's work and will be recognized as his **sons.**

Persecuted: Ridiculed, denounced, ill-treated; perhaps even injured and threatened with death. **On account of righteousness:** Because they are dedicated to God's will and by their confession, way of life, and open witness show their dedication to God's righteous cause. The world is a battleground. The forces of evil strike back at those who actively serve God's cause, which will advance only when his people stand steady in loyalty. **Theirs is the Kingdom:** God will preserve and welcome into the Kingdom those who in the conflict of life pay the cost of discipleship.

Vss. 11 f. expand the thought of vs. 10. Persecution and slanderous reproach must not intimidate or surprise God's people. **Falsely:** The disciples must be careful to give no basis in attitude or action for such hostile charges and ill-treatment. Then they may **exult** even when persecuted. The great **reward** that awaits them **in heaven** is to share in the Kingdom of Heaven. Jesus does not mean that the persecuted earn their salvation; their final privilege is a blessing given by God; but faithfulness is necessary to qualify for it; in that sense Jesus here and elsewhere speaks freely of a reward for the righteous (so do Paul and other N.T. writers). **The prophets:** The persecuted are in a noble succession; Israel had persecuted the O.T. prophets; cf. Heb. xi. 32-38. To remember this fellowship of suffering will steady those who suddenly find their faith and loyal service made the object of hostile, vicious attack. God who cared for his prophets will preserve and reward the ill-treated disciples.

v. 13-16. THE DISCIPLES' MISSION

'You are the salt of the earth. But if the salt becomes 13 tasteless, with what will it be seasoned? It no longer is good for anything but to be thrown out and walked on by men. You are the light of the world. A city situated on a 14 hill cannot be hid. Neither do men light a lamp and put 15 it under a peck-measure, but on the lampstand, and it shines on all who are in the house. Just so let your light 16 shine before men, that they may see your good works and praise your Father in heaven.'

Cf. the similar use of these illustrations in Mk. iv. 21; ix. 50; Lk. viii. 16; xiv. 34-35. Jesus frequently uses the homely conditions of the created world of nature to illustrate the life of men under God. In this paragraph his point is that the disciples have a ministry, a task to perform. They do not live for themselves alone; they do not receive God's gifts merely for personal enjoyment. True disciples are **the salt of the earth.** Salt may be thought of as having food value, as giving taste to food, or as a preservative. Since Jesus is here speaking of the disciples'

79

mission in the world, he seems to mean that they give tone to life and, even more, preserve human life and society. If they possess the qualities mentioned in the Beatitudes, they are truly the salt of the earth. But salt become **tasteless** cannot be restored to its original quality (Jesus may refer to the saline deposits by the Dead Sea, which, drenched by rain, lose their saltiness though still looking like salt; or he may think of salt which, heavily taxed, was adulterated by being mixed with cheap white powder and so lost its strong salty taste); so a disciple who has lost his faith and loyalty is useless and to be discarded.

True disciples are also **the light of the world.** Without forgetting the necessity of inner integrity, they must give a witness to the world by word and especially by life; they must visibly attest God's life-changing power and outgoing goodness. For a moment this illustration is dropped to take up another: **A city situated on** the top of **a hill** or mountainous ridge is inescapably visible. The good life of the disciples must be equally visible and attractive. Returning to the light illustration, the **lamp** is used to make the same point. Men do not hide it under a basket or tub (holding about a peck), but put it on a **lampstand,** where it gives maximum light to **all** in **the house** (the illustration implies a one-room house). Jesus' meaning is clear. The light (not of verbal witness but here) of **good works** must shine out so that men see it and thereby are led, not to praise the one who does the good deeds, but to praise the Father in heaven whom it is the disciple's single and constant purpose to honour and serve. **Father in heaven,** a favourite phrase in Matt., refers to God not as remote, inaccessible, and indifferent towards men, but as exalted, majestic, rightfully man's Lord, and so entitled to all honour and obedience. Man lives not to glorify and promote himself but to bring glory and honour to God.

v. 17-48. JESUS FULFILS THE LAW (AND THE PROPHETS)

17 'Do not suppose that I came to abolish the Law or the
18 Prophets. I did not come to abolish but to fulfil. For truly I tell you, until heaven and earth pass away, not one iota

or one part of a letter will pass away from the Law, until
all things take place. So whoever breaks one of the least 19
of these commandments, and teaches men to do so, will
be called least in the Kingdom of Heaven; but whoever
does and teaches them will be called great in the Kingdom of Heaven. For I tell you that unless your righteous- 20
ness greatly surpasses that of the scribes and Pharisees,
you will not enter the Kingdom of Heaven.

'You have heard that it was said to the men of ancient 21
times, "You shall not kill; whoever kills will be liable to
the court". But I tell you that every one who is angry with 22
his brother will be liable to the court; whoever says to his
brother, "Empty-head", will be liable to the Sanhedrin;
and whoever says, "Fool", will be liable to the Gehenna
of fire.

'If therefore you are offering your gift at the altar and 23
there remember that your brother has something against
you, leave your gift there before the altar and first go and 24
effect a reconciliation with your brother, and then return
and offer your gift.

'Make friends quickly with your opponent, while you 25
are with him on the way, lest your opponent deliver you
to the judge and the judge to the attendant, and you will
be put in prison. Truly I tell you, you will not be released 26
from there until you have paid the last quadrans.

'You have heard that it was said, "You shall not com- 27
mit adultery". But I tell you that every one who looks at 28
a woman with lustful desire for her has already committed adultery with her in his heart.

'If your right eye causes you to sin, tear it out and throw 29
it from you; for it is better for you that one of your
members perish than that your whole body be thrown
into Gehenna. And if your right hand causes you to sin, 30
cut it off and throw it from you; for it is better for you that
one of your members perish than that your whole body
go to Gehenna.

'It was said, "Whoever divorces his wife, let him give 31
her a certificate of release". But I tell you that every one 32
who divorces his wife except on the ground of unchastity

causes her to commit adultery, and whoever marries a divorced woman commits adultery.

33 'Again, you have heard that it was said to the men of ancient times, "You shall not commit perjury, but shall perform to the Lord the things you swear you will do".
34 But I tell you not to swear at all—neither by heaven, for
35 it is the throne of God, nor by the earth, for it is his footstool, nor by Jerusalem, for it is the city of the great
36 King; neither shall you swear by your head, for you can-
37 not make one hair white or black. But let your word be "Yes", "Yes", "No", "No". What exceeds this comes from the Evil One.

38   'You have heard that it was said, "Eye for eye" and
39 "Tooth for tooth". But I tell you not to resist the evil man; rather, whoever slaps you on your right cheek—turn to
40 him also the other one; and to him who is determined to go to law against you and take your tunic—let him have
41 also your outer garment; and whoever impresses you for
42 one mile of transport duty—go with him two. To him who asks you, give, and from him who wishes to borrow from you, do not turn away.

43   'You have heard that it was said, "You shall love your
44 neighbour and hate your enemy". But I tell you: Love
45 your enemies and pray for those who persecute you, that you may be sons of your Father in heaven, for he causes his sun to rise on the evil and the good, and sends rain on
46 the righteous and the unrighteous. For if you love those who love you, what reward is due you? Do not even the
47 tax collectors do the same? And if you greet your brothers only, what are you doing more than others do? Do not
48 even the Gentiles do the same? You therefore shall be perfect, as your heavenly Father is perfect.'

If disciples are to let men see their good works and so bring praise to the Father (vs. 16), what is the relation between the gospel of forgiveness and divine help and the moral demand of God? Jesus is conscious of a unique mission; sent of God, he can speak with authority. Will he use his authority to relax the demands of the Law and soften the stern words of the prophets?

Vss. 17-20, further explained in vss. 21-48 answer that question. Jesus accepts the Scripture (indicated by **the Law** and **the Prophets**) as God's revelation and demand. His main concern here is with the Law. It stands; he supports it. The freedom he exercises in interpreting and applying the Law does not **abolish** it but rather fulfils it, that is, gives the fullest expression to the divine intent in the ancient utterances. The changes he makes are conservative, true to the aim of Scripture; they more clearly express the full purpose and will of God. Vss. 21-48 will give six examples of this. But first note a difficulty.

Vss. 18 f. (cf. Lk. xvi. 17) raise a problem. They seem to express an extreme literalism which requires rigid conformity to the exact wording of every command in the Mosaic Law. But Jesus in vss. 21-48 freely alters the literal meaning of commandments in order to give a full expression of the divine intent present in the ancient Law; he often disregarded ceremony when human need was at stake; he cannot have said that men must always live exactly as they did in the early Mosaic period. Has 'Matthew' here inserted Jewish-Christian ideas and thus altered the teaching of Jesus? Is this paragraph a fierce blast at Paul? The situation is not that simple. Undoubtedly Matt. reflects the Jewish-Christian understanding that Jesus wanted his followers to be loyal to the Law. But as Lk. xvi. 17 shows, Gentile churches also knew teaching of Jesus that the Law remains valid. Abundant evidence proves that Jesus lived as a Jew, wore Jewish clothing, accepted the Law and the Prophets as Scripture, and confined his ministry almost entirely to Jews even though multitudes of Gentiles lived in Palestine. He was no rebel against his Jewish heritage. He understood his message and work as a loyal support of Scripture. He justified his answers to special needs and his more penetrating statements of God's will by appeal to the Law itself. Matthew may have grouped together sayings spoken on various occasions. May we take vs. 18 not with wooden literalness and unbending legalism, but as an emphatic expression of Jesus' deep loyalty to his heritage? The Law (this rather than the Prophets is the real concern in this section) will remain valid while the world lasts. **Iota:** The smallest letter of the Greek alphabet; here used to indicate the smallest letter in Hebrew. **Part of a letter:** Probably refers to the part of a Hebrew letter which distinguishes it from other letters which look somewhat similar. Thus the least detail of the Law will stand **until all things take place;** this repeats in substance the earlier clause, **until heaven and earth pass away.**

Jewish rabbis found 613 commandments in the Law and divided them into two groups, heavy and light. Jesus rejects any such division and the tendency it could easily foster to pay no attention to apparently unimportant commands. He does not rule out of the Kingdom one who disregards such a commandment and teaches others to do so; he simply assigns such a disciple the lowest place; he **will be called,** and will be, **least.** The disciple must not only do but also teach even the apparently unimportant commands.

Thus Jesus asks not less but more than the scribes and Pharisees were asking. He will not tolerate moral laxity or indifference. He wants a **righteousness,** an obedience to the revealed will of God, that is far more complete and faithful than that which **the scribes and Pharisees** show. As vss. 21-48 will explain, the disciple must have a truer understanding of God's will and so express more complete obedience. Such a righteousness, greater than that of the scribes and Pharisees, is necessary even to **enter the Kingdom.** The gospel brings mercy, comfort, and divine help, but it does not cancel the demand of God for faithful and complete obedience to his will.

'Matthew' now presents six examples to show how Jesus both preserved and fulfilled the Law. The opening words are: **You have heard that it was said to the men of ancient times** (vss. 21, 33); **You have heard that it was said** (vss. 27, 38, 43); **It was said** (vs. 31). In each case the contrasting teaching of Jesus begins: **But I tell you that,** etc. The pattern is expanded by appending topically related material (vss. 23-24, 25-26, 29-30) or by more extensive development of Jesus' position, as in the last three examples. Jesus' examples are familiar; his hearers had **heard** them in the Scripture lessons of synagogue services. He recalls things **said to the men of ancient times,** in the Mosaic generation. In vs. 21 he adds to the quotation from the Law a statement based on the Law and known in oral tradition; the commandment forbids murder (Ex. xx. 13; Deut. v. 17), but such passages as Ex. xxi. 12; Num. xxxv. 16-33 indicate that the murderer is liable to the court and will be punished. **I tell you:** As God's Son, entrusted with the decisive role in establishing the Kingdom, Jesus has authority to interpret the Law. He keeps what the Law says; murder is condemned and will be punished. But hostility and ill-treatment find expression not only in murder but also in anger, outspoken scorn, and furious contempt. These too are wrong. It is not clear that the three instances of anger and contempt represent an ascending series of wrongs, but possibly the three courts are placed in an ascending scale; first the (local) **court** (if, as seems probable, κρίσει here means 'court' rather than 'judgment' generally); then **the Sanhedrin,** the highest Jewish court; and finally **the Gehenna of fire,** the place of God's final punishment of the wicked. Gehenna, the name of the valley west and south of Jerusalem, became the symbol of the fiery place of eternal punishment. That words of scorn and contempt lead to such final punishment clearly indicates their wickedness.

In themselves vss. 23 f. seem to refer simply to the need of amicable human relations. 'Matthew' found in them teaching against anger and contempt. These faults imperil man's eternal welfare. If a man making a **gift at the altar** remembers that he has thus wronged another, he should interrupt the offering and promptly take the initiative in **reconciliation;** that is more important than to preserve the smoothness and dignity of the altar rites.

With vss. 25 f. cf. Lk. xii. 58 f. An **opponent** or legal adversary is taking his fellow to court to get judgment against him. The implication is that the opponent has a strong case. Jesus says to **make friends quickly** with the opponent before it is too late to settle out of court. We cannot recover the original setting of these verses, but Jesus was not giving advice on how to win friends and influence people for personal advantage. This is a parable. The Kingdom is at hand; it has begun to come; man is on the way to the final judgment; God will punish the man who does not seek at once the forgiveness that Jesus offers to the penitent. The passage implies the sinfulness of man, his need of forgiveness, and the ruin that would strike him if he had to meet his debt in full. **Quadrans:** the smallest coin; as we might say, 'the last penny'.

Adultery was forbidden in the Ten Commandments (Ex. xx. 14; Deut. v. 18). This demand that men live pure lives and respect marriage ties Jesus fully supports. But God wants something more: purity of thought and desire. Lustful looks and thoughts are as certainly adulterous and sinful as is the act of adultery (Jesus speaks of the man, but his teaching applies to all people). Jesus does not discuss here the serious social consequences of the actual deed; he simply states plainly that the lustful look and desire are sinful, for God wants purity of heart as well as of act. This includes but goes deeper than the tenth commandment (Ex. xx. 17; Deut. v. 21).

With vss. 29-30 cf. xviii. 8 f.; Mark ix. 43-48. In themselves these two verses have no reference to sex life. They say in figurative wording that whatever in one's life tempts one to sin should be discarded, promptly and decisively, just as surgeons today amputate an arm or leg to save life. Jesus' words are obviously figurative. Even without the **right eye** (mentioned perhaps as the more important one), evil and lustful looks would still be possible with the other eye. Even without the **right hand,** evil acts could be done with the left hand. Jesus means that whatever tie or practice leads to sin and so to ruin should be given up at once. Applying this to sex impulses, 'Matthew' means that one must not dwell on the desire to do wrong, or carry out in imagination the adulterous act; one must limit the eye, the imagination, and the desire to lawful and worthy things.

This negative teaching to cut out of life what may lead to sin has limited validity. It could lead—wrongly—to complete avoidance of social relations, to a self-quarantine due to paralysing fear of getting involved in evil. Jesus went to sinners; he ate with them; he befriended them. For him the real protection from evil was not in flight but in commitment to God's will and in genuine concern for the welfare of others. It remains true, however, that it is wrong to dwell on the possibility of unlawful indulgence and it is dangerous to put oneself in a position where wrong-doing is the easy outcome.

With vss. 31 f. cf. xix. 9; Mk. x. 11 f.; Lk. xvi. 18; 1 Cor. vii. 10 f. Jesus spoke strongly against divorce, as did Mal. ii. 16: 'I hate divorce, says the Lord'. Exactly what Jesus said is not so clear. 'Matthew' twice indicates that divorce is proper if the wife is guilty of **unchastity** (πορνεία), which probably means her unfaithfulness after marriage rather than pre-marital illicit relations with another man. Mark, Luke, and Paul know of no such exception.

Did these three assume a universally accepted exception which 'Matthew' is careful to state? Or, since Rabbi Hillel approved divorce for various flimsy pretexts while Shammai approved it only for marital unfaithfulness, was Jesus saying in effect that he agreed with the stricter rule of Shammai? Such explanations mistake Jesus' aim. He was stating the purpose of God, who, as Gen. i.-ii. show, created man and woman for a permanent monogamous union. To fulfil the O.T. law about marriage requires more than reducing the number of valid reasons for divorce; it requires a married life of unbroken mutual love and faithfulness which leaves no room for divorce.

Apparently the Church had to decide what to do when married couples failed to fulfil the purpose of the Creator. 'Matthew', or his source for this teaching, evidently held that the Church must hold divorce to a minimum, but that the spirit of Jesus' teaching could best be realized by permitting divorce where the wife was guilty of unchastity. (In Jewish practice only the man could divorce; this is assumed in all the gospel passages except Mk. x. 12, which may reflect Roman law.)

The O.T. background of this teaching of Jesus is different from that of the other passages where Jesus contrasts the ancient teaching with his own. The other passages are explicit commandments. Deut. xxiv. 1-5, the background of this passage, does not prescribe divorce; it assumes divorce as a common and legitimate practice; it forbids a man to remarry his divorced wife after she has remarried and later become free from her second husband. However, it reflects the common practice of divorce in Israel, and so Jesus can quote it to show what the Mosaic Law permitted.

The practice of giving the wife a written **certificate** of divorce was a protection for her. A capricious husband might drive her from his home with an oral declaration of divorce and later insist that she was still his wife. With a written certificate, however, she could remarry, as Jewish custom permitted, and could not be accused of adultery. Jesus shares this condemnation of capricious divorce, but goes deeper to say that before God all divorce is a failure to live up to the divine purpose of the Creator. **Causes her to commit adultery:** It is assumed that she will marry again, and since her marriage bond is still valid, she will be guilty of adultery. **Whoever marries a divorced woman commits adultery:** Because he marries a woman who is still another man's wife. (Does this seem stern and make sinners of many divorced and remarried people? Vs. 28 makes sinners of far more people; how many completely avoid the lustful look and impulse there condemned?)

Again (πάλιν) introduces the fourth contrast between what Moses said in the Law and Jesus says to fulfil the Law. As in the first contract (vs. 21), the full formula is used: **You have heard that it was said to the men of ancient times;** thus each group of three contrasts is introduced by the full formula, and the other contrasts more briefly.

Vs. 33 does not quote the O.T. literally, but it summarizes faithfully Lev. xix. 12; Num. xxx. 2; Deut. xxiii. 21. The Mosaic Law assumes that men take oaths, calling God to confirm and judge what they say, and it insists that men must **perform** what they swear they will do. This shows a concern for truth when God is seen to be directly involved. But God is concerned in every area of life, and man is always responsible to speak truthfully and live honestly. The trouble with oaths is that they introduce a double standard of truth and honesty; if God is specifically involved, man must deal honestly, but otherwise he may speak and act dishonestly if that suits his purpose. This double standard then leads men to devise oaths which sound impressive but since God's name is not used are not thought binding. How far such evasive dishonest invention could go is seen here and in xxiii. 16-22.

By heaven: This avoids using the name of God, but heaven is his throne (Isa. lxvi. 1; Acts vii. 49), so to refer to heaven is to refer to him and be responsible to him. **By the earth:** Earth seems remote from God in heaven, but it is God's creation, his footstool (Isa. lxvi. 1), a part of his realm. **By Jerusalem:** An oath by this **city of the great King** (a title used of human kings, 2 Kings xviii. 19, and of God, Ps. xcv. 3; on Jerusalem as God's city, cf. Ps. xlviii. 2) involves God and is binding. **By your**

head: Man cannot control his life and destiny; he has a divine Head, his Creator and Lord.

Since in all of life man is dealing with God, he is always obligated to complete integrity in word and act. Therefore the use of oaths is misleading; **swear not at all;** simply say 'Yes' or 'No'. Repeating these words here may be a form of emphasis, which some rabbis regarded as in effect an oath; or Jesus may have said something like Jas. v. 12, 'Let your Yes be Yes, and your No be No'; or it may mean that at various times one will say Yes and at other times No. The use of solemn-sounding oaths instead of simple, truthful speech is a concession to a double standard and comes from **the Evil One,** Satan, the 'father of lies' and dishonesty (Jn. viii. 44).

Lk. vi. 27-36 parallels much of vss. 38-48, but with a different order and interest. In Lk. the basic theme is love of enemies; in Matt., fulfilment of the Law by avoiding retaliation and by showing love of enemies.

Jewish hearers knew the principle of equal retribution from Ex. xxi. 23-25; Lev. xxiv. 19-21; Deut. xix. 21. Possibly the ancient law dictated full punishment to deter men from crime, but probably it intended chiefly to curb blind fury that might seek unlimited revenge. Jesus rejects all idea of revenge and even of exact justice.

Jesus gives five examples of how the disciple should react to unfair or unreasonable treatment. (1) Physical violence. It is not clear whether a back-handed blow **on the right cheek** was thought especially insulting, or whether **the right cheek** was mentioned as the important side (cf. the right eye and right hand in v. 29 f.). Man's usual impulse is to strike back, but the disciple must 'overcome evil with good' (Rom. xii. 21), offer the other cheek for a second blow, seek no revenge. (2) Litigation. In Lk. the wrongdoer takes the outer garment by violence; the disciple must let him take the tunic also. In Matt. the wrongdoer goes to law to take the **tunic;** the disciple must let him have both tunic and **outer garment.** (3) Forced service. Ancient armies and government agents forced natives to carry supplies of passing armies or officials. Evidently the Romans in Palestine compelled Jews to render such service. Jesus tells his disciples not to resent this but to do twice what they are asked to do. (4) Demands for gifts of money or property. Jesus says to **give** what is asked. (5) Demands for loans. The disciple is to give a would-be borrower what he wants.

Does this teaching undermine social order? Is it harmful to both the wrongdoer and the wronged person? Jesus is not legislating for all men or telling the state what laws to pass; he is telling his disciples what they are to do when wronged. Even if one cannot always live literally and mechanically by these instructions (cf. John xviii. 22 f.), they carry important truth: the disciple is not to let selfishness or ill-will determine his response to mistreatment or excessive demands; any limitation on this renunciation of retaliation must come from the demands of a humane, wholesome society and from consideration of what will be fair, helpful, and redemptive for the wrongdoer.

Every Israelite knew from Lev. xix. 18 that he should love his neighbour. No doubt he usually took **neighbour** to mean essentially his fellow-Jews, or those living near by, or those congenial with himself. But note that Lev. xix. 34 explicitly goes beyond the brotherhood of race: 'The stranger who sojourns with you . . . you shall love him as yourself', and no O.T. passage explicitly commands hate of enemies. However, the idea occurs; cf. Deut. vii. 2; xxiii. 3-6; xxv. 17-19; Ps. cxxxvii. 7-9. In these passages a national enemy is in mind, but the attitude could pass over to personal enemies, who are in mind in Matt.

The disciple's goodwill is tested precisely in his treatment of those who show none to him. He proves himself a true disciple by loving his enemies and persecutors (here, as often in the Gospels, the disciple's life is not expected to be easy). **Sons of your Father:** Like him, showing his impartial goodwill in your lives. God is holy, 'the Judge of all the earth' (Gen. xviii. 25), but he gives many blessings—such as sunshine and rain—to **good** and **evil** men alike. To be true sons of God, the disciples must not limit their love and greetings to their own group, who will return their kindness and courtesies. Even the groups most despised among the Jews—**the tax collectors,** who serve the hated Roman government, and **the Gentiles,** thought inferior to God's chosen people—love and greet their own brotherhood. The love that fulfils the will of God is a kindly, sympathetic, steadfast, intelligent, active, resourceful goodwill which in every possible way seeks the good of every man, particularly one's enemy.

This is indeed a high standard. But to fulfil the Law (v. 17) the disciple cannot take a lower standard than Lev. xix. 2, 'You shall be holy, for I the Lord your God am holy'. **Perfect:** Luke says 'merciful'; **perfect** emphasizes the measuring of all life by the perfect holy love of God himself, and makes vs. 48 a fitting conclusion and summary of all that vss. 17-47 have said. To fulfil the Law is to express the Father's will in all of life's tasks and relationships.

CHAPTER VI

---

vi. 1-18. WORSHIP WITHOUT PARADING YOUR PIETY

'Be careful not to practise your piety before men to be 1 seen by them; if you do that, you have no reward with your Father who is in heaven.

'When therefore you give alms, do not sound a trumpet 2 before you, as the hypocrites do in the synagogues and in the streets, that they may be praised by men. Truly I tell you, they have their reward in full. But when you give 3 alms, do not let your left hand know what your right hand is doing, that your almsgiving may be done in secret; and 4 your Father, who sees in secret, will recompense you.

'And when you pray, you shall not be like the hypo- 5 crites; for they love to pray while standing in the synagogues and on the street corners, that they may be seen by men. Truly I tell you, they have their reward in full. But when you pray, go into your inner room and shut your 6 door and pray to your Father who is in secret; and your Father who sees in secret will recompense you.

'But in praying do not babble on as the Gentiles do; for 7 they suppose that they will be heard just because they multiply words. Do not then become like them, for your 8

9 Father knows what you need before you ask him. This
then is the way you are to pray:
"Our Father who art in heaven,
May thy name be held in reverence;
10   May thy Kingdom come;
May thy will be done, as in heaven, so also on earth.
11   Give us today our bread for the coming day;
12   And forgive us our debts, as we also have forgiven our debtors;
13   And do not lead us into temptation, but deliver
us from the Evil One."
14 For if you forgive men their misdeeds, your heavenly
15 Father will forgive you also; but if you do not forgive men,
neither will your Father forgive your misdeeds.
16   'And when you fast, do not put on a gloomy look as the
hypocrites do; for they disfigure their faces that they may
17 be seen by men to be fasting. Truly I tell you, they have
their reward in full. But when you fast, anoint your head
18 and wash your face, that you may not be seen by men to
be fasting but by your Father who is in secret; and your
Father who sees in secret will recompense you.'

Vss. 1-18 deal with the most prominent practices of Jewish
piety: almsgiving, prayer, and fasting. These are the aspects of
righteousness (δικαιοσύνη, here translated **piety**) which the
Jew could perform in regular acts. Some manuscripts read not
'righteousness', **piety**, but 'almsgiving' (ἐλεημοσύνη), perhaps
because the Aramaic word translated 'righteousness' may also
mean 'almsgiving', but probably because 'almsgiving' was read
back from vss. 2-4 into vs. 1. The original reading is 'righteousness', 'piety'. In each of the three examples (vss. 2-4, 5-6, 16-
18) the same pattern occurs: Jesus warns against acting like **the
hypocrites,** whose aim is to win human praise; he asserts that
such parade and pretence are spiritually futile; he commands a
practice of piety with the utmost secrecy, which will have God's
blessing. These three practices, Jesus assumes, the disciples
rightly observe; the religious life has outward expression and
duties; but piety paraded for human notice and praise gets no
recognition from God. The disciple must let his light shine; men

must see his good works (v. 16); but he must not seek honour for himself. **Reward:** Not that man earns his salvation, but that God recognizes and blesses the life lived in gratitude and loyalty to God. **Your Father who is in heaven:** These words do not mean that God is remote from human life; they express his majesty and transcendent greatness.

Almsgiving was honoured in Jewish life. God cares for widows, orphans, and all unfortunate, needy people; his worshippers will actively help such people, either by direct gifts or by contribution to community funds. But such giving can be wrongly used to advertise one's pretended goodness. **Sound a trumpet:** Not literally; the words mean: 'give in a way that gets maximum publicity and praise'. **Hypocrites:** Cf. ch. xxiii. The word, derived from the theatre, denoted an actor, then one who played a part or acted a false role in public life; here used of people who want to be known as pious and so help the needy not in generous sympathy but in selfish effort to win praise from men. They may do it **in the synagogues,** where worshippers will see their giving, or **in the** (narrow) **streets,** where residents and passers-by will notice their act. They get what they want, not God's blessing and the joy of sharing his concern for the needy, but the praise of men. But that is all they get; the Greek word ἀπέχω, used in giving receipts, means: 'Received in full'. When these self-centred pretenders receive praise from men, they have been paid in full; they will get no blessing from God. He sees through their pretence.

The disciple's attitude in almsgiving is entirely different. He keeps his giving as secret as possible. **Do not let your left hand know what your right hand is doing** means: Avoid all scheming for human attention and praise, give in filial obedience to God and with brotherly concern for those in need. He to whom the 'darkness is as light' (Ps. cxxxix. 12) will know the deed and spirit of the giver, and will reward him.

Strong manuscript evidence favours including 'openly' (ἐν τῷ φανερῷ) at the end of vs. 4; secret almsgiving will receive open recognition and reward. Equally strong evidence favours omitting the word, which seems out of place here unless it refers to the final judgment, when all things are made public. Even if we omit 'openly', it is probable that 'Matthew' rightly understood

Jesus to mean **recompense** by praise and recognition at the final judgment.

Prayer, like almsgiving, could be used to parade pretended piety. Jesus speaks not of the common prayers of Jewish worship, when all took part, nor of leading the common prayers, as a layman might do in the synagogue service, but of the Jewish practice of individual praying at regular times (cf. Dan. vi. 10). One could manage to pray surrounded by a large and admiring audience; he could time his movements and prayer schedule so that he prayed **in the synagogues** or **on the street corners** and so appeared unusually pious. **Standing:** The usual posture for prayer among first-century Jews. Jesus is emphatic; a prayer offered to win human attention and praise has no spiritual worth and wins no praise from God.

Prayer is reverent worship, the expression of adoration, gratitude, praise, petition, and dedication. True prayer is offered in humility, with no desire to impress men or God. Prayer does not exist where man's aim is self-promotion; such parade is not prayer to God but self-worship. Therefore the disciple (cf. Isa. xxvi. 20), to avoid the temptation to use the form of prayer to impress others, should enter his **inner room,** shut the door, and pray to God His Father. God will be present to hear and bless him who prays sincerely. Such prayer in private is a test of sincerity; if the disciple prays only in public, public custom and attention mean too much to him; if he prays also in private, he worships without the need of man's praise and custom.

Vss. 7-15 break the literary pattern of general warning (vs. 1) and three examples (vss. 2-4; 5-6; 16-18); they were inserted by 'Matthew' or his source because of their topical connection with vss. 5 f. 'Matthew' often groups material topically, and this is legitimate, for much of the material was preserved without any indication of the place and time when it was spoken, and it was helpful to arrange it in topical order for convenience in teaching.

Quantity of words does not determine the value of prayer. Jesus knew the rightful place of persistent prayer (cf. his own urgency in xxvi. 39-44, and the widow's in Lk. xviii. 1-8). But to **babble on,** as **the Gentiles** were known to do, and expect an answer just for talking so much, is not real prayer and will win no answer.

Such long prayers are not necessary to inform God of man's needs. God the **Father** cares for man and already **knows** his needs. It is essential for man to ask, for God can give his spiritual blessings only to those who know their need, trust his power and goodness, and ask in grateful commitment to his will. But he who knows all things does not need detailed information bulletins.

In the prayer we call The Lord's Prayer Jesus gave his disciples guidance on how to pray. The Gospels give us this prayer in two forms, similar in pattern but different in wording. Lk. xi. 2-4 is much shorter, but includes the main themes found in Matt. Both forms have simplicity, conciseness, intellectual clarity, and spiritual comprehensiveness.

The Prayer falls into three parts. The first is the address, in Lk. only 'Father', but in Matt. the characteristically Jewish **Our Father who art in heaven.** If Lk. is closer to the wording Jesus taught, Matt. is faithful to the meaning. **Our:** The prayer can only be used by the group or by one aware he is one of the group. **Father** expresses the grace and active concern of God. **In heaven:** Does not picture God as inaccessible, but expresses his transcendent greatness and sovereign majesty. An ancient form of Jewish prayer begins: 'Our Father, our King'; 'Father' recognizes his personal concern and active grace, 'King' his authority and power. Precisely because he is the Lord and King, his Fatherhood gives promise of trustworthy and adequate help, and thus gives ground for confidence in prayer.

The second part of the Prayer contains three petitions that God may be honoured and his will fully realized. This is the basic attitude and test of true prayer, 'Not as I will, but as thou wilt' (xxvi. 39). The three separate petitions are: (1) **May thy name be held in reverence. Name:** Means God as he has made himself known. **Held in reverence:** Calls for more than a feeling of reverence or awe, more than cautious avoidance of profanity or irreverent talk; means to respond to God with reverent worship, grateful faith, and humble acceptance of his claim and promise. (2) **May thy Kingdom come.** The Kingdom is the full and effective reign of God. The disciples are not to think first or mainly of their own needs and wishes, but are to pray for the quick realization of the effective rule of God their Father. It will mean security for all good, exclusion of all evil, and privilege for all who share the blessings of their Father's gracious sovereign rule. (3) **May thy will be done.** The disciple who prays for the full coming of the Kingdom must ask that first in himself and then in others and in all social relations the will of God may be fully understood and willingly done. His will is done **in heaven,** as the Prayer gratefully recalls. May it be done equally **on earth;** may earth see the full accomplishment of what God wills. This phrase, **as in heaven, so also on earth,** is best taken with all three petitions that have just been spoken.

The third main part of the Prayer, like the second, consists of three petitions. They refer to needs of the disciples. God is concerned with all human needs, desires, and struggles. Disciples may pray for God's help in every aspect of their lives.

The disciples may pray for **bread,** food to sustain life, provision for their physical needs; bread not for far-off future needs, but **for the coming day.** The word $\epsilon\pi\iota o\acute{u}\sigma\iota o\varsigma$ has puzzled scholars; its earliest occurrence in Greek is in the Lord's Prayer, from whose influence may come the one later occurrence known (on a sort of ancient shopping list found in the sands of Egypt). The word is variously translated: 'for the coming day', 'for today', 'for our essential need', 'for our spiritual (supersubstantial) need'. The first three alternatives all refer to immediate and essential physical need. **For the coming day** may be preferred; it was a prayer that could be used in the morning or evening, to ask for food for the meals just ahead.

The disciples may pray for forgiveness. Judaism knew the description of sins as **debts** owed to God (we owe him complete obedience; every failure to obey puts us hopelessly in debt). Only God can **forgive** sins. And he is ready to do so, when his forgiveness is sincerely wanted. But if we refuse to forgive others who wrong us, our unforgiving spirit makes us unable to receive the forgiveness God is ready to grant. This important point is doubly emphasized in vss. 14 f. **Have forgiven:** Those who ask God for forgiveness cannot really want it or receive it until they are ready to forgive others who wrong them. It is not that man earns God's forgiveness by forgiving others first, or that God's requirement that men forgive others is merely a

formal, legalistic condition, but that God cannot forgive and
renew and use in a ministry of reconciliation those who stubbornly cling to grudges, harbour hate, and refuse to be sons of
God by being merciful peacemakers (v. 7, 9).

The disciples may pray for deliverance from **temptation**.
This final petition seems to contradict life, which inevitably
involves choices between good and evil, and so brings us into
temptation. We cannot ask God to keep us from life's struggles
and decisions. Jesus himself was tempted (iv. 1-11) to the end
of his life (xxvi. 36-46). The disciples likewise must face temptation, but they must not delight in it or be over-confident about
it. They must ask God to spare them from temptation as far as
possible, and to **deliver** them when they must face it. **The Evil
One**: τοῦ πονηροῦ may be neuter, the evil in the world that tries
to drag men down, but it probably is masculine, **the Evil One**,
Satan, who actively tries to seduce men from loyalty to God and
finds in life's trials opportunities to tempt men away from
obedience. When temptation must come, do not let it become
the means by which the Evil One gets control of us; help us face
it so as to achieve deeper and more mature loyalty.

In the early Church Matt.'s longer form of the Lord's Prayer
commended itself for use in common worship. The ending was
felt to be abrupt. Not later than the early second century a
doxology was added. The *Didache* (Teaching of the Twelve
Apostles) adds: 'For thine is the power and the glory forever'.
The later, fuller form, found in most later manuscripts of Matt.,
reads: 'For thine is the kingdom and the power and the glory
forever. Amen.' This ending, not from Jesus and not originally
in Matt., evidently was based on 1 Chron. xxix. 11, but with a
new conciseness which forms a fitting and worshipful conclusion.

Vss. 14 f. emphatically restate, in both positive and negative
form, the condition of forgiveness given in vs. 12b. Cf. xviii.
21-35, the parable of the forgiven servant who would not forgive
his fellow-servant, and therefore lost the forgiveness his master
had granted; also Mk. xi. 25. **Misdeeds**: This term, like 'debts',
is a word for sin, a wrong done to God which only God's
forgiveness can remove.

After inserting the added teaching concerning prayer (vss.
7-15), 'Matthew' presents the third religious practice in which

public parade must be avoided. **Fasting** was not specifically commanded in the Mosaic Law, but the command to afflict oneself on the annual Day of Atonement (Lev. xvi. 31) was taken to involve fasting. Other days were observed by later enactment, and earnest Jews in Jesus' day fasted twice a week (cf. Lk. xviii. 12). Jesus does not forbid fasting; he opposed fasting by rule; it was in place as an expression of sorrow (ix. 14 f.). He here assumes the practice is legitimate, but denounces its use to win a reputation for piety. Evidently some persons not only fasted but disfigured their faces, not to express to God deep inward sorrow over the sins or trials of themselves or their people, but to impress people and win praise. Their act was not worship; it could expect no reward or praise from God.

In contrast, **you** (the emphatic σύ opens the sentence) must give no outward sign, use no uglifying cosmetics, to advertise that you are fasting. Appear cheerful and normal; if your sorrow for sin and suffering is sincere, God will know it; he will recognize it and bless the worshipper who in agony of spirit commits his life to God. When the true disciple gives alms, prays, or fasts, he is not seeking publicity; he is seeking God. He will not shun men; he will let his light shine; but he will make no pretentious parade of his worship and commitment.

vi. 19-34. SERVE GOD RATHER THAN POSSESSIONS

19 'Do not lay up treasures for yourselves on earth, where moth and rust destroy and where thieves dig through and
20 steal. But lay up treasures for yourselves in heaven, where neither moth nor rust destroys and where thieves do not
21 dig through nor steal; for where your treasure is, there also will be your heart.

22   'The lamp of the body is the eye. If then your eye is
23 sound, your whole body will have light; but if your eye is bad, your whole body will be dark. If then the light in you is darkness, how great is the darkness!

24   'No one can serve two masters. For he either will hate the one and love the other, or will be devoted to one and

despise the other. **You cannot serve God and mammon.**

'For this reason I say to you: Do not worry about your 25
life, what you are to eat or what you are to drink, nor about
your body, what you are to wear. Is not the life more than
food and the body more than clothing? Consider the birds 26
of heaven, for they do not sow nor reap nor gather into
storehouses, and yet your heavenly Father feeds them.
Are you not worth much more than they? Which of you 27
by worry can add one cubit to his span of life? And why 28
do you worry about clothing? Observe the wild lilies, how
they grow; they do not labour or spin, but I tell you that 29
even Solomon in all his splendour did not dress as well
as one of them. Now if God so clothes the wild grass which 30
is here today but tomorrow is thrown into an oven, will
he not much more surely clothe you, you men of little
faith? So do not worry, saying, "What are we to eat?" 31
or "What are we to drink?" or "What are we to wear?"
For the Gentiles strive to get all these things, and your 32
heavenly Father knows that you need all these things.
But seek first the Kingdom and his righteousness, and 33
all these things will be given you in addition. So do not 34
worry about tomorrow, for tomorrow will worry about
itself; sufficient for the day is its trouble.'

The rest of ch. vi. falls into five parts: vss. 19-21; 22 f.; 24;
25-33; 34. Lk. parallels the first four, but not in the same order
or in one continuous passage. A common source lies behind
Matt. and Lk. 'Matthew' presents the material in topical grouping; his theme is that true loyalty to God excludes any rival
loyalty; in particular, it excludes concern for possessions and
material comfort and security.

Vss. 19-21 (cf. Lk. xii. 33 f.) contrast earthly and heavenly
treasures. In true ancient oriental style earthly treasures con-
sist in part of costly clothing, which **moths** may ruin. **Rust:** So
βρῶσις (literally, 'eating') may mean; if so, Jesus speaks of
things made of iron that rust; but the word may mean 'worm',
in which case Jesus meant: 'where moth and worm consume'
(garments and woven things). Another danger is **thieves,** who
dig through house walls made of mud brick. Such earthly

treasures are easily and quickly destroyed or stolen. It is foolish to centre life and hope on such fragile, transient treasures. **Treasures in heaven: Heaven** points to God and the approval, blessings, and rewards he gives. Present privilege is not excluded, but thought centres on the secure and richer privilege with God in the coming Kingdom.

Man sets his heart on what he counts important. If one centres on earthly treasures, so transient, so easily lost, one becomes thing-minded and self-concerned. To make possessions one's consuming concern is eternally ruinous; the life with a future is life centred in God and his will.

Vss. 22 f. (cf. Lk. xi. 34-36) is a parable. To act effectively the body must have clear, **sound** vision (ἁπλοῦς means 'single', and so **sound**, 'clear'; πονηρός means **bad**, 'diseased', 'not able to focus clearly'). Just so man must have sound, clear vision in spiritual things, or he will live in spiritual **darkness.** That would be ruinous.

By placing the parable here, 'Matthew' applies it specifically to man's view of possessions. If man divides his interest and tries to focus on both God and possessions, he has no clear vision, and will live without clear orientation or direction. Life not focused on God's claim and command is lost in spiritual darkness. This use of light and darkness in a spiritual sense is frequent in the Bible (especially in Jn.), and occurs in the Dead Sea Scrolls.

Vs. 24 (cf. Lk. xvi. 13) states clearly the intent of the two previous paragraphs: God claims complete loyalty; the disciple cannot divide his loyalty between God and possessions. A slave (Luke says 'house-servant') owes full service and loyalty to his master. If he tries to **serve two masters,** he will soon favour one. **God** claims to be Lord, but **mammon** (wealth, possessions) presses its claim for full attention. Man must make a choice. It seems indicated that mammon will win the major loyalty of the 'double-minded man' (Jas. i. 8) who lets concern for wealth get hold of him. In any case, such divided loyalty will prove ruinous to man; God will not accept partial or part-time service.

Vss. 25-34 (cf. Lk. xii. 22-31) warns against **worry.** It is wicked, and a danger signal that conflict between loyalty to God and concern for material security threatens the spiritual life. The wrong thing is not to 'take thought' but to **worry** (μεριμνᾶτε), to be so anxious and disturbed about material needs that we distrust God and are distracted from faithfully doing his will.

Perhaps those manuscripts are right to omit **or what you are to drink** (but cf. vs. 31); the general meaning remains the same; the fatal fault in worry is that man thinks his real need is physical. Jesus does not despise the physical side of life, but it is wrong to make the means of life one's main concern. Reference to the birds teaches not idleness but freedom from anxiety; they live with unconscious trust in their Maker. Moreover, worry is futile; no amount of worry will add **a cubit** (literally, about eighteen inches) to one's **span of life** (ἡλικία usually means 'age', and so **span of life,** total age; it sometimes means 'stature'; but here the meaning seems to be that a man cannot by worry lengthen his life). Modern medical science would go further; worry shortens life and makes it miserable while it lasts. The **wild lilies** which briefly adorn Palestine in spring receive from their Maker incomparable beauty; even **Solomon,** proverbial for his splendour of court and dress, did not match them with his royal robes. They last only a short time; the dry weather and early summer heat soon wither them; then they serve only to heat the simple **oven** of the common people. If God cares for such transient plants, how **much more** for his people whom he made to live with him in faith and obedience now and in the age to come! What is back of worry? Lack of faith; men do not really believe in God; they do not believe that if they trust and serve him, he will provide for them what they need; they are 'feeble believers', **men of little faith.** To ask anxious questions about what to eat, drink, and wear is wrong for two further reasons. (1) It is pagan. **The Gentiles,** who do not understand God's power and goodness, worry about material needs, but God's people know his concern for them; so they cannot justify worry. (2) It is an affront to God. He **knows** the needs of his people. Worry suspects him of forgetting them or of overlooking their need. It is practical atheism.

The basic necessity is always to put God and his will **first.** Constantly **seek** (the Greek present imperative indicates unceasing quest) as your first and ever dominant concern (πρῶτον) **the Kingdom.** Many manuscripts add 'of God' after **Kingdom,** but in the original text the reader understands from vs. 32

that Jesus means God's Kingdom, his sovereign, righteous, and effective rule. This Kingdom man will not establish, but by loyalty to God man proves fitted to receive it; it is right for man to seek what is basically the gift and work of God. To seek God's **righteousness** is an unusual idea; is righteousness used here, as in Second Isaiah, of the vindicating salvation by which God saves those who seek him? In any case, food, clothing, and other material provision for needs will be added to the blessing which God gives to those whose first and constant quest is the Kingdom.

Vs. 34 has no parallel in Luke; 'Matthew' put it here because he thought it consistent with what precedes. The concern for earthly treasures and possessions is largely or mainly a restless anxiety for the unknown future, it is a worry about **tomorrow** and the days ahead. So the warning not to worry about tomorrow continues the thought of vss. 25-33. The two reasons given, however, are not so basic as those that have preceded. (1) Tomorrow will bring its own anxiety. That is, no one knows today just what tomorrow will bring, and no one can devise in advance a sure protection against its uncertainties. (2) Today brings enough **trouble,** without borrowing hypothetical trouble from tomorrow. Concern yourself with today's problems; they call for all your strength and resourcefulness; deal with your real problems and not with anticipated troubles. The whimsical note in these reasons has a spiritual wisdom that should not be despised; face the actual problem of living in the present instead of crippling the present by fear of the imagined future.

CHAPTER VII

vii. 1-29.   JUDGE KINDLY; PRAY IN FAITH;
OBEY THIS TEACHING

1, 2 'Do not judge, lest you be judged. For with the judgment
you use you will be judged, and with the measure you use
3 things will be measured out to you. Why do you see the

speck in your brother's eye, but do not notice the wooden
beam in your own eye? Or how can you say to your 4
brother, "Let me remove the speck from your eye",
when behold, the wooden beam is there in your own eye?
You hypocrite, first remove the wooden beam from your 5
own eye, and then you will see clearly to remove the
speck from your brother's eye.

'Do not give to dogs what is sacred, nor throw your 6
pearls down before swine, lest they trample them under
foot and turn and tear you in pieces.

'Ask, and your request will be granted; seek, and you 7
will find; knock, and the door will be opened to you. For 8
everyone who asks receives, and he who seeks finds, and
to him who knocks the door will be opened. Or what man 9
is there among you whose son will ask him for bread—he
will not give him a stone, will he? Or again, he will ask 10
for a fish—he will not give him a serpent, will he? If you 11
then, although you are evil, know how to give good gifts to
your children, how much more will your Father who is in
heaven give good things to those who ask him!

'All things therefore that you wish men to do to you, 12
you also must do to them; for this is the Law and the
Prophets.

'Enter through the narrow gate, for wide is the gate and 13
broad the way which leads to ruin, and many are they
who enter by it; for narrow is the gate and straitened the 14
way which leads to life, and few are they who find it.

'Beware of false prophets who come to you in sheep's 15
clothing but inwardly are ravenous wolves. You will re- 16
cognize them by their fruits. Men do not gather grapes
from thorn-bushes, do they? Or figs from thistles? So 17
every good tree bears good fruit, and the decayed tree
bears bad fruit. A good tree cannot bear bad fruit, nor can 18
a decayed tree bear good fruit. Every tree which does not 19
produce good fruit is cut down and thrown into the fire.
So you will recognize them by their fruits.   20

'Not everyone who says to me "Lord! Lord!" will enter 21
the Kingdom of Heaven, but only he who does the will of
my Father who is in heaven. Many will say to me in that 22

day, "Lord! Lord! Did we not prophesy in your name, and
in your name drive out demons, and in your name per-
23 form many miracles?" And then I will openly declare to
them, "I never knew you. Depart from me, you doers of
lawlessness."

24   'Everyone therefore who hears these words of mine
and does them will be compared to a prudent man who
25 built his house on solid rock. And the rain fell and the
floods came and the winds blew and dashed against that
house, but it did not fall, for it had been founded on solid
26 rock. And everyone who hears these words of mine and
does not do them will be compared to a foolish man who
27 built his house on sandy soil. And the rain fell and the
floods came and the winds blew and beat against that
house, and it fell, and great was its fall.'

28   And it happened when Jesus had finished these words
29 that the crowds were astounded at his teaching, for he
taught them with the note of authority, and not as their
scribes did.

With vss. 1-5 cf. Lk. vi. 37 f., 41 f. Every man must make
judgments concerning others; vs. 2 recognizes this. But men
have a chronic tendency to be lenient in judging their own
actions and callously harsh in judging others. (Note Rom. ii. 1.)
In the light of this purpose vs. 1 means: **Do not judge** in a harsh,
censorious spirit. **You will be judged:** By whom? By others?
Jesus probably means here: You will be sternly judged by God
if you are severe in judging others. Cf. v. 7; xviii. 33; Jas. ii. 13.

Verses 3-5 enforce this point by vivid exaggeration and dry
humour. Think first of your own faults; be most severe in dealing with them; be kindly with your brother's failings. Man's
chief and most exacting criticism should be self-criticism.

What makes the man a **hypocrite?** He is self-deceived, self-
complacent, prone to see the faults of others rather than himself. Not that he consciously and deliberately conceals his true
nature; his concern to criticize and reform others is marred by
uncritical moral complacency as to his own life.

'Matthew' uses the puzzling vs. 6 to say: In presenting the
gospel message, use discrimination; do not insist on speaking

when beastly hostility is the only answer. The saying is figurative. Just as **dogs** cannot respect **what is sacred** and **swine** cannot value **pearls,** so some people cannot appreciate the Gospel. Instead of **what is sacred** (τὸ ἅγιον) some would read 'ear-ring', since the Aramaic *qādhshā* can have either meaning, and 'ear-ring' would be a neat parallel to **pearls.** This is possible. The sentence has limited relevance; Jesus went to the outcasts among his people, and found ways to appeal to quite unpromising folk; he did not withhold his teaching for fear of a hostile response.

With vss. 7-11 cf. Lk. xi. 9-13. Elsewhere Jesus indicates important conditions for receiving what one asks of God: be ready to forgive (vi. 12, 14 f.); avoid outward show (vi. 6); persevere in asking (Luke xviii. 1-8); one's consuming concern must be God's rule and will (vi. 10; xxvi. 39). But here Jesus teaches another basic point: God hears and answers prayer. Note the emphasis: the threefold **ask—seek—knock,** twice repeated, and the threefold assurance, twice repeated, that everyone who prays is answered. Imperfect, sinful human fathers (Jesus clearly indicates here the sinfulness of all men) **know how to give good gifts** to their children, and do so. How much more will God, **your** righteous, gracious **Father,** answer your prayers and **give good things** when you ask him! Any problem about answer to prayer is not due to lack of goodness or ability in God; he is ready to give; he does give. If prayer seems to win no answer, the one praying may be at fault, or, as Gethsemane shows (xxvi. 36-46), God may have a wise purpose not yet understood.

The Golden Rule is not original with Jesus. Tobit iv. 15 says, 'What you hate, do not do to any one'. Philo is reported to have written, 'What any one dislikes to experience, he should not do'. Rabbi Hillel said, 'What is hateful to you, you must not do to your neighbour; this is the whole Law'. Various expressions similar in content are found in independent Gentile sources. Such examples usually state the Golden Rule in negative form. Some think a negative statement stronger than the positive form Jesus uses, but it is difficult to concede this.

This is the Law and the Prophets: It is what the O.T. teaches, and so what God requires of man. For Jesus, for 'Matthew', and for the Church this was a deeply religious statement. The Golden Rule by itself, however, is neither the full statement of O.T. teaching nor the adequate summary of what Jesus taught. Its actual wording any atheist might accept; it deals only with fair and helpful relations between men. xxii. 34-40, love to God and neighbour, is a far better summary of what the O.T. and Jesus teach, and xvi. 24, which puts the cross at the centre of life, is a still more adequate expression of the spirit Jesus wanted his disciples to have.

Each of the closing paragraphs of the Sermon on the Mount presents a contrast: the broad and narrow way; the bad and good fruit of religious leaders; doing and failing to do what Jesus teaches.

With vss. 13 f. cf. Lk. xiii. 24. The contrast of two ways of life was a familiar pattern of teaching; cf. Jer. xxi. 8, 'the way of life and the way of death', and the way of light and the way of darkness in the Dead Sea Scrolls. 'Matthew', however, mentions both **the way** and **the gate** through which one who has travelled the road enters the permanent situation to which his choice of road leads. (The manuscript evidence for **the gate** in vs. 13 is fairly strong, and including the phrase keeps the thought balanced.)

Those who take the **broad,** spacious **way** resent the limiting demands of loyalty and discipline; their way seems comfortable and sensible, but it leads to full and final spiritual disaster. There is no faith, character, or salvation without discipline, obedience, and willing concentration on life's true aim and work. But **many,** the majority, take the spacious way; **few,** the minority, find and follow the narrow way. Is Jesus only reporting that most of his generation are indifferent to his message? Or is he saying what will prove true of all generations of mankind? Probably the former. In either case, the fact of divine judgment and the danger of missing eternal **life** are terribly real.

With vss. 15-20 cf. Lk. vi. 43 f.; with vss. 21-23 cf. Lk. vi. 46; xiii. 26 f. But in Matt. the reference to **false prophets** (vss. 15, 22) makes the entire passage apply to these false teachers. They do the characteristic work of a preacher and healer; they wear the outward attitude, the **sheep's clothing,** of pious living; they say **Lord! Lord!** to Jesus. But they are like **thorn-bushes** or **thistles** or a **decayed tree** that bears bad fruit instead of good; they fail to do God's will in their personal lives; on the

contrary, they do **lawlessness**. Because of this lack of integrity,
obedience, and fruitfulness, they will not enter the coming
Kingdom; at the judgment Jesus will refuse to recognize them
as his (vs. 23 assumes, as does xxv. 31-46, that Jesus will speak
the decisive word at the last judgment).

When Jesus upheld the demand of God for faithful obedience
in daily life, he was in harmony with all the O.T. and apostolic
writings. The term **false prophets** reminds us that in the O.T
the true prophets of God were a minority, and in Paul's
churches ecstatic utterances did not always mean that the
speakers were guided by the Spirit (i Thess. v. 20 f.). In what
way the false prophets do evil Jesus does not explicitly state, but
the description **ravenous wolves** implies that they use every
opportunity to dupe and despoil those who hear and trust them.
The general statement that they do **lawlessness** echoes Ps. vi. 8.

The use of **Lord! Lord!** in address to Jesus is striking, and
the Church no doubt felt in this address a fuller content than it
carried to hearers of Jesus during his ministry. But the assumption of Jesus here and elsewhere is that he will speak the decisive word at the final judgment; this indicates clearly that he
did not think of himself or want others to think of him merely
as a good man. He held a unique position of authority and
leadership; he made a demanding claim on men to follow him;
the germ of later high Christology is present in his Synoptic
teaching. His name carries a remarkable effect, even when used
by unworthy men (vs. 22). Incidentally, the reference to exorcisms and other **miracles** (physical healings?) indirectly attests
the occurrence of remarkable deeds of power in the ministry both
of Jesus and of those who witnessed for him.

With vss. 24-27 cf. Lk. vi. 47-49, which concludes the Sermon
on the Plain. **Therefore** marks this section as the conclusion of
the entire Sermon; **these words of mine** here mean all those
in chs. v.-vii.; the claim is that the life of the hearers of the
Sermon will stand firm or collapse according to whether they
do or fail to do what Jesus has taught.

The illustration reflects climatic conditions in Palestine. Most
of the year there is no heavy rain; few streams run the year
round. In the rainy season heavy rains fall, sudden torrents rush
down the valleys of the hilly regions, and what had been dry

level places are flooded. **A prudent man** will build to withstand conditions of the rainy season. He will build on **solid rock**; then the sudden flood waters cannot damage the firmly based house. **A foolish man** (Matt. is the Gospel which most often contrasts prudent and foolish men) builds on pleasant ground, where sudden flood waters swirl away the **sandy soil** and let the house collapse. So, Jesus teaches, obedience to his teaching is the one solid basis for withstanding the future crisis. Probably he means not recurrent crises or trials in life, but as in vss. 21-23 the final crisis at the last day. Only the life built on the solid rock of faithful obedience to his teaching will stand in the final judgment. Without that obedience fatal collapse will occur.

Each of the five main discourses in Matt. ends with some such formula; compare xi. 1; xiii. 53; xix. 1; xxvi. 1. (For a partial parallel to this pattern cf. Lk. vii. 1, and with the note of surprise cf. Mk. i. 21 f.; Lk. iv. 31 f.) This formal ending shows that 'Matthew' consciously builds his Gospel to make these discourses prominent in his outline. For him the teaching of Jesus has basic importance; it confronts the readers of the Gospel with a crucial challenge.

Crowds: Cf. iv. 25; v. 1. **Astounded:** Because the teaching differed from that of the scribes, in content, or in Jesus' note of direct authority, or, probably, in both respects. **The note of authority** warns the readers of the Gospel that they cannot ignore or reject Jesus' teaching without ruinous consequences. **Scribes:** They copied, explained, and applied the Mosaic Law. They did not speak with direct authority but based their explanations on what rabbis before them had taught.

CHAPTER VIII

viii. 1-17. THE HEALING POWER OF JESUS

1 **When he had descended from the mountain, great crowds**
2 **followed him. And behold, a leper approached and fell down in reverence before him, saying, 'Lord, if you will,**

you can cleanse me'. And he stretched out his hand and 3
touched him, saying, 'I will it; be cleansed'. And at once
his leprosy was cleansed. And Jesus said to him, 'See that 4
you tell no one, but go and show yourself to the priest
and offer as a testimony to them the gift which Moses
prescribed'.

When he entered Capernaum a centurion approached 5
him, entreating him and saying, 'Lord, my servant lies 6
paralysed at home, suffering terrible torture'. He said to 7
him, 'Shall I come and heal him?' The centurion an- 8
swered and said, 'Lord, I am not worthy to have you enter
under my roof, but just say the word, and my servant will
be healed. For I myself am a man under authority, with 9
soldiers under me, and I say to this one, "Go", and he
goes, and to another, "Come", and he comes, and to my
slave, "Do this", and he does it.' When Jesus heard this 10
he marvelled and said to those following, 'Truly I tell
you, in no one in Israel have I found such great faith. I tell 11
you that many will come from east and west and recline
at table with Abraham and Isaac and Jacob in the Kingdom of Heaven; but the sons of the Kingdom will be cast 12
out into the outer darkness; there the weeping and gnashing of teeth will occur.' And Jesus said to the centurion, 13
'Go! Let it be done for you as you have believed.' And the
servant was healed that very hour.

And Jesus went into the house of Peter and saw his 14
wife's mother bedfast and burning with fever; and he 15
touched her hand and the fever left her, and she rose and
waited on him.

When evening came they brought to him many who 16
were demon-possessed; and he expelled the spirits with
a word, and all who were ill he healed, that the word 17
might be fulfilled which was spoken through Isaiah the
prophet, who said, 'He himself took our sicknesses and
bore our diseases'.

Chs. viii. and ix. contain mainly ten miracles which Jesus
did in answer to human need. In addition, viii. 16 and ix. 35
refer to other healings. This work fulfils prophecy (viii. 17),

expresses compassion (cf. ix. 36), and by effective use of the Spirit's power shows that the Kingdom has begun to come (see xii. 28).

With viii. 1-4 compare Mk. i. 40-45; Lk. v. 12-16. Matt. is shorter; he does not mention Jesus' emotions (compassion, indignation) or the healed man's disregard of instructions to **tell no one**. **Great crowds:** Presumably those who have heard the Sermon on the Mount. They must follow at a little distance, for an unclean **leper**, not permitted to mingle with crowds, can approach Jesus and ask for help. His reverent attitude and address express faith; Jesus, whose authority and power warrant the title **Lord,** can heal if he wishes. Jesus not only speaks the word; he touches the leper, perhaps to aid in healing. Jesus thereby becomes ceremonially unclean; however, this act of sympathy is more important to him than ceremonial laws, which he usually kept. **At once:** Indicates divine power effectively at work. The Gospels in telling of Jesus' miracles almost always note explicitly that the miracle really occurred. This challenges the reader to believe in him who so plainly has divine power.

Jesus tried to keep his miracles from becoming widely known. Here the healing could hardly have escaped the notice of the crowds present with Jesus. But 'Matthew' knew that Jesus tried to hold publicity about his miracles to a minimum; he sensed that Jesus wanted to keep his message of the Kingdom from being submerged beneath a wave of emotional excitement; so even here he found the traditional instruction fitting: **Tell no one.**

Though Jesus disregarded ceremonial rules to express sympathy and give help, he expected the Jews to live within the framework of the Mosaic Law. He told the healed leper to **go and show yourself to the priest** (in Jerusalem? or in his own city?), and offer the prescribed gift (Lev. xiv. 10 would place this at Jerusalem). **A testimony to them:** Either to the people, that he was now clean and could mingle with them, or to the priests, that Jesus had not disowned the O.T. Law.

With vss. 5-13 cf. Lk. vii. 1-10 (xiii. 29), where the sick person is a slave (δοῦλος). παῖς in Matt. probably means **servant,** but could mean 'child', 'son'. **Centurion:** Evidently an officer under Herod Antipas, tetrarch of Galilee and Perea; he is a

humane and responsible Gentile (vs. 10). The servant has a
form of paralysis which involves extreme pain; the centurion
hopes Jesus can give relief (physicians presumably have failed).
The address **Lord** implies that Jesus has the power to help.
Jesus' reply may be a promise, 'I will come and heal him', but
probably is a question, 'Shall I, a Jew, come and heal him in a
Gentile home?' Never in the Gospels does Jesus enter a Gentile
home or heal a Gentile by personal touch; the few healings of
Gentiles are done at a distance. The centurion tactfully understands Jesus' reluctance, but he firmly believes that Jesus can
heal by a word spoken at a distance.

The Greek of vs. 9 could imply that Jesus is under authority
just as the centurion is: 'For I also (καί) am a man under authority'. In the context we expect the centurion to contrast his
subordinate position and limited power with the far greater
dignity and power of Jesus as **Lord.** So we may translate the
καί 'myself': **For I myself am a man under authority,** etc.
If he, a subordinate military officer, can give commands that are
instantly obeyed, surely Jesus can help his servant by a simple
word of command.

Jesus marvels at such **faith** in a Gentile. In this confident,
unparalleled faith in Jesus' power to heal regardless of distance,
Jesus sees promise of a wide response by Gentiles. He does not
say that they will become Israelites, but he implies that they will
show faith in him, and when the final Kingdom comes and the
great Messianic banquet occurs, **many** Gentiles **will come
from east and west** and share in that banquet (cf. Isa. xlix. 12,
which, however, refers to the return of scattered Israel, and lix.
19) with the patriarchs of Israel, **Abraham and Isaac and
Jacob** (who, xxii. 32 indicates, will share in the resurrection).
The sons of the Kingdom, the Jews, who by ancestry and long
privilege would naturally be expected to share in the final Kingdom, will be rejected. Literally, Jesus implies that all Jews will
be rejected; this undoubtedly excepts those who respond to the
Gospel, but it anticipates a wide rejection of (unresponsive)
Jews. **Weeping and gnashing of teeth:** This figurative expression of disappointment and pain occurs six times in Matt.
and only once (Lk. xiii. 28) in the other Gospels; it need not
imply physical punishment.

The centurion, it is implied, accepted Jesus' assurance, and returned home to find that the healing had occurred at the very **hour** when Jesus spoke his word of power. 'Matthew', in many ways the most Jewish of the evangelists, shows here and elsewhere that he expected wide Gentile reception of the gospel message, and this incident gave to him and to Gentiles who read his Gospel the assurance that Jesus himself approved such reception.

With vss. 14-17 cf. Mk. i. 29-34 and Lk. iv. 38-41, in which these events follow a Sabbath healing; in Matt. no Sabbath setting appears. Peter lived in Capernaum (vs. 5; cf. iv. 13, 18). He was married (cf. 1 Cor. ix. 5), and his wife's mother was sick and feverish. On his own initiative (in Matt.; in Mk. and Lk. Jesus is asked to heal her), Jesus touched her hand, showing sympathy and making his healing purpose clear. The fever promptly left her, and she was able to minister to the needs of Jesus (**him;** many manuscripts read **them,** αὐτοῖς, the entire group present).

The coming of **evening** in Mk. and Lk. marks the end of the Sabbath; people could then carry their sick to Jesus without breaking Sabbath rules against work. In Matt. it is simply a convenient time for the crowd to gather and ask Jesus to help their sick. **Demon-possessed:** Includes those mentally ill, and possibly others with severe physical illness. **Spirits:** Unclean spirits, demons (elsewhere Matt. always has the adjective 'unclean' when **spirits** means demons). **Ill:** The addition of this group shows not all of the sick were **demon-possessed.** 'Matthew' says that people brought **many,** and Jesus healed **all** the sick; this avoids Mark's view that they brought all the sick and Jesus healed many (but not all).

In this healing ministry 'Matthew' sees the fulfilment of Isa. liii. 4, quoted by direct translation of the Hebrew or from a non-LXX Greek translation faithful to the Hebrew. The words **took** and **bore** have here the unusual meaning: took away, removed, healed. The use of Isa. liii. seems to identify Jesus as the Suffering Servant of that chapter (cf. the quotation of Isa. xlii. 1-4, another Servant passage, in xii. 18-21). The present passage, however, does not imply that Jesus suffered vicariously for the sick; it refers only to the removal of illnesses by his healing power.

When Jesus saw a crowd around him he gave the com- 18
mand to depart to the opposite shore. And a scribe ap- 19
proached and said to him, 'Teacher, I will follow you
wherever you go'. And Jesus said to him, 'The foxes have 20
holes and the birds of heaven have nests, but the Son of
Man has no place to lay his head'. Another of the dis- 21
ciples said to him, 'Lord, permit me first to go and bury
my father'. Jesus said to him, 'Follow me, and let the 22
dead bury their own dead'.

And when he had boarded the boat, his disciples fol- 23
lowed him. And behold, a great storm rose on the sea, so 24
that the boat was being submerged by the waves; but he
was sleeping. And they approached and roused him, say- 25
ing, 'Lord, save us; we are perishing'. And he said to 26
them, 'Why are you cowardly, you men of little faith?'
Then he rose and rebuked the winds and the sea, and
a complete calm followed. The men marvelled, saying, 27
'What sort of man is this, that even the winds and the sea
obey him?'

And when he came to the opposite shore, to the country 28
of the Gadarenes, two demoniacs coming out of the tombs
met him; they were dangerously violent, so that no one
could pass by on that road. And behold, they cried out, 29
saying, 'What have we to do with you, Son of God? Have
you come here before the appointed time to torment us?'
Now at a distance from them was a large herd of swine, 30
grazing. The demons kept entreating him, saying, 'If you 31
drive us out, send us into the herd of swine'. And he said 32
to them, 'Go'. They came out and went into the swine,
and behold, the entire herd rushed down the steep bank
into the sea, and drowned in the water. The herdsmen 33
fled, and going into the city they reported everything,
including the facts about the demoniacs. And behold, the 34
entire city went out to meet Jesus, and when they saw
him they entreated him to leave their district.

With vs. 18 cf. Mk. iv. 35; Lk. viii. 22. Vs. 16 implies a night departure from Capernaum (vss. 5, 14) for the **opposite** (eastern) **shore.** The connection of the departure with the preceding events in Matt. is editorial grouping, but true to Jesus' practice of withdrawing from **a crowd** too excited over his miracles to think of his message. Jesus here replies to two volunteers, the first two of the three in Lk. ix. 57-62. Luke's setting, when Jesus has determined to leave Galilee and go to Jerusalem, is more suitable; in Matt. Jesus presumably is leaving only for a temporary visit. Both volunteers, vs. 21 indicates, are disciples of Jesus.

The **scribe** impulsively volunteers to go with Jesus. Jesus tests his sincerity and firmness. Has he counted the cost? Can he face homelessness? Jesus here refers to himself, for the first time in Matt., as **the Son of Man.** This favourite self-designation occurs in all four Gospels (Matt., 31 times; Mk., 14; Lk., 25; Jn., 13), always used by Jesus; outside of the Gospels the N.T. has it only in Acts vii. 56 (without the article, Heb. ii. 6; Rev. i. 13; xiv. 14). At times, as here, it reflects his humble, homeless lot; at other times, his mission of suffering and death; and at other times, his final triumph and glory. It has a partial background in Ps. ii, in Ezekiel's use of 'Son of Man', in Dan. vii. 13, and in the non-canonical Book of Enoch, but we owe to Jesus the merging of the Son of Man with the Suffering Servant figure of Second Isaiah.

The second volunteer has heard Jesus in his own city, but does not want to leave home till his father dies. His father was not dead; had he been, the son would have been at home preparing for the burial, which in Palestine followed soon after death. Jesus' reply is startling. **Let the dead,** those not alive to the crucial importance of the Kingdom message, care for the father; let the son follow Jesus. The cause of the Kingdom ranks first.

With vss. 23-27 cf. Mk. iv. 35-41; Lk. viii. 22-25. Jesus entered a **boat,** perhaps that of Peter and Andrew, or of Zebedee and his sons. His disciples boarded it after him; here as on the road Jesus literally led the way.

A severe sudden **storm** (σεισμός is literally an 'earthquake') rushes down from the hills surrounding the Sea of Galilee, which lies about 700 feet below sea level. The mounting **waves** seem to cover the boat; these experienced sailors cannot control it. In desperation they ask Jesus for help; the use of **Lord** implies faith that he can save them.

In Matt. men in need repeatedly call Jesus **Lord.** No doubt 'Matthew' senses more in this title than did Jesus' disciples during his ministry. Yet in the Gospels Jesus claims authority now and at the last judgment; his teaching is the standard for men's eternal destiny; he has power to heal and transform life. His words and work give a basis for the later use of the title **Lord.**

Jesus, awakened from trustful sleep, rebukes the disciples' fear and cowardice; they should show more **faith** when with him. His rebuke of **winds** and **sea** treats these stormy conditions as demonic. Since sudden storms on the Sea of Galilee may also subside quickly, the calming of the storm has been considered a fortunate coincidence. 'Matthew' and the Church, however, confidently believed that the power and act of Jesus caused the change.

The men, the disciples in the boat, could only marvel in the presence of such power. They ask in grateful wonder: **What sort of man is this?** 'Matthew' has indicated that they know the answer in part; they called Jesus **Lord** in vs. 25. (xiv. 33 is more explicit: 'the Son of God'.) They sense God's presence and power; though 'Matthew' may give a more explicit impression than the disciples then had in Galilee, already they vaguely know that Jesus is doing things that are the work of God; see Pss. lxxxix. 9; cvii. 23-30.

With vss. 28-34 cf. Mk. v. 1-20; Lk. viii. 26-39; the story in Matt. is greatly shortened, but it alone tells of **two demoniacs,** just as only in Matt. does Jesus heal two blind men at one time (ix. 27; xx. 30). The incident clearly occurred on the eastern shore of the Sea of Galilee, where a steep incline runs down to the Sea. But the exact spot and name of the place are uncertain. Three readings appear in the manuscripts of all three Gospels: (1) **Gadarenes** (the probable reading in Matt.). Gadara, however, was six miles south-east of the Sea; the city of vss. 33 f. was presumably close to the Sea. (2) 'Gergesenes' (has considerable support in Matt., and may be original). This may suggest modern Khersa, suitably located on the eastern shore of the Sea. But can the name Khersa be derived from Gergesa? (3) 'Gerasenes.' This refers to Gerasa, thirty miles south-east of the Sea, which hardly suits the geography of the story.

The story assumes that **demons** exist and have power, and speak through the men they possess. The demons know that Jesus is their enemy, the unique **Son of God** who will vanquish them at **the appointed time,** the end of the age. That Jesus can expel them from the hapless men indicates to Christian readers that the Kingdom has begun to come.

The presence of **swine** implies a Gentile region or partly Gentile population. The territory east and south-east of the Sea of Galilee had many Gentiles. Why the demons desired to go into the swine is not stated; perhaps it was their shrinking from homelessness. That the owners suffered financial loss does not trouble 'Matthew'; he rejoices in the victory over the demons and the liberation of previously haunted men. Obviously the story uses patterns of thought not satisfactory to modern men, who would call these demoniacs mentally deranged. Perhaps neither viewpoint is adequate. Mysterious forces of evil are at work in the world; life is a conflict between good and evil; evil is a more real and active thing than mere absence of good.

The near-by **city** was stirred by the report of what had happened. But when the people actually met Jesus, he made them uneasy. There is no hint given that this was due to the financial loss. The people sensed a mysterious power in Jesus. They did not know what to make of him, so they asked him to leave their district.

CHAPTERS IX AND X

ix. 1-17. A NEW MESSAGE OF MERCY

1 And he went on board a boat and crossed over, and came
2 to his own city. And behold, men came bringing to him
a paralytic placed on a bed. And when Jesus saw their

faith he said to the paralytic, 'Courage, son! Your sins are forgiven.' And behold, some of the scribes said inwardly, 3 'This man is blaspheming'. And Jesus, knowing their 4 thoughts, said, 'Why do you think evil thoughts in your hearts? For which is easier, to say, "Your sins are for- 5 given", or to say, "Rise and walk"? But that you may 6 know that the Son of Man has authority to forgive sins on earth'—then he said to the paralytic—'Rise, take up your bed and go to your house'. And he rose and departed to 7 his house. When the crowds saw this, they were afraid 8 and praised God, who had given such authority to men.

And as Jesus went on from there he saw a man named 9 Matthew sitting in the tax office, and he said to him, 'Follow me'. And he rose and followed him. And it hap- 10 pened that as he was reclining at table in the house, be- hold, many tax collectors and sinners came and reclined with Jesus and his disciples. And when the Pharisees saw 11 this, they said to his disciples, 'Why does your teacher eat with the tax collectors and sinners?' He heard this, and 12 said, 'It is not those in good health who need a physician, but those who are sick. Go and learn what this means, "I 13 desire mercy and not sacrifice". For I came to call not righteous men but sinners.'

Then the disciples of John came to him, saying, 'Why 14 is it that we and the Pharisees fast, but your disciples do not fast?' And Jesus said to them, 'The wedding party 15 cannot fast, can they, while the bridegroom is with them? But days will come when the bridegroom will be taken from them, and then they will fast. No one sews a patch 16 of unshrunk cloth on an old garment; for the patch that covers the hole tears out some of the garment, and a worse tear occurs. Nor do men put fresh wine into old 17 wineskins; if they do, the wineskins burst, and the wine is spilled and the wineskins are ruined. But they put fresh wine into new wineskins, and both are preserved.'

With vss. 1-8 cf. the longer version in Mk. ii. 1-12; Lk. v. 17-26. In Matt., Jesus returns by boat to **his own city**, Capernaum (cf. iv. 13). The imperfect tense ($\pi\rho\sigma\acute{\epsilon}\phi\epsilon\rho\sigma\nu$) suggests that **men**

came bringing the paralysed man to Jesus as he came to land; in Mk. and Lk. the scene is laid in a house.

The real interest of 'Matthew' in this story is not in the miracle, but in showing Jesus' **authority to forgive sins.** The men bringing the invalid (**their** probably includes the sick man) believed Jesus could heal. Jesus sensed also a latent faith that he was God's messenger of the coming Kingdom. He turned the man's attention to his need of forgiveness. Jesus does not do this in other healings, so we should not say that Jesus thought sickness was always due to sin (cf. Lk. xiii. 1-5; Jn. ix. 1-3). In this case he could have seen such a connection, but quite likely he simply used the occasion to make the point that what even sick men need most is forgiveness of sins.

To **scribes** present this confident word of forgiveness was blasphemy; only God could forgive sins (Isa. xliii. 25); Jesus was wickedly assuming God's prerogative. Here first hostile scribes appear in Matt.; the scribe in viii. 19 was a (thoughtless) disciple. Jesus knew their inward **thoughts,** which, being wrong and hostile to his God-given beneficent ministry, were evil. He proposes a test. It would be **easier** to say **Your sins are forgiven,** since no doubter could objectively disprove this statement; a command to **Rise and walk** could be tested by watching to see whether the man does so. Jesus undertakes the more difficult task, where failure would promptly discredit him; he says, **Rise and walk;** if the man does walk, all will know that Jesus has divine power and authority, and that his verbal assurance of forgiveness has divine approval. When the healing happened, the crowd feared; they sensed the presence of divine power in Jesus and accepted his claim that he had authority to forgive sins.

Son of Man in vs. 6 must refer to Jesus himself. He is the one challenged; he heals; he has authority to forgive. So **men** in vs. 8 cannot mean that all men have this authority. The authority was given to the man Jesus to exercise on behalf of mankind.

With vss. 9-13 cf. Mk. ii. 13-17; Lk. v. 27-32, where the tax collector's name is Levi (see Introduction on the name **Matthew**). **The tax office** may have been near the beach (cf. vs. 1) to handle business connected with ships coming to Galilee from the east side of the lake, which was not under Herod

Antipas as Galilee was. **In the house:** Either of Jesus, whose home was now in Capernaum, or, as Luke plainly says, of Levi (Matthew). The latter would explain the presence of **many tax collectors and sinners** (**sinners** meant Jews who ignored or broke the Mosaic Law in either moral or ceremonial aspects; **tax collectors** likewise, since they dealt with all people, including Romans and other Gentiles, did not keep all Jewish regulations). **The Pharisees** first appear here (as the scribes did in vs. 3) as sharp critics of Jesus; they condemn lax table fellowship with people who do not observe carefully Jewish food laws and other regulations. They speak **to his disciples;** perhaps they cannot approach Jesus in the crowded house, but probably they hope to undermine the disciples' loyalty to Jesus. Their question implies that Jesus cannot eat with such lax-living people and be loyal to the Law. Jesus, overhearing their question, answers with a brief parable: Who needs **a physician?** Not the healthy, but the sick. Who needs a spiritual physician? Not men with no spiritual need, but those whose lives are damaged by sin. Jesus does not gloss over the sin of the tax collectors and sinners. He cannot help them, however, by quarantining himself from them but only by going to them in outreaching friendship. (Religion which stresses ceremonial purity and externally correct associations forces its adherents to avoid and disdain the people they might and should help.)

Go and learn: Implies that the Pharisees do not really understand the Scriptures. Hosea vi. 6 (cited only here and xii. 7 in the Gospels) literally excludes all sacrifice, but this may merely mean emphatically that mercy is vastly more important than ceremonial correctness. There is here, however, the germ of a break with the Law, which gives sacrifice and ritual an essential place. **Righteous men:** Ironical; these tax collectors and their friends, who know they are sinners, Jesus can help, but he cannot help people who think they are righteous.

With vss. 14-17 cf. Mk. ii. 18-22; Lk. v. 33-39. Here as in vi. 16-18 Jesus criticizes mechanical fasting but honours fasting which really expresses one's spiritual state. The issue arises when Jesus' followers (and Jesus by inference) are criticized by a group we expect to be sympathetic to Jesus. **The disciples of John** the Baptist are fasting, as are **the Pharisees.** Pharisees fasted two days each week (Lk. xviii. 12); perhaps John's disciples adopted their practice. Jesus' disciples (and Jesus) are not fasting; no ascetic touch marks their life; so they are accused of lacking piety and earnestness.

Jesus replies with a parable. No one expects a **wedding party** to fast. During the wedding festivities, fasting would introduce a discordant note. Should **the bridegroom** later be taken away by death, the party would mourn, and fasting would express their real feelings.

Jesus here says four important things: (1) He rejects the authority of current traditions. Frequent fasting was not commanded by the Mosaic Law; Jesus rejects the oral tradition which prescribed it. (2) The form of religious worship and observance should fit the actual situation of the worshippers. Fasting is out of place when the dominant note of the group is grateful joy. (3) Jesus and his group lived in a spirit of joy. The power of the Kingdom was beginning to be manifest; people were responding to the good news; God's power was healing ailing minds and bodies; hope was strong. (4) Jesus has no shallow optimism that expects an easy triumph. He faces the fact of gathering opposition and the possibility if not certainty that rejection lies ahead.

Jesus next illustrates by a double parable the impossibility of expressing the life of the new movement in the old forms of Judaism. When an **old garment** has a hole and a **patch of unshrunk cloth** is sewed over it, that patch, when the garment is washed, will shrink and pull out the weakened threads of the old garment to which it was sewed; the result is a still larger hole. When old animal skins, which have received **fresh wine,** stretched as the fresh wine fermented, and then hardened, are filled again with fresh wine, the hardened skins will burst as the wine ferments, and the wine will be lost. Judaism cannot be helped or made adequate merely by patchwork, by trying to instil new life into rigid old forms. The new must find forms that express its true nature and vitality. Jesus did not reject the O.T. (v. 17); but current religious practice, even when literally supported by the O.T., would have to yield to new forms fitted to express the life of the dawning Kingdom.

ix. 18-34. JESUS' POWER OVER DEATH, ILLNESS, AND DEMONS

As he was saying these things, behold, a ruler approached 18 and fell down in reverence before him, saying, 'My daughter has just died. But come and lay your hand on her, and she will live.' And Jesus with his disciples rose 19 and followed him.

And behold, a woman who for twelve years had suf- 20 fered from a discharge of blood approached him from behind and touched the tassel of his robe, for she said to 21 herself, 'If I only touch his robe, I shall be healed'. Jesus 22 turned and seeing her said, 'Courage, daughter! Your faith has healed you.' And the woman was healed from that hour.

And when Jesus entered the house of the ruler and saw 23 the flute players and the crowd in distress, he said, 'De- 24 part, for the girl has not died but is sleeping'. And they ridiculed him. But when the crowd had been driven out, 25 he went in and took her hand, and the girl rose. And the 26 report of this spread through all that land.

And as Jesus went on from there, two blind men fol- 27 lowed, calling out and saying, 'Show mercy to us, Son of David'. When he went into the house, the blind men 28 came to him, and Jesus said to them, 'Do you believe that I can do this?' They said to him, 'Yes, Lord'. Then he 29 touched their eyes, saying, 'Let it be done for you as you have believed'. And their eyes were opened. And Jesus 30 sternly warned them, saying, 'See that no man knows'. But they went out and spread the news about him in all 31 that land.

As they went out, behold, men brought to him a dumb 32 man possessed by a demon. And when the demon had 33 been expelled, the dumb man spoke. And the crowds marvelled, saying, 'Nothing like this has ever been seen in Israel'. But the Pharisees said, 'It is by the ruler of 34 the demons that he expels the demons'.

With vss. 18-26 cf. Mk. v. 21-43; Lk. viii. 40-56, both more detailed than Matt. 'Matthew', who likes to link events closely, says the **ruler approached** before Jesus finished the foregoing teaching; he does not name the father or call him a synagogue official; he says the **daughter** was **dead** before the ruler came to Jesus; he does not mention the woman's healing until Jesus has assured her of it; he alone mentions the **flute players** at the ruler's house—in his account the girl has been dead longer and formal mourning ceremonies have had time to begin; he gives no word of Jesus to the dead girl; he alone reports that the news of the raising of the girl spread widely.

The daughter of a **ruler** (Jewish official) in the local synagogue or community has just died. He has heard of Jesus' healing ability. In his desperate need he finds courage to believe that Jesus can help; **she will live** means: be brought back to life (not, be spared death). Jesus and his disciples go to the stricken home.

As Jesus went, **a woman who for twelve years had suffered** from continuous menstruation approached and touched his robe's **tassel** (the word κράσπεδον may mean 'border', 'hem', or, if Jesus dressed in characteristic Jewish manner, **tassel,** attached to the corner of the robe). Her action, and her conviction that the touch would bring healing, bordered, to say the least, on the superstitious. But Jesus sensed a faith in it, even if not the purest faith. By feeling the pull on the tassel or by special insight Jesus knew her action and need. He encouraged her (cf. vs. 2), and announced that her **faith** had **healed her** (σώζω, usually translated 'save' in the N.T., means 'heal' here and in other healing stories); while healing is the work of God's power, that power cannot work where faith is lacking. (This is the one miracle story which the Gospels enclose within another such story.)

At the ruler's home the mourning ceremonies were in full swing. **Is sleeping:** Jesus does not deny that she has died; but it is a brief state, like the short sleep after which one wakes. Jesus shuts out the mourners; there is no place for despair and ridicule as he goes to bring the girl life. Without a word, by taking her hand, Jesus brings to the girl the power of God that calls her back to life. In the briefest possible way the miracle is reported: **the girl rose.** This time no (futile) command to keep silence is mentioned. **All that land:** Around Capernaum.

With vss. 27-31 cf. the similar story in xx. 29-34; Mk. x. 46-52; Lk. xviii. 35-43, where only Matt. mentions **two blind men.** Cf. viii. 28: two demoniacs. Do these double healings mean that 'Matthew' knows more stories than he tells, and indicates it by speaking of two men where the other Gospels say one?

In Matt. this event is part of a busy day in Capernaum (cf. ix. 1); **the house** may be Jesus' home in that city. The blind men know of Jesus and hear that he is passing by; they follow, crying out for help from one known for his healing power. **Son of David:** They accept him as the expected Messianic leader who will do wonderful deeds of mercy mentioned in Isa. xxxv. 5; this implies that such ideas were being discussed among the people, though 'Matthew' may tend to antedate the advance in popular thought about Jesus. It was important to him (cf. i. 1) that Jesus was the Son of David. Jesus takes no notice of the outcry or title. When the blind men come to him in the house, he does not discuss the title they used, but asks whether they really **believe** he can heal them. On their affirmative reply he speaks the healing word and touches their eyes; more than once he uses such a touch to bring his healing power actively to bear on human need, and the touch would be especially helpful with blind men, who thus could sense better his merciful purpose. But the central thing is not the words or the touch, but the faith, and the divine power that only faith can receive.

Sternly warned: A startling phrase; ἐμβριμάομαι usually suggests anger or irritation. It expresses Jesus' emphatic desire to reduce to a minimum the publicity from his healings. But his attempt, here as often, was futile. The men cannot keep from telling the glad news of their miraculous healing **in all that land** around Capernaum.

Vss. 32-34 might seem a duplicate of xii. 22-24. But in the latter healing the demoniac was both blind and dumb; Luke xi. 14 is closer to ix. 32-34 than is xii. 22-24. **They** (probably not the blind men of vs. 31, but Jesus and his disciples) **went out;** the group bringing the demoniac met Jesus as he left the house; so **the crowds** outside witnessed the healing. The story assumes but does not mention the faith of those who brought the man to Jesus. The Gospel's interest centres on how the healing affected the onlookers. The general reaction was enthusiastic amazement at such unparalleled working of divine power. But **the Pharisees**, who could not deny the healing, declared that the power in Jesus was the chief demon, Satan (cf. x. 25). This explanation Jesus answers in xii. 22-36. Here it is merely mentioned as preposterous.

ix. 35-x. 4. THE MISSION OF THE TWELVE: THE NEED AND PREPARATION

35 And Jesus went about all the cities and villages, teaching in their synagogues and preaching the gospel of the King-
36 dom and healing every disease and every illness. When he saw the crowds he felt compassion for them, because they were harassed and dejected, as sheep that have no
37 shepherd. Then he said to his disciples, 'The harvest is
38 abundant, but the workers are few. So pray the Lord of the harvest to send out workers into his harvest.'
x. 1 And he summoned the twelve disciples and gave them power over unclean spirits, to expel them, and to heal
2 every disease and every illness. Now these are the names of the twelve apostles: first Simon called Peter and Andrew his brother, and James the son of Zebedee and
3 John his brother, Philip and Bartholomew, Thomas and Matthew the tax collector, James the son of Alphaeus
4 and Thaddaeus, Simon the Zealot and Judas Iscariot, who also betrayed him.

ix. 35-38 is an editorial report stressing Jesus' wide ministry, the need of additional workers, and the urgency of the task. It first parallels Mk. vi. 6, then repeats iv. 23, goes on to parallel Mk. vi. 34, then parallels closely Lk. x. 2 (cf. Jn. iv. 35). The paragraph shows the need for the mission of the Twelve (ch. x).

The itinerant ministry apparently covered all of Galilee. Its work was threefold: teaching, preaching, healing (iv. 23). Jesus used the synagogue, where a visiting Jew might speak following the prayers and reading of the Law and Prophets. His basic

message was **the Kingdom** (iv. 17; cf. x. 7); God's effective rule
is at hand; men must repent and prepare. Two words practically identical here in meaning (νόσος, 'disease'; μαλακία,
'weakness', 'illness') describe the wide and effective healing
ministry to all kinds of physical suffering.

So much human need, both spiritual and physical, aroused
compassion in Jesus. He used the **sheep** and **shepherd** figure,
familiar from the O.T. (cf. Num. xxvii. 17; 1 Kings xxii. 17; 2
Chron. xviii. 16), and meaningful to Jesus (x. 6; xviii. 12; Lk. xv.
3-7; Jn. x. 1-18) and the early Church (Eph. iv. 11; Heb. xiii. 20;
1 Pet. ii. 25; v. 4). The common people, **harassed and dejected,** needed leaders to give them the Kingdom message and
help them in their needs (ἐρριμμένοι, taken literally, means
thrown to the ground and so lying helpless, but here probably
means 'downcast' or **dejected**). Jesus is a shepherd; the disciples are to become active shepherds.

The next saying, from another source, changes the figure to
that of a large **harvest** that urgently calls for many labourers.
An eschatological note is heard; the time is short, more **workers**
are needed at once; Jesus must send out the Twelve to extend
his outreach (ch. x). Is the harvest figure a clue that Jesus said
this in spring, the time of the grain harvest? Perhaps, but that
does not tell us what year, since the saying occurs in such different (editorial) contexts in Matt. and Lk. The illustration
implies in the people a readiness to hear the Kingdom message
which the disciples are to preach (x. 7). The disciples are to pray
God to send workers. Jesus will send them to answer that prayer.

With vs. 1 cf. Mk. vi. 7; Lk. ix. 1. The Twelve will be named
in vss. 2-4, but they have already been chosen. (Mk. iii. 16-19
places the choice of the Twelve some time before their mission
in vi. 7. Lk. vi. 13-16 puts it just before the Sermon on the
Plain.) Jesus now prepares them for their mission. He gives
them power to **expel** demons and **heal** disease (x. 1); he tells
them what to say and how to act (x. 5-42). The demons (x. 8) are
here called **unclean spirits,** unclean because hostile to God's
purpose and harmful to men's mental and physical well-being.
Vs. 1 could mean that the demons cause all illness and the
disciples by expelling them will heal the sick. But probably
demon possession is thought to affect mental health and cause

especially troublesome physical ailments; other physical ailments are separate cases.

Apostles: The Twelve are so called here only in Matt., and fittingly, for ἀπόστολος means one sent out on a mission or definite errand; the usual term for the Twelve in the Gospels is disciple (μαθητής: learner, pupil, follower). Some think Jesus never used the word Apostle of the Twelve, but the tradition of their specific mission is deeply rooted in the tradition, and the title is appropriate if we do not read into it all the meaning given to it later, in the Apostolic Age.

Though 'Matthew' does not say (Mark does) that the Twelve were sent out two by two, he implies this by arranging the names in pairs. Every list of the Twelve names first the four disciples called first, the two pairs of brothers (iv. 18-22). The brothers are paired in Matt. and Lk.; in Mk. and Acts the inner trio appear together (Mk.: Peter, James, John; Acts i. 13: Peter, John, James). **Peter,** always named first, is here called **first.** This recognizes a fact; chosen first, actively the leader, Peter was the key man of the group. When Jesus named him Peter (Rock) 'Matthew' does not say; xvi. 18 probably means that this name had been given earlier. Simon is a Greek name parallel to Symeon, and Andrew and Philip are Greek names; this shows the Hellenistic influence in Galilee, but all of the Twelve are Jews. The designation of **James** as **son of Zebedee** marks him off from other prominent men of that name, and the mention of John as **his brother** shows that the Church knew these brothers were close in their personal relationships.

No others of the Twelve are prominent during Jesus' ministry or in the Apostolic Church. **Philip:** Cf. Jn. i. 43 f. for his call and original residence at Bethsaida. **Bartholomew:** Means Son of Tolmai or Tolomai. **Thomas:** Means Twin; cf. Didymus, Jn. xi. 16. **Matthew:** Called **the tax collector** to recall ix. 9. **James:** Called **the son of Alphaeus** to distinguish him from James the son of Zebedee; Mk. ii. 14 (parallel to Matt. ix. 9) calls Levi, the tax collector, the son of Alphaeus; is it the same Alphaeus? **Thaddaeus:** Many manuscripts read Lebbaeus here; the early Church, it seems, was uncertain who this man was. **Simon:** His title **Cananaean** transliterates an Aramaic word meaning 'zealous' or 'Zealot' (cf. Lk. vi. 15; Acts i. 13,

126

'the Zealot'). Does this mean that before he became a disciple
he had been a member of the Zealot party opposing Rome's rule
(it is uncertain whether that party existed as early as Jesus'
ministry), or that he was zealous and notably energetic in dis-
position? **Judas:** Always named last in the Synoptic lists of
the Twelve, and his betrayal of Jesus is always mentioned. If
Iscariot means 'man of Kerioth', a place in Judea, he probably was the one non-Galilean among the Twelve. This is more
likely than the theory that the name comes from 'dagger', and
identifies him as a former 'dagger-man', a Zealot type of plotter
against Rome's rule over Palestine.

These men, apart from Judas, were no doubt loyal and helpful
men. But apart from the martyred James, son of Zebedee (Acts
xii. 2), and Peter and John, specifically mentioned as active
leaders (though John only accompanies Peter), none plays an
individual role in Acts. The others were known only from
trusted gospel tradition.

x. 5-42. THE MISSION OF THE TWELVE: INSTRUCTIONS

These twelve Jesus sent forth, after he had instructed 5
them, saying: 'Take no road that leads to Gentiles, and
enter no Samaritan city, but go rather to the lost sheep 6
of the house of Israel. As you go, preach, saying, "The 7
Kingdom of Heaven has drawn near". Heal the sick, 8
raise the dead, cleanse the lepers, expel demons; freely
you received, freely give. Get neither gold nor silver nor 9
copper money for your money-belts, nor knapsack for 10
your trip nor two tunics nor sandals nor traveller's staff;
for the worker deserves his food. In whatever city you 11
enter, inquire who in it is worthy, and lodge there until
you depart. When you enter the house, greet it; and if the 12, 13
house is worthy, let your greeting of peace rest upon it;
but if it is not worthy, let your greeting of peace return to
you. And whoever does not welcome you nor hear your 14
words, go out of that house or city and shake off the dust
that clings to your feet. Truly I tell you, it will be more 15

tolerable for the land of Sodom and Gomorrah in the day of judgment than for that city.

16 'Behold, I send you forth as sheep among wolves; so be
17 shrewd as serpents and innocent as doves. But beware of men, for they will hand you over to sanhedrins, and flog
18 you in their synagogues; and you will be led away to trial before governors and kings on my account, for a testi-
19 mony to them and to the Gentiles. When they hand you over, do not worry how to speak or what to say; for in that
20 hour you will be given what you are to say; for it is not you who speak but the Spirit of your Father which speaks
21 in you. Brother will hand his brother over to death, and father his child, and children will rise up against their
22 parents and put them to death. And you will be hated by all because you bear my name; but he who endures to the
23 end will be saved. When they persecute you in this city, flee to the other; for truly I tell you, you will not finish visiting the cities of Israel before the Son of Man comes.
24 'A disciple is not superior to his teacher nor a servant
25 to his master. It is enough for the disciple to become as his teacher, and the servant as his master. If they have called the master of the house Beelzebul, how much more will they so call the members of his household!
26 'So do not fear them, for nothing is hidden which will not be disclosed, nor secret which will not be made
27 known. What I tell you in the darkness, speak in the light; and what you hear whispered in your ear, preach from
28 the housetops. And do not fear those who kill the body but cannot kill the soul; fear rather him who can destroy both
29 soul and body in Gehenna. Are not two sparrows sold for an assarion? And yet not one of them will fall to earth
30 without your Father's knowledge. As for you, even the
31 hairs of your head are all numbered. So do not fear; you
32 are worth more than many sparrows. Everyone therefore who will confess me before men, I in turn will confess
33 him before my Father who is in heaven; but whoever denies me before men, I in turn will deny him before my Father who is in heaven.
34 'Do not suppose that I came to bring peace on the earth;

I came to bring not peace but a sword. For I came to turn 35
a man against his father, and a daughter against her
mother, and a daughter-in-law against her mother-in-
law, and a man's enemies will be the members of his own 36
household. He who loves father or mother more than he 37
loves me is not worthy of me, and he who loves son or
daughter more than he loves me is not worthy of me; and 38
whoever does not take up his cross and follow after me is
not worthy of me. He who finds his life will lose it, and 39
he who loses his life on my account will find it.

'He who receives you receives me, and he who re- 40
ceives me receives him who sent me. He who receives 41
a prophet because he is a prophet will receive a prophet's
reward, and he who receives a righteous man because
he is a righteous man will receive a righteous man's reward. And whoever gives to one of these little ones just a 42
cup of cold water because he is a disciple, truly I tell you,
he will not lose his reward.'

With vss. 5-15 cf. Mk. vi. 8-11; Lk. ix. 3-5; x. 4-12. Instructions to the Twelve in Matt. and Mk. are divided between the
Twelve and the Seventy in Lk. Matt. and Lk. seem to depend
partly on Mk. and partly on Q. x. 5-42, the second main discourse in Matt., has six sections: vss. 5-15; 16-23; 24 f.; 26-33;
34-39; 40-42. The first deals with destination, message, healing,
travel without baggage or funds, and hospitality.

Sent forth: Has the same root as Apostle (ἀποστέλλω). The
Twelve are to go only to Jews (cf. xv. 24). This instruction
occurs only in Matt., but Jesus limited his work to Jews; he
helped Gentiles rarely, and then without entering their homes.
Lost: Need not mean out of touch with the synagogue; suggests
basically their great spiritual need.

The Twelve are to preach the nearness of **the Kingdom** (and
urge prompt repentance). The healing acts are such as Jesus has
been doing (chs. viii, ix). **Raise the dead:** May not be original;
many manuscripts, including important early versions, omit the
words; those which have them vary in where they place them.
The most trusted manuscripts have them placed as in the above
translation. Since the evangelists were certain that even physical

death could not resist the divine power Jesus possessed, 'Matthew' could have written that Jesus spoke thus. In any case the general instruction is to go and do what he himself has been doing. They have **received**, without deserving and without paying for it, the gift of forgiveness and the power to heal; they are to **give** the message and healing to others without payment. What they give was a free gift of which they are only the stewards.

They are to take no **money**, not even the cheapest copper coins, no extra equipment, not even a traveller's **staff** (permitted in Mk.). To travel quickly they must travel light and let their hearers supply their needs. **The worker**, etc.: Cf. Lk. x. 7, cited in 1 Tim. v. 18.

Worthy: Likely to hear the gospel and act as host. **Lodge there:** Do not keep changing lodging to get a more comfortable situation. Vss. 12 f. tells how to test information received on who is worthy; **greet** the home in some such form as 'Peace to this house'. This **greeting** was thought to **rest upon** the **house** if it was worthy and hospitable to the Apostles and their message; otherwise it would **return** to the Apostles, and they must leave the unresponsive house or city after a stern warning. **Shake off the dust:** An acted witness that the Apostles have discharged their responsibility and that the house or community will suffer judgment for their wicked rejection of the gospel. **Sodom and Gomorrah:** Proverbial examples of extreme wickedness (Gen., ch. xix). They will be judged on the imminent last day, but to reject the gospel of the Kingdom and the offer of forgiveness is a more serious sin and will bring a heavier **judgment.** Note the thought of family and community responsibility.

With vs. 16 cf. Lk. x. 3. From this point the discourse continually anticipates opposition and active persecution. Without resources and unarmed, the Apostles are as helpless **as sheep among wolves.** They must not fight back, but be prudent, tactful, like the proverbially **shrewd** serpent (cf. Gen. iii. 1), and **innocent,** free from wrongdoing, like gentle, innocent doves.

With vss. 17-22 cf. xxiv. 9, 13; Mk. xiii. 9-13; Lk. xxi. 12-17. The long discourses in Matt. are editorial groupings of material. Most of this section does not fit a swift preaching tour in

Galilee; it assumes a later, more developed situation, though opposition to Jesus appeared early (cf. ix. 3, 11, 14, 34). The passage here instructs the Apostles to continue to declare their message regardless of opposition.

The Apostles in place after place will be handed over to the local courts, **sanhedrins,** and as punishment for preaching will be flogged **in their synagogues.** Even more severe measures will be taken; they will be seized and handed over to **governors** of provinces and special districts under Rome and to puppet **kings** such as Herod the Great had been and the younger Herods (actually tetrarchs) were popularly called. This appearance before rulers will give opportunity to witness to these rulers and so **to the Gentiles;** the message will be spread by the persecution that seeks to suppress it. The Apostles of the gospel have a message for every situation; they need not worry how to defend themselves in hostile situations. In such unpredictable crises the Holy Spirit, **the Spirit of your Father,** will speak in and through them (Lk. xii. 11 f.).

They will need such comforting help. Even more difficult to bear than official persecution will be family divisions over the claim of Christ. Members of the disciples' own families will betray them in time of persecution and feed the hostility that brings about their death; **put them to death** means in effect to hand them over to the officials or mob that will kill them. When even **brother, father,** and **children** thus betray their loved ones (cf. vss. 35 f.; Mic. vii. 6; Mal. iv. 6), the Apostles may expect to be hated **by all** men 'on account of my name', that is, **because you bear my name** and are loyal to me even when persecuted. In such trials physical deliverance cannot be promised; **be saved** does not mean spared persecution, but saved and given a place in the coming Kingdom. This salvation and eternal privilege is only for him **who endures to the end,** no matter how terrible and long the trials are.

Vs. 23 is difficult. It says that before the Apostles, on their hurried preaching tour, visit all **the cities of Israel,** the **Son of Man** will come. Was Jesus mistaken? Certainly 'Matthew' and the early Church did not so understand the saying. Our first task is to inquire what it meant to them. Cf. xii. 28; xvi. 28; xxvi. 64. Does 'Matthew' mean that as the Apostles do the works of

Christ and win men to accept his Kingdom message, the Kingdom comes and the Son of Man is manifested? A full coming
is still ahead, but a real coming already occurs. No doubt
'Matthew' uses the saying to suggest also to the Apostolic
Church that before it can finish its urgent gospel mission, the
full and final manifestation of the Son of Man will occur.

Lk. vi. 40 offers a partial parallel to vss. 24 f., but differs in
two main respects: (1) It speaks only of the disciple-teacher
relationship. (2) The conclusion it draws is that the disciple
should not expect to surpass his teacher in knowledge and teaching ability. In Matt. **a disciple** is subordinate to **his teacher,**
and so is **a servant** or slave (δοῦλος) to **his master.** The subordinate cannot expect better treatment than his superior receives. Jesus the Teacher and Master (Lord; κύριος) has been
ridiculed and opposed; the prospect of the cross already begins
to appear. The Apostles may expect similar treatment, and must
be ready to suffer what he suffers. Changing the figure, Jesus
notes that his opponents have called him (the head of the **household** of those committed to the Kingdom) Beelzebul; his
followers **(the members of his household)** can expect the
same treatment. **Beelzebul** obviously is related to Beelzebub
(2 Kings i. 2, 6), god of Ekron; his name means 'lord of flies'.
In the Gospels Beelzebul or (as ℵ B read) Beezebul refers to
the 'prince of demons', Satan (xii. 24). Cf. xii. 22-32.

With vss. 26-33 cf. Lk. xii. 2-9; with vs. 26 cf. also Mk. iv. 22;
Lk. viii. 17; and with vss. 32 f. cf. also Mk. viii. 38; Lk. ix. 26.
The key phrase is **Do not fear** (vss. 26, 28, 31). Rather, fear God
(vs. 28); at the last day the testimony of Jesus will determine
men's eternal destiny, and so, if the Apostles withhold their
witness because they fear men rather than God (cf. Acts v. 29),
the honest witness of Jesus will seal their doom.

The Apostles must not fear hostile men and so become silent
or distort their witness. At the judgment day, all that is **hidden**
now (the wickedness of opponents; the loyalty or cowardice of
the disciples) will be **made known.** The Apostles have received
Jesus' teaching **in the darkness,** in comparative privacy, as
though **whispered in your ear.** Now they must **preach** it
openly **from the housetops,** seeking maximum attention.

Life does not permit neutrality. If the Apostles shrink from preaching for fear of **those who kill the body,** they neglect far more important considerations. The forces of evil **cannot kill the soul,** man's true self; only man's cowardly concern for bodily safety and comfort can bring that ruin, in which God the Lord and Judge will **destroy both soul and body in Gehenna,** the hell of final, unalterable punishment. Jesus here implies that man will be raised and the entire man will fall under complete and final judgment.

Vss. 29-31 use an *a fortiori* argument. God cares for **sparrows,** common birds sold for the cheapest price (an *assarion*, a small copper coin, worth about a halfpenny or an American cent), and used for food by poor folk. Thus God is purposeful, alert, and active in all that occurs. Much more will his personal care attend his witnesses. He knows every detail of their life, even the number of **hairs** on the head; if they serve and trust him, nothing will ever really hurt them. They are **worth far more** to him than sparrows; his concern for their welfare far surpasses his care for the birds. He does not promise escape from suffering; in the N.T. loyalty never delivers from trials; on the contrary, God's loyal people will surely suffer (2 Tim. iii. 12). But the loyalty of faithful witnesses will be honoured, and God's faithful care will keep them in all the trials of this life.

The fearless preaching or cowardly silence of the Apostles will have eternal consequences. If they **confess** Jesus by faithful preaching and loyalty, he at the last day will **confess** them, testify that they have been faithful and worthy. If they **deny** him, let fear silence them or dilute their message, he in turn will **deny** them, declare that they have not been faithful and worthy of life in the Kingdom. The Father will render judgment in accord with the testimony of the Son. The Matthean phrase, **my Father who is in heaven,** expresses Jesus' sense of unique filial relation to God; it also expresses God's majesty and authority and here implies fatherly care of all his loyal servants. The entire section stresses the eternal importance of faithful witness and fearless confession of Jesus as teacher and Lord.

Legitimate lesser loyalties may become harmful when they take the supreme place and deny the claim of Jesus. Particularly in time of persecution this problem may become acute. Its most painful form is family divisions (vs. 21); family circles can echo community opposition to disciples (situations later than the mission of the Twelve are in mind in vss. 34-36, whose general idea Lk. xii. 51-53 parallels). **Do not suppose:** Wards off a possible misunderstanding; cf. v. 17. Jesus cannot accept a minor role in the lives of his followers. His message and personal claim must take the controlling place. Jesus' real aim was not to **bring a sword**; it was to reconcile men to God and to each other. But while to make God's claim supreme may reconcile family members (cf. Mal. iv. 6), it may divide families (cf. Mic. vii. 6), and disciples must not yield to family opposition. For Jesus the family has a basic role in society, but it is what God means it to be only when loyal to God. xii. 46-50 shows where Jesus finds the stronger tie.

With vss. 37-39 cf. Lk. xiv. 26 f.; xvii. 33; cf. also xvi. 24 f.; Mk. viii. 34 f.; Lk. ix. 23 f. Two concerns may displace loyalty to Jesus as the disciple's supreme motive. One is love of parents and children. To love them more than he loves Jesus is to become unacceptable as a disciple. The other rival is concern for personal safety and comfort. The disciple must **take up his cross** in active and costly loyalty to Jesus. The Roman use of crucifixion was well known in Palestine; Jesus could use the cross as at least a vivid figurative reference to the cost which he and a disciple must be ready to pay for fearless loyalty to his mission.

Self-seeking is self-defeating. Only self-sacrifice for Jesus and his cause finds real **life**. Vs. 39 has a word-play: He whose aim is to preserve his physical life will lose his real life; he who sacrifices physical safety in loyal service to Jesus will find true life.

With vss. 40-42 cf. xviii. 5; Mk. ix. 37, 41; Lk. ix. 48; x. 16; Jn. xii. 44 f.; xiii. 20. This passage continues the high personal claim made by Jesus in all four Gospels; they know no gospel of the Kingdom without a high Christology. This passage also honours the faithful Apostle, and all who serve Christ by receiving and helping his messengers. To receive them is to receive him, and so to receive God who sent him. To welcome and support a **prophet** or **righteous man** working for Christ, and do so because he represents Christ, will receive the same blessing and **reward** that the prophet and righteous man receive. For

Jesus, who followed John the Baptist, prophecy was not extinct; the Spirit of the Father was present and active in his spokesmen (x. 20); so he could speak of prophets in his movement. **A cup of cold water,** given to **little ones,** outwardly unimportant disciples, because they are serving Jesus, will bring a reward; it is a simple but real service to Christ.

CHAPTER XI

---

xi. 1-19. JOHN THE BAPTIST AND JESUS

And it happened that when Jesus had finished instructing 1 his twelve disciples, he departed from there to teach and preach in their cities.

Now when John heard in prison the words of the Christ, 2 he sent by his disciples and said to him, 'Are you the 3 Coming One, or are we to wait for someone else?' And 4 Jesus answered and said to them, 'Go tell John what you hear and see: the blind receive their sight and the lame 5 walk, lepers are cleansed and the deaf hear, and the dead are raised and the poor hear the gospel preached. And 6 blessed is he who does not take offence at me.'

As these men were leaving, Jesus began to say to the 7 crowds concerning John, 'Why did you go out into the wilderness? To see a reed shaken by the wind? But why 8 did you go out? To see a man clothed in soft clothing? Behold, those who wear soft clothing are found in the houses of kings. But why did you go out? To see a prophet? 9 Yes, I tell you, and more than a prophet. This is he con- 10 cerning whom it is written:

"Behold, I send my messenger ahead of you,
    who will prepare your way before you".
Truly I tell you, there has not appeared among those born 11 of women a man greater than John the Baptist; but he who is least in the Kingdom of Heaven is greater than he

135

12 is. From the days of John the Baptist until now the Kingdom of Heaven suffers violence, and violent men seize it.
13 For all the prophets and the Law prophesied until John;
14 and if you are willing to accept it, he is Elijah who was to
15 come. He who has ears, let him hear.
16   'But to what shall I compare this generation? It is like
children sitting in the market places, who call to their
17 comrades and say:
       "We played the flute for you, but you did not dance;
       we sang a dirge, but you did not mourn".
18 For John came neither eating nor drinking, and men say,
19 "He has a demon". The Son of Man came eating and
drinking, and men say, "Behold, a glutton and drunkard,
a friend of tax collectors and sinners". And yet wisdom
is justified by its works.'

With vs. 1 cf. the similar formal conclusions of the four other
major discourses: vii. 28 f.; xiii. 53; xix. 1; xxvi. 1. Jesus had sent
out the Twelve because the need was urgent; he himself must
continue his active ministry. **Teach and preach:** Cf. iv. 23;
ix. 35. **Their cities:** Vague; means the Jewish cities of the
region.

With vss. 2-6 cf. Lk. vii. 18-23. **John** the Baptist was still alive
but **in prison.** Josephus (*Antiquities*, xviii. 5. 2) says he was kept
at Machaerus, east of the Dead Sea, at the southern border of
the tetrarchy of Herod Antipas, who had arrested him (xiv. 3).
Some at least of his disciples continued loyal to him and through
them he heard what Jesus was doing. **The works of the Christ:**
This title comes from 'Matthew'; John the Baptist was not clear
that Jesus was the Christ; 'Matthew' wants to indicate that the
miracles of Jesus were works befitting the Christ and sufficient
to mark him as such if John faces facts. John has preached, all
four Gospels emphasize, that One greater than himself was
coming. Is Jesus that Coming One? The Greek ἕτερον could
mean: Are we to wait for a 'different' one, a different type of
leader? But probably it means only: **Are we to wait for someone else?** There is no clear evidence that 'the Coming One'
was a common title for the expected Messiah, but John, it is
clear, had spoken of a Coming One.

If Jn. i. 29-36 is chronologically accurate, then John, once certain that Jesus was the Coming One, the Lamb of God, the Son of God, had begun to doubt. More likely the Gospel of John has antedated this Christological view of Jesus for dramatic effect, and the view in Matt., that the report of Jesus' mighty works aroused hope in John, is historically correct. In reply to John, Jesus calls attention to his preaching and especially to his miracles. **What you hear and see**: Implies, as Luke specifically states, that healings occurred while the messengers were present; they can give John a first-hand report. No specific healings of lame or deaf people have been described in Matt.; the types named come from general tradition and are listed to recall Isa. xxix. 18 f.; xxxv. 5 f.; lxi. 1. He who understands Jesus' miracles and recalls these O.T. passages which promise God's decisive, beneficent work, will not **take offence** at Jesus, but will know that divine power is at work, that the Kingdom has begun to come, that Jesus, the Coming One John announced, is now doing God's decisive work. If John recognizes this, he will take his place among Jesus' followers and so find God's blessing. There is no convincing evidence that John did this.

With vss. 7-15 cf. Lk. vii. 24-30; xvi. 16. In Lk. Jesus comments on John after the messengers have left; in Matt. he does so **as these men were leaving.** In both, the crowds hear Jesus' message to John; the beatitude of vs. 6 was thus a challenge to both them and the Baptist. Jesus' hearers, it is assumed, had previously heard John.

In vss. 7 f. the Greek can be translated, 'What did you go out into the wilderness to see? A reed shaken by the wind? But what did you go out to see? A man clothed in soft clothing?' But the translation that parallels vs. 9 more closely seems better. The earliest manuscripts had no punctuation or sentence division, and τί can mean either 'What?' or 'Why?' There is no way to be certain. The questions imply that people would not have hurried into the wilderness to see and hear a man who had no courage or vigour and thought only of his own comfort. That kind of man fawns on rulers and lives at ease, instead of thinking of God's will and men's need. These crowds knew John was a sturdy, fearless man, who sacrificed personal comfort to be loyal to God and to speak the prophetic word men needed. They rightly considered him **a prophet,** sent of God and speaking for God. But he was **more than a prophet,** not because of personal worth, but because he lived at the dawn of the final crisis period of history and had the unique task of announcing the near coming of the Kingdom. He was the forerunner who announced the coming of **the Christ** (vs. 2); he was the **messenger** whose coming Mal. iii. 1 had prophesied. This quotation does not agree precisely with either the Hebrew or the LXX; it is taken here as God's words to the Messiah concerning his forerunner. As vs. 14 will add, John is the **Elijah** whom Mal. iv. 5 said would come before the final day of the Lord. With solemn emphasis Jesus declares that **a man greater than John the Baptist** has never appeared, and none has had so unique a role.

All this shows Jesus' answer to his later question whether the baptism of John was from heaven or from men (xxi. 25). But great as John was, the **least in the** dawning **Kingdom** was **greater,** not in personal achievement and worth, but because by God's gift he, unlike John, was in the Kingdom. For as vss. 12 f. show, John was the end of the old era. He announced the imminence of the Kingdom, but he himself still stood within the old order.

In the brief time since John's imprisonment ended his prophetic ministry, the power of the Kingdom had begun to show itself in the gospel preaching and mighty works of Jesus (vss. 5 f.). That the Kingdom had not fully come was clear, first, from the fact that God still had much to do through Jesus and the mission of his followers, and secondly, as vs. 12 seems to say, from the violent opposition that the dawning Kingdom was meeting. Vs. 12 is admittedly difficult; it certainly indicates that divine power is now at work to establish God's Kingdom; but whether the **violent men** vigorously press into the Kingdom, or violently oppose it, is disputed. If the former is true, vs. 12 means: 'From the days of John the Baptist until now the Kingdom of Heaven exercises its powerful force, and forceful men seize it' to share its privileges. But the last three words of the Greek seem to say that violent men grasp it with hostile intent. So it seems better to interpret as in our translation above; the great final struggle has begun; God's power is at work through

Jesus to establish his reign, but his Kingdom is suffering violence; violent men are trying to seize or snatch away this blessing
and keep men from accepting God's rule. In this crisis time of
history, great with opportunity but full of danger for those not
alert to respond at once, Jesus says with stern emphasis, **He
who has ears, let him hear.**

With vss. 16-19 cf. Lk. vii. 31-35. Jesus warned men to heed
the teaching (vs. 15); this parable shows how greatly such warning is needed. Most people have responded to neither John nor
Jesus. They use the limitations or peculiar methods of God's
spokesmen as an excuse for evading God's claim. The excuses
sound plausible, but the result is comfortable evasion of God's
urgent claim. In the parable, **children** play at weddings and at
funerals; that is, some play, but most refuse to join in. So with
men's response to **John** and **Jesus.** John was ascetic; he stood
aloof from common pleasures in stern reminder that his generation faced a crisis. But people thought such serious self-denial
unnatural; John must have **a demon.** Jesus joined in common
meals and social joys; his concern for people, and his outgoing
friendliness, expressed itself in sharing the common life. But as
people exaggerated John's sternness, so they caricatured, indeed
slandered, Jesus' friendliness; he was **a glutton and drunkard;**
he could not be God's spokesman. This parable shows how
differently John and Jesus lived, how widely rejected both were,
and how cleverly and wickedly people excused their spiritual
irresponsibility. But the divine **wisdom,** Jesus said, **is justified
by its works;** it can use agents of different types; the serious
will listen and the irresponsible must bear their guilt.

xi. 20-30. THE REJECTED SON OF MAN IS
THE SON OF GOD

**Then he began to reproach the cities in which the most 20
of his mighty works had been done, because they had not
repented: 'Woe to you, Chorazin; woe to you, Bethsaida; 21
for if the mighty works done in you had been done in Tyre
and Sidon, they long ago would have repented in sack-
cloth and ashes. But I tell you, it will be more tolerable 22**

for Tyre and Sidon on the day of judgment than for you.
23 And you, Capernaum, will you be exalted to heaven? You
will descend to Hades. For if the mighty works done in
you had been done in Sodom, it would have survived until
24 this day. But I tell you that it will be more tolerable for the
land of Sodom on the day of judgment than for you.'
25   At that time Jesus answered and said, 'I praise thee,
Father, Lord of heaven and earth, because thou hast hidden these things from the wise and intelligent and re-
26 vealed them to children. Yes, Father, for that was what
27 was pleasing to thee. All things have been committed to
me by my Father, and no one knows the Son except the
Father, nor does any one know the Father except the Son
28 and he to whom the Son may choose to reveal him. Come
to me, all who are weary and burdened, and I will give
29 you rest. Take my yoke upon you and learn from me, for
I am meek and humble of heart, and you will find rest
30 for your souls. For my yoke is easy and the load I impose
is light.'

With vss. 20-24 cf. Lk. x. 13-15; both writers draw the basic
sayings from Q. **Then:** Frequent in Matt. to connect incidents;
in topical grouping here it indicates that Jesus' words fit the
preceding context of opposition and rejection. Jesus has done
many **mighty works** by divine power. (Vs. 20 seems to fit best
the closing days of the Galilean ministry.) **Most** of these miracles
(δυνάμεις, works of power, **mighty works**) were done in three
cities north of the Sea of Galilee; **Chorazin** was little more than
two miles north-northwest of Capernaum (the Gospels relate no
specific miracle done there); **Bethsaida** was on the north shore,
just east of the Jordan; **Capernaum** (*Tell Hum*) was on the
north-west shore. If most of his mighty works were done in these
cities, he must have spent much of his time in them rather than
in itineration around Galilee.

Thus these cities had repeatedly seen events which indicated
divine power at work in their midst. But **they had not repented** as Jesus implies he had summoned them to do. **Tyre
and Sidon,** which O.T. prophets denounced and condemned
to doom for their wickedness, had not repented, but Jesus is

certain that had these pagan cities heard him and seen his
miracles, they **would have repented.** They will be judged
more leniently on the final judgment day than these cities which
have rejected Jesus. Note that cities have a corporate responsibility; they as well as individuals can fall under doom.

In condemning **Capernaum,** most favoured of all the Galilean cities since Jesus made it his home during his Galilean
ministry (iv. 13), he uses the taunt song directed against Babylon
in Isa. xiv. 13-15. He does not quote literally either the Hebrew
or the LXX of Isaiah. He goes on to compare **Sodom** with
Capernaum, with the same point as before: Neither city repented, but Capernaum, with the greater opportunity, will
suffer the greater penalty. The passage reflects the widespread
rejection of Jesus even in the Galilean cities to which he gave the
most attention.

With vss. 25-27 cf. Lk. x. 21 f.; the close agreement shows use
of a common source (Q), which implies early knowledge of this
passage in the Church. Because of its high Christology, it is often
called the 'Johannine' passage of the Synoptics, with the inference that it is late and was not spoken by Jesus. However, this
consciousness of divine Sonship appears here in two Synoptic
Gospels and in Q, one of their two main sources (cf. also Mk. i.
11; xiii. 32; xv. 39). The usage is frequent in Matt. (the Son: ii.
15; iii. 17; iv. 3, 6; viii. 29; xvi. 16; the absolute use of Father and
Son: xxiv. 36; cf. Jesus' reference to 'my Father', e.g. in x. 32).
The evangelists no doubt varied in their understanding of this
unique Sonship, but all four Gospels ascribe to Jesus the consciousness of such a unique filial relationship to the Father.

Vss. 28-30 need not have been spoken at the same time as
vss. 25-27, but they reflect the same unique consciousness in
Jesus. Some claim that the direct source of this entire paragraph
is Sirach, ch. 51. Were that so, the parallels with Sirach should
be much closer than they are. Jesus could have reflected knowledge of Sirach, or the Church (or the writer of the Q source)
could have arranged Jesus' ideas in a pattern suggested by
Sirach, or the points akin to Sirach could have been known
through general oral tradition.

The phrase **at that time** (cf. xii. 1; xiv. 1) connects the
entire passage with the preceding ones. **Answered:** Need not

imply a previous question; it is a common formula in Matt. to introduce another item of teaching. **Father:** Jesus' frequent usage, and in particular vs. 27, show that this address expresses his unique relation as Son to the Father. The Father is **Lord of heaven and earth,** and he can commit or entrust this Lordship, this authority, to **the Son,** as is stated in vs. 27 and xxviii. 18 (here to the risen Christ, called Son in the baptismal formula).

Vss. 25 f. are a prayer of thanksgiving and praise (ἐξομολο-γοῦμαι can mean 'confess' or 'acknowledge', but here means **praise**). In Matt. the clause beginning **because** refers back to the rejection of Jesus noted in vss. 12, 19, 20. Jesus is glad that if rejection must occur the Father has **hidden these things,** the meaning of his message and healings, **from the wise and intelligent,** those ready to trust their own ability to understand God's will and ways (cf. Isa. xxix. 14; 1 Cor. i. 19), and has **revealed them to children,** who in trusting innocence are ready to hear and accept the gospel and do not let preconceived ideas of what God's way should be keep them from responding to Jesus' preaching and mighty works. Vs. 26 repeats and emphasizes vs. 25: Jesus praises the Father because he was pleased to work in that way. The religious leaders are kept from responding to Jesus by their pride in their supposed spiritual knowledge, but the common people are responding far more than are the leaders.

The heart of Jesus' claim is in vs. 27. **All things,** not merely authority to do mighty works, but the entire ministry of revealing and carrying out the Father's purpose, **have been committed** by the **Father** to him, the **Son.** (The text of the rest of the verse varies in the manuscripts, but the overwhelming mass of good evidence supports the text back of our translation.) To most people Jesus seems a misguided or good man, but not the unique agent and revealer of the Father; only **the Father** really knows him and how fully he reveals and fulfils God's purpose; even the disciples (included in the **children,** vs. 25) are still so limited in understanding of the Son that they can be disregarded; only the Father really **knows the Son.** Nor do people know the Father any better than they know the Son. Only the Son really knows the nature, purpose, power, and grace of the

Father; only as others link their lives with the Son and let him reveal the Father to them (Jn. xiv. 9 f.) will they really know him. **Choose** (βούληται): Does not imply that the Son is arbitrary or capricious in choosing which people he permits to know the Father; it rather emphasizes that it is only by the free act and gracious work of the Son that men come to know the Father (cf. Acts iv. 12). The Son knows the Father now in a full and complete way; others may receive that knowledge, to the extent of their need and capacity, through the revealing work of the Son.

This verse comes close to stating the Logos idea of the role of Christ. If it meant that the Son mediates knowledge of the Father to all generations of mankind, this would be a full parallel to the Logos as the Light of the world (Jn. i. 1-18). However, the reference in Matt. has no clear reference to former generations, and so does not yet seem to contain the fully developed Logos teaching of the Prologue of Jn. But at least for the present (and the future), knowledge of the Father comes through the Son, who, as xxviii. 18-20 shows, carries forward that work through his commissioned representatives.

The work of the Son is not merely to reveal truth or give a vision of the Father; it includes meeting the needs of burdened humanity (vss. 28-30). It is doubtful whether these verses were originally spoken by Jesus in close connection with vss. 25-27. Those who see in vss. 25-30 direct literary dependence on the apocryphal wisdom book Sirach, especially li. 1, 23-27, may regard this passage as a literary unity composed by some early Christian. But while the similarities in language to the Sirach passage are noteworthy and show the Jewish background of this passage, they do not show real agreement in thought; they relate to vss. 28-30 for the most part. Luke, who closely parallels vss. 25-27, has no parallel to vss. 28-30. These last verses may thus have been spoken at a different time. Moreover, vss. 25-27 are a direct prayer to the Father, while vss. 28-30 are not a prayer, but an invitation spoken directly to needy people. They imply the same unique relation of the Son to the Father which vss. 25-27 explicitly state, but have no literary unity with vss. 25-27.

Jesus invites the **weary** (κοπιῶντες) and **burdened** (πεφορ-τισμένοι) to come to him; he promises to refresh them and give them **rest.** Curiously enough, in describing the promised blessing he makes only one point: that rest will not be idleness or inaction; it includes a **yoke,** a **burden,** and a learning. There is no discipleship without a task. Those who come to him must by their own decision accept the yoke he places on them. Jewish hearers were familiar with the yoke of the Law, which they had to learn and fulfil. The yoke he places on his followers will include learning God's will, as his continual teaching shows, and obeying it in active service. But this yoke and burden will not be irksome or crushing. He who imposes it is himself **meek** (cf. v. 5) **and humble of heart;** he has sympathy for all in need or bowed by burdens; his yoke and burden, willingly accepted and carried with his companionship and help (cf. xxviii. 20), will prove **easy** to endure, **light** to carry; and in carrying this load, as Jer. vi. 16 suggests, they will find **rest for** their **souls,** that is, for themselves. This service will not gradually drain away their strength; from their tie with Jesus they will draw refreshment and renewal that will enable them to carry their load without finding it irksome or crushing (cf. 2 Cor. iv. 16). If they will only be responsive children (vs. 25), open-minded, ready to receive what only the Son can give, all the blessings of God are open to them.

CHAPTER XII

xii. 1-21. JESUS THE MERCIFUL SERVANT IS LORD OF THE SABBATH

1 At that time Jesus went through the grain fields on the Sabbath. His disciples became hungry, and began to pick 2 heads of grain and eat them. When the Pharisees saw this they said to him, 'Behold, your disciples are doing what 3 it is not lawful to do on a Sabbath'. But he said to them, 'Have you not read what David did when he and his 4 companions became hungry, how he entered into the house of God and ate the loaves of presentation, which

it was not lawful for him or his companions to eat, but
only for the priests? Or have you not read in the Law that 5
on the Sabbath the priests in the temple desecrate the Sabbath and are guiltless? I tell you that something greater 6
than the temple is here. But if you had realized what this 7
means, "I desire mercy and not sacrifice", you would
not have condemned the guiltless. For the Son of Man is 8
Lord of the Sabbath.'

And he departed from there and went into their syna- 9
gogue. And behold, a man with a withered hand; and 10
they asked him, saying, 'Is it lawful to heal on the Sabbath?'—that they might accuse him. He said to them, 11
'What man of you will there be who will have one
sheep, and if it falls into a pit on the Sabbath, will not take
hold of it and lift it out? Now a man is worth far more 12
than a sheep! So it is lawful to do good on the Sabbath.'
Then he said to the man, 'Stretch out your hand'. And he 13
stretched it out, and it was restored to the same healthy
condition as the other one. But the Pharisees went out and 14
plotted against him to destroy him.

When Jesus learned of it, he departed from there, and 15
many followed him, and he healed them all, and he 16
sternly charged them not to make him known, that the 17
word might be fulfilled which had been spoken through
Isaiah the prophet, who said:
'Behold, my Servant, whom I have chosen,   18
    my Beloved, in whom my soul has been well pleased;
I will put my Spirit upon him,
    and he will proclaim justice to the Gentiles.
He will not quarrel or cry out,   19
    nor will any one hear his voice in the streets.
A bent reed he will not break,   20
    and a smouldering wick he will not extinguish,
until he has led the right to victory.
    And Gentiles will put their hope in his name.'   21

With vss. 1-8 cf. Mk. ii. 23-28; Lk. vi. 1-5 (but neither
parallels vss. 5-7, placed here in Matt. to show Jesus' attitude
toward the Sabbath). There is only formal connection (at that

time) with ch. **xi**; the essential is the day: **the Sabbath.** The ripened grain shows that it was late spring. Vs. 9 implies that Jesus was on the way to a synagogue. On the right to **pick heads of grain,** cf. Deut. xxiii. 25; the alleged wrong here was in doing it on the Sabbath, when work was not permitted. The Pharisees' tradition defined many activities, including reaping, as work and so forbidden on the Sabbath. They criticized the disciples, but addressed Jesus as responsible for what his followers did.

Jesus appeals to 1 Sam. xxi. 1-6, which the objectors surely had read. Had they understood it, they would know that human need is more important than their ruling that to pick a few heads of grain was work. 1 Samuel does not say that **David** actually entered the sanctuary at Nob, but that Ahimelech the priest gave David **the loaves of presentation;** these loaves, placed before the Presence of the Lord in the sanctuary (Lev. xxiv. 8 f.; 1 Sam. xxi. 6) and set aside when fresh loaves replaced them, could only be eaten by **the priests.** But hunger justified David and his men in eating them. If David (and his men) could do this, even more can the Son of David (i. 1) and his followers.

Vss. 5 f. give another situation that warrants violating usual rules against doing work on the Sabbath. **The Law** itself prescribes work for priests **on the Sabbath;** e.g. **the priests** must offer sacrifices 'every sabbath' (Num. xxviii. 9 f.). They thus **desecrate the Sabbath,** that is, do work on the day when men must not work. But they are **guiltless;** the necessity of performing the sacrifices takes precedence over the prohibition of work. If priests can do this, even more can the Son of Man, who has come to serve and give his life as a ransom for many (xx. 28). Jesus and his work are more important than the temple; **something greater than the temple** refers to Jesus, but the neuter (μεῖζον) may include the Kingdom movement which Jesus heads (cf. vss. 41 f., 'something greater than Jonah' and 'than Solomon').

The two illustrations about the **bread of the presentation** and the Sabbath duties of priests may not seem decisive; the disciples' need for food was not acute, and picking heads of grain hardly seems so important to God's people as the prescribed sacrifices. In vs. 7 Jesus presents a deeper point. Referring again (cf. ix. 13) to Hos. vi. 6, he indicts the Pharisees for losing sight of kindness and **mercy** (cf. v. 7; xxiii. 23). Their traditions, blind to human need and special situations, have no validity; the disciples in disregarding them do not really violate the will of God. In fact, if rulings about Sabbath observance are to be made, it is not the Pharisees but **the Son of Man,** as **Lord of the Sabbath,** who has authority to say how to observe properly the day of rest.

This passage uses or reflects three titles of Jesus: the Son of David (vss. 3 f.); the Suffering Servant (vss. 5 f.); the Son of Man (vs. 8). For Jesus and 'Matthew' these three unite in one portrait.

With vss. 9-14 cf. Mk. iii. 1-6; Lk. vi. 6-11; xiii. 15 f.; xiv. 5. In Matt. Jesus goes from the grain fields to the synagogue of the neighbouring town or city. **Their synagogue:** The one with which the Pharisees of vs. 2 were connected. They, it is implied, ask the question of vs. 10, and in vs. 14 plot against Jesus. However, this plot sounds like the work of more than a local group. In any event, they here take the aggressive, and to get a charge against him, try to get him to contradict current rules on Sabbath observance. The implication is that to heal on the Sabbath is work and violates the Law (Ex. xx. 8-11).

Jesus' reply cites an act of work done on the Sabbath which all agree would be justified. The **sheep** might live until the next day, but it is humane and right to rescue it **on the Sabbath.** Even more should **a man** in need have sympathy and active help. He need not be in danger of dying; it still is right to give him full health and happiness on the Sabbath. **It is lawful to do good** (to heal a man and give him normal use of his hand) **on the Sabbath.**

The man's faith is not mentioned, but in stretching out his hand he shows faith, and he receives healing. **The Pharisees** plot against Jesus' life; they consider that both their standing and God's truth are at stake. They see a beneficent act and think only of the sacredness of their tradition.

With vss. 15-21 cf. Mk. iii. 7-12; Lk. vi. 17-19; Isaiah is quoted only in Matt. Jesus **learned,** by information brought him or by his own discernment, of the plot against his life (vs.

14). **Departed:** To continue his ministry where opposition had not crystallized against him. **Many followed:** Since **he healed them all,** the **many** were sick people seeking help (the word **all** emphasizes the effective power of Jesus). Though his healings could not be kept secret, Jesus honestly wanted the minimum of public attention (vs. 16). He wanted to centre attention on his Kingdom message. He lived and worked in the spirit of the Servant of Second Isaiah; the purpose expressed in vs. 17 is not simply the divine purpose, seen later by the Gospel writer, but also the purpose of Jesus.

'Matthew' takes Jesus to be the chosen **Servant** of Isa. xlii. 1-4. He will avoid quarrels when possible (vs. 15); he will not call attention to his works (vs. 16); he will be gentle with broken and damaged lives, and will work patiently to bring to full victory the divine rule with judgment on evil and salvation for the poor. The Gentile response, foreshadowed in the Magi (ch. ii) and anticipated in viii. 11 f. and xxviii. 18-20, is predicted here rather unexpectedly in the midst of the Galilean ministry.

xii. 22-37. JESUS ACCUSED OF SERVING BEELZEBUL

22 Then a demoniac, blind and unable to speak, was brought to him; and he healed him, so that the dumb man could
23 speak and see. And all the crowds were astonished, and
24 said, 'Is this perhaps the Son of David?' But when the Pharisees heard it, they said, 'This man expels demons
25 only by Beelzebul the ruler of the demons'. Knowing their thoughts, he said to them, 'Every kingdom divided against itself is devastated, and every city or house divided
26 against itself will not stand. And if Satan expels Satan, he is divided against himself; how then will his kingdom
27 stand? And if I by Beelzebul expel demons, by whom do your sons expel them? Therefore they will be your judges.
28 But if by the Spirit of God I expel demons, then the King-
29 dom of God has just come to you. Or how can anyone enter the house of the strong man and seize his property unless he first ties up the strong man? And then he will

plunder his house. He who is not with me is against me, 30
and he who does not gather with me scatters. Therefore 31
I tell you, every sin and blasphemy will be forgiven men,
but blasphemy against the Spirit will not be forgiven.
And whoever says a word against the Son of Man will be 32
forgiven for it; but whoever says it against the Holy Spirit
will not be forgiven for it either in this age or the coming
one.

'Either make the tree good and its fruit good, or make 33
the tree bad and its fruit bad; for the tree is known by its
fruit. You brood of vipers, how can you, evil as you are, 34
speak good things? For the mouth speaks from the abundance of the heart. The good man brings forth good things 35
from his good treasure, and the evil man brings forth evil
things from his evil treasure.

'I tell you that for every careless word which men will 36
speak they will render an account on the day of judgment;
for by your words you will be acquitted, and by your 37
words you will be condemned.'

With vss. 22-32 cf. Mk. iii. 20-30; Lk. xi. 14-23; xii. 10. The
occasion in Matt. and Lk. is an exorcism; but the interest centres
on the blasphemous charge against Jesus (vs. 24) and on his
reply. When speech and sight had been restored to the demon-
possessed man, onlookers were affected in two ways. **All the
crowds were astonished;** in a cautious question they consider
whether Jesus is **the Son of David,** the expected Messiah (for
the Gospel answer, given thus far, cf. i. 1; ix. 27). The Pharisees
(cf. ix. 34) say that Jesus can control demons in other people
only because he himself is possessed by **Beelzebul** (Satan), **the
ruler of the demons,** who naturally controls all the other
demons. Jesus is not sent of God; he is the tool of the devil, and
so can perform these exorcisms.

Jesus first shows that the charge against him is nonsense. A
divided kingdom, city, or **house** is doomed. If Satan in him
drives Satan's helpers out of other lives, Satan destroys his
control over mankind and dooms his own rule or kingdom. So
it makes no sense to say that these exorcisms are Satan's doing.
Vs. 27 is an *argumentum ad hominem;* not only Jesus but

disciples of the Pharisees were expelling demons; if he does it by the power of Beelzebul, then the Pharisees must say that their own disciples do so by the same Satanic power. This they dare not admit. So he suggests the logical and true explanation. He does these beneficent acts by the power of **the Spirit of God.** God has begun to establish his **Kingdom;** these mighty works of Jesus show that his effective rule has begun to appear; the aorist ἔφθασεν suggests that the Kingdom has just begun to come.

To make his point clearer Jesus uses a short parable. A **strong man** can only be bound and **his property** seized by one still stronger. If, then, the demons have met their master, a stronger one than any demon is acting through Jesus. That stronger one is the Holy Spirit, by whose power Jesus expels the demons.

Such issues, Jesus sternly warns, permit no neutrality (cf. Mk. ix. 40; Lk. ix. 50). As used here, vs. 30 means: Either Satan or the Holy Spirit is back of Jesus' mighty, beneficent works. To be neutral is to reject and oppose Christ.

Vss. 31 f. are among the sternest words Jesus ever spoke. By the power of **the Spirit** he has given health to needy people. Yet the Pharisees call these healing acts the work of Beelzebul (the devil); they identify the Holy Spirit as Satan. Jesus sees no hope for such people, because their moral vision is so confused and reversed as to be past remedy. All other sins, even **blasphemy,** will be forgiven. Indeed, though he is **Son of Man,** human in lot and situation but destined for triumph and glory, forgiveness and eternal salvation are open to those who blasphemously berate him. But he knows the Spirit directs his life; to call these Spirit-effected healings the work of Satan reveals the speaker's hopeless bankruptcy.

With vss. 33-35 cf. vii. 16-20; Lk. vi. 43-45. These sayings are put here in Matt. to teach that such an accusation as vs. 24 comes from an evil heart and reveals deep-seated wickedness. The tree inevitably produces its own kind of fruit. This may challenge the Pharisees to be consistent in judging Jesus; they must say he is demon-inspired, and his healings are evil, or that he is Spirit-led and his works are good. But probably the imperative **make** means that the Pharisees necessarily show the nature of their lives in their actions. As a **brood of vipers** (iii. 7; xxiii. 33), evil in nature, they cannot **speak good things;** their wicked attack on Jesus shows their true nature. A good man's **heart** or inner **treasure** of faith and character will express itself in good words (and acts); an evil man's inner wickedness will express itself in wicked, harmful words (and acts). A man may try to conceal his true motives and nature by an outward pretence of goodness, but his true nature will come out; his words and deeds will make clear what kind of person he is.

Only Matt. has vss. 36 f. Jesus condemns idle, **careless,** irresponsible (ἀργόν) speech. Men must answer at the last day for all that they have said. God will justify, acquit, those responsible, reverent, sympathetic, and friendly in speech. But he will condemn men irresponsible, profane, hostile, and harmful in speech. This underlines the wickedness of the false and irresponsible charges made by the Pharisees. On the importance of honest, responsible speech cf. v. 33-37; xxiii. 16-22.

xii. 38-50. AN EVIL GENERATION REJECTS JESUS

Then some of the scribes and Pharisees answered him, 38 **saying, 'Teacher, we wish to see a sign from you'. But** 39 **he answered and said to them, 'An evil and adulterous generation desires a sign, but no sign will be given it except the sign of Jonah the prophet. For just as Jonah was** 40 **in the belly of the sea-monster three days and three nights, so the Son of Man will be in the heart of the earth three days and three nights. Men of Nineveh will rise up** 41 **at the judgment with this generation and will condemn it, for they repented in response to the message of Jonah, and behold, something greater than Jonah is here. The** 42 **queen of the south will rise up at the judgment with this generation and will condemn it, for she came from the ends of the earth to hear the wisdom of Solomon, and behold, something greater than Solomon is here.**

'Whenever the unclean spirit goes out of the man, it 43 **wanders through waterless places, seeking rest, but does not find it. Then it says, "I will return to my house from** 44 **which I came", and it goes and finds it empty, swept,**

45 and put in order. Then it goes and takes with it seven
   other spirits more evil than it is, and it enters and dwells
   there; and the last state of that man is worse than the
   first. So also it will happen to this wicked generation.'
46   While he was still speaking to the crowds, behold, his
   mother and brothers stood outside, wishing to speak with
47 him. Someone said to him, 'Behold, your mother and
   your brothers stand outside, wishing to speak with you'.
48 But he answered and said to the one who told him, 'Who
49 is my mother, and who are my brothers?' And stretching
   out his hand toward his disciples he said, 'Behold, my
50 mother and my brothers! For whoever does the will of
   my Father who is in heaven, he is my brother and sister
   and mother.'

With vss. 38-42 cf. Lk. xi. 29-32. **Sign:** Here means a striking
miracle which gives compelling proof that his power and authority are God-given. In xvi. 1, 4 and Mk. viii. 11 f. Jesus flatly
rejects the request for a sign. Here the desire for signs is condemned as evil, but one sign is given, **the sign of Jonah.** Since
the scribes and Pharisees make the request, Jesus probably
thinks mainly of them as the **evil and adulterous generation**
(cf. xii. 24). **Adulterous:** Refers here not to marital unfaithfulness, but to unfaithfulness to God; this idea is familiar from the
O.T. prophets. The **sign of Jonah:** In Lk. xi. 30, Jonah's
preaching to the Ninevites; but in Matt., deliverance from **the
belly of the sea-monster** (Jon. i. 17). Jonah thus becomes a
sign of Jesus' resurrection; the length of the burial, **three days
and three nights,** seems at odds with such passages as xvi. 21,
'on the third day', but agrees with xxvii. 63, 'after three days';
the evangelist regards these expressions as equivalent. Jesus tells
his opponents that the only sign he will ever give them is his
resurrection. But only a repentant and receptive spirit will know
that the resurrection has occurred, and such a spirit these
opponents and most of their generation do not have. In **the
judgment** therefore they face final condemnation for their
wickedness.

Two examples contrast **this** wicked **generation** of Jews and
responsive Gentiles of O.T. times. **The men of Nineveh** re-

pented when **Jonah** preached God's judgment on their sins, and
were forgiven (Jonah, ch. iii; Jesus seems to accept the Book of
Jonah as a record of actual history). **The queen of the south**
(from Sheba; 1 Kings x. 1-10) **came from the ends of the
earth** (Arabia was then a long journey from Jerusalem) **to hear
the wisdom of Solomon.** These Gentiles heeded what Jonah
and Solomon, God's spokesmen, said. **At the** final **judgment**
they will **rise up** and **condemn** Jesus' Jewish contemporaries.
This does not mean that they will determine the final verdict
on these wicked and unrepentant Jews; God will do that, or do
it through Jesus (xxv. 31); but their repentant response to God's
spokesmen will condemn the unrepentant attitude of the Jews,
who in Jesus and the dawning Kingdom have **something
greater** than Jonah or Solomon and therefore will receive
greater condemnation for rejecting their greater opportunity (cf.
xi. 20-24).

With vss. 43-45 cf. Lk. xi. 24-26. This parable describes the
grim destiny awaiting the generation which is rejecting Jesus'
appeal. A demon is called **unclean** since it defiles the life it controls. It may go out of a man, either by choice or because
exorcised by some stronger power. While restlessly seeking a
new home, it roams, so men thought, in desert **waterless
places.** Finding no new home, it returns to the man it formerly
possessed. That life, no longer 'unclean', is cleansed of evil and
put in order. But nothing good and strong has taken the
demon's place. The life is empty. Nothing prevents its recapture
by the demon; he enlists allies, seven demons worse than he is,
and together they take control of the luckless man, now worse
off than before.

Does Jesus mean only that each man must let active forces of
good rule his life? In Matt., and for Jesus, the point is more
specific. Jesus has driven demons from the lives of harassed
people. Something greater than the temple (vs. 6), than Jonah
(vs. 41), than Solomon (vs. 42), is here; the stronger one has
proved his power (vs. 29); the Spirit in Jesus has broken the
grip of evil and the Kingdom has begun to come (vs. 28). The
Kingdom of Satan is in retreat, but the demons Jesus has routed
can and will return unless Israel accepts Jesus and his message,
repents, and enters the dawning Kingdom. If Israel is liberated

11   153

from evil powers but not committed to Jesus, the forces of evil will recapture this generation, which has had the greatest opportunity ever offered mankind.

Jesus and 'Matthew' thought in terms of actual evil spirits which seized and harmed human lives. Today these stories are often explained in terms of psychological maladjustment, to be remedied by skilled counselling. But while we need not believe in demons just as first-century people did, the forces of evil are more real, more deeply rooted and more difficult to control, than is often understood. The power of God, and not merely the skill of trained counsellors, is needed to resolve the deep-seated crisis which evil brings to man.

With vss. 46-50 cf. Mk. iii. 31-35; Lk. viii. 19-21. In Matt. successive incidents or items of teaching are often said to follow one another closely; here the next incident begins before the preceding teaching is completed (cf. ix. 18). This hints that the writer sees a connection in thought; throughout ch. xii Israel's failure to respond to God's will has been prominent; even the family of Jesus has failed to understand his mission and support it. It is not suggested (as in Mk. iii. 20 f.) that to the family his urgent preaching marked him as mentally unbalanced. But they stand outside; they want to see him but do not come in.

Early and important manuscripts and versions omit vs. 47; it may be a later addition. But vs. 48 implies some such statement as vs. 47 gives. Since both vss. 46 and 47 end with the same Greek word (speak), a situation which often leads to omissions, this may have led an early scribe to skip the entire vs. 47, which would explain the omission in some manuscripts and versions.

Jesus' reply implies that his family are not in sympathy with his work (cf. Jn. vii. 5). 'Matthew' does not say why **his mother and brothers** came, but they clearly are not active followers of Jesus. His stronger ties are with his disciples, described as those who do the will of God. **Whoever:** Shows that this close tie is open to all, including his family, who respond to God's will. This reference to obedience reminds us that God was not considered morally indifferent; as **Father** he is to be obeyed, respected, and loved.

CHAPTER XIII

xiii. 1-52. PARABLES OF THE KINGDOM

On that day Jesus went out of the house and sat beside the 1
sea; and large crowds gathered and came to him, so that 2
he entered a boat and sat there, and all the crowd stood
upon the shore.

And he spoke much to them in parables, saying, 'Behold, 3
the sower went out to sow. And as he sowed some seeds 4
fell beside the road, and the birds came and ate them.
Others fell upon the rocky places, where they did not have 5
much soil, and at once they sprang up, because they had no
depth of soil; but when the sun rose they were scorched, 6
and because they had no root they withered. Others fell 7
among the thorns, and the thorns grew up and choked
them. But others fell upon the good soil and yielded fruit, 8
one a hundredfold, another sixtyfold, and another thirtyfold. He who has ears, let him hear.' 9

And the disciples approached and said to him, 'Why do 10
you speak to them in parables?' He answered and said, 11
'To you it has been given to understand the mysteries of
the Kingdom of Heaven, but to them it has not been given.
For whoever has, more will be given him and he will have 12
abundance; but whoever does not have, even what he has
will be taken away from him. For this reason I speak to 13
them in parables, because though they see they do not
really see and though they hear they do not really hear
or understand. And with them is fulfilled the prophecy 14
of Isaiah which says,

"You will indeed hear and yet you will not understand,
    and you will indeed see and yet you will not perceive.
For the heart of this people has become dull,   15
    and with their ears they hear with difficulty,
    and their eyes they have closed,
lest they see with their eyes
and hear with their ears

and understand with their heart and turn back,
and I shall heal them."

16 But your eyes are blessed, for they see, and your ears, for
17 they hear. For truly I tell you that many prophets and
righteous men desired to see what you see but did not see
it, and to hear what you hear but did not hear it.

18,19 'You therefore hear the parable of the sower. From
every one who hears the word about the Kingdom and
does not understand it the Evil One comes and snatches
away what has been sown in his heart; this is the seed
20 sown by the road. That sown on the rocky places—this is
he who hears the word and at once receives it with joy;
21 however, he has no root in himself but lasts only a little
while; when affliction or persecution comes on account
22 of the word he at once falls away. That sown among the
thorns—this is he who hears the word, and the worry the
world excites and the deception wealth exercises chokes
23 the word, and it proves unfruitful. But that sown on the
good soil—this is he who hears the word and understands
it, who bears fruit and produces one a hundredfold, another sixtyfold, another thirtyfold.'

24 Another parable he put before them, saying, 'The Kingdom of Heaven may be compared to a man who sowed
25 good seed in his field. But while men slept his enemy
came and added a sowing of darnel among the wheat,
26 and went away. When the stalks grew up and began to
27 produce fruit, then the darnel appeared also. The servants
of the master of the house came and said to him, "Lord,
did you not sow good seed in your field? From what source
28 then comes darnel?" He said to them, "An enemy has
done this". His servants said to him, "Do you wish us,
29 then, to go and gather them?" And he said, "No, lest in
gathering the darnel, you uproot the wheat with them.
30 Let both grow together until the harvest, and at harvest
'time I will say to the reapers, 'Gather first the darnel and
tie them in bundles to burn them, but gather the wheat
into my storehouse'.""

31 Another parable he put before them, saying, 'The Kingdom of Heaven is like a mustard seed which a man took

and sowed in his field; it is smaller than all the seeds, but 32
when it has grown, it is larger than garden vegetable
plants and becomes a tree, so that "the birds of heaven"
come and "nest in its branches"'.

Another parable he spoke to them, 'The Kingdom of 33
Heaven is like leaven, which a woman took and hid in
three measures of wheat flour, until the whole was leavened'.

All these things Jesus spoke to the crowds in parables, 34
and he spoke nothing to them without using a parable,
that the saying might be fulfilled which was spoken 35
through the prophet, who said,

'I will open my mouth in parables,
I will proclaim things hidden from the beginning'.

Then he left the crowds and went into the house. And 36
his disciples came to him, saying, 'Explain to us the parable about the darnel of the field'. He answered and said, 37
'He who sows the good seed is the Son of Man; the field 38
is the world; the good seed—these are the sons of the
Kingdom; the darnel are the sons of the evil one; the 39
enemy who sowed them is the devil; the harvest is the
end of the age; and the reapers are angels. As then 40
the darnel are gathered and consumed by fire, so it will
be at the end of the age. The Son of Man will send forth 41
his angels and they will gather out of his Kingdom all
things that give offence and those who do lawless deeds,
and they will throw them into the fiery furnace; there 42
the weeping and gnashing of teeth will occur. Then the 43
righteous will shine as the sun in the Kingdom of their
Father. He who has ears, let him hear.

'The Kingdom of Heaven is like a treasure hidden in 44
the field, which a man found and hid, and because of his
joy he goes and sells what he owns and buys that field.

'Again, the Kingdom of Heaven is like a merchant look- 45
ing for beautiful pearls. When he found one very valuable 46
pearl he went and sold everything he owned and bought it.

'Again, the Kingdom of Heaven is like a dragnet which 47
was thrown into the sea and enclosed fish of every kind;
when it was full they pulled it up on the beach and sat 48

down and gathered the good ones in containers, but
49 threw out the bad ones. So it will be at the end of the age;
the angels will go forth and separate the wicked from
50 among the righteous, and will throw them into the fiery
furnace; there the weeping and gnashing of teeth will
occur.

51   'Have you understood all these things?' They said to
52 him, 'Yes'. He said to them, 'Therefore every scribe who
has become a disciple of the Kingdom of Heaven is like a
master of a house who takes out of his treasure things new
and old'.

With vss. 1-9 cf. Mk. iv. 1-9; Lk. viii. 4-8. Matt. closely
parallels Mk.; Lk. differs from both and is much shorter. Jesus
goes from **the house** (his home in Capernaum?) to the seaside;
xii. 46, which implies that Jesus was in a house, may be in mind,
though the connection is editorial. To avoid being jostled by **the
crowd,** or to see the people better, Jesus got into **a boat** moored
at the shore; perhaps it was a fishing boat such as Peter and
Andrew and James and John had used in the past.

Jesus taught in **parables.** A parable is an illustration: a proverb (Lk. iv. 23), a comparison (x. 24 f.), or a story from the
realm of nature (xiii. 3-9) or human life (xxv. 1-12). It usually
aims to teach one point, but it may have allegorical traits, as
Jewish stories often had. It was not a new form of illustrating
truth, but Jesus used it with a mastery never surpassed. The
Synoptic Gospels contain about five dozen separate parables; the
Gospel of John has almost none of these; the rest of the N.T.
offers no real parallels. This is fatal to the idea that the early
Church created the parables; no one in the Church even attempted to rival Jesus in this teaching method. He used parables
not only to illustrate and clarify truth but also to capture the
imagination, direct the will, and lead to obedience.

In this parable interest centres not on **the sower** or the **seeds**
but on the varied situation in the soils. The seed sown on **the
road** or path that borders or crosses the field cannot penetrate
the hard ground, trodden down by passers-by; **the birds** eat it;
it produces no harvest. On **rocky places** a shallow layer of soil
covers the ledge of rock; roots cannot go deep and the sun's heat

bakes the moisture out of the shallow ground; the grain plants soon wither and die. Where **thorns** spring up in good, deep soil, their roots take the moisture and nourishment; their rapid growth takes the light and air; the grain plants do poorly and yield no harvest. But in **good,** deep, thorn-free **soil** the grain plants show amazing fruitfulness. **Hear:** Listen, understand, and heed, because this story illustrates important truth.

With vss. 10-17 cf. Mk. iv. 10-12; Lk. viii. 9 f.; x. 23 f. **The disciples,** Matt. assumes, bring their question to Jesus apart from the crowds (Mk. states this); the crowds are still present in vss. 24, 31, 33, 34; Jesus leaves them at vs. 36; all this shows that the evangelist has grouped these parables in one editorial collection. In Mk. and Lk. the disciples ask Jesus to interpret the parables to them; in Matt. the disciples ask **why** he speaks to the crowds in parables (the plural implies that he has spoken more than one), but Jesus goes on, as in Mk. and Lk., to explain the parable to the disciples. Before Jesus answers the question (vs. 13 ff.), he explains how the disciples differ from other hearers: God has given the disciples ability **to understand the mysteries of the Kingdom of Heaven** (which is the subject of the parables and of Jesus' teaching as a whole). To understand the divine purpose and working is beyond man's power; this understanding has not been given to all but only to the disciples; their repentance, faith, and obedience to Jesus are presupposed. Vs. 12 (cf. Mk. iv. 25; Lk. viii. 18) adds that he who has and cherishes the beginning of true understanding and loyalty will be given still clearer insight, while those who lack the basic gift and commitment will lose what they hear but only vaguely understand. Vs. 13 describes the latter type, vs. 16 the former.

In explaining why he speaks to the crowds **in parables,** Jesus uses the ironical passage in Isa. vi. 9 f. (cf. also Jer. v. 21); it lies back of vs. 13 and is quoted from the LXX in vss. 14 f. Though the theme of fulfilment of prophecy is characteristic of 'Matthew', the formula of citation used in vs. 14 and the exact copying of a long quotation from the LXX are unique in Matt. In Isa. God tells the prophet that though the stubborn people will not heed his message, he must preach. In Matt. this passage is taken to predict that the mass of the Jewish people will not understand or receive Jesus' teaching. They **hear,** but do not grasp the truth. Why? Because their **heart,** which in Hebraic manner includes intellectual capacity, **has become dull** (literally, thick, calloused); they are not sensitive or attentive; they hear with difficulty and do not keep alert. Now comes the ironical note; Jesus states that the result of their callousness and indifference (which he tries to overcome by his parable illustrations) is unresponsiveness. With sad irony, Jesus says that they fear they may **see** and **hear** and **understand,** and **turn back,** that is, repent, and receive from God healing, salvation, and blessing. Their guilty callousness leads them to turn away from the very thing they need. **Because** of the immense difficulty of arousing such people to their spiritual need, Jesus uses parables; this way of presenting truth may penetrate the dullness and incomprehension which is leading people to doom. (Mark seems to say that Jesus used parables to conceal truth from the masses; Jesus hardly did that. 'Matthew' is nearer the truth of Jesus' purpose, but the passage is exceedingly difficult. In general, Jesus used parables to illustrate, clarify, and enforce truth and lead men to right decision as they faced his Kingdom teaching.)

In strong contrast to this callousness, the disciples see and hear; **your** stands first in the Greek of vs. 16 (and **You** in vs. 18) to make this contrast emphatic. But Jesus intends another contrast, on which Luke focuses. **Many prophets and righteous men** of former times, living in yearning hope, **desired** in vain **to see** God's promise realized. It should make the disciples grateful and alert to know that they live in dramatic days of powerful fulfilment. The effective reign of God is being established. Cf. 1 Pet. i. 10-12.

With vss. 18-23 cf. Mk. iv. 13-20; Lk. viii. 11-15. Whether Jesus spoke these words is doubtful; he was not accustomed to explain his parables in allegorical detail. Does this parable teach only that in spite of loss of labour and seed the sower still reaps an abundant harvest? No; the varied soils in which the seed falls also have point; if so, the teaching includes the hearer's responsibility; the explanation, if not original with Jesus, catches the meaning. He describes four classes of hearers: (1) The unresponsive hearer. The seed gets no understanding. **The Evil One,** Satan, ever alert to block acceptance of the gospel,

snatches it away; the man loses his opportunity. (2) The shallow hearer. He lacks deep roots. He understands that the message is important; it takes root; but his faith and commitment lack depth and persistence; his promising initial discipleship proves transient. (3) The hearer who lets concern for material things crowd out his loyalty to God. He lets life get cluttered up with material wants and worries; deceived by the apparent importance and worth of wealth, he tries to serve God and Mammon (vi. 24) and lets Mammon crowd God out. (4) The intelligent, fruitful hearer. He **hears, understands,** maintains steady loyalty to God, and yields the **fruit** of worship and obedience. The harvest may vary with the individual disciple. No blame is attached to the lesser harvest (cf. xxv. 20-23). Good soil, cultivated and kept free from damaging distractions, will yield a rich harvest.

The darnel parable, only in Matt., is interpreted in vss. 36-43. The introductory formula, **Another parable he put before them, saying,** is repeated in vs. 31 and in part in vs. 33. The phrase, **The Kingdom of Heaven may be compared to,** gives way to the similar formula, **The Kingdom of Heaven is like,** in vss. 31, 33, 44, 45, and 47 (with **Again** prefixed in vss. 45, 47).

The parable concerns not the soils but the kind of seed sown. The farmer **sowed good seed; his enemy came** later and sowed **darnel** (tares; perhaps *lolium temulentum*), a useless weed which somewhat resembles the wheat plant. **Slept:** Men are not blamed for sleeping; the point is that the enemy acts in secrecy, and the wrong becomes apparent only as the plants grow. **The servants,** when they notice the darnel, ask a natural question; surely the farmer sowed **good seed,** free from seeds of useless plants; how then did the darnel get into the field? (This implies that the field had been well cared for; the darnel cannot have come from previous crops; but nothing is made of this.) The farmer knows that this can only come from an enemy's work. The servants offer to gather the darnel plants so that only the good wheat plants will remain; **gather,** vs. 29 shows, means pull up.

But pulling up the darnel plants will uproot the wheat plants also, for their roots are intertwined with the darnel roots. The only practical thing is to **let both grow together until the**

harvest, and then, in cutting the grain, separate the darnel plants, with their heads of seeds, into bundles which can be burned (cf. iii. 12). This will destroy the darnel so that its seeds cannot damage the next crop planted in that field. The wheat can then be threshed and the grain stored safely in the **store-house** or barn. See vss. 36-43 for an interpretation.

With vss. 31-33 cf. Mk. iv. 30-32; Lk. xiii. 18-21. Mk. has only the mustard seed parable; Lk. has both parables, as does Matt., and in their source Q these two parables may have been a unit, twin parables with double emphasis on one basic point.

In ancient Judaism the **mustard seed** was proverbially, as here, the smallest seed, which produces a remarkably large plant; it becomes so large and sturdy that it may be called **a tree.** Some interpret **the birds** nesting in its branches as a reference to the coming of Gentiles into the Church, but this feature probably shows only how large and sturdy a growth results from so small a seed. The closing words of vs. 32 recall Dan. iv. 21; Nebuchadnezzar in his dream sees a tree which reaches to heaven and is visible to the end of the earth; this emphasizes the size of the tree, and in the parable indicates immense growth from small beginnings. The Kingdom of Heaven has begun to come in Jesus' ministry (xii. 28); it will grow and in full form attain amazing dimensions.

The second parable speaks of the permeation of a large mass of dough by a small amount of **leaven.** Does the point vary in the two parables, the former stressing visible outward growth, the latter, inner permeation? Probably both parables make one point, the great development from small beginnings. **Leaven:** Regularly in the Bible means an evil penetrating force, but here refers in a good sense to the spread of the Kingdom. The size of the baking is amazing; the **measure** contains about a peck and a half; **three measures,** leavened, would make a very large baking. Yet a little leaven penetrates so large a mass of dough. Gen. xviii. 6 and 1 Sam. i. 24 (an ephah contained three measures) show that three measures was a traditionally large baking. The Kingdom, now small, will spread and permeate the world. The parables do not mean that all men will accept the gospel, but the Kingdom will show an amazing growth from modest beginnings.

With vss. 34-35 cf. Mk. iv. 33 f., which makes no reference to fulfilment of prophecy. **All these things:** In vss. 3-33. Much of Jesus' teaching is direct and plain statement; that he always spoke to the crowds only in parables is not true, but perhaps he did on a special occasion. The use of two concluding formulas in this discourse (vss. 34 f., 51 f.) shows that this parable collection grew by stages; it is a literary device to group parables on the Kingdom.

The quotation does not name **the prophet.** Some manuscripts insert wrongly the name of Isaiah; the quotation is from Ps. lxxviii. 2. Others insert the name of Asaph, whom the Psalm heading names as author. 1 Chron. xxv. 2 calls him a prophet. 'Matthew' need not have thought of 1 Chron. xxv. 2; any O.T. passage which pointed forward to Jesus was a prophecy. The Psalmist is commenting on God's past dealings with Israel; in Matt. the word parable becomes a prophecy of Jesus' teaching method; the **things hidden from the beginning** of the world are the truth Jesus now proclaims about the Kingdom.

Vss. 36-43 give a detailed allegorical interpretation of vss. 24-30; it may well be, at least in this form, a later creation of the Church. However, the parable calls for some such interpretation, and allegorical features appear in vss. 18-22, 49 f.; xxi. 33-46, and other parables. That Jesus included more or less of allegorical detail in parables may be freely conceded, although the Church later tended to sharpen up details and apply them to its life.

Into the house: Cf. vs. 10. Indoors, his disciples could talk to him privately. **The field is the world:** Contrast x. 5 f.; xv. 24. Jesus here identifies the preaching and teaching commanded in xxviii. 18-20 as the extension of his own preaching. Curiously, he identifies the **good seed** with the people who accept it, and the **darnel** with those who accept the devil's teaching. The **harvest,** the final judgment, is carried out by **angels** (cf. vs. 49) at the command of **the Son of Man,** whose role at the judgment is decisive. All evil conditions that hinder good living, and all lawless persons (cf. Zeph. i. 3), will be removed from the Kingdom. **Fiery furnace** (cf. Rev. xx. 14): A figurative description of the terrible ruin which awaits the wicked. **Weeping and gnashing of teeth** indicate their continued existence and miserable lot. In the final **Kingdom,** unmarred by the presence and active hostility of the wicked, the loyal **righteous** will reflect the light of God **their Father.**

The final words warn hearers to **hear** and heed this teaching and not be confused by the present ambiguous situation, in which evil appears strong and often seems likely to triumph.

The parables in vss. 44-46 both teach that **the Kingdom of Heaven** is worth more than every alternative life offers. It is wisdom to surrender everything else to obtain the joy and privilege of sharing in the Kingdom. Some note that one man found the hidden **treasure** by chance, while the other was definitely seeking valuable **pearls;** they take Jesus to mean that one may either stumble onto the Kingdom or find it by a deliberate spiritual quest. This distinction probably is artificial; the two parables emphasize one truth, that in view of the Kingdom's supreme value it is profitable to give up whatever conflicts with complete and single-minded loyalty to Jesus and the cause of the Kingdom.

In ancient times safe places to deposit money or valuables were hard to find. Many thought it wisest to bury their treasure in a field. In the parable **a man** found such a treasure, buried **in the field** by someone other than the present owner, who did not suspect its presence. The finder could obtain legal title to the treasure by buying the field. The parable does not discuss whether the buyer was morally obligated to tell the owner of the field that it contained a treasure. Jesus tells how men would act to get material treasures; he uses the story to illustrate the supreme worth of the Kingdom.

In the second parable the **merchant** makes it his business to look for the best **pearls.** He finds available one beautiful pearl of immense value. To get funds to buy it he has to sell everything he owns. The parable does not imply that one can buy the Kingdom or earn it. It teaches that the Kingdom is of such enormous worth that giving up everything else to gain admittance to it is well worth while.

Vss. 47-50 teach that some people outwardly connected with the Kingdom will be found unworthy at the judgment and be rejected. This idea, found in the parables of the soils (vss. 3-9) and the darnel (vss. 24-30), recurs in xxii. 11-13. It seems incongruous for unworthy people to have even a temporary place in the Kingdom. But Judas was one of the Twelve until the Last Supper.

The **dragnet** was familiar to hearers near the Sea of Galilee. Thrown into the sea and then pulled to the shore, it enclosed any fish caught between the net and the shore. Many fish were edible, but some were not. The fishermen (**they** in vs. 48) picked out and kept the **good ones;** the rest they threw away.

The interpretation begins in words which echo vs. 40b, and closes with words found in vs. 42. If the interpretation, similar in teaching to vss. 36-43, is entirely secondary, and not from Jesus, the same may be true of the parable itself, for the interpretation corresponds to the parable content. But if Jesus thought of the Kingdom as beginning in his work and recognized that, as Judas illustrates, a neat immediate separation of the worthy from the unworthy was not possible, he could have spoken what these parables assert. 'Matthew' certainly held that **at the end of the age** not only the obviously evil but also the pretenders to goodness will be identified for what they really are and given their eternal place in keeping with their own decision. Their close touch with the servants and outward life of the Kingdom will only make their guilt the more heinous and their condemnation the more certain.

All these things (vs. 51) refers to the parables editorially grouped in vss. 3-50. But the origin of these words may have been some occasion when Jesus commented more generally on the results of his teaching in the understanding and equipment of his disciples. In Matt. they have heard the entire series of seven parables and the explanations of three, and are the only hearers from vs. 36 on. Have they understood his teaching? Their answer, **Yes,** implies that they can understand at least some parables without specific interpretation. This leads Jesus to describe the true and well informed disciple as a **scribe** (for favourable uses of **scribe** see viii. 19; xxiii. 34), who knows and passes on the message of the Scriptures as his Master has interpreted them. By this training this scribe has become instructed in and dedicated to the **Kingdom of Heaven.** So he now, like a householder, has a store of **things new and old;** he knows his heritage in Israel and has the new understanding of it which

Jesus has given in his Kingdom teaching. His duty, it is implied, is to hand on both aspects of truth.

xiii. 53-58. JESUS REJECTED AT NAZARETH

53 And it happened that when Jesus had finished these par-
54 ables, he departed from there, and came to his home town and taught them in their synagogue so that they were astounded and said, 'From what source does this
55 man get this wisdom and these miracles? Is not this the carpenter's son? Is not his mother named Mary and his
56 brothers James and Joseph and Simon and Judas? And are not all of his sisters here with us? From what source then
57 does this man get all these things? And they took offence at him. But Jesus said to them, 'A prophet does not lack
58 honour except in his home town and in his home'. And he did not perform many mighty works there, on account of their unbelief.

Cf. Mk. vi. 1-6, rather closely parallel, and Lk. iv. 16-30, placed much earlier and considerably different in content. In Matt. the incident follows the parable discourse, which as one of five great discourses has the formal ending (vs. 53) found also in vii. 28 f.; xi. 1; xix. 1; xxvi. 1. Jesus **departed from there,** probably Capernaum, and **came to his home town** Nazareth. (πατρίς means fatherland or ancestral home.) There he **taught** (the imperfect tense ἐδίδασκεν suggests more than one occasion) **in their synagogue,** where any Jewish man might speak when invited. The people are **astounded** at both his wise teaching and his mighty works (done in Nazareth? or elsewhere?). They admit his wisdom and power, but are amazed at such abilities in a son of an ordinary good home in their own small town. A great man, it seems, should come from a distance or from a prominent family! Jesus is just a **carpenter's son;** from the way the mother and brothers are named, it seems that Joseph was already dead. Presumably the four brothers are named in order of age, beginning with the oldest. xii. 46-50 shows that they did not at this time sympathize with Jesus in his work. The word **all** implies that the number of sisters was more than two.

Three views are held as to the relation of these **brothers** to Jesus and Mary: (1) The Helvidian view: children of Joseph and Mary, born after Jesus was (cf. i. 25; Lk. ii. 7). (2) The Epiphanian view: children of Joseph by a former marriage, and so older than Jesus. (3) The Hieronymian view (after Jerome; Latin, Hieronymus): children of a sister of Mary, and so cousins of Jesus. The first view seems the natural meaning of the N.T. The other two views avoid the idea that Mary had other children besides Jesus. These brothers did not believe in Jesus during his ministry (xii. 46-50; Jn. vii. 5), but early became active leaders in the Church (Acts i. 14) and carried on some travelling ministry (1 Cor. ix. 5); James, the most prominent, became the resident leader at Jerusalem (Acts xii. 17; xv. 13; xxi. 18). James and Judas and even Simon were later identified as members of the Twelve, and James and Judas (Jude) were reported to have written epistles which later became canonical.

Jesus replied to the sceptics, who could not see that his wisdom and power came from God, with a proverbial saying. In it he accepts the title of **prophet,** given him by others. The one place a prophet fails to win a response is **in his home town and in his home;** the latter phrase proves that his brothers were not then supporting his mission. It takes a special spiritual openness and gift to see the divine mission of those known to us in their early years and humble human origin. In Matt. Jesus could not do **many mighty works** in Nazareth (Mk. says none). The lack of faith he encountered shut the door to blessings his needy townsmen might have received.

CHAPTER XIV

xiv. 1-12. HEROD KILLS JOHN THE BAPTIST

At that time Herod the tetrarch heard of the fame of 1 Jesus, and said to his attendants, 'This is John the 2 Baptist; he has risen from the dead, and therefore

these powers are at work in him'.

3 For Herod had seized and bound John and put him in
prison because of Herodias the wife of Philip his brother,
4 for John said to him, 'It is not permissible for you to have
5 her'. And although he wanted to kill him he feared the
6 people, because they regarded him as a prophet. But when
Herod's birthday celebration occurred, the daughter of
7 Herodias danced in the midst and pleased Herod; therefore he promised with an oath to give her whatever she
8 asked. Urged on by her mother, she said, 'Give me here
9 on a platter the head of John the Baptist'. And the king,
though distressed, because of his oaths and his dinner
10 guests commanded it to be given, and he sent and be-
11 headed John in the prison. And his head was brought
upon a platter and given to the girl, and she carried it to
12 her mother. And his disciples came and carried away the
body and buried him, and they went and told Jesus.

With vss. 1 f. cf. Mk. vi. 14-16; Lk. ix. 7-9. In Matt. this connects closely with Jesus' visit to Nazareth, in Mk. and Lk. with
the preaching and healings of the Twelve. xiv. 1 correctly calls
Herod Antipas tetrarch (of Galilee and Perea); vs. 9 and Mk.
6:14-29 use the popular (incorrect) title king.

While Herod is surrounded by attendants or courtiers (παισίν
could mean slaves or menial servants, but probably, as in ancient
oriental thought, refers to members of his court), some visitors
or informants brought word of the wide **fame of Jesus.** Herod
identifies Jesus as **John the Baptist . . . risen from the dead.**
This suggests that the ministries of John and Jesus did not overlap; Herod could hardly have identified the two if they had
worked publicly at the same time. What made him identify the
two? Vs. 2 indicates that it was the mighty works of Jesus. Yet
John made his impression as a prophetic teacher; as Jn. x. 41
says, and with this all N.T. evidence agrees, 'John did no sign'.
It is odd that Jesus reminded Herod of John by doing something
John did not do. It has been said that John, once risen from the
dead, would have added power and could perform miracles; but
was there no more specific reason for saying that Jesus must be
John? At the least the likeness in prophetic message must have

aided the guilty, superstitious Herod to identify the two; given that common bond, the miracles could have seemed to Herod an ominous added power given to the risen John. (The passage attests the current belief in resurrection.)

With vss. 3-12 cf. Mk. vi. 17-29, skilfully abbreviated in Matt. Vs. 13 suggests that John's execution occurred shortly before Herod heard about Jesus, of whom he heard while his guilt for executing John was still fresh in his mind.

Josephus reports that Herod imprisoned John because he feared John might arouse the Jews to political revolt (*Antiquities*, xviii. 5. 2). In Matt. and Mk. the arrest is ascribed to more personal reasons. **Herod** Antipas, son of Herod the Great, had left his wife, daughter of Aretas, to marry **Herodias**, granddaughter of Herod the Great and wife of Herod Antipas' half-brother, called Herod by Josephus but **Philip** in Matt. and Mk. Was his full name Herod Philip or is this Herod confused with Philip the tetrarch (Lk. iii. 1) in Matt. and Mk.? To **John the Baptist** it was doubly immoral for Herod Antipas to leave his wife to take the wife of another man, and he denounced the tetrarch. In Matt. (not in Mk.) Herod promptly desires to **kill** John. But throughout the story Herod acts in fear and cowardice; he fears John; he fears the Jews who approve John's preaching; he fears to break an unholy oath; he fears to seem weak before his guests; he fears Herodias, whose merciless scheming and hatred are apparent. Probably his hatred of John was prompted and bolstered by the purposeful Herodias. The immense popularity of John is reflected (cf. xxi. 26); to the people he was **a prophet,** sent of God to speak to ruler and ruled alike. Herodias achieved what Herod was too weak to do; the no doubt immodest and provocative dance of her **daughter** (Salome) before the drunken Herod and his guests was part of her plan. It achieved its intended aim; with no trace of feminine gentleness, Salome demanded that John be beheaded and the head delivered to her **on a platter, here,** at once. Herod complied. Where did this happen? Matt. does not tell; Josephus says, at the fortress Machaerus, east of the Dead Sea, an unlikely place for Herodias and Salome to be.

But Herod's memory could not get rid of John; when he heard of Jesus he sensed that Jesus was continuing the work of

John. The reader realizes that the hope of Israel is not in the Herods, or in Rome which approves their rule, but in the prophetic voice now heard in Jesus.

John's loyal **disciples** by courageous request received and **buried** the **body**. Only in Matt. do they then report to Jesus. This indicates that the prophetic mantle and central leadership now belong clearly to Jesus.

xiv. 13-36. JESUS' POWER OVER NATURE

13 When Jesus heard it, he departed privately from there in a boat to a desolate place; and the crowds heard of it and

14 followed him on foot from the cities. And when he disembarked, he saw a large crowd, and he felt sympathy for them and healed their sick.

15 When evening came, the disciples came to him, saying, 'The place is desolate and the hour has already passed; dismiss the crowds, therefore, that they may depart to the

16 villages and buy food for themselves'. But Jesus said to them, 'They need not depart; you give them something

17 to eat'. They said to him, 'We have nothing here except

18 five loaves and two fish'. And he said, 'Bring them here

19 to me'. And after commanding the crowds to recline on the grass, he took the five loaves and the two fish, and looking up to heaven he blessed them, and broke the loaves and gave them to the disciples, and the disciples to the

20 crowds. And they all ate and were filled; and they took up

21 what was left over in fragments, twelve baskets full. Now those who ate were about five thousand men, besides women and children.

22 And at once he compelled the disciples to embark in the boat and precede him to the other side, while he dis-

23 missed the crowds. And when he had dismissed the crowds, he went up into the hill country by himself to pray.

24 When evening came, he was there alone. But the boat was already many stades distant from the land, harassed by

25 the waves, for the wind was against it. In the fourth watch

26 of the night he came to them, walking on the sea. When

the disciples saw him walking on the sea they were terri-
fied, saying, 'It is a ghost', and they cried out for fear. But 27
Jesus at once spoke to them, saying, 'Courage! It is I. Do
not be afraid.' Peter answered him and said, 'Lord, if it 28
is you, command me to come to you on the water'. He 29
said, 'Come'. And Peter stepped down from the boat and
walked on the water and came toward Jesus. But as he 30
saw the wind he became frightened, and he began to sink
and cried out, saying, 'Lord, save me'. At once Jesus 31
stretched out his hand and took hold of him, and said to
him, 'You feeble believer, why did you doubt?' And when 32
they stepped up into the boat, the wind ceased. Then those 33
in the boat worshipped him, saying, 'You are in truth
God's Son'.

And when they had crossed over, they came to land at 34
Gennesaret. And when the men of that place recognized 35
him, they sent out into all the surrounding region and
brought to him all who were sick, and they implored him 36
that they might touch just the tassel of his garment; and
as many as touched it were cured.

With vss. 13-21 cf. Mk. vi. 30-44; Lk. ix. 10-17; Jn. vi. 1-13.
Note also the feeding of the four thousand in Matt. xv. 32-39;
Mk. viii. 1-10. In the O.T. cf. 2 Kings iv. 42-44 (and Ruth ii.
14). Jesus is near the Sea of Galilee, perhaps at Capernaum.
(The last place mentioned in Matt. was Nazareth; xiii. 54.)
Jesus left the territory of Herod Antipas, who had just executed
John the Baptist, and landed on the north-east shore, governed
by the tetrarch Philip; his aim seems to be to avoid for the
time being a public clash with Herod. But his attempt to withdraw unnoticed failed; his departure was noted, his destination
foreseen, and people streamed eastward across the Jordan to
meet him **when he disembarked.** In compassion he **healed
their sick.** No doubt he also taught them, as Mark and Luke
say.

The disciples' suggestion that Jesus **dismiss the crowds**
seems reasonable. The people had no food; it was past time for
supper; villages were near where food could be bought. Jesus
denies that this plan is necessary; the disciples have resources

to meet the need. They protest that they have only **five loaves** of bread and **two fish**. His reply, **Bring them here to me**, implies that if what they have is freely given to him he can use it to meet the need. **Recline:** As for a feast; reclining was the position at table for feasts. **Grass:** Suggests a time in spring, before early summer drouth withers the green vegetation. The occasion reminded 'Matthew' of the Last Supper and the later Lord's Supper, and was a foretaste of the Messianic banquet which Jews expected to share in the coming Kingdom. **Looking up to heaven:** The wonderful gift, like all good gifts, comes from the Father. **Blessed:** He gives thanks to the Father, praises him for his goodness, and asks him to use the meagre supply to feed the many hungry persons. **Broke the loaves:** A sign of table fellowship and of adequate provision for all (cf. also xxvi. 26). How the five loaves (and the two fish, which are not mentioned further) became enough to feed thousands is not explained; no question is felt about God's ability to meet the total need. The gathering of the **fragments** emphasizes not frugality but the fact, adequacy, and immensity of the miracle. This latter point is underlined by giving the number fed; the number is larger in Matt.; besides **five thousand men,** a large but uncounted number of **women and children** were fed.

No doubt this story meant to 'Matthew' that spiritual food and strength, given through Jesus' filial link with the Father, made effective through his death, and available in the Lord's Supper, is fully adequate for the needs of those who trust in him. But it meant more. The story, found in all four Gospels and plainly part of the original gospel tradition, was not merely a parable of spiritual truth; it intended to tell of an astounding increase of food supply. The miraculous element is not played up but assumed, as though the fact could not be denied. The problem arises for the modern Christian; such things do not happen today. To those who believe in the living God and his active Lordship, possibilities of unusual events may be recognized. Even so, the Christian may reserve judgment here. The centre of the gospel is not in amazing miracles but in suffering love by which Jesus Christ makes effective God's righteousness and love. Not to amaze people, but possibly to help people in physical need and to give them an acted parable of the sufficiency of God's provision in Christ for their need, Jesus could have done such an act.

With vss. 22-33 cf. Mk. vi. 45-52; Jn. vi. 15-21. All three accounts follow immediately the feeding miracle, but the narrative in Jn. differs in many details.

Compelled, a strong word, suggests that **the disciples** did not want to go. Jesus wanted to remove them from the popular enthusiasm the miracle had roused. Whatever we think of Jn. vi. 15 (the people wanted to make Jesus king), the atmosphere focused attention on the miraculous and in so far as the feeding miracle pointed to the Messianic banquet and Kingdom, it could stir thoughts of political freedom and external glory, things hostile rather than integral to Jesus' purpose. **The other side** (cf. vs. 34): The western or north-western side of the Sea of Galilee; the feeding had occurred on the north-east shore. Jesus was conscious of a critical situation; here, as at Gethsemane, he went apart for prayer; only on these two occasions is he said to pray in Matt. and Mk.; he wanted to keep his purpose clear and guide his disciples and the crowds aright. There are no real mountains near the north-eastern shore of the lake; Jesus went up into the **hill country** (ὄρος), higher land away from the shore. **When evening came:** The same clause used in vs. 15; 'Matthew' crowds the feeding and dismissal of the people into an unnaturally brief time.

The disciples, sailing westward against a stiff (north-west?) wind, are not in Matt. close to the northern shore, but **many stades** from land (stade: about 600 feet). As they see Jesus **walking on the sea,** they think him **a ghost;** no human could be walking on the water so far from shore. They take fright at their one true source of courage and confidence. Jesus challenges them to take heart and banish their fear; **It is I,** a statement vague in itself, occurs only in the Gospels in the N.T., and implies that the speaker has authority and embodies God's power and claim. Jesus brings the answer to their need if only they perceive and believe that in him God is at work to save them.

Only Matt. tells how **Peter** unsuccessfully attempts to walk **on the water.** This has been understood as an acted parable of Peter's career: pride, fall, rescue, and restoration. But it is told as actual event. Peter, still not certain that he sees his Lord, but reassured by Jesus' word of command, starts bravely forth, actually walks on the water, but then, his first confidence challenged by the wind and waves, begins to sink, and calls despairingly for help. Jesus can reach out and save him; he lost his courage just when he had almost reached his Lord safely. Safe now, he hears his rebuke: **feeble believer;** he need not have yielded to dismay and doubt. Upheld by Jesus, he safely reaches the boat.

Three miracles occur: Jesus walks on the water; so does Peter, temporarily; the wind ceases (this to 'Matthew' is no chance event). Jesus' coming to his disciples brings outward calm; it also brings inward calm and a deeper faith. No mere man could work these wonders. The disciples worship Jesus, confessing their grateful insight that he is in actual fact the **Son** of God. With him as their Lord they may have faith, courage, and strength to meet the storms of life.

It may seem startling to find so full and explicit a confession of faith so early in Matt. In xvi. 17 Peter is praised for his fresh and crucial insight that Jesus is 'the Christ, the Son of the living God'. But for 'Matthew' Jesus has been the Son of God from childhood (ii. 15); he has known it at least since his baptism (iii. 17; iv. 3, 6); the demons know it (viii. 29); and Jesus has spoken of it to his disciples (xi. 27). We must protect the real advance in discernment that came at Caesarea Philippi (xvi. 16), and recognize that 'Matthew' anticipates at times insight that took full form more slowly, but we must not think that before xvi. 16 the disciples regarded Jesus as only another good man. They were groping for a title and understanding adequate to express the unique authority and power which they saw active in Jesus. These miracle stories have grown in the telling, but they are nearer the truth than a gospel narrative stripped of miracles and high faith.

With vss. 34-36 cf. Mk. vi. 53-56; note also iv. 24; viii. 16; ix. 35. **Gennesaret:** A fertile plain, thickly populated, just south-west of Capernaum. **Surrounding region:** Probably means not all Galilee but the region of Gennesaret. **Tassel:** Worn by Jews on the edge of their outer garment; cf. ix. 20. Touching it may have had a superstitious aspect, but it gave a sense of contact with the healer. Jesus himself is said to touch

the sick or even use saliva (Mk. vii. 33; viii. 23; Jn. ix. 6). These
acts symbolized and promised healing, and made vivid the
healer's active sympathetic outreach. Note the stress on the completeness of Jesus' ministry: **all** the vicinity; **all** the sick; **as
many as touched.** For 'Matthew' these healings brought the
power of the dawning Kingdom to Gennesaret.

CHAPTER XV

xv. 1-20. WHAT REALLY DEFILES HUMAN LIFE

**Then Pharisees and scribes came to Jesus from Jerusa-
lem, saying, 'Why do your disciples transgress the** 1
tradition of the elders? For they do not wash their hands 2
**when they eat bread.' He answered and said to them,
'Why do you yourselves transgress the commandment** 3
**of God for the sake of your tradition? For God said,
"Honour your father and mother", and "Let him who** 4
**speaks evil of father or mother die without fail". But you
say, "Whoever says to his father or mother, 'The thing** 5
**by which you might have received help from me is a
gift', shall not honour his father or his mother." And you
have made the word of God void for the sake of your** 6
**tradition. Hypocrites, well did Isaiah prophesy concern-
ing you, saying,** 7
　　**"This people honours me with their lips,
　　　　but their heart is far distant from me;** 8
　　**In vain do they worship me,
　　　　teaching what are merely human command-** 9
　　　　ments".'
**And he summoned the crowd and said to them, 'Hear
and understand. It is not what enters the mouth that de-** 10
files a man, but what goes out of the mouth, this defiles 11
a man.'
Then the disciples came and said to him, 'Do you know 12
that the Pharisees, when they heard what you said, were

13 offended?, He answered and said, 'Every plant which my
   heavenly Father has not planted will be pulled up by the
14 roots. Leave them alone; they are blind guides of the
   blind; if a blind man guides a blind man, both will fall
   into a pit.'
15 Peter answered and said to him, 'Explain the parable
16 to us'. He said, 'Are you also still without understanding?
17 Do you not understand that everything which enters the
   mouth goes into the digestive system and is evacuated in
18 the latrine? But what goes out of the mouth comes from
19 the heart, and those things defile a man. For out of the
   heart come evil thoughts and acts of murder, adultery,
20 fornication, theft, false witness, and slander. These are
   the things that defile a man; but to eat with unwashed
   hands does not defile a man.'

Cf. Mk. vii. 1-23. The coming of opponents to challenge
Jesus is followed by a withdrawal (vs. 21), a challenge by
Pharisees and Sadducees (xvi. 1), a withdrawal to the region of
Caesarea Philippi (xvi. 13), and other signs that the Galilean
ministry is nearing its end. The dispute over Jewish oral tradition and food laws did not interest Luke or his Gentile readers,
but for Jewish Christians it was a burning issue. **From Jerusalem:** Indicates the widespread knowledge of Jesus. **Pharisees and scribes:** Jewish leaders especially active in the synagogues and in teaching the common people. Most scribes were
Pharisees, who had developed and cherished the oral **tradition.**
The Sadducees did not recognize its validity, but to Pharisees
it was an integral part of the Law of God, equally authoritative
with the written Mosaic Law. The specific criticism here, that
the disciples did not practise the prescribed washing of the
hands before eating, rested on such an oral tradition, binding
for the Pharisees, but not required in the O.T.

Jesus boldly denies the validity of such oral traditions because
they actually annul the Law of God contained in Scripture.
God said (sharpens up Mark's 'Moses said'): Ex. xx. 12; xxi.
17; Lev. xx. 9; Deut. v. 16. **But you say:** The oral tradition lets
heartless, ungrateful children avoid fulfilling God's command
that they should honour (this includes giving financial support

to) their parents. The tradition let a man dedicate part of his property to God as **a gift**, 'earmarked' for God; the 'giver' still possessed and could use it, and could piously refuse to give any of it to support his parents. Many rabbis, like Jesus, denounced this evasion of filial duty; but their discussion shows that the subterfuge was then current though not unchallenged. To Jesus, legalizing by oral tradition this evasion of filial duty nullifies the explicit will of God expressed in the Pentateuch, which Jesus accepts as Scripture. The oral tradition must be rejected.

Hypocrites: Does not mean that they consciously set out to nullify the Law of God, but their concern for traditions and outward forms leads them to a way of life which belies their expressed concern to do God's will and obscures God's demand for human kindness and family love. With irony Jesus applies to them Isa. xxix. 13. This rebuke to people of Isaiah's day fits perfectly Jesus' opponents. In **heart** they are quite remote from loyalty and devotion to God; their man-made teaching lacks divine sanction. This entire passage shows how far apart Jesus and the Pharisees really were. It is sometimes said that he agreed with them in all essentials. In many points he sided with them against the Sadducees. But he rejected their oral tradition and their legalistic formalism. The gulf between them was deep. Wherever in the Church tradition and forms gain ascendancy over the Scripture, the Pharisee position has won control.

To the surrounding crowd, whom he urges not to be dull-minded (cf. xiii. 14), Jesus speaks a **parable** (vs. 15), an enigmatic saying, paradoxical in form, challenging the hearer to look for the real meaning behind the puzzling words. How could something coming from within **defile** (literally, make common, and so ceremonially unclean) a person, while nothing (even pork?!) taken into the mouth could defile him? Vs. 15 suggests the perplexity of the disciples.

The disciples are worried at the hostile reaction of the Pharisees to Jesus' teaching about oral tradition. **What you said**: Probably refers not to vs. 11 but to vss. 3-9. Jesus warns the disciples not to follow, even unconsciously, the leadership of the Pharisees; they are **blind** leaders who cannot guide their own lives aright. If blind people, who do not see that the oral tradition nullifies God's will, follow the blind Pharisees, only disaster can befall both leaders and led. **The pit:** An O.T. expression for spiritual catastrophe. Judgment will fall upon the Pharisees and all who follow them (xxi. 43).

Jesus explains the **parable** of vs. 11. **Peter** speaks for the group; Jesus replies to the group of disciples (**you** is plural). He grieves that they, like the crowds (cf. **also), still** do **not understand.** Food eaten and digested cannot defile. This statement is astounding. Jesus has defended the Mosaic Law against a nullifying oral tradition; now, as Mk. vii. 19 notes, he undermines the validity of the Pentateuchal system of food laws. His reading of Scripture finds no binding validity in ceremonial rules and ritual purity. He is concerned with what comes from **the mouth** and **the heart.** An evil heart, a corrupt tree, an evil inner treasure (xii. 33-35) will produce evil words and deeds, of which Jesus names seven (the last word may mean blasphemy, but probably means here **slander** of one's fellow-man). Cf. Prov. iv. 23: 'Keep your heart with all vigilance, for from it flow the springs of life'. This corruption of the whole life by an evil mind, will, and imagination **defiles a man,** makes him thoroughly unclean and unacceptable to God.

xv. 21-39. JESUS HEALS AND FEEDS THE NEEDY

21 **And Jesus left that place and departed to the region of**
22 **Tyre and Sidon. And behold, a Canaanite woman came out from that district and called out repeatedly, saying, 'Have mercy on me, Lord, Son of David. My daughter is**
23 **completely possessed by a demon.' But he answered her not a word. And the disciples came to him and kept requesting him, saying, 'Dismiss her, for she keeps calling**
24 **out after us'. But he answered and said, 'I was not sent**
25 **except to the lost sheep of the house of Israel'. But she came and fell reverently before him, saying, 'Lord, help**
26 **me'. He answered and said, 'It is not good to take the**
27 **children's bread and toss it to the puppies'. She said, 'Yes, Lord; for even the puppies eat of the crumbs that fall**
28 **from their masters' table'. Then Jesus answered and said, 'O woman, great is your faith. Let it be done for you as**

you wish.' And her daughter was healed from that hour.

And Jesus departed from there and came to the shore 29 of the Sea of Galilee, and he went up into the hill country and sat there. And there came to him large crowds who 30 had with them lame, crippled, blind, and dumb people and many others, and they placed them at his feet; and he healed them, so that the crowd marvelled, for they 31 saw the dumb speaking, the crippled made sound, and the lame walking, and the blind seeing; and they praised the God of Israel.

And Jesus summoned his disciples and said, 'I feel 32 compassion for the crowd, because they have already stayed three days with me and have nothing to eat; and I am unwilling to dismiss them hungry, for fear that they may collapse on the way'. And the disciples said to him, 33 'Where can we, in an uninhabited place, get loaves enough to feed so large a crowd?' And Jesus said to them, 34 'How many loaves have you?' They said, 'Seven, and a few small fish'. And when he had directed the crowd to 35 recline on the ground, he took the seven loaves and the 36 fish, and after giving thanks he broke them and gave them to the disciples, and the disciples to the crowds. And they all ate and were satisfied, and they took up what 37 was left over in fragments, seven baskets full. Now those 38 who ate were four thousand men, besides women and children. And he dismissed the crowds, embarked in the 39 boat, and came to the district of Magadan.

With vss. 21-28 cf. Mk. vii. 24-30, parallel in essentials, but parallel in wording only at Matt. xv. 26 f. In Matt. Jesus goes north-westward from Gennesaret (xiv. 34) to Phoenicia, whose chief cities are **Tyre and Sidon.** But the woman **came out from that district** to appeal to Jesus; this places the incident (in Matt.) on the eastern borders of Phoenicia. **Canaanite:** Since Canaan, originally used of Palestine, could include Phoenicia, the term could describe a Phoenician woman not a Jewess. She followed Jesus and the disciples (vs. 23) and kept **calling out** (imperfect tense: ἔκραζεν) for help. She knew of Jesus' healing power and Davidic descent and addressed him with reverent respect **(Lord)**. What physical ailment or mental trouble her demon-possessed daughter suffered is not said. Vss. 23 f. are in Matt. only. Do the disciples ask Jesus to send her away without help, or to do what she asks and then send her home? Their words seem to favour the former view, but Jesus seems to imply that he has been asked to help her and get it over with, for he objects that he has been **sent** not to Phoenician non-Jews, but only **to the lost sheep** (cf. xviii. 12-14) among the Jews. The trip to Phoenicia seems a time of withdrawal with his disciples, and he has no commission from the Father to open a ministry among Gentiles. Cf. x. 6. Both these sayings occur only in Matt., but in all four Gospels Jesus systematically confines his ministry to Jews; he only rarely responds to a Gentile plea for help, and then heals, as here, at a distance. God's chosen people must first hear and respond to his message, and become God's instruments in whatever wider work God has for them.

Still persistent (imperfect tense: προσεκύνει), the woman repeats her plea; the title **Lord** implies that he can **help** her if he wishes. His blunt answer is not a literal statement, calling her and her countrymen dogs, but a parable or proverbial statement used to make clear that his work is with his own people. Its effect would depend much on the speaker's tone and facial expression. The woman senses that his word is not final, and she is quick to show him that he can help her without giving up his concentrated mission to fellow-Jews. Jesus cannot resist her great **faith** and persistent love; he praises her faith and assures her that her daughter will be healed. The story is more a lesson in faith than a miracle story, but it closes with the briefest possible statement that the daughter was **healed** at once.

With vss. 29-31 cf. Mk. vii. 31-37, which tells of but one healing (a deaf mute). Jesus returns from the borders of Phoenicia; strangely, no event near **the Sea of Galilee** is reported; Jesus goes up into the mountain or **hill country,** which in Matt. is a special place of divine revelation. **Sat there:** We might expect to hear of teaching; the Jewish teacher sat down to teach. The bringing of numerous sick people shows faith, to which Jesus responds with healing power, thus fulfilling the promises of **the God of Israel** (Isa. xxxv. 5 f.).

With vss. 32-39 cf. Mk. viii. 1-10, and also the feeding of more than five thousand, Matt. xiv. 13-21 and parallels. Are the two feeding stories variant accounts of the same event? They have important points in common: the **uninhabited place**; lack of food, except a few **loaves** and **fish**; **the crowd** reclining to eat; the thanks and breaking of bread, anticipating the Last Supper, the early Lord's Supper, and the future Messianic banquet; the food left over; the crossing of the lake. But the two accounts differ: Jesus here takes the initiative, and the numbers all differ. The strongest argument that this second narrative is a variant of the former is the question in vs. 33; after seeing Jesus feed more than five thousand with five loaves and two fish, the disciples might well say: You fed more than five thousand on less food than we have now; you surely can feed this smaller crowd.

Jesus' guiding motive is stated: sympathy. The place is not near a city (vs. 33); the people are far from home; without food they might **collapse on the way.** The story emphasizes again that through Christ God can provide abundantly for his people; such powerful provision manifests the beginning of the Kingdom and promises its full coming.

Vs. 39 does not state but implies that the disciples accompanied Jesus. **The boat:** Probably one that he and his disciples regularly used. Apparently the (north-east shore of the) lake was near the scene of the feeding. **Magadan:** Unknown, as is Dalmanutha (Mk. viii. 10). A poorly attested variant reading in both Gospels gives the destination as Magdala, on the western shore of the lake. The reading cannot be trusted, but it rightly infers that Jesus would sail to a place on the western shore.

CHAPTER XVI

xvi. 1-12. WARNING AGAINST THE PHARISEES AND SADDUCEES

And the Pharisees and Sadducees came to him, and 1 tempting him asked him to show them a sign from heaven. But he answered and said to them, ('When 2

evening comes you say, "Fair weather, for the sky is glow-
3 ing red ", and in early morning, "Stormy today, for the sky
glows with ominous red ". You know how to interpret the
appearance of the sky, but you cannot interpret the signs
4 of the times.) An evil and adulterous generation desires
a sign, but no sign will be given to it except the sign of
Jonah.' And he left them and departed.
5   And when the disciples came to the other side, they
6 had forgotten to take loaves of bread. Jesus said to them,
'Take care and be on guard against the leaven of the
7 Pharisees and Sadducees'. They discussed this among
8 themselves, saying, 'We took no bread'. Jesus realized
this and said, 'Why are you discussing among yourselves,
9 you feeble believers, the fact that you have no bread? Do
you not yet understand or remember the five loaves of the
10 five thousand and how many baskets you took up? Nor
the seven loaves of the four thousand and how many
11 hampers you took up? How is it that you do not understand that I did not speak to you about loaves? But be
on guard against the leaven of the Pharisees and Saddu-
12 cees.' Then they understood that he had not said to be on
guard against the leaven found in bread but against the
teaching of the Pharisees and Sadducees.

With vss. 1-4 cf. Mk. viii. 11-13; Lk. xi. 29. Cf. Matt. xii.
38 f., where Jesus gives to a similar demand an almost identical
reply. The religious leaders demand that Jesus do some marvellous deed possible only to divine power (**from heaven**), and
so prove that God has sent him. Mark and Luke do not mention
the **Sadducees,** who have not appeared in Matt. since iii. 7;
their appearance here would indicate an official delegation,
Jesus' widespread fame, and official awareness that Jesus presents a challenge to the Jewish leaders.

Vss. 2b, 3 probably were added to Matt. by a scribe at an
early date; the connecting idea is the urgent need to interpret
signs of the times. The passage says: You are expert weather
prophets; but now you ask for a sign when signs enough warn
the spiritually alert that a crisis is here, judgment lies ahead, and
repentance is an urgent option you should be quick to take.

The very demand for an overpowering, undeniable proof of his message marks this **generation** and its leaders as **evil and adulterous,** loyal to forces that oppose God. Jesus did not do his miracles to compel faith; external wonders cannot create or compel real faith. In the conflict of life, faith finds God at work, not in massive proofs, but in the 'still small voice' and the movements of justice and love. In the temptation (iv. 5-7), Jesus rejected the temptation to compel faith by astounding marvels. But he does give one exception, **the sign of Jonah** (xii. 39). For Luke Jonah's preaching at Nineveh is the sign. Jonah preached judgment; the Ninevites repented; so Jesus' generation should repent. But in Matt. the sign is the resurrection. It will help only the spiritually responsive; but the sign will be there if they are able to see it.

With vss. 5-12 cf. Mk. viii. 14-21; Lk. xii. 1. Luke, with a different setting, interprets the leaven as hypocrisy. **Come to the other side:** Presumably from the western (xv. 39) to the north-east shore (cf. vs. 13). On landing, the disciples remember that they brought no **bread.** Jesus uses the situation to warn against the **leaven,** the teaching and influence, **of the Pharisees and Sadducees** (vs. 1). The disciples misunderstand him. He, as often, knows, without being told, what they think and say. He rebukes their misplaced attention: 'You are thinking of the wrong thing. You show a lack of faith. Twice you saw food provided when there was need (xiv. 19-21; xv. 36-38). I was speaking not of literal bread but of a real danger; beware of letting the teaching and influence of these leaders win a hold in your minds; it will permeate and corrupt your whole life.' Perhaps the warning refers directly to the recent demand for an authenticating sign (vs. 1). The reference to **leaven** warns the disciples not to let unconscious influence from his opponents destroy their loyalty to him.

xvi. 13-28. JESUS THE CHRIST; PETER THE ROCK; THE IMMINENT CROSS

When Jesus came into the district of Caesarea Philippi, 13 he was asking his disciples, saying, 'Who do men say that

14 the Son of Man is?' They said, 'Some say, John the Baptist; others, Elijah; and others, Jeremiah or one of the
15 prophets.' He said to them, 'But you—who do you say
16 that I am?' Simon Peter answered and said, 'You are the
17 Christ, the Son of the living God.' Jesus answered and said
to him, 'You are blessed, Simon Barjonah, for flesh and
blood has not revealed this to you, but my Father who is
18 in heaven. And I say to you that you are Peter, and on
this rock I will build my church, and the gates of Hades
19 will not prove victor over it. I will give you the keys of the
Kingdom of Heaven, and whatever you bind on earth will
be bound in heaven, and whatever you loose on earth will
20 be loosed in heaven.' Then he sternly warned his disciples not to tell anyone that he was the Christ.

21   From that time Jesus Christ began to explain to his disciples that he must depart to Jerusalem and suffer much
at the hands of the elders and chief priests and scribes,
22 and be killed, and on the third day be raised. And Peter
took him aside and began to reprove him, saying, 'Mercy
23 on you, Lord! This will never happen to you.' But he
turned and said to Peter, 'Get behind me, Satan. You are
a temptation to me, for your thinking reflects the thoughts
not of God but of men.'

24   Then Jesus said to his disciples, 'If any one wishes to
come after me, let him deny himself and take up his cross
25 and follow me. For whoever wishes to save his life will
lose it, but whoever loses his life for my sake will find it.
26 For what benefit will a man get if he gains the whole
world but forfeits his life? Or what will a man give in
27 exchange for his life? For the Son of Man is about to come
in the glory of his Father, accompanied by his angels, and
then he will recompense each one according to what he
28 has done. Truly I tell you, there are some of those standing here who will not taste of death until they see the
Son of Man coming in his Kingdom.'

With vss. 13-20 cf. Mk. viii. 27-30; Lk. ix. 18-21. In Jn. the
disciples have known all along that Jesus is the Son of God and
the Christ (i. 34, 41). But in the Synoptics, Peter's confession

marks a turning-point. It opens the way to teaching about what kind of Messiah Jesus is; he begins to teach his disciples about the Cross.

Caesarea Philippi: Slightly over twenty miles north of the Sea of Galilee; formerly called Paneas, after the god Pan; the tetrarch Philip rebuilt and renamed it. It continued to be a pagan city, and Jesus did not enter it; he only entered its *district* (in Mk., its villages; Luke does not mention the city at all). The journey into this mainly pagan region was evidently a time of withdrawal with **the disciples.** Jesus had important teaching to give the disciples if they were ready. So he persistently (ἠρώτα, imperfect tense) questioned them concerning popular Jewish views of him. He refers to himself as **the Son of Man,** according to the probable Greek text; many manuscripts in Matt. read **I the Son of Man,** but this **I** probably slipped into manuscripts of Matt. from Mk.

The disciples report four identifications: (1) **John the Baptist** (cf. xiv. 2). (2) **Elijah,** expected to return before the final day of judgment (Mal. iv. 5). Cf. xvii. 10-13, which identifies John the Baptist as Elijah. (3) **Jeremiah.** The only Gospel to refer to him and report that some thought Jesus was Jeremiah is Matt. (cf. ii. 17; xxvii. 9). (4) **One of the prophets.** All four popular views identify Jesus as a prophet, a stirring, fearless spokesman for God. He accepted the title (Lk. iv. 24), but was conscious of a unique role. So he turns directly to the disciples, and with emphatic challenge—**But you**—asks what they think. As usual, Peter speaks for the group; but this is no ordinary occasion, so his double name, **Simon Peter,** is used for solemn emphasis. Its use here suggests that Jesus had given Simon the name Peter before this occasion.

In Peter's answer **Christ** is the crucial word. Matt. alone adds, **the Son of the living God.** This may be simply a Messianic designation, synonymous with Christ. But in Matt. Jesus has more than once been called Son or Son of God (ii. 15; iii. 17; iv. 3, 6; viii. 29; xi. 27; xiv. 33), marking his unique nature and filial relation to the Father; it thus must have that meaning here. In one sense, therefore, it seems an anti-climax to designate Jesus as the expected Messiah (the Hebrew word Messiah and the Greek word Christ both mean 'anointed'); usually this great spiritual and political leader of Israel was not expected to be divine. Why then is the identificaticn of Jesus as the Christ so climactic in the Synoptic Gospels? Partly because Jesus was sent to Israel (xv. 24), and to fulfil his mission needed recognition as their authoritative head; and partly because he needed a group aware of his crucial role in Israel and banded together to witness to it. Death is impending (vs. 21); his remaining time for ministry is limited; Israel as a whole has not responded to his message (xi. 20-24); he needs a core group, convinced that he is Israel's God-sent leader, to carry his work forward among Israel and in the world. Peter's confession shows that the disciples have reached a stage at which he can begin to teach them what lies ahead.

Vss. 17-19 occur only in Matt. For three main reasons many deny that Jesus spoke these words: (1) They seem to imply that Peter has fully understood Jesus, but vs. 22 proves otherwise. (2) They seem to speak of a Church separate from Judaism, yet apart from xviii. 17, which simply refers to a local congregation of believers, the word does not occur again in the Gospels. (3) The granting of complete authority to Peter has no parallel in the Gospels, and the Book of Acts shows that he possessed no such authority in the Apostolic Church. The wording of these verses no doubt reflects a special interest in Peter in the community where Matt. was written. But if we avoid reading modern conceptions of the Church into the passage, recognize that nothing is said about successors to Peter, and remember that for Jesus all authority ceases when obedience ends, we may agree that Jesus here praises Peter for his basic though partial understanding that Jesus fulfils Israel's hopes. The verses need not all have been spoken at one time; Matt. often presents editorial grouping of material. But Jesus could have said essentially what Matt. contains.   If so, what did he mean?

Peter is praised because he has expressed clearly for the first time the Messianic role of Jesus. This pioneer insight enables him to receive a unique place among the disciples. **Flesh and blood:** Human beings. No human has given Peter this insight; it came from God.   **Barjonah:** Aramaic for 'Son of Jonah'.

Peter (Greek Πέτρος): means Rock, as does Cephas in Aramaic. This name, probably given earlier, is now used by

Jesus in a word play. He calls this disciple Cephas, Petros, Rock, and says that he will build his Church on this **Petra** (this feminine form used here in Greek for a ledge of rock would be Cephas in Aramaic; speaking in Aramaic, Jesus would say: You are Cephas . . . and on this Cephas I will build, etc.). What is meant by this Rock? Hardly Jesus himself; it is something in Peter. Is it simply Peter's faith, so that he receives no personal role in the Church? Probably Jesus means Peter himself, but Peter as the first believer in Jesus as the Christ. On this first explicit confessor of Jesus as the rightful Messianic leader of Israel Jesus can build his Church, which in one sense begins right here. Moreover, Jesus clearly counts on Peter to exercise basic leadership (cf. Lk. xxii. 31 f.). And the story of Acts i-v shows that Peter did so in the critical first days of the Church.

The word **church** has deep roots in its O.T. use to designate the congregation of Israel. Jesus does not think of a Church which rejects all ties with Israel, but of a congregation within Israel which represents what all Israel should be and seeks to win all Israel. It accepts Jesus as the Christ and tells all Israel that he is their Christ. This congregation will not fail; **the gates of Hades,** the power of death to hold the dead, **will not prove victor** over this Church; Peter's faith will not be belied by the impending death of the Christ; Jesus will rise from the dead and the Church will go forward under its living Lord.

The reference to **the keys** is figurative. A master gives his servant the keys to his house as a trust. Jesus says nothing of successors to Peter; and he gives the same trust not only to the group of disciples, but to any two who pray in faith and loyalty (xviii. 18 f.). But he expects Peter to exercise prominent leadership. His decisions, when made in loyalty, will have God's approval; **in heaven** means 'with God'. **Bind** and **loose** do not refer, as Jn. xx. 23 does, to excluding from or admitting into the Kingdom, but to teaching what is forbidden or permitted.

Peter and his fellow-disciples are **not to tell** others that Jesus is the Christ. Not even the Twelve fully understand his Messianic role. They do not see that suffering is integral to the role of the Christ. Until he can establish by teaching and suffering what it really means to be the Christ, and what this means for the faith and life of his followers, to tell people that he is the

187

Christ would arouse false nationalistic hopes; it could lead the Romans to seize him as a rebel claimant to earthly kingship before he could challenge his people at Jerusalem, the centre of Jewish religious life.

With vss. 21-23 cf. Mk. viii. 31-33; Lk. ix. 22. **From that time:** Here begins the second half of Jesus' teaching. Since iv. 17 he has centred on public preaching about the Kingdom of Heaven; now he points the disciples to the Cross, and defines Messiahship essentially in terms of the Suffering Servant of Second Isaiah. If **Jesus Christ** is the original text (many authorities read only **Jesus**), the word **Christ** appropriately recalls Peter's decisive confession which opened the way for this essential new teaching. **Must:** Indicates not mere outward necessity, imposed by human scheming, but the divine will and purpose. **To Jerusalem:** The full and final appeal to Jewish leaders and people can only be made there, at the very centre of the religious life of this people. **Elders, chief priests, scribes:** These make up the Sanhedrin, the highest court of the Jews; they will bring about his suffering and death.

Jesus' words are usually called a prediction of his passion; this is misleading, for they close with brief but clear assurance of his resurrection. The suffering is emphasized because that was not expected of the Messiah. **The third day:** This agrees with the resurrection story; Mark's 'after three days' means the same thing, but is less exact.

This prediction is given three times (xvi. 21; xvii. 22 f.; xx. 18 f.). Each time the disciples fail to grasp its truth and necessity, Jesus reiterates his teaching, and tells the disciples they must show the spirit with which he faces the Cross. Here Peter rebukes Jesus, and Jesus rebukes Peter and teaches that self-denial and the cross are obligatory for all true disciples.

Peter's rebuke expresses the common Jewish outlook. They expected their Messiah to triumph easily and completely. Peter takes Jesus **aside** (or, possibly, pulls him close to speak quietly). **Mercy on you:** Literally: '(God) be gracious to you', that is, God forgive you for saying so mistaken and shocking a thing. For the Christ to suffer is unthinkable. Jesus faces Peter squarely and no doubt speaks so that the other disciples hear. **Get behind me:** Get out of my sight; I will have nothing to do with you when you talk like that. **Satan:** Withering epithet. In the words of his friend Jesus hears the temptation to avoid the Cross. The intensity of the rebuke indicates the courage it takes to face death; he does not want his close friend Peter to make it harder. **Temptation:** Literally, a stumbling-block, which makes one fail in obedience. Peter's thinking, his life outlook, is still wrong. The way of suffering, which men selfishly seek to avoid, is God's way to save men.

With vss. 24-28 cf. Mk. viii. 34-ix. 1; Lk. ix. 23-27. **His disciples:** Here the Twelve. After his prediction of his death (and resurrection) and his rebuke of Peter, he reiterates his teaching and applies it to his disciples. **Follow me:** Not only to Jerusalem but more generally, in faithful discipleship which banishes selfish concern and is ready for self-sacrifice even to death. The present imperative ($\dot{a}\kappa o\lambda o\upsilon\theta\epsilon\acute{\iota}\tau\omega$) calls for steady continuing faithfulness in the way of costly obedience.

Vs. 25 and x. 39 have the same word-play on **life** ($\psi\upsilon\chi\acute{\eta}$). To save physical life and further physical comfort and safety at all costs is to lose real life; to give up physical comfort and safety and if necessary accept martyrdom will lead to true life with God. Present loss or gain may be partly the meaning, but the major reference, vs. 27 suggests, is to the final loss or gain at the final judgment.

To sacrifice permanent spiritual welfare for temporary physical safety or comfort is a bad bargain (Jesus gave a place to common sense). Suppose a man neglects his spiritual welfare to acquire all the material advantages this world can give; he ends with an infinite deficit. He has missed a priceless privilege to get a transient and corrupting advantage. He has no business sense! The second question in vs. 26 is rhetorical; nothing that man can get or gain equals the privilege and blessings God can give now and in all time to come. A final reckoning and revelation of the value of what men have chosen will come at the last day; it will make crystal clear the colossal lack of sense in those who have lived in scheming worldliness.

For judgment is coming. It is near. The Greek $\mu\acute{\epsilon}\lambda\lambda\epsilon\iota$ means that something is 'about to', 'going to', or 'certain to' happen. Here it probably means judgment is **about to** occur (an added reason to shun worldly choices). Jesus as **Son of Man** will come visibly, with power, with the splendour that surrounds the Father in heaven. He will appear as divine judge, and act for the Father. **Recompense each one:** Ps. lxii. 12 says God will do this; here again the Son of Man carries out the divine work; Jesus is conscious that he plays a more than human role.

The nearness of judgment (vs. 27) is further emphasized. **Truly I tell you:** A formula of emphasis. The Son of Man will not come at once to judge; some present will be dead before that. But he will come soon; **some** present will still be alive. Mark's reference to the Kingdom's coming might (but probably does not) refer to some preliminary spiritual triumph; in Matt. Jesus unmistakably refers to his coming to establish the full **Kingdom** and execute the final judgment. Vs. 28 implies that some eye-witnesses of Jesus' ministry were still alive when Matt. was written.

CHAPTER XVII

xvii. 1-27. THE TRANSFIGURATION; ELIJAH HAS COME; HEALING BY FAITH; THE COMING CRISIS; FREE SONS

1 And after six days Jesus took Peter and James and John his brother, and led them up on a high mountain apart.
2 And he was transfigured before them, and his face shone as the sun, and his clothing became white as light.
3 And behold, Moses and Elijah appeared to them, con-
4 versing with him. Peter answered and said to Jesus, 'Lord, it is good that we are here; if you wish, I will make here three booths, one for you and one for Moses and one for
5 Elijah'. While he was still speaking, behold, a bright cloud covered them, and behold, a voice from the cloud, saying, 'This is my beloved Son, with whom I was well
6 pleased; hear him'. And when the disciples heard this,
7 they fell on their faces and were much afraid. And Jesus came to them, touched them, and said, 'Rise and do not

be afraid'. When they lifted their eyes they saw no one 8
except Jesus alone.

And as they were descending from the mountain Jesus 9
commanded them, saying, 'Tell the vision to no one
until the Son of Man has risen from the dead'. And the 10
disciples questioned him, saying, 'Why then do the
scribes say that Elijah must come first?' He answered 11
and said, 'Elijah indeed comes and will restore all things.
But I tell you that Elijah already has come, and they did 12
not recognize him, but did with him as they wished. So
also the Son of Man is about to suffer at their hands.' Then 13
the disciples understood that he had spoken to them concerning John the Baptist.

And when they came to the crowd a man approached 14
him, kneeling before him and saying, 'Lord, have mercy 15
on my son, for he is epileptic and very sick; for often he
falls into the fire and often into the water. And I brought 16
him to your disciples, but they were unable to heal him.'
Jesus answered and said, 'O unbelieving and perverse 17
generation, how long shall I be with you? How long shall
I put up with you? Bring him here to me.' And Jesus re- 18
buked him, and the demon came out of him, and the
child was cured from that hour. Then the disciples came 19
to Jesus privately and said, 'Why were we unable to drive
it out?' He said to them, 'Because you had so little faith. 20
For truly I tell you, if you have faith like a mustard seed,
you will say to this mountain, "Move from here to there",
and it will move, and nothing will be impossible for you.'

As they were gathering in Galilee, Jesus said to them, 22
'The Son of Man is about to be delivered into the hands
of men, and they will kill him, and on the third day he 23
will rise'. And they were greatly grieved.

When they came to Capernaum those who collected 24
the double drachma came to Peter and said, 'Does not
your teacher pay the double drachma?' He said, 'Cer- 25
tainly'. And when he entered the house Jesus anticipated
him by saying, 'What do you think, Simon? From whom
do the kings of the earth collect revenues or poll-tax?
From their sons or from aliens?' When he said, 'From 26

aliens', Jesus said to him, 'Then the sons are exempt.
27 But in order that we may not offend them, go to the sea,
throw in a fishhook, and pull in the first fish that comes
up; and when you open its mouth you will find a stater.
Take that and give it to them for me and yourself.'

With vss. 1-8 cf. Mk. ix. 2-8; Lk. ix. 28-36. This mysterious
event, dated **six days** (Luke says eight) after xvi. 13 ff., Jesus
shared with the inner trio of disciples. In this trio **Peter** is
always named first, as in lists of the Twelve. **John his brother:**
So called to distinguish him from John the Baptist? Or from
another John? **High mountain:** Could be Mt. Hermon, since
Caesarea Philippi was at its foot. The high mountain in Biblical
times was a place of divine revelation.

Jesus' **face shone** with flashing radiance; his garments were
brilliant **white**; the word 'vision' (vs. 9) does not deny the
reality of the revelation, but suggests that no physical trans-
formation need be inferred. The experience of **light,** however,
indicates the presence and working of God, and implies, as the
Gospels often do, that though Jesus was human, the divine was
mysteriously present and active in him.

Moses and Elijah represent the Law and the Prophets; the
O.T. witnesses to Jesus and he fulfils what it says (v. 17). What
do the two discuss with Jesus? He has just spoken of his impending death; a suffering Christ is unacceptable to the disciples; the vision means that the Law and the Prophets confirm
the teaching of Jesus about the Cross.

Peter as usual is first to speak and act. He is sharing a rich
and blessed privilege on the mountain. So he says **I will make,**
etc. (in many manuscripts, however, he makes the offer for all
three disciples present: Let us make, etc.). In the **three booths**
he thinks that the three central figures may stay with proper
dignity. He seems to fear that this brilliant vision will fade; he
would like to prevent that.

Jesus does not answer. **A bright cloud**—traditional symbol
of the divine presence—covers the group, and from it **a voice**
—it can only come from the Father—uses again the words
spoken at Jesus' baptism. Then it approved his humbly coming
to baptism; here it confirms his teaching that he must go to

Jerusalem and suffer. **Hear him:** The voice refers to what Jesus has just been teaching; the Cross is the Father's will for him.

Knowing that they hear the voice of God, the disciples, in intense fear, fall face down on the ground; they dare not see the awful majesty of God. But with the voice the vision has reached its climax and fulfilled its purpose. Jesus comes to the cowering disciples, touches them reassuringly, and tells them to rise and cease to fear; the glorious manifestation of the Father has ended. So they dare to raise their eyes; now they see no signs of the divine majesty or the ancient leaders of Israel. They see **Jesus alone** in his familiar human form. Now they should understand him better; they have the answer to their deep inward rebellion at the idea of a suffering Christ: the O.T. supports his teaching; the Father wills the Cross; they should listen to what Jesus says about it.

With vss. 9-13 cf. Mk. ix. 9-13. Jesus tells the three disciples not to tell the vision until after his resurrection (already promised in xvi. 21). The Cross is not public teaching during his ministry. **Vision:** Suggests a real experience of the divine presence, a real revelation of truth, but perhaps not something that a modern camera could have caught.

On the basis of Mal. iv. 5, coupled no doubt with Mal. iii. 1, **the scribes,** the scholars of the Pharisee sect, teach that Elijah must return to prepare for the Lord's final judgment. But now Peter has identified Jesus as the Christ; Jesus is about to suffer, die, rise (xvi. 21), and carry out the final judgment (xvi. 27). If the end is so near, is it not too late for Elijah's preparatory ministry?

Jesus in answer first quotes the scribal expectation (vs. 11); but he does not stop to note that **Elijah** has not restored all things. He at once states his position (vs. 12); Elijah has a role in the final events at the end of history, but the scribes have failed to recognize that Elijah **has come.** No one recognized him for what he was; **they,** used twice in vs. 12, may mean only the scribes, or may be, as often in Greek, the indefinite subject, 'men', which would include the scribes, whose failure to recognize John the Baptist as Elijah made it possible for Herod Antipas to act against John and put him to death.

In Matt. (not Mk.) Jesus concludes by saying that the Son of Man is about to suffer at the hands of the same people who have already failed to recognize Elijah. Here too **their** may mean the Jewish religious leaders or include both the religious and the political leaders, combined to effect Jesus' death.

Then the disciples understood the pattern of history in which they were living. It is implied that previously they had not understood the true relation of John to Jesus.

With vss. 14-20 cf. Mk. ix. 14-29; Lk. ix. 37-43a. Matt. and Lk. are much more concise than Mk. When Jesus, Peter, James, and John descend from the mountain, a **crowd** and the other nine of the Twelve meet him (vs. 16). A father with an **epileptic** son (called demon-possessed in vs. 18) appeals to Jesus for help. The nine **disciples** waiting at the foot of the mountain had been unable to heal the victim. Jesus' rebuke (vs. 17) hardly applies to the father, who showed faith in bringing the boy to be healed, or to the crowd, drawn by knowledge of Jesus' healing power; it appears to apply directly to the nine; they had power to heal (x. 8). However, Jesus finds in his **generation** as a whole the fault so glaringly manifest in the nine disciples. **Unbelieving and perverse:** May recall Deut. xxxii. 5, 'a perverse and crooked generation', but Jesus denounces a fault not stated there, the lack of faith that does not see the power of God at work in Jesus. The repeated **How long?** expresses impatience with his generation's slow growth in learning and loyalty. In the temptation he determined to try to win people's minds and wills to voluntary full loyalty to him and his cause. But he has found the progress painfully slow.

Rebuked him: Means rebuked the demon in the boy. **The disciples:** The nine who had tried to heal the boy but had failed. **Little faith:** Explains their inability; cf. **unbelieving** in vs. 17.

Vs. 20b has no parallel in Mk. (cf. Lk. xvii. 6). 'Matthew' groups it here topically; so far Jesus has said that more faith is needed; this says that even a very small amount of faith, no larger than a mustard seed (supposed to be the smallest seed; xiii. 32), can work wonders; it can move a mountain as large as **this mountain** of transfiguration (xvii. 1). Indeed, faith can do anything. This sweeping statement warns men not to let cynicism and scepticism determine their outlook; faith can increase immensely their ability to serve God and bless men.

Many manuscripts add vs. 21: **This kind does not come out except by prayer and fasting.** This later addition attempts to excuse the disciples who had failed to cast out the demon. Only special prayer and earnest fasting could conquer so formidable a demon.

With vss. 22-23 cf. Mk. ix. 30-32; Lk. ix. 43b-45. This is the second of three explicit predictions (cf. xvi. 21; xx. 18 f.). The first occurred near Caesarea Philippi; the third, on the way to Jerusalem (xix. 1); this second one, **in Galilee,** as **they** (Jesus and the Twelve) **were gathering** for the journey to Jerusalem. The repetition shows that this theme was important in Jesus' teaching of the Twelve in this latter part of his ministry, and that they found it hard to accept the fact that Jesus was to die a violent death. But Matt. differs from Mk. and Lk. in indicating that the disciples, even if reluctantly, accepted this teaching with some understanding and **were greatly grieved.**

The story of vss. 24-27 occurs only in Matt. Every male Jew twenty or more years old owed a half shekel each year (Ex. xxx. 11-16; Neh. x. 32 says a third of a shekel) for the maintenance of the temple services. It apparently was collected in early spring. In current money a half shekel was a **double drachma.** The collectors **came to Peter** about Jesus' payment because Jesus was staying with Peter or because of Peter's close ties with Jesus. Peter impulsively assures them that Jesus will pay. **Anticipated:** Peter intended to confirm his impression by asking Jesus, but Jesus brought the matter up first and used a parable to settle it. **Kings** do not impose taxes, such as customs duties or the capitation tax, on their own family; they raise money for government and military expense by taxing **aliens,** peoples subject to them. (The Jews knew well that Rome levied heavy taxes on subject peoples.) So the **sons** of the king of the dawning Kingdom of Heaven are by right **exempt** from taxes for the temple. This saying shows a keen consciousness of division between the followers of Jesus and supporters of the traditional temple system. Contrast Jesus' zeal for the temple in xxi. 12 f. But Jesus does not tell Peter to break with the temple. In full freedom, to keep those loyal to the temple from being offended and so prevented from seeing the truth of the gospel, he and Peter may pay the temple tax.

Vs. 27 apparently reports a miracle. In the mouth of the first fish Peter catches he will find a **stater** (worth four drachmas or one shekel); this will pay the half shekel temple tax for both Jesus and Peter. (This implies that other disciples will pay this tax, and that Jewish Christians later may pay it, though with no feeling that their standing with God depends on it.) All other gospel miracle stories conclude by telling of the actual performance of the marvellous act. Since this story does not, possibly the words of Jesus are figurative, instructing Peter to fish and get the money to pay the tax by selling the fish he catches. But this interpretation seems forced; the narrative seems to promise a marvellous provision of the tax money and a marvellous pre-vision of its finding. A figurative statement of Jesus may have developed into a miracle story in the course of transmission. If so, this could happen only because the Church knew that Jesus had done many remarkable things, and this did not seem an impossible addition to the list.

CHAPTER XVIII

xviii. 1-35. HUMILITY, DISCIPLINE, AND FORGIVENESS

1 **At that hour the disciples came to Jesus, saying, 'Who**
2 **then is the greatest in the Kingdom of Heaven?' And he**
3 **summoned a little child, placed him in their midst, and said, 'Truly I tell you, unless you turn and become as little children, you will not enter the Kingdom of Heaven.**
4 **Whoever therefore humbles himself as this little child,**
5 **he is the greatest in the Kingdom of Heaven. And whoever receives one such little child in my name, receives**
6 **me; but whoever causes one of these little ones who believe in me to sin, it would be better for him to have a**

large mill-stone hung around his neck and be drowned
in the deep sea.

'Woe to the world because of temptations to sin. For it 7
is necessary that the temptations come, but woe to the
man through whom the temptation comes. If your hand 8
or your foot tempts you to sin, cut it off and throw it from
you; it is better for you to enter into life maimed or lame
than to have two hands or two feet and be thrown into the
everlasting fire. And if your eye tempts you to sin, tear 9
it out and throw it from you; it is better for you to enter
into life one-eyed than to have both eyes and be thrown
into fiery Gehenna.

'See that you do not despise one of these little ones; for 10
I tell you that their angels in heaven always see the face
of my Father who is in heaven. What do you think? If a 12
certain man has a hundred sheep and one of them strays
away, will he not leave the ninety-nine on the mountains
and go and look for the stray one? And if he happens to 13
find it, truly I tell you, he rejoices over it more than over
the ninety-nine which have not strayed away. So it is not 14
the will of your Father who is in heaven that one of these
little ones should perish.

'If your brother sins, go and reprove him between you 15
and him alone. If he listens to you, you have gained your
brother. But if he refuses to listen, take with you one or 16
two others, in order that everything may be established
by the word of two or three witnesses. If he refuses to 17
listen to them, tell it to the church; and if he refuses to
listen even to the church, let him be to you as the Gentile
and the tax-collector.

'Truly I tell you, whatever things you bind on earth will 18
be bound in heaven, and whatever things you loose on
earth will be loosed in heaven. Again, truly I tell you, if 19
two of you agree on earth concerning anything they may
ask, it will be done for them by my Father who is in
heaven. For where two or three are gathered in my name, 20
I am there in their midst.'

Then Peter approached and said to him, 'Lord, how 21
many times shall my brother sin against me and I

22 forgive him? As many as seven times?' Jesus said to him, 'I do not say to you as many as seven times, but as many as seventy-seven times.

23 'Therefore the Kingdom of Heaven may be compared to a king who decided to settle accounts with his ser-
24 vants. When he began to settle accounts, one was brought
25 to him who owed ten thousand talents. Since he had nothing with which to pay, the master commanded that he be sold, with his wife and children and all that he had,
26 and payment made. Then the servant fell prostrate before him, saying, "Be patient with me, and I will pay you
27 everything". Stirred by compassion, the master of that
28 servant released him and forgave him the debt. But that servant went out and found one of his fellow-servants who owed him a hundred denarii, and he seized him and
29 choked him, saying, "Pay what you owe". Then his fellow-servant fell down and entreated him, saying, "Be
30 patient with me, and I will pay you". But he refused, and instead went away and threw him in prison until he
31 should pay the debt. When therefore his fellow-servants saw what had happened, they were greatly grieved, and went and reported to their master all that had happened.
32 Then his master summoned him and said to him, "Wicked servant, I forgave you all that debt, since you
33 entreated me; should not you also have shown mercy to
34 your fellow-servant, as I showed mercy to you?" And his master was angered and handed him over to the torturers
35 until he should pay him the whole debt. So also my heavenly Father will do to you, unless you each forgive your brother from your heart.'

Ch. 18, the fourth of five formal discourses (v-vii; x; xiii; xviii; xxiv-xxv), collects in topical form various teachings of Jesus concerning relations between disciples.

With vss. 1-6 cf. Mk. ix. 33-37, 42; x. 15; Lk. ix. 46-48; xvii.
1 f. **At that hour** may be only a formal link with the preceding incident, but 'Matthew' may mean a real connection; if sons of the Kingdom are free and the full Kingdom will be so great a privilege, who will have top rank in it? In Mk. the disciples have

been disputing as to which of them is the **greatest;** Matt. says nothing of this, but Jesus' words in vs. 3 are stern and show that the disciples are thinking along wrong lines.

Jesus, taking a **child** as an object lesson of trustful humility, says with emphasis: If you do not change your attitude and become humble instead of ambitious to get top rank, you will have no place **in the Kingdom.** A trustful humility that accepts a place in the Kingdom as a gift is necessary for entrance; scheming for the highest rank is out of place. Vs. 4 then answers the question of vs. 1. Humility, necessary for entrance, is also the measure of greatness in the Kingdom; the trustful humility of the child who readily came to Jesus when called is the attitude that marks true greatness and fulfils God's will. Cf. xxiii. 12. Brazen or cleverly concealed selfishness and ambitious self-promotion indicate unworthiness rather than greatness.

Vss. 5 f. deal with how the true disciple treats children. It is wrong to be too busy and important to pay attention to a child. The disciple must welcome the child, Jesus says, **in my name,** that is, as a person so dear to Jesus that a welcome to the child is a welcome to Christ. Jesus so identifies himself with all who need friendship that such friendship is really shown to Jesus (xxv. 40).

To cause **little ones** who trust in Jesus to sin is unspeakably wicked (perhaps **little ones** here includes not only children but also apparently unimportant people, as in vss. 10, 14). Jesus implies that it will bring the guilty man to divine condemnation and eternal ruin. It would seem a cruel thing to tie a heavy **mill-stone,** the upper stone used in grinding grain between two stones, around a man's neck and throw him, helplessly weighted down, into the deep sea to drown. But this would be better for the man than if he were to mislead a child and bring eternal condemnation on himself.

The theme (vs. 6) of causing others to sin is continued in vs. 7; cf. Mk. ix. 43-48; Lk. xvii. 1 f. Vss. 8 f. is linked with vs. 7 by the catchword 'cause or tempt to sin' (σκανδαλίζει). **The world** here means mankind, subject to the lure and traps of evil. The 'offences' (σκάνδαλα) are **temptations to sin,** traps for the unwary or weak. In the providence of God evil is temporarily tolerated. Moral choices must be made and possibilities exist of being misled. But as the second **woe** shows, the fact that possibilities of sin exist in life's moral struggle does not relieve from responsibility one who misleads his fellow-men. He will suffer heavy penalty for that.

One must remove from life at any cost things that may lead him to sin (cf. v. 29 f.). The three examples: **hand, foot, eye,** are figurative; the impulse and practice of sin cannot be removed by removing a part of the body. One must remove from his life anything—even something as important for normal living as a hand, foot, or eye—if it would lead to sin and so to spiritual ruin. **Everlasting fire** and **fiery Gehenna** both point to the everlasting consequences of moral collapse. **Gehenna:** See on v. 22. **Fiery:** This is a figurative reference to the threatened punishment and anguish.

In vss. 10-14 the concern of Jesus for children and apparently unimportant people is the connecting thread. It is clearer in vs. 10 than in vs. 6 that **little ones** includes persons whom the world thinks of little importance; in vs. 14 this reference is certain. Persons of no apparent influence or importance are important to God and are under his care, and they will be important to anyone who follows Jesus and shares his mind. They have direct access to God; **angels in heaven** individually represent each of these **little ones** (cf. Dan. x. 13, 20 f.; Rev. i. 20; ii. 1, 8, etc.). That these angels have direct access to God (see his face) means that God always knows the plight of his **little ones,** cares for them, and will vindicate them if they are despised or ill-treated. This reference to such angels expresses God's constant awareness of the needs of all his people, and his prompt action to protect and bless them when they need his help. How literally Jesus meant this reference to an angelic counterpart of each needy person is not easy to say, but it vividly assures humble believers that God their Father is gracious and alertly protective.

Many manuscripts include vs. 11: 'For the Son of Man came to save what was lost'. This was borrowed from Lk. xix. 10; it does not belong in Matt.

Vss. 12-14 parallel Lk. xv. 3-7. Back of the parable is the O.T. thought of God as a shepherd, used in the N.T. of Jesus as the seeking pastor, the Good Shepherd (Jn. x. 11). The shepherd, to save the straying sheep from danger and final loss, leaves the other sheep (probably thought to be safe, but **on the mountains** may suggest they are exposed to some risk) and goes to look for the lost **one**. If he finds it, his joy is so sincere and great that for the moment he forgets what all the other **ninety-nine** mean to him. His joy is not mere delight in recovering valuable property; he cares for each one of his sheep; the loss of one brings sorrow; its recovery brings joy.

Vs. 14 applies the parable. God is like that shepherd (so is Jesus, as ix. 13 shows). He does not want even the least important or most humbly situated of his people to be lost. Lost here means out of right relation to God and in danger of eternal ruin unless sought out and restored. God cares for each; he seeks to recover each lost one; those who share his mind and follow his Son will do the same; they cannot despise any one of those for whom God cares so much and so constantly (cf. vs. 10).

To vss. 15-17 only Lk. xvii. 3 offers a (partial) parallel. **Brother** in Matt. means fellow-disciple; Jesus probably was thinking of relations among his followers. (A similar method of dealing with differences within a religious fellowship, with maximum consideration for the offender, appears in the Qumran *Manual of Discipline* v. 24-vi. 1.) The passage is Jewish and early in character; the only basis for assigning it a late origin is the use of the word **church,** which here means not the later hierarchical Church of Gentile Christianity, but the local group of believers in which two disciples are at variance. Nothing justifies the view that Jesus could not have spoken the words.

Jesus outlines four steps: (1) Try first to clear up the problem by private conference with the wrongdoer. **Sins:** Most manuscripts add 'against you'. This may well have been original in Matt.; but even if added later, it probably is a correct interpretation. If the sinner regrets his fault, the person who went to him has **gained,** won back, his fellow-disciple, and there need be no public exposure of the sin. (2) If the sinner **refuses** to repent, Deut. xix. 15 suggests the next step: bring in **one or two others** as conciliating witnesses. (3) If these quiet methods, which cause the sinner as little public shame as possible, fail, the entire local congregation must know the facts and use its influence. (4) If this fails, the congregation must exclude the

14   201

wrongdoer from its fellowship. **Gentile, tax-collector;** Jesus personally does not scorn such people; he here uses current Jewish terms of reproach to describe the wrongdoer as an unworthy outsider. Only a Gospel with a Jewish-Christian setting could comfortably use such terms, which sound strange on Jesus' lips (but cf. v. 46 f.).

With vs. 18 cf. xvi. 19; Jn. xx. 23. Vs. 17 directs the church to exclude the unrepentant sinner. Vs. 18 confirms its authority to do this. It assumes that the disciples (**you** is plural—the full group) meet in loyalty to Jesus, seek divine guidance, and act with sincere concern for the good of individuals and the church. **Bind, loose:** In xvi. 19 seemed to refer to teaching and rulings on what is prohibited or permitted; they may mean this here, but in discipline the rulings practically become judicial decisions controlling church life. The Father will sanction decisions made in a loyal, loving spirit, for they express his judgment and purpose.

The hierarchical tendency in Matt. is limited if present at all. The entire church is here given the authority given Peter in xvi. 19; and vs. 19 gives equal authority to any **two** disciples, who may ask anything and God will grant it. To find a rigid church organization in Matt. and ignore vs. 19 is to play fast and loose with evidence. Vs. 19, vs. 18, and xvi. 19 all depend on the presence and leading of Christ, promised in vs. 20 to any **two or three** assembled in his **name,** that is, as disciples seeking earnestly to know and do his will. The power of Christ to work in the Church, and the authority to act for him, are promised to any group of disciples, however small (or large), which is awake to the presence of Christ and responsive to his leading. This does not nullify the place and value of organization, but the acts of corrupt or unworthy leaders are not sanctioned. The acts of disciples are authoritative in so far as they conform to God's will.

All three Synoptic Gospels teach the disciple to forgive others (Mk. xi. 25; Lk. vi. 36; xi. 4; xvii. 3 f.); 'Matthew', though sternly warning of judgment, lays particular emphasis on the necessity of a forgiving spirit (v. 7, 43-48; vi. 12, 14 f.). Peter's question shows that he understands this teaching (had he already heard Lk. xvii. 4?); but **how many times** is he to forgive? He is generously ready to forgive the same wrongdoer **seven times** (cf. a Talmudic injunction to forgive three times). Jesus says **seventy-seven times,** or, as the Greek may mean, seventy times seven times. This reverses the spirit of unlimited revenge in the song of Lamech (Gen. iv. 24); the disciple must never refuse to forgive when the wrongdoer repents and asks forgiveness.

In the parable which follows (Matt. only) Jesus teaches that God will not forgive an unforgiving person. An unforgiving spirit blocks his readiness to forgive.

Therefore: Since the obligation to forgive is unlimited, God's dealings with an unforgiving person will be like those described in this parable. Man must undergo judgment before admission to the final Kingdom, and since all men are sinners—as this parable clearly assumes (cf. vi. 12; vii. 11)—they must rely on God's gracious leniency, which he will show if they have forgiven their fellow-men who have wronged them.

King: A slight reminder that the story deals with the Kingdom and God's role as King. The **servants** or slaves have been entrusted with resources and responsibilities, and the king decides to settle accounts. **Ten thousand talents** (a talent was worth 6000 denarii): Roughly 3,500,000 pounds or ten million dollars, too immense a debt for a servant to repay (a hint that man can never make up for his sin against God). The man, his property, and his family are to be sold (cf. 2 Kings iv. 1); the proceeds, it is implied, will not clear the debt. The servant, in agonized and repeated entreaty (imperfect tense: προσεκύνει), asks the master for time and freedom, and promises to pay **the debt.** This promise seems fantastically optimistic, but the master does more than asked. He releases the servant and cancels the immense debt.

But the servant promptly proves heartless towards a fellow-servant who owes him only seven pounds or twenty dollars. He refuses to grant to the fellow-servant the favour he had just asked of his master (vs. 26). He puts his fellow-servant **in prison** until **the debt** is paid, and thereby takes from the debtor freedom to work and earn.

Greatly grieved: At the plight of the imprisoned servant. **Wicked servant:** Not to forgive after being forgiven is wicked.

Having received forgiveness, the servant should have been not merely grateful but forgiving. In fact, had he been really grateful he would have been forgiving. **Torturers:** This hardly suggests that the man had hidden away the money he owed, and might be forced by torture to disclose where it was; it hints rather of punishment following the final judgment. The immensity of the debt leaves the prisoner no real hope of paying it and obtaining release. His future is hopeless; he has forfeited his new privilege by proving unworthy of it.

Vs. 35 draws the lesson; it only makes explicit what the story itself has clearly implied. God's readiness to forgive, the immensity of the wrong which man's sin does to God, the obligation of every forgiven man to forgive others to whatever extent they need and ask it—these points are clear. But is God really like the king, who first forgave and then cancelled his forgiveness? The king forgave freely until the servant proved himself unworthy by misusing his freedom and acting in callous heartlessness. Jesus taught that the misuse of God's gracious gifts leads to their loss, not because God is capricious, but because man cannot really receive and hold God's blessings unless he catches and reflects God's spirit in his own relations to other people (cf. vi. 14 f.). One must share the attitude of God to be capable of entering into restored fellowship with him. Salvation transforms the saved person's attitudes and social relations.

CHAPTER XIX

xix. 1-15. ON MARRIAGE AND JESUS' LOVE OF CHILDREN

1 **And it happened when Jesus had finished these sayings that he departed from Galilee and came into the region**
2 **of Judea across the Jordan. And large crowds followed him, and he healed them there.**
3 **And Pharisees came to him, testing him and saying, 'Is it permitted for one to divorce his wife for any and**

every cause?' He answered and said, 'Have you not read 4 that from the beginning the Creator made them male and female?' And he said, '"For this reason a man shall leave 5 his father and mother and be joined to his wife, and the two shall be one flesh". So they are no longer two but one 6 flesh. Therefore let no man separate what God has joined together.' They said to him, 'Why then did Moses com- 7 mand to give a certificate of divorce and dismiss her?' He said to them, 'Because of your hardness of heart 8 Moses permitted you to divorce your wives, but from the beginning it has not been so. I tell you that whoever 9 divorces his wife except for unchastity and marries an- other woman commits adultery.'

The disciples said to him, 'If the relationship of the 10 man with his wife is like this, it is better not to marry'. He said to them, 'Not all men can receive this saying, 11 but only those to whom it is given. For there are eunuchs 12 who were born that way from their mother's womb, and there are eunuchs who were made eunuchs by men, and there are eunuchs who made themselves eunuchs for the sake of the Kingdom of Heaven. He who can receive this, let him receive it.'

Then children were brought to him, that he might lay 13 his hands on them and pray. His disciples rebuked them, but Jesus said, 'Permit the children to come to me, and 14 do not forbid them, for the Kingdom of Heaven is for such as they are'. And he laid his hands on them and departed 15 from there.

With vss. 1 f. cf. Mk. x. 1. The composite discourse concerning relations between disciples closes with the usual formula (cf. vii. 28; xi. 1; xiii. 53; xxvi. 1). **Departed:** The final departure from Galilee for Jerusalem. Jesus crossed the Jordan below the Sea of Galilee, journeyed southward on the east side, and re-crossed the Jordan near Jericho (xx. 29). **Judea across the Jordan:** An unusual geographical description; Judea was commonly regarded as west of Jordan, south of Samaria. The region east of the Jordan, ruled by Herod Antipas, was called Perea; peopled largely by Jews, it here is considered part of Judea.

Crowds: Going to the Passover, as Jesus and his disciples were, or coming to Jesus for help. **Healed them:** Hyperbole; literally implies that all were sick and were healed. To Jesus and 'Matthew' these healings attested the beginning of the Kingdom.

With vss. 3-9 cf. v. 32; Mk. x. 2-12; Lk. xvi. 18; 1 Cor. vii. 10-12. **Pharisees,** present to observe Jesus, hear his teaching, and test him. They had long disputed over the meaning of Deut. xxiv. 1; they agreed it permitted **divorce,** but differed over what 'some indecency' meant. The strict school (so Shammai) limited it to immorality by the wife; the more liberal view (so Hillel) said it meant anything in the wife that displeased her husband. Did Jesus agree with Hillel, that the Law permitted divorce **for any and every cause?**

Have you not read: They surely have read this clear teaching of Scripture, that God created man and woman to live together in monogamous marriage (Gen. i. 27). Jesus then cites Gen. ii. 24; a man is to **leave** his parents and be united with his bride in a union so complete that they are **no longer two** independent individuals but **one flesh,** a new creation that has its life only in their union. God has made them one; the husband must not break by divorce this permanent monogamous union (in Jewish law only the man could divorce; he had to give the woman a written certificate for her protection).

Jesus leaves no place for divorce. The Pharisees appeal to Deut. xxiv. 1, arguing that **Moses** there clearly sanctions divorce. Jesus replies first that while Moses permitted divorce, he did so only in view of man's **hardness of heart.** Divorce is wrong; a right attitude would avoid it and so fulfil the Creator's purpose and will.

Vs. 9, like v. 32, recognizes one valid ground for divorce, **unchastity** on the part of the woman. Mark, Luke, and Paul know no such exception; vss. 4-8 leave no room for one. Vs. 9 makes Jesus agree with Shammai against Hillel. But Jesus' point is that God intends man and woman to live together in a permanent monogamous union. It has been argued that Matt. gives the implied meaning of Jesus, who said nothing of the exception, but assumed that actual immorality on the part of the wife would break the union and warrant divorce. But Jesus was con-

cerned to state and defend the permanent nature of true marriage; 'Matthew' adapts his teaching to support the stricter line
of Jewish teaching. Vss. 4-8 imply just what Mark, Luke, and
Paul say: to break the marriage union is to fail of God's purpose;
the disciple, set free from hardness of heart, will not think of
divorce.

Vss. 10-12 discuss the proper place of celibacy. The disciples are astounded at the high standard of marriage just
presented. If marriage is so permanent and binding, **it is better
not to marry**; the disciples see too many possibilities of discord
or failure. **This saying:** The disciples' remark about remaining
single by choice. A deliberately chosen celibate life is not for all
men; as Paul saw (1 Cor. vii), marriage is normal and desirable
for most men, who could not remain single without undue
emotional and moral strain. Jesus clearly implies that his cause
needs some persons to forgo marriage. He mentions three
groups of **eunuchs** (meaning here persons who live without
normal marriage relations). One group is born unable to fulfil
the marital functions. Another has been made unable by human
action; in royal courts men were made eunuchs so that they
would not threaten sex violence to women of the court. Others
have made themselves eunuchs by their own decision, in order
to serve the cause of **the Kingdom.** Because the first two
types were physically incapacitated for marriage, this third type
was understood literally by a few ancient Christians, including
Origen. But undoubtedly Jesus meant not a physical operation
but the deliberate decision to refrain from marriage to be free
to devote one's entire time to the cause of the Kingdom. This
does not deny the normal place of marriage in God's created
order. But the work of the Kingdom is so urgent that a few must
forgo normal family ties. Jesus, and apparently John the Baptist and Paul, did not marry. Since marriage was normal among
Jews, this must have been by deliberate choice. But Jesus recognizes that only a small minority, by personal choice and for
dedication to a particularly demanding work, could and should
live in this way.

With vss. 13-15 cf. Mk. x. 13-16; Lk. xviii. 15-17. Just as
marriage belongs to God's created order and is sacred (vss.
3-9), so **children** have the blessing of God and of Jesus, and

represent the attitude that must mark members of the Kingdom. Attention centres entirely on the children. The parents
who brought them wanted Jesus to **lay his hands on them
and pray,** and so mediate or give God's blessing to them. The
disciples wanted to protect Jesus. The children seemed unimportant; their coming seemed an intrusion into his vital work of
teaching and healing. Their officious act, Jesus saw, misunderstood who and what are important. These children are precisely
the kind of person that belongs in **the Kingdom** (cf. xviii. 3).
They come with trusting faith and simple openness; in their
simplicity, trust, and humility they represent what all members
of the Kingdom must be.

xix. 16-30. TEACHING ON POSSESSIONS

16 **And behold, one came to him and said, 'Teacher, what
17 good thing shall I do to obtain eternal life?' He said to
him, 'Why do you ask me concerning the good? There is
one who is the Good One. But if you wish to enter into life,
18 keep the commandments.' He said to him, 'Which ones?'
Jesus said, 'You shall not kill, You shall not commit adultery, You shall not steal, You shall not bear false witness,
19 Honour your father and mother, and You shall love your
20 neighbour as yourself.' The young man said to him, 'All
21 these things I have kept. What do I still lack?' Jesus said
to him, 'If you wish to be perfect, go and sell your possessions and give the money to the poor, and you will have
22 treasure in heaven; and come and follow me'. When the
young man heard this saying he went away sorrowing, for
he had great possessions.**

23 **Jesus said to his disciples, 'Truly I tell you, only with
difficulty will a rich man enter the Kingdom of Heaven.
24 Again I tell you, it is easier for a camel to go through the
eye of a needle than for a rich man to enter the Kingdom
25 of God.' When the disciples heard this, they were greatly
26 amazed, saying, 'Who then can be saved?' Jesus looked
at them and said, 'With men this is impossible, but with
God all things are possible'.**

Then Peter answered and said to him, 'Behold, we have 27 left everything and followed you; what then will we receive?' Jesus said to them, 'Truly I tell you, in the world 28 renewal, when the Son of Man sits on his glorious throne, you also who have followed me will yourselves sit on twelve thrones judging the twelve tribes of Israel. And 29 every one who has left houses or brothers or sisters or father or mother or children or fields for the sake of my name will receive many times as much and will inherit eternal life. But many now first will be last, and ones now 30 last will be first.'

With vss. 16-26 cf. Mk. x. 17-27; Lk. xviii. 18-27; only Matt. says the man was **young** (vs. 20); only Lk. calls him a 'ruler'. In Mk. and Lk. Jesus is called 'Good Teacher', and Jesus rejects the adjective **good**. Matt. partly avoids this apparent reflection on Jesus' character by using **good** of the **things** the man might do. But when Jesus says, **There is one who is the Good One,** he implies that the Father is good in a sense that even Jesus may not claim. Jesus is not confessing sin, but saying where the clear standard of perfect holiness, undimmed by sin or human limitations, is found.

Eternal life: This final blessing and privilege, pointed to by the words **life** (vs. 17), **treasure in heaven** (vs. 21), **Kingdom of Heaven** (vs. 23), **Kingdom of God** (vs. 24), and **be saved** (vs. 25), is the reception of those who trust and obey God into full and permanent fellowship with Him; while this may begin in man's earthly life, the reference here is to the full and final gift of rich life with God at the end of the age. The man's question need not express complacent satisfaction; although he has lived as a faithful member of God's people Israel, he feels that something is lacking.

Jesus in Matt. says that he is not the one to ask about what is good; the only **Good One,** God, is the authority on that; the way to qualify for life is to **keep the commandments** God has given (cf. vii. 21). The rich man asks **which** commandments (possibly but not probably ποίας means 'what sort of' commandments). Jesus quotes five of the Ten Commandments (Ex. xx), and adds Lev. xix. 18. All six commands quoted deal with

relations with other people, rather than with worship or ceremonies; does this hint that the man's problem is lack of sensi-
tiveness towards the needs and rights of others? The young man
is aware of no such failures, but still feels deficient.

Vs. 21 raises two main questions: (1) Is Jesus dividing his
followers into two classes, ordinary and perfect? τέλειος, **perfect,** mature, fully developed, may seem to suggest so. But
Matt.'s other use of this adjective (v. 48) refers to the disciples
generally; Jesus here tells the man what to do to be a true
disciple. (2) Must every disciple give up all his possessions? In
the Essene-type sect at Qumran this was a definite requirement
(cf. also the early Jerusalem church: Acts ii. 44 f.; iv. 32). But
this is required of would-be disciples nowhere else in Matt.;
Jesus made no rigid rule. His answer to this man is a potential
answer to every disciple, and may apply to many.

The man is not willing to depend for support on the gener-
osity of others, as Jesus does. His **possessions** mean too much
to him; he chooses them instead of the insecurity of a wandering
life with Jesus. His wealth leaves him with an unmet need, but
he cannot give it up for discipleship. His possessions still remain
his first loyalty (cf. vi. 24).

Jesus sees the hold that money and possessions can get on a
man, and how difficult the rich can find it to respond to the
gospel of the Kingdom. But his clear demand is that his disciples must put the Kingdom first (vi. 33). With earnest emphasis, Jesus twice states (vss. 23 f.) that **only with difficulty**
can a **rich man** be saved. Vs. 24 uses exaggeration. **Eye of a
needle:** Sometimes thought to be a low gateway in the wall of
Jerusalem, which a **camel** could barely pass through with no
load on its back; so a rich man must discard his wealth to get
through the gateway into eternal life. But no such gate is known.
The saying is rather a deliberate exaggeration; cf. a rabbinical
saying to someone telling a tall tale: 'Oh! You're from Pumbe-
ditha, where they put elephants through needles' eyes.' Jesus
means by vs. 24 what he says in vs. 26. It is beyond human
power for a rich man to resist the pull of possessions, but God
can enable a rich man to break the grip that possessions have on
him, and save him. Matthew gave up his lucrative work as tax
collector; Zaccheus used his money for justice and mercy (Lk.

xix. 8); Joseph of Arimathea became a disciple (xxvii. 57). But
when God saves a rich man, it is a miracle.

With vss. 27-30 cf. Mk. x. 28-31; Lk. xviii. 28-30; xxii. 28-30;
xiii. 30. The Twelve have left their possessions; though **Peter**
still has a house (viii. 14) and a fishing-boat (Jn. xxi. 3), and
probably others still have property, they have given up home
life, work, and income to go with Jesus. What will they get for
their sacrifice?

Jesus replies with two promises and a warning, probably
grouped in Matt. by topical interest. The Twelve, for all their
slowness and mistakes, have been loyal, and when the new age
comes and all things are renewed (Rev. xxi. 5), their sacrifice
and faithfulness will be honoured. The **Son of Man** will act as
judge (cf. xxv. 31); **his glorious throne** and role as judge mark
him as more than human. On the judgment day the Twelve will
be his deputies in **judging the twelve tribes of Israel** (cf.
I Cor. vi. 2 f.). (A less likely interpretation is that after the new
age begins, he will rule and govern for the Father and his twelve
disciples will govern Israel as his representatives; the verb
'judge' often means govern in the O.T.) The saying recalls
that Jesus' ministry was confined to Israel and that the Jewish-
Christian Church in the Apostolic Age felt strong ties with
other Jews.

The second promise (vs. 29) connects with vs. 27. All who,
like the Twelve, have given up home ties and possessions will
receive privileges worth many times as much as those they left
for work with Jesus. Jesus does not mean gifts separate from
eternal life in the Kingdom. This Kingdom will bring gifts
vastly richer than the dearest of human ties and the richest of
possessions; the greatest gift will be eternal life with God. Whoever receives this privilege will never regret his decision to
follow Christ.

The stern warning of vs. 30 is supported by xx. 1-15 and
repeated in xx. 16. After saying that for their sacrifices the
disciples will be honoured with places of decisive importance at
the judgment, and that rich gifts and eternal life will be given
to all who leave family and property to follow Jesus, the warning
is given that in many cases present ranks will be reversed; those
now holding chief places may have the humblest place in the

Kingdom, while those now seemingly unimportant will take front rank when true worth and loyalty are revealed. The final honours and highest ranks in the Kingdom will not be determined by men's external position in this life; the standards at the end will include the humility, active usefulness, kindness, and obedience which Jesus continually emphasized.

CHAPTERS XX AND XXI

xx. 1-16. THE WORKERS IN THE VINEYARD

1 'For the Kingdom of Heaven is like a farm owner who went out early in the morning to hire workers for his
2 vineyard. When he had agreed with the workers to pay them a denarius for the day, he sent them into his vine-
3 yard. And about the third hour he went out and saw others
4 standing idle in the market-place, and he said to them, "You also go into the vineyard, and I will pay you what-
5 ever is right". So they went. He went out again about the
6 sixth and ninth hour and did likewise. And about the eleventh he went out and found others standing there, and said to them, "Why do you stand here all day idle?"
7 They said to him, "Because no one has hired us". He
8 said to them, "You also go into the vineyard". When evening came the owner of the vineyard said to his steward, "Call the workers and pay the wages, beginning
9 with the last ones and ending with the first". When those hired about the eleventh hour came, they received a de-
10 narius apiece. And the first ones, when they came, supposed that they would receive more, but they too received
11 a denarius apiece. On receiving it they grumbled against
12 the farm owner, saying, "These last ones worked one hour, and yet you have made them equal to us who have
13 borne the burden of the day and the burning heat". But he answered one of them and said, "Comrade, I am doing

you no injustice. Did you not agree to work for me for a denarius? Take your pay and depart; I choose to give to 14 this last man just what I gave to you. Am I not permitted 15 to do what I choose with what is mine? Or is your eye evil because I am good?" So the last ones will be first and the 16 first ones last.'

Both vs. 16 and **For** in vs. 1 show that this parable (Matt. only) is put here to illustrate xix. 30. The Kingdom will show unexpected reversals of rank. The parable itself says only that at the end, regardless of the length of service, all will receive the same pay (vs. 12). Yet Peter (xix. 27) thinks that the Twelve may well expect a favoured position, as the workers who work all day think they deserve the most pay. If some disciple joins the group later and receives notable recognition, Peter and the Twelve may think positions are being reversed, just as the workers who worked all day thought that equal pay really meant they were the poorest paid of all. This at least is how 'Matthew' understands Jesus. The older brother in Lk. xv. 11-32 interprets the Father's equal love for two sons of unequal service as a putting last of the one who deserved to be first; in other words, Luke shows that Jesus taught just what 'Matthew' understands to be the meaning of this parable. Rankings based on time of service or outward prominence will be disregarded and the resulting grace to all may seem a reversal of what is fair and just.

The way this employer deals with the men he hires illustrates one aspect of **the Kingdom.** At vintage time he urgently needs workmen for his vineyard. He hires free men, and must pay at the end of **the day. Denarius:** A normal day's wage for labourers (about 1s. 6d. or 20 cents). At about 9 A.M., noon, and 3 P.M., others are hired and promised fair pay. The urgent need for help is suggested by the hiring of men about 5 P.M. **No one has hired us:** The story does not blame them for earlier idleness.

At **evening,** according to Jewish law (Lev. xix. 13), the employer pays the workers. He instructs the steward to pay the men in the reverse order from that in which they were hired, and to give every man **a denarius.** Those who have worked all day expect more, because they have worked more, but they receive the same pay. They object openly; they feel that they deserve more than men who have worked one hour. The employer replies to one man, the spokesman or a prominent objector. The men who worked all day have received what they had agreed was fair; they cannot justly complain. The owner, who chooses to pay the others a full day's pay, asks the tired worker: **Is your eye evil,** are you jealous and resentful, **because I am good,** because I choose to be generous? This question forms the climax and may embody the real point of the parable.

The parable is introduced (xix. 30) and closed (vs. 16) by a general pronouncement which fits Jesus' teaching but is used here in Matt. as an editorial framework. Those whom the disciples think **last** will share God's gifts so richly that though only sharing what all enjoy they seem to enjoy preferential treatment. Those who by common estimate are **first** and important, though sharing the gifts on an equal basis, will actually feel less favoured. The Twelve have made sacrifices (xix. 27), will have special privileges (xix. 28), and may want the chief places in the Kingdom (xx. 21), but only the Father can assign them, and the only greatness consists in unselfish, faithful service to others (xx. 26 f.).

xx. 17-28. 'A RANSOM FOR MANY'

17 As Jesus was about to go up to Jerusalem, he took the
18 Twelve aside, and on the way said to them, 'Behold, we are going up to Jerusalem, and the Son of Man will be handed over to the chief priests and scribes, and they will
19 condemn him to death, and will hand him over to the Gentiles to mock and scourge and crucify, and on the third day he will rise'.
20   Then the mother of the sons of Zebedee came to him with her sons; she fell reverently before him and made a
21 request of him. He said to her, 'What do you want?' She said to him, 'Command that these my two sons shall sit one at your right side and one at your left in your King-
22 dom'. Jesus answered and said, 'You do not know what you are asking. Are you able to drink the cup that I am
23 about to drink?' They said to him, 'We are'. He said to

them, 'My cup you shall drink, but to sit at my right side and at my left is not mine to give, but is for those for whom it has been prepared by my Father'.

And when the Ten heard it, they were indignant at the 24 two brothers. But Jesus summoned them and said, 'You 25 know that the rulers of the Gentiles lord it over them and their great men tyrannize over them. It shall not be so 26 among you, but whoever wishes to become great among you shall be your servant, and whoever wishes to be first 27 among you shall be slave of all, just as the Son of Man 28 came not to be served but to serve and to give his life as a ransom for many.'

With vss. 17-19 cf. Mk. x. 32-34; Lk. xviii. 31-34. In this, as in the two preceding explicit predictions (xvi. 21; xvii. 22 f.), Jesus emphasizes the suffering, so unexpected in popular views of the Messiah, but clearly predicts the resurrection. In Matt. (cf. xix. 1; xx. 29) this third prediction occurs east of the Jordan, or at Jericho west of the Jordan. In all three predictions, Jesus speaks only to the Twelve. Three new points emerge in this third prediction: (1) The Jewish leaders will definitely condemn Jesus to death. (2) **The Gentiles** (the Roman ruler and staff) will execute the sentence. (3) The manner of Jesus' death is stated; after mocking and scourging he will be crucified, a Roman form of execution. **On the third day:** so xvi. 21; Mk.'s 'after three days' seems to mean the same thing; Mk. xvi. 2 puts the resurrection on the third day.

The threefold prediction aims to combat the Jewish view, which the disciples were all too ready to share, that the Messiah would achieve quick triumph. Evidently Jesus' coupling of the Suffering Servant figure with the Messiah and Son of Man figures was new and offensive to those who first heard it. Thus his originality emerges; in his rejection by the leaders and most of his people, he had found not defeat for himself and God's purpose, but God's deeper way to fulfil his plan.

With vss. 20-28 cf. Mk. x. 35-45; with vss. 24-28 cf. Lk. xxii. 24-27. In Matt., as usual more concise than Mk., the request for the highest places is made not by James and John **the sons of Zebedee,** but by their **mother.** xxvii. 56 shows that she followed Jesus to Jerusalem; from Mk. xv. 40 it seems that her name was Salome. Since Jesus replies not to her but to her sons, and the indignation of the Ten is directed at her sons, they were at least parties to the request, and probably actually made it, as Mark says.

The mother is asking the Messiah-King to promise her sons the highest places in his Kingdom, the places of honour and authority next to the King (cf. Ps. cx. 1). The request assumes that even now Jesus can assign these places. In effect, this request seeks a higher rank than Peter, for apart from the sons of Zebedee he is the prominent one of the Twelve.

Jesus replies to James and John (the verbs are plural). **The cup**: Might suggest the Messianic feast, but following Jesus' clear prediction of his impending passion they know that he means his coming suffering. Can they share that? They confidently reply that they can. (When Jesus is arrested in Gethsemane, they flee in panic.) Jesus predicts that they will indeed suffer. This seems to predict their martyrdom. Acts xii. 2 reports the martyr death of James. Certain lists of martyrs and a doubtful late tradition, allegedly going back to the second-century Papias, indicate that John too suffered a martyr death, but the prevailing tradition of the Church, from the late second century on, was that John lived to old age in Ephesus and died a natural death. This verse is often considered strong evidence that John did die a martyr's death. This difficult question affects chiefly the debate whether John could have written the Gospel of John in his old age.

Jesus declares that the **Father** will assign the chief places in his Kingdom according to the divine plan. Whether Jesus knows what that plan is, we do not learn (cf. xxiv. 36). But the sons of Zebedee get no promise of preference. Vss. 26 f. give the basis on which to qualify for honour. Ambitious scheming for chief places will not help.

Clearly the sons of Zebedee have the wrong spirit. But the other **ten** disciples are no better. Their indignation shows the same self-interest and desire to protect their own position. To rebuke and correct them (**them** means primarily the ten, but in effect includes all twelve), Jesus states the right way to greatness. **You know**: Contains a rebuke; they know too well; their thinking accepts the world's standard. The Gentile rulers make pomp and outward power their way of life. Greatness to them means power to dominate and dictate to other people. But Jesus defines greatness as continual service to others, serving their interests and doing everything possible to honour and help them. Vs. 27 repeats and sharpens this teaching; to rank **first** of all, be the **slave of all,** living only to serve their good and happiness. (By worldly standards this really puts the last first and the first last! Cf. xix. 30; xx. 16.)

This principle of greatness is the spirit of the Kingdom and its King. It has been the spirit of Jesus' ministry. He came not to seek outward honour or exercise arbitrary power over others, but **to serve,** help, and benefit others. This spirit of his ministry finds climactic expression in his death, which he faces not because he must or because he is helpless or weak, but because it will benefit **many.** As **a ransom** redeems a captive from his bondage, so Jesus' obediently accepted death, in a way not defined, will further his cause and benefit his followers. It will bring release and new life to many. **Many:** Cf. Isa. liii. 12; as the Suffering Servant, Jesus will save his people from their sins (i. 21). The word **many** does not limit the number but promises that the benefit will be widely effective.

xx. 29-xxi. 17. JESUS COMES TO JERUSALEM TO CLEANSE THE TEMPLE AND HEAL THE SICK

And as they were leaving Jericho a large crowd followed 29 **him. And behold, two blind men who were sitting by the** 30 **road, when they heard that Jesus was passing by, cried out, saying, 'Lord, have mercy on us, Son of David'. The** 31 **crowd sternly charged them to keep quiet, but they cried out still louder, saying, 'Lord, have mercy on us, Son of David'. And Jesus stopped, called them, and said, 'What** 32 **do you wish me to do for you?' They said to him, 'Lord,** 33 **that our eyes may be opened'. In compassion Jesus** 34 **touched their eyes, and at once they received their sight and followed him.**

And when they neared Jerusalem and came to xxi. 1

Bethphage at the Mount of Olives, then Jesus sent two
2 disciples, saying to them, 'Go into the village opposite you, and at once you will find an ass tied, and a colt with her;
3 loose them and bring them to me. And if anyone says anything to you, you shall say, "The Lord needs them",
4 and he will send them at once.' This happened that the saying might be fulfilled which was spoken through the prophet, who said,

5   'Say to the daughter of Zion,
               "Behold, your King comes to you,
                 humble and mounted on an ass,
                 and on a colt of a beast of burden"'.

6 So the disciples went and did as Jesus had commanded
7 them; they brought the ass and the colt, and placed their
8 garments upon them, and he sat on them. The immense crowd spread their garments on the road, and others were cutting branches from the trees and spreading them on
9 the road. The crowds that preceded and followed him were calling out, saying,

          'Hosanna to the Son of David!
               Blessed is he who comes in the name of
               the Lord!
          Hosanna in the highest heaven!'

10 And when he entered Jerusalem the entire city was
11 stirred, saying, 'Who is this?' The crowds said, 'This is the prophet Jesus from Nazareth in Galilee'.
12   And Jesus entered the temple and drove out all who were selling and buying in the temple, and he overturned the tables of the money-changers and the seats of those
13 who were selling the doves, and he said to them, 'It is written, "My house shall be called a house of prayer",
14 but you are making it "a den of robbers"'. And blind and lame people came to him in the temple, and he healed
15 them. But when the chief priests and the scribes saw the wonders he did, and the children calling out in the temple and saying, 'Hosanna to the Son of David', they were
16 indignant, and said to him, 'Do you hear what these are saying?' Jesus said to them, 'Yes; have you never read that "Thou hast prepared praise for thyself from the

mouths of babes and sucklings "?'. And he left them and 17 went out of the city to Bethany, and spent the night there.

With vss. 29-34 cf. Mk. x. 46-52; Lk. xviii. 35-43. Mark and Luke speak of one blind man, 'Matthew' of **two** (cf. viii. 28; ix. 27; his series of twos may indicate knowledge of more healing stories than space permits him to narrate). **Jericho:** The first definite location of an event since Jesus left Capernaum (xvii. 24); xix. 1 was general, xx. 17 quite vague. **A large crowd:** Mainly pilgrims going to Jerusalem for the Passover celebration. **Lord:** Three times in these verses (two, if, as some good evidence favours, the word is omitted in vs. 30); it confesses that Jesus has divine power and authority to heal. **Son of David:** A common rumour known to the blind men identifies Jesus as the expected Messiah, the great God-sent ruler who will free the Jews and rule them in justice (cf. ix. 27; xii. 23; xv. 22). The blind men think that Jesus is going to Jerusalem to declare himself King of his people; they assume that even now he can help them.

The impatience of **the crowd,** usually thrilled by Jesus' miracles, suggests that their thought now centres on the hope that at Jerusalem Jesus will free his people from Roman rule. But Jesus hears the persistent cry for help, and gives the blind men an opportunity to express their implicit faith that he can heal them. Only Matt. mentions Jesus' **compassion** and touching the eyes of the men. The story concludes, as the gospel healing stories regularly do, with a clear statement that the healing occurred. The men follow Jesus to Jerusalem. Their presence with Jesus will increase the popular Messianic expectations when they join in the acclamation of Jesus as the rightful King of Jerusalem, the Son of David (xxi. 5, 9); their grateful following of Jesus will contrast with the stubborn refusal of the leaders to see in Jesus the God-sent leader of his people.

With xxi. 1-11 cf. Mk. xi. 1-11a; Lk. xix. 28-38; Jn. xii. 12-19. Jesus, his disciples, and the crowd travelled up the rather steep road from Jericho (xx. 29) to **Jerusalem.** Just east of Jerusalem, across the Kidron Valley, lay the **Mount of Olives.** The road either came up over this mountain ridge or skirted the slopes of its southern end. **Bethphage:** Lay either on the ridge directly east of Jerusalem, or a little east of Bethany, on the south-east slope of the Mount. In the latter case, **the village opposite you** was Bethany, to which they had not yet come. **You will find:** Does Jesus know this by special divine insight? Or (especially if Bethany is the village) has he prearranged this with friends? **An ass, a colt:** Two animals in Matt. only. Probably 'Matthew' or his source thought of two animals because of Zech. ix. 9. In this poetic verse the prophet speaks in parallel lines of the animal the king will ride; both lines refer to the same animal. But the double reference seems to have led to the prosaic assumption that there were two animals.

If no previous arrangement has been made, vs. 3 refers to the natural objection of the owner or his friends; if a previous arrangement has been made, the challenge to the two disciples is a prearranged means of identification. **He will send them at once:** This translation means that the owner will promptly send the animals when he learns who needs them. But the words may be the words of the disciples; when challenged, they are to say: 'The Lord (Jesus) needs them, and will send thém back promptly'.

In this use of these animals 'Matthew' sees prophecy fulfilled. **The prophet:** Actually two are quoted; the first line recalls Isa. lxii. 11; the rest is from Zech. ix. 9, emphasizing the rider's humility (but omitting, as does the LXX, the reference to his triumph and victory). Does the quotation express Jesus' intention as well as the Church's later insight? The entire passage implies that Jesus used the animals to make a point; the acted parable said what kind of leader he was and on what basis he offered himself to his people. He was indeed the Messiah, the King of Israel, but he came not with political and military ambitions, but to serve and give his life a ransom for many (xx. 28). The event was an acted Messianic confession intended to show to the discerning that the Suffering Servant figure defined the kind of Messiah he was.

Sat on them: On the **garments** or on the two animals; taking Zech. ix. 9 to mean riding on two animals does not work out well. Thrilled with Messianic expectation, the crowd, undeterred by Jesus' humble manner, treated him as a triumphant

kingly leader coming to take his throne. Spreading on the road
their cloaks and **branches** cut from trees was a further tribute.
The entire crowd, all along the procession, cried out in Messianic expectation. Of their reported words only the middle line
is a real quotation (Ps. cxviii. 25 f.). **Hosanna:** Originally transliterated the Hebrew, meaning as in Ps. cxviii. 25: 'Save now!'
But the expression had become a shout of joyous praise and
acclaim, to which a dative of the person acclaimed could be
added. The praise of Jesus as **the son of David** repeats the
thought of **your King** (vs. 5); Jesus comes, the approaching
pilgrims shout, as the expected Davidic Messiah; he comes **in
the name of the Lord** God, and so deserves all honour and
praise, not only from men, but from the angelic host **in the
highest heaven.** Matt. announces the Son of David title at the
outset (i. 1) and reports statements suggesting or asserting the
Son of David role of Jesus (ix. 27; xii. 23; xv. 22). Jesus did not
encourage this usage; he avoided it, and warned his disciples
not to call him Messiah because it would make people think in
political and military patterns; his manner of entering Jerusalem
attempted to draw attention away from such aspects of Messiahship. He fulfilled the deepest meaning of his people's hopes but
knew that he must avoid and even reject wrong aspects of that
expectation. What the crowd said contained truth, but his acted
parable meant that their enthusiasm was largely focused on
wrong aims.

When the jubilant procession entered Jerusalem, **the entire
city** (i.e. its residents) was **stirred,** shaken as by an earthquake
(ἐσείσθη). Note the two groups: pilgrims largely from Galilee,
praising Jesus as they come to Jerusalem for the Passover, and
the Jerusalem people, not actively involved in the tribute to
Jesus. The latter, perplexed, ask: **'Who is this?'** In answer the
pilgrims do not call Jesus King or Son of David. They say he is
the prophet Jesus from Nazareth in Galilee. Jesus accepted
this title of prophet (Lk. iv. 24). One Jewish expectation was
that a prophet like Moses would be sent by God to Israel (Deut.
xviii. 15, 18); this role of Messianic prophet was considered so
important that even John the Baptist dared not claim to fulfil it
(Jn. i. 21). This role of the Messianic prophet of the last days
was obviously not a minor one to the crowds or the gospel

writer; here, at the climax of the entry scene, it calls attention away from political Messiahship to the prophetic Kingdom message of Jesus.

With vss. 12-17 cf. Mk. xi. 11, 15-19; Lk. xix. 45 f.; Jn. ii. 13-22. In Jn. the temple cleansing is placed early in Jesus' ministry, to symbolize the cleansing and renewal Jesus brought to Judaism. In Mk. the event occurs the day after the entry into Jerusalem. In Matt. and Lk. Jesus cleanses the temple immediately after the entry. **Temple** (ἱερόν): The entire temple area; here particularly the large outer court, called the Court of the Gentiles, the only court the Gentiles could enter. There for convenience (and profit to priestly leaders) sacrificial animals were sold; foreign money was exchanged for coins acceptable in temple offerings; and doves for offerings by the poor (Lk. ii. 24) were sold. Jesus drives out both sellers and buyers; the latter, by making purchases, countenance and encourage the evils this trade causes. Citing Isa. lvi. 7 and Jer. vii. 11, he denounces the sellers: (1) The temple is a sacred place; God calls it **my house;** it must be respected. (2) The temple is the central place of **prayer,** even in this one court which Gentiles could enter (cf. Isa. lvi. 7); the confusion of business, the haggling over prices, ruins the atmosphere of prayer. (3) In greed for profit the sellers are a band of **robbers.**

Did this event recall Mal. iii. 1, 'The Lord . . . will suddenly come to his temple' in judgment? Certainly Jesus clearly assumed authority over temple practices. The enthusiasm of the crowd no doubt supported him (cf. vs. 15), and his moral indignation and personal authority enabled him to correct things, at least temporarily.

'Matthew' mentions no teaching this first day, but in healings God's power was at work in his temple through his anointed leader. The event was a challenge and an offer to Israel and its leaders. **The chief priests,** heretofore mentioned rarely, now appear often; the temple is their chief centre of ministry and influence. They and the **scribes,** active here as in the synagogues, see in the temple cleansing an unauthorized intrusion; they find no work of God in Jesus' healings. **The children** still echo the words of the crowds (vs. 9); this shocks the leaders. **Do you hear,** etc.: Means, How can you let them utter such false words without protest? He answers, **Yes;** this fulfils Ps. viii. 2 (cited here from the LXX): God has prepared suitable **praise** for himself and caused it to be uttered by children. Thus here Jesus accepts the designation **Son of David,** and rebukes the Jewish leaders for not seeing in the children's praise a God-inspired tribute.

The lines are drawn. Jesus has asserted his authority over even the temple, has exercised God's power there in healing, has accepted as essentially true the tribute of the pilgrims and children, and has been rejected by the temple leaders. The hostile reception he predicted while still in Galilee has at once appeared. But he has friends in **Bethany.** At the close of the day he goes there for safety and rest before the conflict resumes the next day.

xxi. 18-46. THE AUTHORITY OF JESUS REJECTED BY THE JEWISH LEADERS

Early in the morning, when he returned to the city, he 18 **grew hungry, and seeing a fig tree by the road he went** 19 **to it, but found nothing on it except leaves only; and he said to it, 'Let nò fruit ever come from you again'. And immediately the fig tree withered. And when the dis-** 20 **ciples saw it, they marvelled, saying, 'How did the fig tree wither immediately?' Jesus answered and said to** 21 **them, 'Truly I tell you, if you have faith and do not doubt, you not only will do what happened to the fig tree, but even if you say to this mountain, "Be picked up and thrown into the sea", it will happen. And if you have faith,** 22 **you will receive all things that you ask in prayer.'**

And when he entered the temple, the chief priests and 23 **the elders of the people came to him as he was teaching; they said, 'By what authority are you doing these things? And who gave you this authority?' Jesus answered and** 24 **said to them, 'I also will ask you a question; if you answer it for me, I in turn will tell you by what authority I do these things. From what source was the baptism of John?** 25 **From heaven or from men?' They reasoned among themselves, saying, 'If we say, "From heaven", he will say**

26 to us, "Then why did you not believe him?" But if we say,
"From men", we fear the crowd, for they all regard John
27 as a prophet.' And they answered Jesus and said, 'We do
not know'. He then said to them, 'Nor do I tell you by
what authority I do these things.

28   'What do you think? A man had two sons. Going to the
first he said, "Son, go and work today in the vineyard".
29 He answered and said, "I will not"; afterward he changed
30 his mind and went. Going to the second he said the same
thing. He answered and said, "I go, sir", but he did not
31 go. Which of the two did the will of his father?' They said,
'The first'. Jesus said to them, 'Truly I tell you, the tax-
collectors and the prostitutes go into the Kingdom of God
32 before you. For John came to you with a way of righteousness, and you did not believe him; the tax-collectors and
prostitutes believed him, but you, although you saw that,
did not even repent later and believe him.

33   'Hear another parable. There was a farm owner who
planted a vineyard, and put a hedge around it, and dug a
wine-press in it, and built a watch tower; and he leased
34 it to tenant farmers, and went on a journey. When the fruit
season drew near, he sent his servants to the tenants to
35 receive his fruit. But the tenants took his servants and
36 beat one, killed another, and stoned another. Again he
sent other servants, more than the first ones, and they
37 treated them the same way. Finally he sent his son to
38 them, saying, "They will respect my son". But the
tenants, when they saw the son, said among themselves,
"This is the heir. Come, let us kill him, and take his in-
39 heritance." And they seized him, threw him out of the
40 vineyard, and killed him. When therefore the owner of
the vineyard comes, what will he do to those tenants?'
41 They said to him, 'He will inflict a miserable death on
those miserable men, and will lease the vineyard to other
tenants, who will deliver the fruit to him in its seasons'.
42 Jesus said to them, 'Have you never read in the Scriptures,

"The stone which the builders discarded,
this has become the capstone.

This has come from the Lord,
and it is marvellous in our sight."
Therefore I say to you that the Kingdom of God will be 43
taken away from you and given to a nation that yields its
fruit. And he who falls on this stone will be dashed to 44
pieces, but on whomsoever it falls, it will crush him.'
And when the chief priests and the Pharisees heard his 45
parables, they realized that he was speaking about them;
but though they wanted to seize him they feared the 46
crowds, since they held him to be a prophet.

With vss. 18-22 cf. Mk. xi. 12-14, 20-24, where the tree is not
seen withered until the following morning. As Jesus returns
from Bethany without having had breakfast, he grows **hungry.**
The **fig tree** he sees cannot have the regular crop of figs (the
time is spring), but such trees may have in spring a small early
growth that is edible. This tree had no such small fruit; Jesus'
hunger and disappointed expectation show his humanity. His
startling words might be translated as a strong negative statement, 'No one will ever eat fruit from you again'; even so, the
words are an utterance with power which dooms the tree.

This story raises serious questions. Jesus elsewhere used his
power for unselfish, beneficent ends; to condemn a tree for not
satisfying his hunger seems to reverse his attitude in iv. 3 f., and
the spiritual purpose of the miracle is hard to see. Has Church
tradition transformed a parable condemning a fruitless fig tree
(Lk. xiii. 6-9) into a supposed act of Jesus? Did an earlier form
condemn Israel for failing to produce the fruit of faith and
obedience?

The gospel author takes the story as an actual historical event.
What meaning did it have for him? (1) It expressed Jesus' power.
The prompt withering of the tree and the amazement of the
disciples stress this. (Had not Jesus repeatedly done acts of
power the Church could not have accepted this story.) (2) It
teaches the lesson of **faith.** Such acts are possible only for one
who has faith and so lets the power of God work through him.
The disciples, too, if they **have faith** (cf. Jas. i. 6) may do
astounding things; these great works (cf. Jn. xiv. 12) are figura-
tively indicated as power to move a **mountain.** Indeed, God will

answer every sincere and trustful **prayer** of the disciples (cf. vii. 7-11; xviii. 19); he will give prompt and powerful response to every worthy prayer.

With vss. 23-27 cf. Mk. xi. 27-33; Lk. xx. 1-8. **The chief priests and elders,** like the chief priests and the scribes (vs. 15), represent the Sanhedrin, the leading Jewish authority. They challenge his right to do **these things,** to cleanse the temple, heal the sick, and accept Messianic tributes, and now to teach with authority in the temple. He has shown a clear consciousness of commanding **authority;** who gave it to him? Their implied answer is that he has no real authority; certainly God gave him none; he is self-appointed and to be condemned. Cf. Jn. ii. 18.

Instead of giving a direct answer, Jesus asks a counter-question. He promises to answer their question if they will answer his. **From what source** came John's preaching of repentance in view of the imminent Kingdom and his **baptism** of those who repented? Was it **from heaven,** i.e. from God, or **from men,** without divine prompting or approval? Jesus knows that his work and John's are connected, and that the Jewish leaders, in failing to see that God had sent John, had forfeited their right to judge John's successor.

The leaders withdraw, discuss the question, and see their dilemma. (ἐν ἑαυτοῖς probably means **among themselves** rather than that they each thought inwardly in themselves and reached the same answer.) If they answer **from heaven,** from God, they condemn themselves for not responding to God's prophet, and Jesus can condemn them. But if they answer **from men,** as they would like to do, the people, who consider that **John** was a God-sent **prophet,** will repudiate them. This passage attests the continuing popular esteem for John the Baptist.

The leaders prefer to profess inability to answer. Actually this is no escape from their dilemma, for they thereby confess incompetence to judge one who except for Jesus has been the most prominent preacher of their day. If they cannot tell whether God was at work in John the Baptist, they are not competent to question and judge Jesus. But in a sense Jesus has answered their question; his authority has the same source as that of John;

those who can discern the divine approval of John will know that God is the source of Jesus' authority.

Vss. 28-32 (Matt. only) give the first of three parables which indict the Jewish leaders for rejecting God's spokesmen. Jesus advances to direct criticism.

The intention of the parable is clear, but the Greek text varies curiously in ancient manuscripts and versions. There are two main problems. Which **son** is first described, the insolent one who later works, or the formally dutiful son who does nothing? Which son do the hearers approve? Logic and manuscript evidence indicate that the Jewish leaders approve the son who actually worked; working, not promising, is decisive. If so, the leaders are forced to agree with Jesus that outwardly pious promises to do God's will are no substitute for responding to God's prophet by actual repentance and obedience.

The opening question is a sharp challenge to **think** attentively about what follows. The **vineyard** may refer, as often in the Bible, to Israel (Isa. v. 7), but probably is simply the scene of a story told to teach the necessity of active obedience. The one **son,** at first impolite and defiant, later changes his mind and does the assigned work. The **second** son, dutifully polite **(Sir!),** does no work. Who did what the **father** wanted done? The outwardly impudent but finally obedient son did his father's will (cf. vii. 21-27; Jas. ii. 14-26).

Jesus himself points the moral. **The tax-collectors and prostitutes** correspond to the impudent, defiant son; their earlier behaviour had rejected God's claim. The Jewish leaders correspond to the polite son who promised but did not obey; they keep the traditional forms of worship but have not really done God's will. For when God sent **John** the Baptist, the tax-collectors and prostitutes obeyed his call and are entering **the Kingdom,** but the Jewish leaders have not responded with repentance and obedience. Jesus may not finally exclude the leaders from the Kingdom; they still could respond to the preaching which he gives in continuation of John's message. But as things now stand, the outcast classes are entering the Kingdom, and there is no evidence that the outwardly respectable leaders will respond. Even the sight of the outcasts streaming into the Kingdom has not changed their attitude.

The parable shows that Jesus is conscious of close ties with John in purpose and message. Both have preached the imminent coming of the Kingdom; those who reject John set themselves against Jesus and exclude themselves from the Kingdom. Vs. 32 could mean that John had come living in a righteous way, but probably means that John came **with** (that is, teaching) **a way of righteousness** that called for repentance and obedience to God.

With vss. 33-46 cf. Mk. xii. 1-12; Lk. xx. 9-19. This, the second of a series of three parables which indict the Jewish leaders for rejection of Jesus, is strongly marked by allegorical features; Israel rejects God's spokesmen and even his Son. Hence some have thought it a creation of the Apostolic Church. But allegorical features appear often in O.T. and rabbinical parables. The real reason scholars deny this parable to Jesus is that it explicitly identifies him as God's **Son** (vs. 37) and plainly speaks of his death. But Jesus has already been identified several times as the Son of God, and has even spoken of himself as such (xi. 27), and he has spoken of his impending death, most explicitly in xx. 17-19. The parable is not what the Apostolic Age would have produced. It offers no real doctrine of atonement or clear mention of the resurrection; its atmosphere is not post-Easter. It can best be understood as coming in essentials from Jesus.

The details quoted from Isa. v. 1 f. show that the **owner** did his part to provide the **tenants** a **vineyard** profitable to him and to them. (The use of the vineyard description of Isa. v. 1 f. may suggest that vineyard in vs. 28 is a figurative reference to Israel.) His departure then left the responsibility with the tenants; it does not mean that God abandoned Israel.

Isa. v centres interest on the yield of the vineyard; this parable's interest is in the tenants, who wickedly refuse to fulfil their obligations. The owner (God) was to receive part of what the vineyard produced, but the tenants (Israel, especially her recognized religious leaders; cf. vs. 45) reject his servants (God's prophetic messengers) and mistreat them (cf. Heb. xi. 32-38). The number of messengers is not defined; the first three (vs. 35) and the larger group (vs. 36) are typical examples of a series (the prophets down to John the Baptist) who are violently rejected.

His son: This singular reference, and the tenants' idea that by killing him they can get permanent possession of the vineyard, indicate that he is the only son (here a reference to Jesus). The tenants, like Joseph's brothers (Gen. xxxvii. 18-20), see in his coming only an opportunity to get their rival out of the way; they falsely assume that the owner will not come and punish them. So they kill him.

The story does not mean that the Jewish leaders clearly know Jesus to be the Son of God. But it makes a tremendous claim for Jesus and may imply that the leaders, in opposing him, are suppressing inner awareness that God's power is really working in him. The climactic murder of the only son is a pointed challenge to the leaders to stop before they commit the greatest possible sin. The parable offers a last warning, with little hope that they will accept it.

Only in Matt. do the hearers answer Jesus' question; they thus condemn themselves and point to new tenants (a new people of God and new leaders) who will give the owner his due. **Have you never read:** Ps. cxviii. 22 f. was known to them; it pointed ahead to the unique and crucial role of the Son in the people of God; as Scripture it was God's warning to the Jewish leaders. A **stone which the builders** had **rejected** as having no place in their building finally proved to be the capstone to finish the building. κεφαλὴν γωνίας, literally 'head of a corner', may mean foundation-stone, but here the stone (the Son) finds use only in the late stage of construction; this favours the meaning **capstone.** The distinguished place finally given the stone implies a prominent role for Jesus following his death, and so his resurrection, but this point is veiled, not explicit as would be expected in a story created after Jesus' resurrection. This vindication of the rejected stone, the quotation implies, was part of God's plan; an incipient theology of the Cross emerges here. **Our sight:** 'Our' means here those with spiritual eyes to see.

Vs. 43 (in Matt. only) need not be original in this context. The **Kingdom** will be **taken** from the disobedient Jewish leaders; their rejection of the prophets and the Son makes them liable to judgment. What is the **nation** which **yields** the **fruit** of repentance (iii. 8) and obedient faith? A renewed Israel under loyal leadership? Another nation? A new people combining the loyal of Israel with faithful people from east and west (viii. 11)? Probably the last (cf. xxviii. 19).

Vs. 44, omitted in some manuscripts and versions, may be an insertion from Lk. xx. 18. The **stone** refers to Jesus; the language may reflect Isa. viii. 14. Those who bitterly oppose Jesus the Son had better take warning; such opposition will bring them to complete spiritual disaster; the Son himself will be the Father's agent in judging them.

The chief priests and the Pharisees: The Sanhedrin, as in vss. 15, 23. They understood Jesus' meaning; he was warning them to accept his claim or face repudiation and disaster. Though determined to get rid of him, they did not dare to act yet, while he was surrounded by enthusiastic pilgrims who held him to be a **prophet** sent by God (vs. 11).

CHAPTER XXII

xxii. 1-46. FINAL DEBATES WITH JEWISH LEADERS

1 And Jesus answered and spoke to them again in parables,
2 saying, 'The Kingdom of Heaven may be compared to a
3 king who made a wedding feast for his son. And he sent
his servants to summon to the wedding feast those who
4 had been invited, but they refused to come. Again he sent
other servants, saying, "Tell those who have been invited, 'Behold, I have prepared my dinner; my oxen and fattened cattle have been slain, and everything is ready;
5 come to the wedding feast'". But they paid no attention
and went off, one to his own field and another to his busi-
6 ness; and the rest seized his servants and insulted and
7 killed them. The king was angered, and sending his
armies he killed those murderers and burned their city.
8 Then he said to his servants, "The wedding feast is ready,
9 but those invited were not worthy. Go therefore to where
the roads leave the city, and whomsoever you find, invite
10 to the wedding feast." So those servants went out to the

roads and gathered all whom they found, both bad and good; and the wedding hall was filled with those reclining at table.

'When the king entered to greet those who were at 11 table, he saw there a man who was not clothed with a wedding garment, and said to him, "Friend, how did you 12 enter here without a wedding garment?" And he was silent. Then the king said to the attendants, "Bind his feet 13 and hands and cast him out into the outer darkness; there the weeping and gnashing of teeth will occur". For many 14 are invited, but few are chosen.'

Then the Pharisees went and plotted to entrap him in 15 his speech. And they sent to him their disciples with the 16 Herodians; they said, 'Teacher, we know that you are truthful and teach truly the way of God, and you care for no one, for you pay no attention to men's outward posi-tion. Tell us therefore what you think. Is it permitted to 17 pay poll-tax to Caesar or not?' Jesus discerned their 18 wickedness and said, 'Why do you test me, you hypo-crites? Show me the coin used in paying the poll-tax.' So 19 they brought him a denarius. And he said to them, 'Whose 20 image and inscription is this?' They said, 'Caesar's'. 21 Then he said to them, 'Then pay back to Caesar the things that are Caesar's—and to God the things that are God's'. And when they heard this they marvelled, and left him 22 and went away.

On that day Sadducees came to him, saying that there 23 is no resurrection, and they asked him, saying, 'Teacher, 24 Moses said, "If any man dies childless, his brother shall marry his wife and raise up children for his brother". Now there were with us seven brothers. And the first, 25 after marrying, died, and since he had no children he left his wife to his brother; so also did the second, and the 26 third, to the seventh. Last of all, the woman died. Of which 27, 28 of the seven, then, will she be the wife in the resurrection? For they all had her.' Jesus answered and said to them, 29 'You err because you know neither the Scriptures nor the power of God. For in the resurrection they neither marry 30 nor are given in marriage, but are like angels in heaven.

31 But concerning the resurrection of the dead, have you not
32 read what was spoken to you by God, who said, "I am the
God of Abraham and the God of Isaac and the God of
Jacob"? He is not the God of the dead but of the living.'
33 And when the crowds heard this they were astonished at
his teaching.

34   Now when the Pharisees heard that he had silenced the
35 Sadducees, they gathered together, and one of them, a
36 lawyer, asked him as a test, 'Teacher, which command-
37 ment in the Law is greatest?' He said to him, '"You shall
love the Lord your God with all your heart and with all
38 your soul and with all your mind". This is the greatest
39 and first commandment. A second one like it is, "You
40 shall love your neighbour as yourself". On these two
commandments hang all the law and the prophets.'

41   While the Pharisees were gathered together, Jesus
42 asked them, saying, 'What do you think concerning the
43 Christ? Whose son is he?' They said to him, 'David's'. He
said to them, 'How then can David in the Spirit call him
Lord, saying,

44   "The Lord said to my Lord, 'Sit at my right hand,
       Until I put your enemies beneath your feet'"?
45 If then David calls him Lord, how can he be his son?'
46 And no one was able to answer him a word, nor from that
day did anyone dare to question him further.

With vss. 1-14 cf. Lk. xiv. 15-24, which differs in many
details and has almost no agreement in wording; it hardly seems
a variant form of the same parable. Both parables teach that
judgment will strike those who reject God's urgent invitation to
share in his coming eschatological banquet. In Matt. this third
parable warning of judgment seems aimed at the Jewish people
rather than simply the Jewish leaders.

In the Kingdom God's dealings with those who are invited
to enter but refuse will be like a king's response to guests who
refuse his invitation. Matt. speaks of a king, a wedding feast,
and the king's son; but all attention centres on the attitude of
the invited guests. Invited previously and now informed that the
feast is ready, they refuse (the parable ignores those Jews who

respond to the gospel and enter the Kingdom). The **wedding feast** represents the joyous privilege of sharing in the Kingdom. The **servants** must be the messengers of the last days, in which Jesus and his disciples are living. The twofold sending of messengers means that the Jewish people have had ample urgent summons to respond by repentance and faith. The insulting and killing of the messengers is a startling allegorical feature; so is the surprising *Blitzkrieg* in which the king, before the feast can cool, destroys the **city** and its inhabitants for not coming. (Has a saying of Jesus about judgment on Jerusalem, expressed in war terms, been combined with a parable about a wedding feast?) Then, amid the smoking ruins, the messengers **go to where the roads leave the city** and find people (refugees from the destroyed city, or outsiders?) to fill the banquet hall.

One man has come without a **wedding garment.** It is assumed that the hastily invited guest could have clothed himself properly, though it is not clear how (that the king provided proper garments is only a conjecture). The incident is told to teach that God will condemn all who try to enter the Kingdom without doing the will of the King. **Outer darkness:** Such utter separation from the king and his feast means exclusion from the Kingdom. **Many are invited:** The Kingdom is preached as widely as possible; but **few are chosen,** only those who earnestly prepare as the King expects will be admitted to the final Kingdom.

The parable condemns the failure of Israel and its leaders to respond to the Kingdom message of Jesus (his followers are clearly a meagre minority). It warns that response to his message is a crucial issue with eternal consequences. Two serious questions remain. (1) Who are those brought in from the highways? Had the Apostolic Age created the parable, they would no doubt be the Gentiles. But to Jesus they more likely were the 'tax-collectors and sinners', considered outcasts by the 'good' people but welcomed by Jesus. (2) Could Jesus possibly have condemned thus the man **without a wedding garment?** Vss. 11-13 may well have been originally a separate parable, in which the lack of a wedding garment represents the failure to fulfil the will of the King who graciously invited the guest. Condemnation of failure to do God's will is frequent in Matt. and in the

16

other Gospels. Jesus never discarded the idea of final judgment; to him forgiveness did not excuse subsequent moral laxity. Judas Iscariot reminds us that a man with every privilege may lack the wedding garment of obedient discipleship. 'Matthew' stresses this judgment aspect more than the other evangelists, but they clearly include it; Jesus wanted both an initial enthusiastic response and ongoing faithful obedience.

With vss. 15-22 cf. Mk. xii. 13-17; Lk. xx. 20-26. **The Pharisees** try to trap Jesus into saying something which can be used against him. **Their disciples:** The leading Pharisees do not come in person, but send less prominent members of their group. **Herodians:** Partisans of the Herodian family; probably Jewish supporters of Herod Antipas, tetrarch of Galilee and Perea, in Jerusalem to forestall supposed revolutionary tendencies of Jesus. The Pharisees, alert to establish Jesus' disloyalty to the Jewish Law and tradition, and the Herodians, at work to remove Jesus from the public scene, are far apart in basic interests, but may band together to oppose Jesus. He has defied the temple authorities; they hope to get him either to disown his people's nationalistic hopes or to defy the Roman authority.

They begin with flattering words, true enough but ironically spoken. Jesus has integrity; he accurately teaches what God wants men to do; he is not intimidated by any person, and refuses to trim his message for fear of anyone (even the Roman governor). So, they imply, he will give an honest answer. After this attempt to make him bold, they ask a question hotly debated by many Jews: Is it in accord with Jewish Law and duty to **pay** the annual **poll-tax** which the Romans levy? The question may imply that God's people should not be subject to pagan Gentiles; the Zealots held this position, and were ready to fight for it. Or it may imply that since some subjects of Tiberius Caesar paid him divine honours, the coin with which the tax was paid bore Caesar's image (in violation of Jewish convictions), and had an inscription bestowing high titles on Caesar, no good Jew could pay the tax without sacrificing his monotheistic faith. The image and titles could seem blasphemous to a Jew.

Jesus sees that the questioners seek only to discredit him. The clash between their pretended respect and their real aim shows

that they are scheming **hypocrites.** If he says, Pay the tax;
Zealots and other Jews hostile to Rome will turn against him,
if he says, Do not pay it, he can be turned over to the Romans
for inciting the Jews to rebel against Rome. He asks to be shown
the coin (denarius) **used in paying the poll-tax.** To prepare
for the point he intends to make, he asks **whose image and
inscription** it bears. They of course say, **Caesar's.** The coin is
marked plainly as his; it represents visibly the fact that he rules
Palestine (through his subordinates). The coin is his; give it back
(ἀπόδοτε) to him. **Pay** the tax. Jesus rejects the Zealot revolutionary position.

But he adds that the Jews should also give back **to God** what
they have from him. Made in God's image, living under him as
their Lord, continually receiving his good gifts, and bound to
him by his covenant with their people, their tie with God is far
stronger than their bond with Caesar. Jesus does not divide life
into two parts, one political, in which Caesar is supreme, and one
religious, in which God has sovereign control. That would rank
Caesar with the Lord God. What Jesus means is that they have
an obligation to the government over them, but they have a
greater obligation to God; it covers all of life; in the present
situation it includes the obligation to pay the tax to the power
that God permits to rule the Jews (cf. Rom. xiii. 1, 7).

Some take this passage to mean that Jesus prescribes the
separation of Church and State, so that life falls into two independent realms, each with a ruling authority. But he says nothing here about the Church. He speaks of Caesar and God; God
is not equated with the Church.

The opponents could not attack Jesus' answer. They did not
dare oppose it, for then they would take the Zealot position. So
they marvelled at his skill and **left him.** But the idea that he
completely evaded the dilemma they posed would be wrong; he
had alienated Jews of Zealot persuasion. But his mission was not
to evade every dilemma; it was to **teach truly the way of God.**

With vss. 23-33 cf. Mk. xii. 18-27; Lk. xx. 27-40. **That day:**
The day after Jesus entered Jerusalem and cleansed the temple
(cf. xxi. 18). The **Sadducees** now undertake to discredit
Jesus. **Saying that there is no resurrection:** That is, they
present an example to discredit the idea of resurrection. As the

conservative priestly party, giving Scriptural authority only to the Pentateuch, and rejecting the oral tradition accepted by Pharisees, they denied the resurrection doctrine (Acts xxiii. 8); it was not in the Pentateuch, and was rare in the remaining O.T., appearing most clearly in Isa. xxvi. 19; Dan. xii. 2. **Asked him:** The question comes in vs. 28.

The Sadducees cite Deut. xxv. 5 (not literally; cf. also Gen. xxxviii. 8). They may have thought that the father's life continues only in his child; compare ἀναστήσει, **shall raise up,** with ἀνάστασις, **resurrection.** Deut. prescribes Levirate marriage; that is, a brother must marry the widow of a childless brother and the children of this marriage are considered the children of the dead brother, so that his family line continues. In the story based on this law **seven brothers** in turn marry the same woman, and the Sadducees think that the question whose wife she will be after the resurrection shows the whole idea of the resurrection to be absurd. They obviously assume that resurrection would restore the dead to their former physical life, so that marriage would continue on a physical basis.

The Sadducees, Jesus replies, **know neither the Scriptures nor the power of God.** God's power will so transform the conditions of life that those raised will no longer live the present physical life; physical marriage relations will have no place. So the dilemma the Sadducees pose will not exist.

The Sadducees also fail to understand **the Scriptures. Have you not read:** They surely have, but evidently have not understood. The words Jesus quotes (Ex. iii. 6), spoken by God to Moses, are preserved in Scripture, so Jesus regards them as also spoken by God **to you** Sadducees. They do not actually mention resurrection. The three patriarchs, **Abraham, Isaac,** and **Jacob,** had been dead for centuries when God spoke to Moses. Yet God says he is their **God.** He is not the God of **dead** men but of **living** men; he has the **power** to keep them in living relation to him; so they are alive when he says this to Moses and when he says it to men as they read the Scripture; these patriarchs are with God, held safe by his power and love. Jesus assumes that God will renew all things and provide a fitting place for the eternal life of his people with him, and he therefore takes it as certain that these men will be raised and given their

place in that perfect eternal Kingdom. That man ceases to exist
at death, or exists thereafter only as a helpless ghost, or lives on
only in his descendants, is an impossible view for anyone who
knows God's power and his people's continuing fellowship with
him after death.

With vss. 34-40 cf. Mk. xii. 28-34; Lk. x. 25-28. The Pharisees again test Jesus (cf. vs. 15). The question is general and
hostile intent is not explicit, but the word **test** ($\pi\epsilon\iota\rho\acute{a}\zeta\omega\nu$ can
mean testing or tempting) shows that for 'Matthew' the aim is
to get some ground of criticism. The lines are too clearly drawn
to expect disinterested discussion. **Together** ($\dot{\epsilon}\pi\grave{\iota}\ \tau\grave{o}\ a\dot{v}\tau\acute{o}$): May
echo Ps. ii. 2 (cf. Acts iv. 26), and indicate hostile attitude.

The question itself is reasonable. It continues a Jewish attempt
to identify the central and most important commandment in
the Mosaic Law; various rabbis had given different but help-
ful answers to this question. **Lawyer** ($\nu o\mu\iota\kappa\acute{o}s$, from $\nu\acute{o}\mu os$,
'law'): This noun, used only here in Matt., is found six times in
Luke and in Tit. iii. 13; the more usual word is scribe, a student
and interpreter of the Mosaic Law. **Teacher:** Cf. vss. 16, 24.
The lawyer asks, **Which** ($\pi o\acute{\iota}a$ could mean 'What kind of')
commandment in the Law (of Moses in the Pentateuch) **is
greatest** ($\mu\epsilon\gamma\acute{a}\lambda\eta$, literally 'great', is used as in Hebrew with
superlative force)?

Jesus quotes Deut. vi. 5 (using, however, the word **mind**
instead of 'might'; some manuscripts and versions, however,
read 'might' ($\mathring{\iota}\sigma\chi\upsilon\iota$), or 'might' and **mind,** instead of simply
mind ($\delta\iota a\nuo\acute{\iota}a$), which seems original); the vs. commands love
of God with all of one's being and powers; the whole life is to
find its unity in this love. This vs. was part of the Shema (a
confession of faith repeated regularly by every Jew; it consisted
of Deut. vi. 4-9; xi. 13-21; Num. xv. 37-41, and began in
Hebrew with the word *shema,* 'Hear'). Its emphasis is not on
the ceremonial and external observance but on the vital relation
of the worshipper with his God, who should receive the willing,
grateful, and complete love of his people. **This,** Jesus says, **is
the greatest and first commandment,** supreme in importance and priority.

But Jesus cites a second command, **like** the first in importance and as unifying background for the entire Law. Lev. xix. 18

is not an alternative to Deut. vi. 5 nor an independent law that controls one area of life while Deut. vi. 5 controls another; it tells what love to God involves in relations with other people. Lev. xix. 18, already quoted in xix. 19, quoted and interpreted in a deepened sense in v. 43 ff., and used in Mk. xii. 31; Lk. x. 27; Rom. xiii. 9; Gal. v. 14; Jas. ii. 8, obviously was a key vs. for Jesus and the early Church. It does not call for taking up one's cross (xvi. 24), but in requiring as much concern for others as a person has for his own welfare it states a far-reaching principle which, if practised, would revolutionize human relations.

These two commandments, Jesus says, are the key commands from which all others derive. The others state specific ways in which love to God and neighbour may find proper expression. Thus these two may be taken as the key and substance of **the** Mosaic **Law;** its aim is the promotion of right relations with God and other people. It is added (cf. v. 17) that the content also of the prophetic books of the O.T. finds in these two commands its centre and creative power; the question put to Jesus (vs. 36) concerned only the Law, but the dominating outreach of the two commands reaches out beyond the Law to include the prophetic books.

Was Jesus the first to combine the two commands of love to God and neighbour? Lk. x. 27 says a scribe combined them, and Jesus approved. In the *Testaments of the Twelve Patriarchs* three passages combine love to God and neighbour (Test. Issachar v. 2; vii. 6; Test. Dan v. 3). They do not cite the two Scripture passages Jesus cites, but they express concisely their content. The date of the *Testaments,* however, is disputed. Often considered pre-Christian writings, with Christian interpolations, they recently have been taken by some scholars as later Christian writings composed on the basis of Jewish sources. This, if Lk. x. 27 is an editorial setting, would leave the way open to hold that Jesus first combined these two verses and made them basic in the way the Gospels suggest.

In any case this passage represents far more fully and accurately than vii. 12 the full scope of Jesus' teaching. Willing and active love to both God and man sums up well the creative demand of the O.T.

With vss. 41-46 cf. Mk. xii. 35-37; Lk. xx. 41-44. **The**

Pharisees, mentioned for the third time in this chapter (vss. 15, 34), will be severely condemned in ch. xxiii. Though the Sadducees oppose Jesus in Jerusalem, even there, 'Matthew' implies, Jesus' deepest conflict is with the Pharisees. They persistently watch him, and in Matt. Jesus now asks them a question before they disperse. The view that **the Christ** is the **Son of David** has O.T. roots (cf. 2 Sam. vii. 12 ff.), but the Gospels give the first explicit statement of it. The Pharisees' reply agrees with what 'Matthew' has repeatedly stated or implied (from i. 1 on), yet Jesus attacks this view. We must return to this problem.

Jesus' interpretation of Ps. cx. 1 rests upon the presupposition that (1) **David** wrote this Psalm (the current view in Jesus' day), (2) he wrote it under the inspiration of the Holy **Spirit** (vs. 43), and (3) **My Lord** refers to the Messiah, whom David reverently mentions as superior to him. Thus for Jesus the verse says: The Lord (God) said to my Lord (the Messiah), Sit on my right hand (on the right hand of God), until I (God) put your enemies (the enemies of the Messiah) beneath your feet (a picture of the Messiah's final victory over all who oppose him). David on this view calls the Messiah his **Lord,** and so, as vs. 45 says, it belittles the Messiah to call him David's **son.** The current Son of David expectation, which looked for a Messiah like David who would repeat David's conquests and rule like David, is disowned. The alternative, not here stated, but already made clear by Jesus, is the Suffering Servant leader, fused with the Son of Man figure and identified with the Messiah. The Messiah will do his work not by the military and political methods of David but by the way of the Servant and the Son of Man.

Without guidance from Jesus, Jewish Christians could hardly have accepted this rejection of the Son of David idea. Certainly 'Matthew', to whom the Son of David Messiah was highly significant as fulfilling the expectations of his people and his Scripture, would never have created such an incident. It reflects Jesus' wrestling with current expectations and shows in part how he grasped God's will for him in the light of his widespread rejection by his people. Essentially he had put aside the popular Son of David idea of Messiahship at the temptation (iv. 8-10); the essential basis of his Suffering Servant interpretation of his

239

work was thus present throughout his ministry; he here publicly challenges the popular view.

Five points are worth noting: (1) Jesus found in the O.T. forecasts of his own time and career; Ps. cx. 1 pointed to his present and future role. (2) He did not deal with literary and historical problems we face; this Psalm was considered David's writing, and he accepted that view. (3) In connecting the title Lord with the Messiah, the Apostolic Church followed his thinking. (4) Basically the Messiah is not explained by Davidic descent, but by his unique link with God (cf. xi. 27). (5) The exaltation and triumph of the Messiah was for Jesus as for the Apostolic Church an integral part of the Messianic hope.

Did Jesus reject the Son of David idea completely? Taken literally, this passage says, Yes. At the very least Jesus declares the freedom of the Messiah to establish the Kingdom by another path than the political and military methods of David. The Messiah can be and will be the Suffering Servant rather than the military conqueror and earthly king. 'Matthew' and the early Church did not understand this to exclude physical descent from David, and for them this descent linked the Messiah with the Jewish heritage and the O.T. promises.

CHAPTER XXIII

xxiii. 1-39. THE SCRIBES AND PHARISEES INDICTED

1, 2 Then Jesus addressed the crowds and his disciples, say-
3 ing, 'The scribes and the Pharisees sit on Moses' seat. So do and observe all that they tell you, but do not do accord-
4 ing to their deeds, for they say but do not do. They bind heavy burdens together and place them on men's shoulders, but they themselves refuse to move them with
5 their finger. All their deeds they do to be seen by men; for they make their phylacteries broad and their tassels long,
6 and they love the place of honour at banquets, and the

best seats in the synagogues, and the greetings in the 7
market-places, and to be called Rabbi by men. But you 8
are not to be called Rabbi, for one is your Teacher and
you are all brothers. And do not call anyone on earth your 9
Father, for you have one Father, the One in heaven.
Neither be called teachers, for you have one Teacher, 10
the Christ. The greatest among you shall be your servant. 11
He who exalts himself will be humbled, and he who 12
humbles himself will be exalted.

'Woe to you, scribes and Pharisees, hypocrites, for you 13
shut the Kingdom of Heaven against men; for you yourselves do not enter, nor do you permit those who are
entering to enter.

'Woe to you, scribes and Pharisees, hypocrites, for you 15
travel about on sea and land to make one proselyte, and
when he has become one, you make him twice as much
a son of Gehenna as you are.

'Woe to you, blind guides who say, "Whoever swears 16
by the temple, it is nothing; but whoever swears by the
gold of the temple is obligated". You are foolish and 17
blind! For which is greater, the gold or the temple which
makes the gold sacred? And, "Whoever swears by the 18
altar, it is nothing; but whoever swears by the gift on it is
obligated". You are blind! For which is greater, the gift 19
or the altar which makes the gift sacred? He therefore 20
who swears by the altar swears by it and by all that is
on it, and he who swears by the temple swears by it 21
and by him who dwells in it, and he who swears by 22
heaven swears by the throne of God and by him who
sits on it.

'Woe to you, scribes and Pharisees, hypocrites, for you 23
tithe mint and dill and cumin, but have left undone the
more important requirements of the Law, justice and
mercy and faithfulness; these you should have done without leaving those undone. You blind guides, who strain 24
out the gnat but swallow the camel.

'Woe to you, scribes and Pharisees, hypocrites, for you 25
cleanse the outside of the cup and the dish, but within
they are full of plunder and self-indulgence. You blind 26

Pharisee, cleanse first the inside of the cup, that its outside also may become clean.

27 'Woe to you, scribes and Pharisees, hypocrites, for you are like whitewashed tombs, which on the outside appear beautiful, but inside are full of dead men's bones and all
28 uncleanness. So you also outwardly appear to men to be righteous, but inwardly are full of hypocrisy and lawlessness.

29 'Woe to you, scribes and Pharisees, hypocrites, for you build the tombs of the prophets and adorn the monuments
30 of the righteous, and you say, "If we had lived in the days of our fathers, we would not have joined with them in
31 shedding the blood of the prophets". And so you testify against yourselves that you are sons of those who mur-
32 dered the prophets. Fill up in your turn the measure of
33 your fathers. You serpents, you offspring of vipers, how
34 could you escape the judgment of Gehenna? Therefore behold, I send to you prophets and wise men and scribes; some of them you will kill and crucify, and some of them you will scourge in your synagues and persecute from
35 city to city, that all the righteous blood shed on the land may come upon you, from the blood of righteous Abel to the blood of Zechariah the son of Barachiah, whom you murdered between the temple building and the altar.
36 Truly I tell you, all these things will come upon this generation.

37 'Jerusalem, Jerusalem, who kills the prophets and stones those sent to her, how often I have wished to gather together your children, as a hen gathers her young chicks
38 under her wings, and you refused. Behold, your house is
39 being abandoned to you. For I tell you, you will not see me henceforth until you say, "Blessed is he who comes in the name of the Lord".'

With vss. 1-12 cf. Mk. xii. 37b-40; Lk. xi. 46; xx. 45-47. With ch. xxiii the public ministry of Jesus closes; in his last address to the crowds Jesus brings out the basic clash between himself and **the Pharisees.** They opposed him during his ministry, and after A.D. 70 were the surviving group of Judaism with which

the Church had to do. The tradition here used comes from the
early Jewish-Christian Church; its criticism of Jewish failures
was of special interest to them. But Lk. contains parallels to most
of ch. xxiii, and though the ch. is an editorial collection, shaped
somewhat by Jewish-Christian conflicts with rabbinical circles,
it nevertheless represents common early Christian tradition. It
falls into three parts: warnings (vss. 1-12); seven Woes (vss.
13-36); closing lament (vss. 37-39).

The scribes, mostly Pharisees, copied, taught, and applied
the Mosaic Law. They were pledged to obey and teach both the
written Law and the oral tradition, which they claimed was an
integral part of the Law, received through a direct succession of
teachers going back to Moses (cf. the Jewish tractate, *Sayings
of the Fathers*, i. 1). **Moses' seat:** A synagogue chair which
symbolized the origin and authority of their teaching. Jesus does
not challenge their claim; he seems here to approve it. After
opposing Pharisaic teaching so many times, could he thus tell
his hearers, including his disciples, to do **all** that the scribes and
Pharisees teach? This is at best doubtful. But the main purpose
in vs. 3 is to contrast the generally good teaching of these people
with their much less commendable living. **They say** what the
will of God is, but they **do not do** it. So Jesus warned against
imitating their lives. Though usually outwardly correct and
formally obedient, they lacked the personal dedication and unselfish integrity of good living (cf. v. 20).

Jesus gives a glaring example of teaching without practice.
They multiply duties, develop strict interpretations of the Law,
burden men with obligations, but leave them to carry the load
unaided (cf. Gal. vi. 2). v. 20-48 shows that Jesus demanded full
obedience to the will of God; but as xi. 30 shows, he had sympathy and compassion, and put the emphasis not on meticulous
detail but on grateful willing obedience.

Jesus denounces the scribes and Pharisees for their bold
parade of pretended piety. **Phylacteries:** Little boxes tied with
a leather thong on the forehead and arm at the time of morning
prayer and containing copies of Ex. xiii. 1-10, 11-16; Deut. vi.
4-9; xi. 13-21. **Tassels,** worn on the corners of the outer Jewish
garment, marked a Jew. Large phylacteries and long tassels were
ways of recommending oneself as pious.

Jesus names four other practices prompted by love of parade and high position. Such people seek honoured places at **banquets,** the prominent seats in **synagogues,** deferential **greetings** in public places and recognition as **Rabbi** ('my teacher'). Use of this title encouraged superficial deference which catered to pride; no one should give or want such deference (cf. vss. 8, 10). The disciples are not to let people call them **Rabbi.** They have one authoritative **Teacher, the Christ** (vs. 10). They are all equal and are dependent on him. They must keep this equality and dependence clear by thinking of each other as **brothers,** and so avoid class lines. No one should be singled out for extreme deference and called **Father.** All disciples are children of the **one Father,** God. Vs. 10 restates vs. 8.

Vss. 11 f. emphasize the greatness of humility and service to others (cf. xviii. 3 f.; xx. 26 f.). Any ambitious attempt at self-advancement is foredoomed to failure; he who willingly accepts humble tasks and ministers to the needs of others will be recognized as **the greatest** among the disciples; he has expressed in life the spirit and will of his Master.

Ch. xxiii, an editorial collection of criticisms of the **scribes and Pharisees,** contains seven Woes, which vary in literary form. Lk. xi. 39-52 parallels five of Matt.'s seven Woes, and has a sixth Woe parallel to vs. 4, in which Matt. does not use the word **Woe.** Luke groups six woes under two headings, three against Pharisees and three against lawyers (scribes). Despite such differences in order and wording, the explicit condemnation of the scribes and Pharisees by using the Woe form of address was part of the early tradition of Jesus' teaching. It was not a mere creation of Jewish Christians reacting against Jewish hostility to the Church.

Woe (cf. Isa. v. 8-23 for an O.T. pattern): Expresses burning condemnation, and implies that Jesus' words express God's attitude towards these leaders. They show no signs of regret and repentance, and stubborn continuance in their present conduct will inevitably lead to final ruin. **Hypocrites:** Need not imply conscious crafty deception, but condemns their inexcusable failure to live up to what they have had full opportunity to know is right.

With vs. 13 cf. Lk. xi. 52. These leaders keep men from

entering **the Kingdom** both by example—they do not respond
to Jesus' preaching by repentance and faith—and by their teaching and active hostility. Their prominence and public influence
induce many otherwise favourably inclined people to turn from
Jesus and his urgent message.

Considerable evidence of Greek manuscripts and ancient versions favours inserting before or after vs. 13 this Woe: 'Woe to
you, scribes and Pharisees, hypocrites, for you devour widows'
houses and in pretence offer long prayers; for this you will
receive greater condemnation'. This is a later addition to Matt.,
derived from Mk. xii. 40; Lk. xx. 47.

Abundant evidence attests Jewish activity in Jesus' day to
make proselytes, that is, win Gentiles to complete adherence to
Judaism. This persistent zeal considered no journey too long if
one proselyte could be won. But the scribes and Pharisees so
train these converts that they make the converts twice as bad
as the evangelists are. Does Jesus imply that proselytes more
narrow and rabid than Jewish leaders had opposed him? **Son
of Gehenna:** Belonging by nature to Gehenna, deserving by
manner of life to be condemned to Gehenna. Gehenna, originally the name of the valley south and west of Jerusalem, became
a name for the place of final punishment of the wicked, perhaps
because smouldering fires in that valley suggested the fires of
the final punishment of the wicked.

Blind guides: Refers to the scribes and Pharisees, who only
in this Woe are not directly named (cf. xv. 14). On vss. 16-22
cf. v. 33-37, which goes beyond this passage by forbidding all
use of oaths. The use of oaths divides speech into two areas, one
in which the person, because under oath, must tell the truth or
God will punish him, and one in which no such obligation is felt
or penalty expected. But in fact one always speaks in God's
presence and is responsible to him for truthfulness. The present
passage exposes a further evil in the use of oaths; men arbi-
trarily divided oaths into those in which the man **is obligated**
(literally, 'owes it') and those in which he is not **(it is nothing).**
Two such vicious distinctions are reported (vss. 16, 18) and
another implied (vs. 22). In each case the oath naming the more
important thing is perversely considered not binding, while
reference to the less important thing gives the oath binding

character. Actually to Jesus **the temple** would be more sacred than **the gold** on it, and **the altar** than **the gift** placed on it; and, vs. 22 implies, **heaven,** often used as a veiled reference to God because of Jewish reluctance to utter the name of God directly, and sometimes called his throne (Isa. lxvi. 1; cf. v. 34), would be a more comprehensive and solemn reference than **the throne of God.** (Note that Jesus does not here criticize the sacrificial system, but seems to assume that it has divine sanction.) Any reference to the temple, the altar, or heaven leads back to God and in effect refers to God, and so any such oath calls God to witness the oath and defend the truth. Any dividing of oaths into those that are binding and those that sound impressive but leave the one who swears them free to do as he pleases is hypocritical and evil.

With vss. 23 f. cf. Lk. xi. 42. Israel owed a **tithe** (tenth) of all that grew as seed or fruit (Lev. xxvii. 30; Deut. xiv. 22 f.). Tradition interpreted this to apply to even the smallest herbs, **mint,** and **dill** (anise?), used for seasoning, and **cumin** (or cummin), used as spice and medicine. Jesus attacks not the painstaking obedience to this tradition but neglect of the far **more important requirements: justice,** honest diligence in doing what is right and fair; **mercy,** active kindness to everyone in need of help; and **faithfulness,** steady integrity in dealings with others (πίστιν can mean faith towards God; if Mic. vi. 8 is in mind, the translation 'faith' must be preferred). Obviously for Jesus the Law is not concerned primarily with ceremonial prescriptions, though he does not condemn attention to lesser details if the greater things are kept central.

With that sense of the grotesque which Jesus often uses to ridicule wrong ways of life, he compares such obsession with minutiae with a concern for good drinking water in which the man carefully strains out a **gnat** and so gets rid of an unclean insect, but gulps down without hesitation a full-size **camel** (for the camel as an example of a huge object cf. xix. 24). Spiritual health and the ability to give spiritual leadership depend on a sense of proportion which keeps the important things central and never lets anxious attention to lesser detail crowd them out.

With vss. 25 f. cf. Lk. xi. 39-41, not in the Woe form or closely parallel in wording. Utensils used for holding food had to be

washed carefully to satisfy Jewish rules of ceremonial purity
(Mk. vii. 4). The scribes and Pharisees observe these rules
strictly, but on the inside their utensils are unclean, because of
what is put in them: **plunder,** food obtained by violent or dishonest practices, and **self-indulgence,** foods that show selfish
concentration on enjoyment regardless of what others need.
Jesus addresses a single **Pharisee** for dramatic effect (this
address suggests that these two verses originally were uncon-
nected with the series of Woes), and tells him what to do: cleanse
first what the cup contains; see that your food is honestly obtained and is not chosen in a spirit of self-indulgence. Injustice
and self-indulgence make meticulous attention to ceremonial
purity a pretence and transparent fraud. (Vs. 26 and Lk. xi. 41
seem to represent two renderings of an earlier Aramaic form;
the rendering in Matt. makes consistent sense.)

With vss. 27 f. cf. Lk. xi. 44, which has a different point: an
unnoticed grave makes ceremonially unclean whoever steps on
it (Num. xix. 16). In Matt. the tomb is plainly marked; this fits
well the situation in Matt., the days immediately preceding Passover, for **tombs** were whitewashed on the fifteenth of the month
Adar, a month before the Passover, so that Jews would clearly
see them and not be defiled and kept from observing Passover
by accidental contact with a grave. The freshly whitewashed
tombs appeared **beautiful** but beneath the pleasing exterior
were the unclean and ceremonially defiling **bones** of the dead.
So the scribes and Pharisees have an outwardly correct and
pious manner of life; but within they are **full of hypocrisy**
(their life may not consciously aim at deception but it is a sham
by its glaring contrast between correct outward forms and inner
selfishness) **and lawlessness** (they outwardly do the rites the
Law commands but inwardly are driven by selfish and unjust
aims and so live the opposite of an obedient life). Wickedness
is only rendered more evil when carried on behind an outward
show of pious worship.

With vss. 29-36 cf. Lk. xi. 47-51. It is assumed here, as in
Jewish tradition (cf. Heb. xi. 32-38), that **prophets** and other
righteous men of earlier days were persecuted and martyred.
The **scribes and Pharisees** recognize the injustice in this and
to make up for it build **tombs** to give belated honour to God's

loyal servants. They thus disown the actions of their ancestors, and think that had they lived then, they would not have shared in such wickedness. Jesus grimly rejects their claim. They kill **the prophets** in their own day, just as their ancestors did; their people have repeatedly persecuted God's messengers and are ready to put to death his Son (cf. xxi. 33-46). **Fill up:** Complete the evil work of your ancestors. Instead of πληρώσατε, **fill up,** a defiant urging, some ancient authorities read πληρώσετε, 'you will fill up', a sad prediction.

Epithets of withering condemnation (cf. iii. 7; xii. 34) show that Jesus sees no hope for them to escape final condemnation, for he sees no sign that they will change their wicked ways. They are sons of **Gehenna** (vs. 15), persons whose nature fits them for the place of final punishment, and they face **the judgment** that will sentence them to that place. They still have their chance to choose the right; Jesus (Luke says, 'the Wisdom of God') will send **prophets and wise men and scribes** (this use of **scribes** for teachers of Jesus' message is unusual); but some will be killed (the crucifixion predicted would involve execution by the Romans; Jews executed by stoning; has 'Matthew' made explicit what Jesus left more vague?) or scourged in **synagogues** (cf. 2 Cor. xi. 24) and hounded **from city to city.**

On **this generation** that rejects Jesus the climactic blows of judgment will fall. The guilt of Israel has already led to exile and loss of national liberty; now the time for divine judgment in its fullness has nearly arrived. That divine judgment will bring just punishment not only for the sins of this generation, but for all the murders of God's **righteous** servants from **Abel,** the first man killed in the Bible (Gen. iv. 8), to Zechariah, the last man martyred in the O.T. narrative (2 Chron. xxiv. 20-22). **Land:** γῆς probably means Palestine here instead of the 'earth'. **Barachiah:** Seems to confuse the Zechariah in 2 Chron. xxiv. 20 with the one in Zech. i. 1, whose father was Berechiah. **You murdered:** These contemporary wrong-doers, who continue the wrongdoing of their ancestors, are held to participate in the sin and guilt of those earlier generations.

This climactic judgment Jesus expected soon, in the lifetime of his **generation** (cf. xvi. 28). The expectation of almost immediate judgment leads Jesus, though he does not profess to

know the exact time (xxiv. 36), to lament over stubborn Jerusalem (vss. 37-39) and then teach about the coming judgment
(chs. xxiv-xxv).

With vss. 37-39 cf. Lk. xiii. 34 f., almost identical in wording
but placed much earlier in the ministry. This sad lament shows
how deeply Jesus felt the stubborn refusal of **Jerusalem** to
accept him. He wanted to shelter her from impending judgment.
How often: Does this mean that he has made several visits to
Jerusalem during his ministry (so in Jn.) to appeal to her to
repent? Or that while in Galilee he has often wished to preach
in Jerusalem, and only now has come to do it? No such earlier
visits are reported in Matt., Mk., or Lk. **You refused:** The
ministry is ended; the Jewish leaders and the holy city have said
No to his appeal. **Your house is being abandoned to you:**
This may mean in part that God is abandoning his house, his
temple (cf. Jer. xii. 7; xxii. 5; Ezek. x. 18 f.; xi. 22 f.). But **for,**
which begins vs. 39, indicates that vs. 38 refers to Jesus' departure. The people of Jerusalem will not see him again until
they welcome him as he **comes in the name of the Lord**
God at the end of history to carry out God's judgment and final
redemption. In Lk. these words of Ps. cxviii. 26 can refer to the
entry into Jerusalem on Sunday of the last week of Jesus' life,
but as placed in Matt. they point forward to Jesus' final coming
in glory to finish God's work.

This stern chapter is a collection of sayings rather than a
discourse Jesus spoke at one time. It certainly reflects the deep
cleavage between Jewish Christians and Pharisaic Judaism. But
it also presents the essential truth that the Jewish leaders definitely rejected and opposed Jesus, and that Jesus, conscious of
being sent by God with a crucial message, could not be indifferent to his rejection by his people and their leaders. Christian
scholars must remember that every fault of the scribes and
Pharisees has been copied by Christian leaders, but they cannot
say that Jesus and the Pharisees were friends.

CHAPTER XXIV

xxiv. 1-51. THE END OF THE PRESENT AGE

1 And Jesus departed from the temple and was going his way, and his disciples came to show him the temple
2 buildings. He answered and said to them, 'Do you not see all these? Truly I tell you, there will not be left here one stone upon another which will not be thrown down.'

3   As he was sitting on the Mount of Olives, the disciples came to him privately, saying, 'Tell us, when will these things occur, and what will be the sign of your coming
4 and of the end of the age?' And Jesus answered and said
5 to them, 'Take care lest anyone mislead you. For many will come in my name, saying, "I am the Christ", and
6 will mislead many. You will soon hear of wars and rumours of wars; see that you are not frightened; for this
7 must happen, but the end is not yet. For nation will rise against nation and kingdom against kingdom, and there
8 will be famines and earthquakes in various places; all these things are only the initial birth-pains.

9   'Then men will hand you over to oppression and will kill you; you will be hated by all the nations on account of
10 my name. And then many will be tempted to sin and will
11 betray one another and hate one another; and many false
12 prophets will arise and mislead many; and because lawlessness has increased, the love of the many will grow
13, 14 cold. But he who endures to the end will be saved. And this gospel of the Kingdom will be preached in the whole earth, as a testimony to all the nations, and then the end will come.

15   'When therefore you see the desolating abomination, spoken of by Daniel the prophet, standing in the holy
16 place—let the reader understand—then let those who are
17 in Judea flee to the mountains; let him who is on the housetop not go down to pick up the things in his house;
18 and let him who is in the field not turn back to pick up his
19 coat. Woe to the women who are pregnant or are nursing

a child in those days. And pray that your flight may not 20
occur in winter or on a Sabbath, for then there will be 21
great tribulation, such as has not happened from the beginning of the world up to now, nor will happen again.
And if those days had not been shortened, no one would 22
be saved; but for the sake of the elect those days will be
shortened.

'If anyone then says to you, "Behold, here is the 23
Christ", or "Here he is", do not believe him; for false 24
Christs and false prophets will arise and perform great
signs and wonders, so as to mislead if possible even the
elect. Behold, I have told you beforehand. So if they say 25, 26
to you, "Behold, he is in the wilderness", do not go out;
"Behold, he is in the inner rooms", do not believe it; for 27
as the lightning flashes forth from the east and shines to
the west, so will be the coming of the Son of Man. Wher- 28
ever the corpse is, there the vultures will be gathered
together.

'Immediately after the tribulation of those days the sun 29
will be darkened and the moon will not shed its light and
the stars will fall from heaven, and the powers of the
heavens will be shaken. And then the sign of the Son of 30
Man will appear in heaven, and then all the tribes of the
earth will mourn and will see the Son of Man coming on
the clouds of heaven with power and great glory. And he 31
will send forth his angels with a loud trumpet call, and
they will assemble his elect from the four winds, from
one end of heaven to the other.

'Now from the fig tree learn the parable. Whenever its 32
branch has become tender and puts forth foliage, you
know that summer is near. So also, whenever you see all 33
these things, know that he is near, at the door. Truly I tell 34
you, this generation will not pass away until all these
things occur. Heaven and earth will pass away, but my 35
words will not pass away.

'But concerning that day or hour no one knows, not 36
even the angels in heaven or the Son, but only the Father.
For just as the days of Noah were, so will be the coming 37
of the Son of Man. For as in the days before the flood they 38

were eating and drinking, marrying and giving in mar-
39 riage, until the day that Noah entered the ark, and they
did not understand until the flood came and swept them
all away, so also will be the coming of the Son of Man.
40 Then there will be two men in the field; one is taken and
41 the other is left. Two women will be grinding at the mill;
42 one is taken and the other is left. Watch therefore, for you
43 do not know at what hour your Lord is coming. But know
this: if the householder had known at what hour the thief
was coming, he would have watched and not have let his
44 house be broken into. Therefore you also must be ready,
for the Son of Man is coming at an hour when you do not
expect him.
45   'Who then is the faithful and prudent servant whom his
master has placed in charge of his household to give
46 them their food at the proper times? Blessed is that servant whom his master, when he comes, will find doing
47 so. Truly I tell you, he will put him in charge of all his
48 possessions. But if that evil servant says in his heart, "My
49 master delays his return", and begins to beat his fellow-
50 servants, and eats and drinks with drunken men, the
master of that servant will come on a day that he does
15 not expect and at an hour that he does not know, and will
cut him in two and assign him his place with the hypocrites; there the weeping and gnashing of teeth will
occur.'

With vss. 1 f. cf. Mk. xiii. 1 f.; Lk. xxi. 5 f. Jesus, in the
temple since xxi. 23, now takes final leave of it. His disciples
point back to the beauty and grandeur of its **buildings** (built by
Herod the Great, beginning 20–19 B.C., and his successors).
Temple (ἱερόν): A term for the entire temple area, with its buildings, gates, porticoes, and walls. What impressed Jesus was the
impending violent destruction of the temple, a divine judgment
on this city and people for rejecting the gospel.

With vss. 3-8 cf. Mk. xiii. 3-8; Lk. xxi. 7-11 (perhaps Mk. xiii,
the basic source of Matt. xxiv, depends on a written collection
and application of Jesus' eschatological teaching). Jesus left the
temple and city, crossed the Kidron Valley east of Jerusalem,

and from the **Mount of Olives** could look down into the temple court. **Privately:** The public ministry has ended; he speaks with his disciples. They ask (1) **when** this temple will be destroyed, and, in Matt., (2) **what will be the sign** (cf. vs. 30) of his **coming,** advent (παρουσία), and of the **end,** consummation, of this present **age.** In all three Synoptic Gospels the discourse is composite, and Jesus speaks of both the fall of Jerusalem and the end of the age.

Jesus first warns against expecting the end at once. It will come in his generation (xxiii. 36; xxiv. 34), but other things must happen first: deceivers (vs. 5), **wars** (vs. 6 f.), natural catastrophes (vs. 7), persecution and dissension (vss. 9-12), and world-wide preaching (vs. 14). The disciples must not be misled by false Messiahs, claiming God-given anointing and authority (cf. false prophets; vii. 15; xxiv. 11). **In my name:** Might suggest that they claim only to continue Jesus' work, but in Matt. they claim to be **the Christ,** to succeed and replace Jesus.

The disciples will hear that **wars,** an expected feature of the last days, have broken out and more are impending. The social order will be tottering; but the disciples must not panic, for these things have their place in God's plan, and God's people will be kept safe if they trust him and hold steady through further trials yet to come.

The reference to large-scale wars may be only traditional language, but it may include war between the Romans and Parthians, in which Palestine, a border region, would suffer terror and confusion. Natural catastrophes, **famines** (because of war) **and earthquakes,** are an added warning and divine punishment on the wicked. But these things are only the **initial birth-pains** connected with the coming of God's perfect Kingdom.

With vss. 9-14 cf. Mk. xiii. 9-13; Lk. xxi. 12-19. Most of Mk.'s parallel has already been used in Matt. x. 17-21 to describe the work and dangers of the disciples in their mission; it is now briefly repeated and expanded by prediction of dissension and apostasy (vss. 10-12). **Hand you over:** To the ruling authorities. The hostility will be general; in the N.T. **the nations** (τὰ ἔθνη) usually means Gentiles (as contrasted with ὁ λαός, 'the people', the Jews), but combined with **all** may mean all nations including the Jews (cf. xxv. 32). **On account of my name** (cf. x. 22): Because you are my disciples and your loyalty to me controls your life. In hating the disciples they hate Christ.

Vss. 10-12 describe the final trials; betrayal, hostility, and persecution will sap loyalty and courage. **Many:** the majority, as in vs. 12. **Tempted to sin:** Literally, caused to stumble, to give up loyalty to Christ and his disciples. **False prophets** (cf. vs. 24 and vii. 15): Christian teachers claiming direct instructions from God, but actually changing their message to avoid hostility. Their smooth compromise with the world will **mislead many** (the majority). **Lawlessness:** Not among the disciples but in their social environment. **Grow cold:** They will desert the Christian fellowship, which will be a loyal remnant. For this remnant endurance until the final Kingdom comes will be the key word and key virtue. The experiences of the persecuted Apostolic Church led 'Matthew' to stress the importance of endurance.

In this final period the faithful remnant must not be passive; they must actively witness for Christ, announcing that **the Kingdom** will soon come and men must repent and believe (iv. 17). The disciples must preach **in the whole earth** (so also xxviii. 18-20). The universal scope of the mission is emphasized by referring first to **the whole earth** ($o\dot{\iota}\kappa o\nu\mu\acute{\epsilon}\nu\eta$, literally 'inhabited', means inhabited earth) and then to **all the nations.** The gospel is to all **a testimony** that God's final action is under way and urgently claims man's repentant response. Such a world mission, which seems long-lasting to us, is here (as in xxviii. 19, it seems) considered the work of a generation.

It is hard to explain why, if Jesus said this (and Acts i. 8), the Twelve stayed in Jerusalem, even when the Church was persecuted (Acts viii. 1), and let Paul and others develop the mission to Gentiles. For all his breadth of outlook, Peter was essentially an evangelist among the Jews (Gal. ii. 7 f.). Did the Twelve hope first to win the Jews before undertaking a mission to Gentiles? Some think that Jesus never spoke of this wider mission, but all four gospel writers say he did, and 'Matthew' as a Jewish Christian would have had no reason to ascribe such words to Jesus unless solid early tradition reported them.

With vss. 15-22 cf. Mk. xiii. 14-20; Lk. xxi. 20-24. The terrible final trial is described as an invasion of Palestine. The key phrase, **the desolating abomination,** referred in Dan. ix. 27; xi. 31 to the pagan altar set up in the temple by Antiochus Epiphanes (168 or 167 B.C.). Here it is reinterpreted to mean the blasphemous invader (the anti-Christ?), who invades **the holy place** (possibly the holy land, Palestine, or the holy city, Jerusalem, but probably, as in Dan., the temple). Such traditional language carries overtones of the final eschatological clash; it is a symbol of the final conflict between the forces of good and evil, a time of unparalleled hardship and danger for God's people. **Let the reader understand:** A parenthesis from the writer of Mk.'s source? Or a warning by Jesus that he is reinterpreting Dan. to apply to the coming crisis?

Vss. 16-18 urge instant and unhesitating flight when the mysterious evil foe appears. **Flee to the mountains:** Where remote spots and numerous caves offer hiding places. A man on his **housetop** or in his **field** when the sudden danger appears must flee without stopping a second to save valuables or clothing. It will go hard with those who cannot flee fast. Pregnant women or mothers with nursing infants cannot flee quickly enough to escape danger. **Woe:** Spoken not in anger but in sorrow at the prospect of their suffering. **In winter:** When cold and bad weather make it harder to flee and to find shelter. **On a Sabbath:** Only in Matt.; reflects Jewish-Christian faithfulness in keeping the Sabbath and dread at having to break it, but implies that even if the crisis comes on a Sabbath, instant flight is necessary.

Using words from Dan. xii. 1, Jesus describes this **great tribulation** as the greatest in the entire course of history. Human nature could not long endure it; to spare his **elect,** his chosen ones, the followers of Christ, **those days will be shortened.** Will each day be made shorter? More likely the meaning is that the number of days of terror will be limited.

With vss. 23-25 cf. Mk. xiii. 21-23; with vss. 26-28 cf. Lk. xvii. 23 f., 37. These two paragraphs, taken from different sources, have a common theme: Do not be misled by rumours that Christ has already come and is at some other place. When he comes, his brilliant appearance will be visible at once to all. These verses, parenthetical between vs. 22 and vs. 29, warn against a wrong and excited expectation that false leaders will promote. **The Christ:** Returned to establish the final Kingdom. Deut. xiii. 1-3 is recalled to warn the disciples that false leaders will arise; Jesus has previously spoken of false Christs (vs. 5) and **false prophets** (vs. 11), who may even work miracles (vii. 15-23); such miracles are no certain sign of divine mission (cf. 1 Cor. xiii. 2). His advance warning should put them sufficiently on guard against excited rumour.

Vs. 26 resumes the teaching of vs. 23. Since Christ will return like a lightning flash, visible from one end of heaven to the other, no journey will be necessary to see him and no report that he is elsewhere, **in the wilderness** or in some secret room, should be believed; his glorious presence will be everywhere and instantly visible.

Vs. 28 quotes a proverb. ἀετός usually means 'eagle' but here means **vulture,** as in other ancient sources. Vultures congregate where a carcass lies. Jesus seems to mean that wherever the disciples are, the returning Christ will appear. They will not have to search for him; he will come visibly to them.

With vss. 29-31 cf. Mk. xiii. 24-27; Lk. xxi. 25-28. Promptly at the end of the unparalleled **tribulation** (vs. 22) the break-up of the previously orderly starry system will herald the imminent end. Building on such passages as Isa. xiii. 10; xxiv. 4, Jewish eschatology expected the darkening of **sun** and **moon,** falling of **stars,** and shaking loose from their fixed places of the heavenly bodies (**the powers of the heavens** means all these heavenly bodies; cf. Deut. iv. 19; xvii. 3; 2 Kings xxiii. 5; Jer. viii. 2). In the darkness left by the loss of their light **the sign** asked for in vs. 3 appears **in heaven,** from which the **Son of Man** is returning. Is the sign this brilliant light of his coming (vs. 27)? As first response to his impending arrival **all the tribes of the earth** lament (cf. Zech. xii. 10-14, used also in Rev. i. 7), aware that his coming means final divine judgment on all. His coming is like that described in Dan. vii. 13 f. His **power** may mean the accompanying angels (vs. 31), or, better, his divine power to judge and save. **Glory:** The splendour of his divine nature and role.

His angels (cf. iv. 6; xvi. 27) not only eliminate the wicked (xiii. 41) but **assemble his elect,** long before chosen and

destined for salvation. At a **trumpet call** (cf. 1 Thess. iv. 16),
the ancient signal for God's people to assemble, they are
gathered from all directions (**the four winds:** cf. Zech. ii. 6)
and from the most remote regions (Deut. xxx. 4), where the
dome of **heaven** touches earth's outer rim. Peoples of every
region will assemble with Christ in the final Kingdom (vs. 14;
viii. 11; xxviii. 19; cf. Rev. vii. 9). The resurrection is probably
implied by the trumpet call (cf. 1 Thess. iv. 16). Where the elect
assemble is not said, but they will be with the Son of Man
(1 Thess. iv. 17).

With vss. 32-35 cf. Mk. xiii. 28-31; Lk. xxi. 29-33. After
describing pictorially the events that precede and constitute the
end, the discourse now discusses the time of the end and how to
prepare for it. The rest of this chapter refers to the period prior
to Jesus' return, i.e. prior to vss. 29-31.

The parable teaches that the nearness (not the exact time)
of the end can be discerned from the events of vss. 4-22 or 15-22.
In spring the sap flows into a fig tree's **branch,** it becomes soft
and **tender,** and puts forth leaves, a sure sign that **summer is
near.** So the disciples should know from the events of vss.
4-22 or 15-22 that Christ's coming is very **near,** as though **at
the** very **door** of the house, ready to enter. γινώσκετε in vs. 33
can be indicative, as in vs. 32, but probably is imperative,
know, a command to be alert and discern the meaning of events.

To stimulate alertness, Jesus states that before his generation
ends all the preparatory events described will occur. Thus the
end, the coming of the Son of Man, will come within a generation. Attempts to translate γενεά as 'human race' or 'Jewish
race', and interpret Jesus to say that the human race or Jewish
race will still exist on earth when the end comes, are misguided;
the word refers to the **generation** living when Jesus spoke. Did
the saying originally speak of the fall of Jerusalem? 'Matthew'
certainly understood **all these things** to refer to the end of
history; this agrees with x. 23; xvi. 28, and what Mark and Luke
say. Even if we say that the persecutions of the Apostolic Age
and the fall of Jerusalem began the fulfilment of Jesus' predictions, the end (**all these things**) did not come as expected. We
have to accept limits of knowledge in Jesus (cf. vs. 36). But his
vivid message of imminent judgment and salvation is truer to

the Biblical faith in the living God than alternatives that discard all affirmations about the future, or comfortably postpone the end so far that the urgency of God's claim is lost, or make of judgment an impersonal process, or deny any future consequences for sin, or assume automatic immortality for individuals with no final vindication of God's rule.

Vs. 35 also speaks of the end of the age; since Jesus' **words** will stand, alert preparation is imperative. But the main interest of this saying is in the permanent validity of Jesus' teaching. It will be found true and valid after this age has ended and the eternal Kingdom has been fully established.

With vs. 36 cf. Mk. xiii. 32; with vss. 37-41 cf. Lk. xvii. 26 f., 34 f.; with vs. 42 cf. Mk. xiii. 35; with vss. 43 f. cf. Lk. xii. 39 f. Obviously Matt. has collected sayings to teach that since **no one knows** the exact date of the last day, and judgment decides man's eternal lot, every disciple must stay alert and be prepared to enter the Kingdom.

The end will come within a generation (vs. 34), but just when, no one knows. (Vss. 42-44 emphasize this same point.) Jesus confesses that even he, the **Son,** does not know. Some ancient authorities omit **or the Son;** either 'Matthew' omitted these words, not wanting to say, as Mark did, that Jesus did not know the day, and a later scribe supplied them from Mk., or, probably, they were included by 'Matthew', and some early scribe left them out to avoid saying Jesus was ignorant. Certainly the words **only the Father** imply ignorance in the Son. Jesus, the unique Son of God (xi. 27), lived a human life limited in knowledge and subordinate to the Father.

The end, unknown in date and sudden in coming (vs. 27), will catch many unprepared and off guard, as **the flood** caught the generation of **Noah.** That generation was not alive to God's claim or to the danger of judgment. Men went about their usual ways, complacently acting as though the world would continue for ever. The masses, with a 'business as usual' and pleasure as usual policy, were taken by surprise. All except the little family that had prepared for the crisis and entered the ark were destroyed. So, Jesus says, most of his generation will treat lightly the grave danger they face, and will be caught by surprise in spite of the preaching of repentance that they have heard.

Two illustrations (vss. 40 f.) repeat the warning that the end
will come suddenly, and add that it will swiftly separate the two
groups alive at the time. (The present tenses, **is taken, is left,**
express vividly the separation certain to occur in the near
future.) **One,** alert and prepared, **is taken,** evidently by the
angels of the Son of Man sent forth to assemble his elect ones
(vs. 31), but **the other,** not prepared and on guard, **is left,** and
so faces condemnation in the final judgment.

So, to avoid surprise and condemnation, **Watch** (present
imperative: be continuously on the watch). Whether Jesus used
the title **Lord** here is a question; he rarely used this title of himself (cf. xxii. 41-45), but often made the claim that the word
expresses. The urgency of the present crisis is emphasized in
both vs. 42 and vs. 44; **Watch** and **Be ready** say much the same
thing. **Watch** means be prepared in spirit and life, keep in mind
that the Lord may return at any time, **be ready** to meet him
when he suddenly comes. Vs. 43 enforces this point by a parable.
What enables a **thief** to dig through the walls of a man's house
and steal the man's property? The man is not on the watch and
so the thief takes him by surprise. This illustration of the sudden
coming of a thief was often used in ancient times to show the
necessity of being ready for a crisis when it comes (1 Thess.
v. 2; Rev. xvi. 15); perhaps Jesus' use of the illustration made
it popular in the Church. The only way to avoid catastrophe at
the sudden coming of the Lord is to be constantly prepared by
living in alert faith, steady loyalty, and faithful obedience.

With vss. 45-51 cf. Lk. xii. 42-46. Another parable to emphasize that the Lord will return suddenly. Even if there is
delay in his coming (no great delay seems suggested; cf. vs. 34),
religious leaders must be constantly faithful in their duties or
they may be caught by surprise and even lose their place in the
Kingdom. The **master** of a house (κύριος, **master,** is elsewhere translated 'lord'), before leaving on a journey, places a
servant in charge of giving food to the other servants at
appointed times. This servant should be **faithful** in his duties
and **prudent** in recognizing that his conduct will be checked on
his master's sudden return. If found faithfully doing his work, he
will be honoured and rewarded. The reward, as in xxv. 21, 23, will
be the privilege of still higher responsibility (not endless rest!).

But if the servant is unfaithful to his trust, mistreating his fellow-servants, carousing with drunkards, and thinking that an apparent delay in his master's return will continue indefinitely (some interval—but not one of centuries—between Jesus' ministry and the actual end of the age is implied), his wickedness will cause him to be off guard when his master suddenly returns, and he will lose his responsible position and also his place in the Kingdom. **Cut him in two:** Probably a strong figurative expression for severe and irrevocable punishment. Vs. 51, especially in the words **assign him his place with the hypocrites,** etc., applies the parable; the Lord on his return at the last day will reward those servants who have been faithful in their assigned duties, but will punish and condemn to eternal ruin those who have misused their trust to harm others and indulge their own lusts. **There** (in the place of punishment for condemned persons) **the weeping and gnashing of teeth will occur.**

If Jesus never wove the application into his parables, this parable, or at least its application, was created by the Apostolic Church. But Jesus, like O.T. and Jewish users of parables, does elsewhere weave his application into the story or comparison, and while we cannot guarantee the exact wording of his parables, this warning that abuse of trust will bring eternal damage agrees with what he has repeatedly stressed in this section: the end is near; the exact time is not known; to gain blessedness and avoid ruin, be constantly ready, faithful in life and service, and alert to welcome the Lord on his return.

CHAPTER XXV

xxv. 1-46. THE ALERT, FAITHFUL, AND HUMANE WILL BE SAVED

1 'Then the Kingdom of Heaven may be compared to ten maidens who took their lamps and went out to meet the 2 bridegroom. Five of them were foolish and five were 3 prudent. For the foolish ones took their lamps but took

along no oil, but the prudent ones took oil in containers 4
with their lamps. When the bridegroom delayed they all 5
became drowsy and slept. At midnight a shout came, 6
"Behold, the bridegroom! Go out to meet him." Then all 7
those maidens arose and trimmed their lamps. The fool- 8
ish ones said to the prudent ones, "Give us some of your
oil, for our lamps are going out". But the prudent ones 9
answered, saying, "No; perhaps there will not be enough
for us and you. Go rather to the dealers and buy some for
yourselves." As they went away to buy some, the bride- 10
groom came, and the maidens who were ready went in
with him to the wedding banquet, and the door was
closed. Later the rest of the maidens came also, saying, 11
"Lord, lord, open to us". But he answered and said, 12
"Truly I tell you, I do not know you". Watch therefore, 13
for you do not know the day or the hour.

'For it is just like a man leaving on a journey; he called 14
his servants and handed over to them his possessions, and 15
to one he gave five talents, to another two, to another one
—to each according to his ability; and he went on his
journey. At once he who had received the five talents 16
went and engaged in business with them, and gained
five more talents. Similarly, he who had received the 17
two gained two more. But he who had received the one 18
went away and dug a hole in the ground and hid his
master's money. After a considerable time the master of 19
those servants came and settled accounts with them. And 20
he who had received five talents came to him and presented five talents more, saying, "Master, you handed
over to me five talents. Behold, I have gained five talents
more." His master said to him, "Well done, good and 21
faithful servant! You were faithful over a few things; I
will place you over many things. Enter into the joy of your
master." He also who had received the two talents came 22
and said, "Master, you handed over to me two talents.
Behold, I have gained two talents more." His master said 23
to him, "Well done, good and faithful servant! You were
faithful over a few things; I will place you over many
things. Enter into the joy of your master." Then he also 24

who had received the one talent came, and he said,
"Master, I knew you, that you are a harsh man, reaping
where you have not sowed, and gathering from places
25 where you have not scattered; and because I was afraid
I went away and hid your talent in the ground. Behold!
26 You have what is yours." His master answered and said
to him, "You wicked and lazy servant! Did you know that
I reap where I have not sowed, and gather from places
27 where I have not scattered? Then you should have de-
posited my money with the bankers, and at my coming
I would have received with interest what belonged to me.
28 So take the talent from him and give it to him who has
29 the ten talents." For to everyone who has, more will be
given, and he will have abundance; but from him who
30 has not—even what he has will be taken from him. And
drive the worthless servant out into the outer darkness;
there the weeping and gnashing of teeth will occur.
31   'When the Son of Man comes in his glory and all the
angels with him, then he will sit down on his glorious
32 throne, and all the nations will be assembled before him,
and he will separate them from one another, as the shep-
33 herd separates the sheep from the goats; and he will place
34 the sheep on his right side, and the goats on the left. Then
the King will say to those on his right side, "Come, you
who are blessed by my Father, inherit the Kingdom
which has been prepared for you from the foundation of
35 the world. For I hungered and you gave me food, I thirsted
and you gave me drink, I was a stranger and you received
36 me as your guest, I was scantily clad and you clothed me,
I became sick and you visited me, I was in prison and
37 you came to me." Then the righteous will answer him,
saying, "Lord, when did we see you hungry and feed
38 you, or thirsty and give you drink? When did we see you
a stranger and receive you as our guest, or scantily clad
39 and clothe you? And when did we see you sick or in
prison and come to you?" And the King will answer
40 and say to them, "Truly I tell you, in so far as you did
this to one of these brothers of mine, the least ones, you
41 did it to me". Then he will say also to those on the left

side, "Depart from me, you accursed ones, into the
eternal fire prepared for the devil and his angels. For
I hungered and you gave me no food, I thirsted and 42
you gave me no drink, I was a stranger and you did 43
not receive me as a guest, I was scantily clad and you
did not clothe me, sick and in prison and you did not
visit me." Then they also will answer, saying, "Lord, 44
when did we see you hungry or thirsty or a stranger or
scantily clad or sick or in prison and did not minister
to you?" Then he will answer them, saying, "Truly I tell 45
you, in so far as you did not do it to one of these least ones,
you did not do it to me". And these will go away to 46
eternal punishment, but the righteous to eternal life.'

Vss. 1-13 appear only in Matt., but Lk. xii. 35 f. teach much
the same point, and Lk. xiii. 25, like vss. 11 f., says that those
who come too late will be rejected. The parable emphasizes the
point of the preceding paragraphs; since no man knows the
exact time of the end, all must be ready to meet the Son of Man
when he returns; the coming may not be quite so soon as some
in their eagerness expect, but the delay must not lull any into
unpreparedness for the crucial event; cf. xxiv. 36, 42, 44, 48.
Vss. 1-13 develop the idea of prudence, and vss. 14-30 that of
faithfulness (cf. xxiv. 45).

Then: The time near the end of the age, when the Lord is
expected but has not yet come. **Ten maidens:** Friends of the
bride, assembled to welcome the groom when he approaches the
home of the bride's father for the wedding feast before taking
his bride to his own home. (Some manuscripts and versions end
vs. 1 with the added words, **and the bride.** This less likely text
means that the maidens waited near the bridegroom's home to
welcome the bridal couple.) **Foolish:** Did not think ahead and
prepare for possible delay. **Prudent:** Because their lamps held
a limited amount of oil, they each took a jar or container with
extra oil to use if the bridegroom came later than expected. The
number **five** in each group indicates not that half of mankind
will be saved, but merely that there were two types of maidens,
and the hearer must decide which type to imitate.

All ten sleep for an undefined time until announcement of the bridegroom's sudden coming startles them into wakefulness. This point is significant; Christ will come suddenly (xxiv. 27). No blame is attached to falling asleep; **all** ten **slept;** but the prudent five were not caught unprepared, while the foolish five had made no provision for possible delay and so were at fault.

The **lamps,** it is assumed, had been burning all the time, and needed more **oil.** The foolish maidens asked the others for some but were refused. This is not described as selfishness; the bridegroom must be welcomed, and the supply may not be enough for all. For Jesus' purpose this refusal has a special point; in the judgment, when Jesus comes at the end of the age, there can be no transfer of spiritual reserves or merit; spiritual preparedness is an individual matter; no one can borrow the resources needed. So the foolish maidens must go and try to buy oil in time to **meet the bridegroom.** But he comes almost at once, and the foolish five are left outside when the five prudent maidens are welcomed to the wedding feast. (A banquet or wedding feast was one current pictorial expression for the privilege and joy of sharing in the final Kingdom.) The point of the parable is largely in vs. 10; those ready **went in** to the feast. **The door was closed:** A note of finality; there comes a time when it is too late. (Some think that the Church later added vss. 11 f. to Jesus' original parable. But the foolish maidens have been prominent throughout the story; these verses present the warning that Jesus wanted people to hear and heed.) The bridegroom seems to answer brusquely and without sympathy, but the five who appeal for entrance had not fulfilled their task; they were not ready to welcome him when he came. The story is told with an eye on the final judgment.

Vs. 13 does not seem to fit the story, which does not say to stay awake. It fits only if **Watch** is understood to mean: prepare and be ready even if the coming of the Lord is delayed. If properly prepared, one may be at his normal work (xxiv. 40 f.), or sleeping, but one must have the resources with which to meet the Lord whenever his sudden coming occurs.

Are vss. 14-30 and Lk. xix. 11-27 two forms of one parable Jesus spoke? The two have many similarities: funds entrusted to servants; the master's journey; two make a profit, the third does not use the money; two praised and given greater responsibility, the third blamed for inactivity and his money given to the man who made the larger gain. But note real differences: in Matt. three servants, in Lk. ten (only three report); in Matt. talents, each worth fifty minas, in Lk. minas or pounds; in Lk. the master goes to receive a kingdom, the people protest, he later takes revenge; in Matt. the servants receive varying amounts according to ability, in Lk. all receive the same; in Matt. the first two each double their capital, in Lk. one makes a tenfold profit, the other fivefold; in Matt. the promised reward is vague, in Lk. it is rule over cities. In Lk. only, the hearers protest at taking the mina from the lazy servant. The verbal agreement between the two parables is not close. Either Jesus told two similar stories to make much the same point, or the parable has been altered considerably in one or both forms. On either alternative we must assume editorial work by the evangelists and the shaping influence of oral transmission.

This parable stresses the need of faithful service (cf. xxiv. 45; xxv. 21, 23). **For** ties the parable to vs. 13 and warns the reader to watch; be constantly prepared for the final judgment by faithful use of gifts received from the Lord. **A journey**: Indicates the time that Jesus, between his exaltation and return, is not visibly with his followers. The three **servants** are typical of three types. The amount entrusted to each matches his ability; no one is asked the impossible, but he must use faithfully what is given him. Two servants prove faithful and diligent, and earn a profit. The third does not squander the money (as the Prodigal Son did; Lk. xv. 13) or lose it by carelessness; but he makes no profitable use of it; using an ancient method of keeping valuables safe, he went to a lonely place, dug a hole, buried the money, and so could produce it when his master returned; he knew he would have to answer for it.

The **master** returned only **after a considerable time** (a hint of delay; cf. xxiv. 48; xxv. 5). Then he calls in his servants for an accounting (cf. xviii. 23). The first two servants have each doubled the sum entrusted to them. Each receives the same praise; for his faithfulness (the key idea) he is promised as a reward not long rest, but still greater responsibility; he is invited to share the **joy** his master has. The story is told with an eye on the joy in the Master's Kingdom; that is the way Semitic

18

parables were normally told—with hints of the application built into the story.

The third servant brings out by contrast the lesson of faithfulness. He has to answer for what was entrusted to him. But he is defiant, and tries to put the blame for his laziness on his master. His excuse is that had he lost the money while using it, he could expect no mercy from his master. Thus he makes of his laziness a necessity and a virtue. With a show of righteous triumph he returns the money, and implies that no more could be asked. But the master brands his laziness as wrong. He should at least have made a cautious but profitable use of his master's money by depositing it at interest **with the bankers.** So the other servants, assumed to be present, are told to **take the talent** from the lazy servant and give it to him who made the larger gain (vs. 20).

Then Jesus states the general principle already found in xiii. 12: abundantly more will be given to everyone who has (and, it is here implied, uses) resources, while the little another has, if not used and increased, will be taken from him. Good living is not negative or static; faithful use of one's gifts, large or small, increases them, brings recognition, and opens the door to greater usefulness, but lazy disuse is blameworthy abuse of one's privileges and will mean the loss of one's gifts and place in the Kingdom. **Outer darkness:** A figurative expression for complete and final rejection. **Weeping, gnashing of teeth:** Painful and futile lament (a favourite expression in Matt.). The negative fault of the lazy servant was deadly; he made no good use of what was entrusted to him; he was not faithful.

Vss. 31-46 give not a parable but a description of the last judgment. The illustration of the **shepherd** separating the **sheep from the goats** is incidental to the main scene. The passage, often praised, and rightly, for its humanitarian emphasis, contains notable Christological teaching. **The Son of Man** returns with divine power and glory to execute the final judgment for his Father; he is called **King** (vs. 34) and **Lord** (vss. 37, 44); whoever deals with any needy person is dealing with the Son of Man (vss. 40, 45). Thus Jesus ends his teaching with an immense Christological claim.

The opening words (ὅταν and the subjunctive) could be

translated: 'Whenever the Son of Man comes'; the time is not known to man. The **Son of Man,** after a lowly life, suffering, and exaltation, will come at the end **in** divine **glory;** the host of **angels** with him mark his unique role; they may help him (as in xxiv. 31) in the judgment. **His glorious throne:** Only the divine Son of Man can thus act for the Father. **All the nations:** Probably implies the resurrection of the dead, and the judgment of all men; **the nations** usually means the Gentiles, but the word **all** seems to make the phrase include all mankind (cf. xxiv. 9, 14; xxviii. 19). Some take **all the nations** to mean only non-Christians, but the phrase seems all-inclusive. The entire passage is true to Jesus' emphasis on human kindness rather than conventional piety.

The Son of Man will **separate** people into two groups. He will know what they have done and what they deserve. **Sheep:** A figure for those given his concern and tender care. **Right side:** Traditionally the place of honour and good fortune. **Goats:** The rejected group, put in the place of dishonour. The **sheep** are welcomed into the Kingdom. The Son of Man as **the King** gives his decree; it is final. But it is the decree of his Father, for the King is the Son of God. **Blessed** ($\epsilon \vec{\upsilon} \lambda o \gamma \eta$-$\mu \acute{\epsilon} \nu o \iota$), perfect passive participle, indicates that the Father had decided the final lot of these people before the creation of the world; they now inherit (cf. v. 5) what has been intended for them all along. This fore-ordination does not exclude but rather includes the human responsibility and activity of those thus chosen for places in **the Kingdom.**

Now comes the surprise; Jesus tells why these people will be welcomed. They have relieved human need and suffering and shown compassion; though they did not realize that they were ministering to the Son of Man, they have done these kind acts to him. They are called **righteous** (vs. 37). But this surprises them. They did not know that they were serving the Son of Man; it was enough for them that they saw and could relieve human need. But every such act of kindness is done to him; he so identifies himself in sympathy and companionship with the suffering and needy that to help them is to serve him (cf. x. 40, 42; xviii. 5). They are all his **brothers,** even **the least** of them, those whose outward position seems to mark them as unimportant; active sympathy for needy people is direct service to him.

Jesus often combines both praise and warning. So here he first gives the positive picture and then presents the contrast as a warning (cf. vss. 11 f.). Calloused, unsympathetic people are **accursed;** their inhuman way of life has served the devil's purposes, and now they are banished from the presence of the King and sentenced to **the eternal fire prepared for the devil and his angels** (cf. Rev. xx. 10, 14 f.; xxi. 8). These people attempt a defence. They call the judge **Lord;** they recognize his power and authority. They insist they had no opportunity to minister to him. They would gladly have done that, but they thought those needy people unimportant; they did not know that the King identified himself with every needy and suffering individual. So they have to hear him say that to fail to help their needy fellow-men was to fail to minister to the King their Lord.

The division and sentence are final. Each group goes where God's will and their choice assign them. Jesus does not describe the punishment of the callously indifferent people (**fire** in vs. 41 is figurative). It is certainly permanent separation from the King (vs. 41: **depart from me**) and a permanently unhappy lot. **Eternal life** is the life of the perfect and permanent Kingdom of Heaven, in fellowship with the Father, the Lord Jesus, and all whom they have welcomed into the life of secure blessedness. The attempt to limit the time of punishment is misguided; the same adjective αἰώνιος is used to describe the everlasting duration of both the **punishment** and the **life.**

CHAPTER XXVI

xxvi. 1-29. THE LAST SUPPER

1 **And it happened that when Jesus had finished all these**
2 **words, he said to his disciples, 'You know that after two days comes the Passover, and the Son of Man is handed**

over to be crucified'. Then the chief priests and the elders 3
assembled in the palace of the chief priest, whose name
was Caiaphas, and they made a plot to seize Jesus by 4
cunning and kill him. But they said, 'Not during the feast, 5
for fear that an uproar may occur among the people'.

Now when Jesus was in Bethany in the house of Simon 6
the leper, a woman came to him with an alabaster flask of 7
very costly ointment, and she poured it on his head as he
reclined at table. When his disciples saw it, they were 8
indignant, saying, 'Why this waste? For this could have 9
been sold for a large sum and given to the poor.' Jesus 10
perceived it and said to them, 'Why do you trouble the
woman? For she has done a good deed to me; for you 11
always have the poor with you, but you do not always
have me. For this woman, in putting this ointment on my 12
body, has done it to prepare me for burial. Truly I tell 13
you, wherever this gospel will be preached in the whole
world, this also which this woman has done will be told
in memory of her.'

Then one of the Twelve, named Judas Iscariot, went to 14
the chief priests and said, 'What will you give me and I 15
will betray him to you?' They weighed out to him thirty
silver coins. And from that time he watched for a suitable 16
opportunity to betray him.

On the first day of unleavened bread the disciples came 17
to Jesus, saying, 'Where do you wish us to prepare for you
to eat the Passover?' He said, 'Go into the city to a certain 18
man and say to him, "The Teacher says, 'My time is
near; I keep the Passover at your home with my disciples'"'. And the disciples did as Jesus commanded 19
them, and prepared the Passover.

When evening came he reclined at table with the 20
Twelve. And as they were eating, he said, 'Truly I tell 21
you, one of you will betray me'. And they, greatly grieved, 22
began each one to say to him, 'Surely it is not I, Lord?'
He answered and said, 'He who has dipped his hand in 23
the bowl with me, this one will betray me. The Son of 24
Man goes as it is written concerning him, but woe to that
man through whom the Son of Man is betrayed. It

would have been better for that man if he had not been
25 born.' Judas, who was betraying him, answered and
said, 'Surely it is not I, Rabbi?' He said to him, 'You
have said'.

26 As they were eating, Jesus took bread, and after pro-
nouncing the blessing he broke it, and gave it to his dis-
27 ciples and said, 'Take, eat; this is my body'. And he took
a cup, and after giving thanks he gave it to them, saying,
28 'Drink of it, all of you; for this is my blood of the cove-
29 nant, shed for many for forgiveness of sins. I tell you,
from now on I will never drink of this fruit of the vine
until that day when I drink it new with you in the Kingdom of my Father.'

With vss. 1-5 cf. Mk. xiv. 1 f.; Lk. xxii. 1 f.; Jn. xi. 47-53.
The last of the five great discourses (chs. xxiv. f.) has just been
concluded. The usual formal conclusion (cf. vii. 28 f.; xi. 1; xiii.
53; xix. 1) leads into the narrative of the passion and resurrection. Jesus himself announces that the betrayal and death of
which he has spoken (xvi. 21; xvii. 22 f.; xx. 17-19) will come at
the Passover, just **two days** away. The Passover was eaten on
Thursday evening, so Jesus said this about Tuesday. **Is handed
over:** The present tense speaks of the future event as a certainty. **Crucified:** Implies execution by the Romans; the Jews
executed condemned persons by stoning.

Then: As soon as Jesus said these words their fulfilment
began. **The chief priests and the elders:** The Sanhedrin.
Caiaphas: High priest from A.D. 18 to 36. **Palace:** αὐλήν could
mean the courtyard of his residence (cf. vs. 58), but here probably means his palace or official residence. **Kill him:** That is,
get him put to death. **Not during the feast:** Jerusalem was
crowded with pilgrims at Passover time. Among them many
from Galilee were enthusiastic supporters of Jesus. Passover
was always a time of intense nationalistic feeling; it recalled
Israel's deliverance from Egypt and aroused hopes of deliverance from the Romans; the presence of Jesus brought added
danger of popular uprising by the volatile crowds, whom the
Sanhedrin did not want to provoke by any overt act. So they
looked for a way to seize him by trickery. There is irony in their

reason: first, they were not concerned for the reverent spirit of the sacred feast so much as for the popular effects of their move against Jesus; and later, in Matt., they actually seize Jesus on the very night of the feast.

With vss. 6-13 cf. Mk. xiv. 3-9; Jn. xii. 1-8 (six days before the Passover). Lk. vii. 36-50 tells of a supper in Galilee at which a Pharisee named Simon was host and a sinful woman anointed Jesus' feet. That story may be a variant of the Bethany anointing, but this is not certain. In Matt. the anointing points to the impending death and burial, and prevents any feeling that this mark of respect had been culpably neglected.

Bethany: Where Jesus spent the last nights before his arrest (cf. xxi. 17). **Reclined at table:** At the evening meal, on Wednesday (or Tuesday). **Simon, the leper:** If present at the meal, he had recovered from the disease; if he was still leprous, he was not at home and others of his family must have acted as hosts.

The **woman** who anointed Jesus is described vaguely; nothing indicates that she belonged to the household or regularly followed Jesus. **An alabaster flask,** itself expensive, was a fitting container for **very costly ointment. Poured it on his head:** As a mark of affection and honour. This unstinted expression of affection and loyalty made the disciples **indignant.** They had learned well Jesus' concern for **the poor** (he approved that; vs. 11), but they lacked the woman's insight that at times costly expression of affection is legitimate. Jesus checks their protest, evidently so audibly expressed as to embarrass the woman. He calls her act **a good deed.** As he has told them (cf. vs. 2; ix. 15; etc.), his time is short and his death is so near that this anointing can be regarded as the customary preparation **for burial.** Vs. 12 seems to say that the woman knew that her act was a substitute for the usual preparation of a dead body for burial. Certainly Jesus, fully aware that his death was close at hand, understood it that way.

Jesus knew that this spontaneous expression of loyal love would not be forgotten. His death was approaching; the gospel story would give a place to the events of his last hours; the act of this devoted woman would be **told** whenever his followers proclaimed the gospel story; and so her act of love would become known throughout **the world.** Jesus thus spoke of the world-wide preaching of the gospel, which would give a prominent place to his death. xxiv. 14 and xxviii. 19 f. likewise refer explicitly to this world-wide preaching, and the coming of the Magi (ii. 1-12) and the forecast in viii. 11 f. give glimpses of a much wider horizon than Judaism. Of all the gospel writers, 'Matthew', as a Jewish Christian concerned to reach Jewish Christians, had least apologetic interest in expanding the horizon of the Christian mission, but the tradition he knew in Jewish-Christian circles was a gospel which told of Jesus' death and was intended for the world. This theme, then, cannot be ascribed to purely Gentile-Christian interest. It roots in very early tradition; origin in Jesus' own teaching best explains it.

With vss. 14-16 cf. Mk. xiv. 10 f.; Lk. xxii. 3-6. **Then:** A frequent word in Matt.; vague. Following vss. 2, 6, the act hardly occurred before Wednesday. **Iscariot:** See on x. 4. **One of the Twelve:** Reflects the Church's horror and sorrow at the betrayal of Jesus by a favoured disciple. He had Jesus' confidence at the beginning. Why then this betrayal? Was he jealous of others of the Twelve? Was he repelled because Jesus accepted suffering rather than undertake militant nationalistic leadership? Did he see that Jesus faced defeat and turn traitor to save himself? We do not know.

Judas takes the initiative. He seeks out **the chief priests** and says in effect, 'If you make me a good offer, I will betray him to you'. To 'Matthew' the act (cf. also xxvii. 9 f.) fulfilled Zech. xi. 12. He is the only gospel writer to say that Judas received **thirty silver coins** and received them at once. If the thirty coins were shekels, the total bribe was about a month's wages, small pay for so great an act of treason. This hardly suggests greed for money. To 'Matthew' fulfilment of prophecy held more interest than ideas of financial profit.

The main fact is clear. Judas agreed to help the chief priests take Jesus prisoner at a time and place where the crowds would not be present to protest or resist. No evidence supports the theory that what Judas betrayed was Jesus' claim to be the Messiah; his agreement, which he kept, was to lead the authorities to a place where they could secretly take Jesus prisoner.

With vss. 17-19 cf. Mk. xiv. 12-16; Lk. xxii. 7-13. (In Jn. the

Last Supper is not a Passover.) Matt. is much shorter than Mk.
and Lk., but the three agree in nearly all essentials.

On the first day of unleavened bread: The Passover was
that evening; the seven-day feast of unleavened bread followed
it. But the two feasts were often thought of as one eight-day
celebration, called (the feast of) unleavened bread. The day
before the Passover, being filled with preparations for it, might
be included, as here, in that feast. On this day all leaven had
to be removed from the homes. The disciples assume or know
that Jesus will observe the Passover. He sends them into Jerusalem (from Bethany?). In Mk. Jesus sends only two; Lk. names
them: Peter and John; in Matt. all Twelve are sent. **A certain
man:** τὸν δεῖνα, Mr. X; 'Matthew' does not know his name
or does not wish to give it. The man seems a follower of Jesus;
he knows the disciples and accepts Jesus as **the Teacher. My
time:** Refers to his impending death, now close at hand. **I
keep:** Present tense for a near future event. **At your home:**
Jesus asks for a separate room where he can preside and be alone
with the Twelve.

Was it a Passover meal? In Jn. Jesus dies before the Passover
is observed; he dies at the very time that the Passover lambs are
being slain and prepared for the feast (xviii. 28; cf. 1 Cor. v. 7).
Do the Dead Sea Scrolls and related literature indicate that the
Essenes had a different calendar, which Jesus used, so that he
and the Essenes ate the Passover on Tuesday evening and the
Sadducees and others ate it on Friday evening? The evidence is
not decisive. The dating in Jn. may well be correct. But the meal
certainly occurred at Passover time, in the atmosphere of Passover thought, and the Church from the beginning interpreted
the event with Passover imagery.

With vss. 20-25 cf. Mk. xiv. 17-21; Lk. xxii. 14, 21-23.
Evening: The Passover had to be eaten at night. The group
included only Jesus and **the Twelve. One of you:** A sad note;
see on vs. 14. **Greatly grieved:** Because Jesus is to be betrayed? Or because one of them will do it? Probably both;
the latter seems their main concern. The form of the Greek
question (μήτι ἐγώ εἰμι) suggests that a negative answer is
cautiously expected, but an affirmative answer is not completely
ruled out. Does this suggest in each an inner fear and sense of

273

personal weakness? Or is the tone, 'You surely do not think that **I** would do such a thing, do you?' All had **dipped** in the same **bowl,** so Jesus' answer does not identify the man; it underlines the guilt of one sharing in this final meal and then by betrayal breaking the close bond that table fellowship was held to establish between friends. Judas' question (vs. 25) shows that Jesus had not clearly identified the betrayer. **Goes:** Departs by death. **Written:** In Scripture. Jesus does not say where. Cf. Ps. xxii.; Isa. liii.; Zech. xi.; they loomed large in later Church thought. That his death was predicted meant that it was in God's plan and had a place in achieving God's purpose. But the traitor must answer for his deliberate act; the plan and working of God do not exclude human freedom and responsibility; the man who betrays the Son of Man will find that the balance of his life record will be a deadly deficit.

The others call Jesus **Lord,** but Judas calls him **Rabbi.** Does 'Matthew' hint that Judas' loyalty is clearly fading? Jesus' enigmatic answer seems to concede that Judas' cautious question expresses the real situation.

With vss. 26-29 cf. Mk. xiv. 22-25; Lk. xxii. 15-20; 1 Cor. xi. 23-25. During the Supper, probably just before the final cup, Jesus alters the usual Passover pattern. Vs. 29 suggests that the cup of vs. 27 was the last cup of the Passover series of four. Before taking this cup Jesus takes unleavened **bread** used at the Passover meal and performs a symbolic act; he gives thanks to God in a spoken **blessing,** breaks the bread (this act is essential to the meaning) and gives it to the disciples with an interpreting statement; as they receive from him and **eat** this symbol of his broken **body,** they symbolize the fact that his death has meaning and benefit for them. This is expressed still more clearly in the explanation of the second acted parable or symbol. Jesus takes a **cup,** probably the fourth and final one of the Passover meal, again gives **thanks** to God, and passes it to the disciples; **all** are to **drink of it.** The wine represents his blood; **is shed** (present participle) suggests that death is close at hand. **Blood of the covenant:** Probably not a reference to the new covenant in Jer. xxxi. 31-34, where no blood is mentioned, but rather to Ex. xxiv. 8, perhaps combined with the thought of the Servant as the covenant with the people in Isa. xlii. 6; xlix. 8. The word

new, found with **covenant** in many ancient authorities, probably was not in the original text, but the idea is implied; God is
making a new covenant with his people by the death of Christ.
The blood, poured out **for many,** on their behalf and for their
benefit, recalls Isa. liii. 12; the Suffering Servant willingly accepts his impending death for the benefit of his followers, who
will be many. The nature of this benefit is not defined in detail;
for the forgiveness of sins is not added in the other accounts,
but was known early in the Church, since Paul was so taught
when he was converted (1 Cor. xv. 3: 'for our sins'). The gospel
had been a gospel of forgiveness from the beginning (iv. 17);
now Jesus dies to make effective the message of the holy and
gracious God who seeks the good of sinful men and provides
in his Servant a means of forgiveness. The words of Jesus do
not explain how his death effects forgiveness, but they assure
men that it does. Jesus did not come to give moral advice and
leave men to work out their own salvation; he died for the purpose he had served in his ministry, to help sinners who needed
the grace of God. Whether Jesus explicitly said at the Supper
that his death provided forgiveness of sins, he implied just that,
and the disciples understood him to mean that, for they so
taught from the early days of the Church.

Vs. 29 is a farewell word. Jesus faces death, but not in despair.
His death is not final defeat; it will further God's plan; beyond
it lies his resurrection and the coming of the complete and final
Kingdom of his **Father.** So at this Last Supper he can speak
of another banquet to come. The Messianic Kingdom, or its
inauguration, was often described as a joyous banquet in which
God's people share. Reunited with his disciples, he and they will
share the glad cup in that triumphant Kingdom. So they may
look beyond the events of the next few hours and steady themselves with the confidence that his death will benefit them and
all who follow their Master; he will not be defeated but will rise
to rejoice with them in the final fulfilment of God's saving purpose. This Supper thus gives them perspective, insight into the
meaning of a dark event and a look beyond to the final triumph.
There is in Matt., Mk., and Lk.'s shorter text no command to
repeat the supper, but these two acted parables were given to
interpret the death of Jesus and to recall in coming days the

meaning of that cross. The Church rightly understood Jesus' intent in these symbolic actions; his apparently futile and barren suffering was the most fruitful event of his ministry for men, and these actions help his people to remember this.

xxvi. 30-56. PRAYER AND ARREST IN GETHSEMANE

30 And when they had sung a hymn they went out to the
31 Mount of Olives. Then Jesus said to them, 'All of you will take offence at me this night; for it is written, "I will strike down the shepherd, and the sheep of the flock will
32 be scattered". But after I have risen, I will precede you
33 to Galilee.' Peter answered and said to him, 'If all take
34 offence at you, I will never take offence.' Jesus said to him, 'Truly I tell you that this night, before a cock crows,
35 you will deny me three times.' Peter said to him, 'Even if I must die with you, I will never deny you'. And like-
36 wise said all the disciples. Then Jesus came with them to a place called Gethsemane, and said to his disciples,
37 'Sit here while I go there and pray'. And he took with him Peter and the two sons of Zebedee and began to be grieved
38 and distressed. Then he said to them, 'My soul is grieved
39 unto death; stay here and watch with me'. And going forward a little he fell on his face and prayed and said, 'My Father, if it is possible, let this cup pass from me; yet not
40 as I will, but as thou wilt'. And he came to the disciples and found them sleeping, and said to Peter, 'So you could
41 not watch with me one hour! Watch and pray, that you may not come into temptation. The spirit is willing, but
42 the flesh is weak.' Again a second time he went away and prayed, saying, 'My Father, if this cannot pass unless I
43 drink it, thy will be done'. And he came again and found
44 them sleeping, for their eyes were heavy. And leaving them he again went away, and prayed a third time, saying
45 again the same thing. Then he came to the disciples and said to them, 'Sleep on now and take your rest! Behold, the hour is near and the Son of Man is being betrayed into

the hands of sinners. Rise, let us go; behold, he who be- 46
trays me is near.' And while he still was speaking, Behold, 47
Judas, one of the Twelve, came, and with him a large
crowd, armed with swords and clubs, from the chief
priests and elders of the people. He who was betraying 48
him had given them a sign, saying, 'The one whom I kiss
is he; arrest him'. And he promptly approached Jesus and 49
said, 'Greeting, Rabbi!' and kissed him. Jesus said to 50
him, 'Friend, why have you come?' Then they came up
and laid hands on Jesus and took him in custody. And 51
behold, one of the men with Jesus stretched out his hand
and drew his sword, and he struck the servant of the high
priest and cut off his ear. Then Jesus said to him, 'Put 52
your sword back in its place, for all who take the sword
will die by the sword. Or do you think that I cannot re- 53
quest my Father and he at once will put at my disposal
more than twelve legions of angels? How then would the 54
Scriptures be fulfilled that thus it must happen?' In that 55
hour Jesus said to the crowds, 'Have you come out armed
with swords and clubs to arrest me, as though you were
after a bandit? Daily I sat in the temple, teaching, and
you did not arrest me. But all this has happened that the 56
Scriptures of the prophets might be fulfilled.' Then the
disciples all left him and fled.

With vss. 30-35 cf. Mk. xii. 26-31; Lk. xxii. 39, 31-34; Jn.
xvi. 32; xiii. 36-38. The Passover eaten, the group sings a closing
hymn, perhaps one of the psalms of the Hallel ('praise') sung
at the Passover celebration. The Hallel consisted of Pss. 113-118;
the first two were sung after the second of the four Passover
cups; the last four followed the fourth and last cup. If a single
other psalm is meant, 'Matthew' means that it followed the last
Hallel psalm. From the house in Jerusalem they went eastward,
out the city gate, down to and across the brook Kidron to the
Garden of Gethsemane (vs. 36), on the lower slopes of the
Mount of Olives. Jesus wanted a time alone for prayer. On
the way he told them they would **take offence,** be caused to
stumble, led into sin by their relation to him; their loyalty to
him would bring them into a danger whose pressure would lead

them to act wrongly. In this coming event is seen a fulfilment of Zech. xiii. 7 (cf. the use of Zech. ix. 9 in Matt. xxi. 5 and of Zech. xi. 12 in Matt. xxvi. 15). The verse as quoted in Matt. agrees with neither the Hebrew nor the Greek of Zech., but it faithfully uses the idea of the scattering effect on a **flock** when its **shepherd** is struck down; the (eleven) disciples are here the flock. But Jesus adds a word of encouragement. Beyond his death, a shattering experience for them, lies his resurrection. When risen he will precede them to Galilee, and meet them there (cf. xxviii. 16, though the prediction here mentions no mountain). προάξω, translated **precede,** might mean go **(to Galilee)** at the head of the group, and thus as their leader. But xxviii. 16 shows that 'Matthew' clearly understood it to mean that Jesus would go to Galilee before they did and see them there. All this assumes that Jesus foresaw not only his death and resurrection but also his reunion with his followers, at least for a brief time, after his resurrection. It presents Jesus not as a naïve and defeated figure but as one possessed of insight, confidence, and power to become the exalted leader of a triumphant Church.

This talk of death and being offended has not shaken Peter's self-confidence. He boldly declares that his courage and steadfastness will prove more than adequate for any impending trial. He will never forsake Jesus. Jesus replies that before dawn, as the reference to the cock's crowing implies, Peter will **three times deny** Jesus. Even this leaves Peter unshaken. He is ready to die to stay loyal to Jesus. The others echo Peter's words. Cf. vss. 56, 69-75. Jesus knew better than they did what was coming and what danger would do to their courage.

With vss. 36-46 cf. Mk. xiv. 32-42; Lk. xxii. 40-46; Jn. xviii. 1. **Gethsemane:** 'Oil-press'. The place apparently was an olive grove, with an oil-press to press the oil from the olives in season. It was just east of the brook Kidron, low on the western slopes of the Mount of Olives (Jn. xviii. 1). Judas had probably left the group before arrival there (cf. Jn. xiii. 30). Jesus leaves eight disciples at the edge of the grove but takes the inner trio further. To these three close friends he speaks of his deep grief in words that recall Ps. xlii. 5, 11; xliii. 5; he is sorrowful enough to die (cf. Jon. iv. 9). It is some comfort to share his trouble with them, but he alone knows the full weight of his inner suffering, so he leaves them to **watch** and warn him when the expected danger approaches, and goes to make the final decision to face the death he has seen approaching for months.

Going forward: Reading προελθών, which makes sense here, rather than the also well attested προσελθών, 'approaching'. **On his face:** the attitude of earnest, humble prayer. **My Father:** So often in Matt. and Jn. He asks that if God's plan can be realized and his own work completed without suffering death, this cup of impending suffering (cf. xx. 22) may pass from him and God's will be realized in some less painful way. The pain is not merely fear of physical suffering and death; it comes from his rejection by his people and their leaders. But his prayer, spoken with agonizing earnestness, is not an ultimatum, which would not be real prayer. The final decision rests with the Father, whose will he loyally accepts. The story reveals the reality of his human life and will, which must choose and do the Father's will.

Jesus prayed for some time. On his return he reproaches the three for **sleeping.** He particularly rebukes **Peter,** who had boasted so confidently (vss. 33-35). His words are a surprised and sorrowful ejaculation: **So you could not,** etc., or a reproachful question, 'Were you thus not able, etc.'. The reproach and desire for companionship are evident. **Watch and pray:** Present imperatives of continuing action; the test is just ahead; it will bring powerful temptation. They should pray that the temptation may not be too great. Their **spirit** he knows is **willing,** but **the flesh,** the physical self with its desires and emotions, shrinks from suffering and may undermine spiritual loyalty.

A second time Jesus prays alone, seeking to know the Father's will. **Thy will be done:** The very words of vi. 10! On returning, no doubt to the inner trio, he finds them **sleeping** again. **Their eyes were heavy:** Their weariness is noted as a partial excuse. He leaves them sleeping and in a **third** period of prayer, in willingness to accept the Father's will, he reaches final inner acceptance of what faces him. He returns probably now to the entire group. His words to them may be a reproachful question or more likely a reproachful command: **Sleep on now; the**

time when you could have helped by watching is past; he will watch now for the traitor's approach, which he expects soon. If the words are a command, there is an interval between vs. 45 and vs. 46, the latter spoken when Jesus sees the arresting party approaching (there was a Passover full moon, and the party no doubt carried torches). Jesus speaks only of the traitor's approach; the words reflect his deep sorrow and disappointment and that of the early Church over Judas' defection.

With vss. 47-56 cf. Mk. xiv. 43-52; Lk. xxii. 47-53; Jn. xviii. 2-12. **One of the Twelve** (cf. vs. 14): Underlines the enormity of Judas' wickedness in betraying Jesus. **Large crowd:** Not Roman soldiers; a party sent out by the Sanhedrin to arrest Jesus secretly; they were hastily armed with swords and clubs to overpower any resistance by Jesus and his disciples (cf. vs. 51).

The **kiss,** which should express respect and affection, is basely used to identify Jesus so that the armed party, who do not know him, can arrest him. Judas calls Jesus **Rabbi** ('My Teacher'); in Matt. he never calls Jesus 'Master', 'Lord'. The Greek word **kissed** may indicate an elaborately affectionate kiss and so emphasize Judas' hypocrisy.

Friend: Not sarcasm but recognition of their past close association. Jesus says (the Greek ἐφ' ὃ πάρει is puzzling) either 'Why have you come?' or 'Do what you have come to do'. The former seems better; it is a reproach to the traitor. At these words the crowd seizes Jesus.

One disciple (Peter in Jn. xviii. 10) had a **sword,** probably not carried regularly but because he sensed danger in Jerusalem (cf. Lk. xxii. 38). **The servant of the high priest:** Probably the leader of the band sent to arrest Jesus. Jesus at once checks this show of resistance. (Only Matt. has vss. 52-54.) Such fighting to defend him is self-defeating; those who fight for power die by the weapons they use. The way of the cross is not a sad second choice but is God's way to achieve his purpose. Jesus' renunciation of external force is not due to lack of power; he is confident that for the asking he could have **more than twelve legions of angels** to crush man's boasted armies. But he has accepted the cross as the Father's will. He acts not in weakness but in strength which by discipline and self-sacrifice will win the victory. He adds (vs. 54) that his arrest, suffering, and death are forecast in Scripture; they have a place in the divine plan and are essential to its realization. Vs. 56 repeats this idea.

In that hour of arrest in the olive grove Jesus taunted the crowd for their method of seizing him. They came out with a great show of force, as though trying to track down and capture an elusive **bandit**. Yet **daily** (does this suggest a longer Jerusalem ministry than the two or three days reported in Matt.?) he **sat in the temple**, publicly **teaching,** and open to arrest. The only sense in their secret night sally was that it fulfilled expectations of **the prophets** (here all O.T. spokesmen who anticipated the coming and suffering of Israel's unique leader).

The eleven **disciples** (Judas is no longer one of them) were in danger of arrest. Jesus had stopped their one attempt to resist; they knew nothing more to do to help him; fear seized them and they **fled.** They did what Jesus had foretold (vs. 31). At the end he had to stand alone; not even his closest friends had the courage to go with him and plead his case or share his lot.

xxvi. 57-75. JESUS CONDEMNED AND DENIED

Those who had arrested Jesus led him away to Caiaphas 57 the high priest, where the scribes and the elders had assembled. Peter followed him at a distance as far as the 58 courtyard of the high priest, and went in and sat with the servants to see the end. The chief priests and the entire 59 Sanhedrin tried to get false testimony against Jesus in order to put him to death, but they found none, although 60 many false witnesses came. Finally two came and said, 61 'This fellow said, "I can destroy the temple of God and build it within three days"'. And the high priest stood up 62 and said, 'Do you answer nothing? What are these men testifying against you?' But Jesus remained silent. And 63 the high priest said to him, 'I adjure you by the living God that you tell us whether you are the Christ, the Son of God'. Jesus said to him, 'You have said. But I tell you, 64 from now on you will see the Son of Man sitting at the right hand of Power and coming on the clouds of heaven.'

19   281

65 Then the high priest tore his garments, saying, 'He has blasphemed. What further need have we of witnesses? 66 Behold, you have now heard the blasphemy. What do you think?' They answered and said, 'He deserves death'. 67 Then they spat in his face and struck him, and some 68 slapped him, saying, 'Prophesy to us, you Christ! Who was it who hit you?'

69 Now Peter was sitting outside in the courtyard. And a servant girl came to him, saying, 'You also were with 70 Jesus the Galilean'. But he denied it before them all, say-71 ing, 'I do not know what you mean'. When he had gone out into the gateway, another servant girl saw him and said to those present, 'This man was with Jesus the 72 Nazorean'. And again, with an oath, he denied it, 'I do 73 not know the man'. After a little while the men standing there approached and said to Peter, 'You really are one 74 of them, for your speech gives you away'. Then he began to curse and to swear, 'I do not know the man'. And at 75 once a cock crowed. And Peter remembered what Jesus had said, 'Before a cock crows, you will deny me three times'. And he went outside and wept bitterly.

With vss. 57-68 cf. Mk. xiv. 53-65; Lk. xxii. 54 f.; 63-65; 67-71 (Luke's order is different; his only trial scene comes after daybreak). **The scribes and the elders:** As vs. 59 shows, this means the Sanhedrin, as do xvi. 21, elders, chief priests, and scribes; xx. 18, chief priests and scribes; xxi. 23 and xxvi. 3, chief priests and elders; xxi. 45, chief priests and Pharisees. They meet at night; dawn comes after vs. 74. It is often argued that the Sanhedrin could not condemn a man to death at night. This no doubt was so, but this was not a formal trial; it was an attempt to find a charge serious enough to enable them to get rid of Jesus. Perhaps 'Matthew' meant xxvii. 1 f. as the time when the Sanhedrin formally acted. The Sanhedrin had to ask Pilate to execute Jesus; they lacked power to do that; they needed a charge which would lead Pilate to pronounce the death sentence.

Peter is often considered a weak coward, but he had the courage to follow the hostile crowd into the courtyard of the high priest. **To see the end:** Suggests hopeless despair and dogged loyalty.

The **chief priests,** part of the Sanhedrin, probably are mentioned first because of their prominence, and **the entire Sanhedrin** is mentioned to indicate that the highest Jewish body acted. **Tried:** Imperfect tense ($\dot{\epsilon}\zeta\dot{\eta}\tau ovv$); the attempt lasted for some time; 'Matthew' says **false testimony** because there was no legitimate basis for a death penalty and so they could only use falsehoods. **Found none:** Either their evidence did not warrant the death penalty or no two witnesses agreed (cf. Deut. xvii. 6). **I can destroy,** etc.: Jesus evidently said the temple would be destroyed (Mk. xiv. 58; Jn. ii. 19; Acts vi. 14), but not that he would destroy it. His statement did not clearly contain a Messianic claim, or usurp divine rights, or commit sacrilege against the holy place. The high priest tried to get from Jesus some clearer ground of action. But Jesus continued silent; in this the Church saw Isa. liii. 7 fulfilled: 'He opened not his mouth'. As a last resort the high priest puts Jesus under oath and asks him whether he is the Christ (**Son of God** here is another title for Messiah; the wording reflects xvi. 16). The high priest has heard this claim from Judas or from popular rumour. Jesus answers, not because under oath (cf. v. 34), but because the decisive moment has come to make clear to the Jewish people his full claim. Yet his affirmative answer is cautious, for the Jewish leaders (and the Romans) can interpret his Messianic claim to mean revolt against existing authorities. **You have said:** You are right, but not in the way you interpret the title. Then, without using the title Messiah or Christ, he says that from now on they will **see** him, **the Son of Man,** exalted to power and rank next to God, and soon they will see him **coming** to establish fully God's Kingdom. This saying, a warning to these sceptical leaders but to the Church a reassuring promise, echoes Dan. vii. 13 and Ps. cx. 1. The Son of Man title is used to interpret what Jesus meant by **Christ** and **Son of God.**

The **high priest** tore his robe, a ceremonial way to express horror and rejection of the answer. But he really was pleased; he now had a basis of action against Jesus, something that expressed **blasphemy,** the pretender's own claim of divine role and power. They can insist to Pilate that such a claim includes the assertion of supreme political power, and so is rebellion against Rome. The rest of the Sanhedrin agree that for his blasphemy Jesus **deserves death.**

To judge by vss. 67 f., the night session was not a formal court session. The entire Sanhedrin, in Matt., expressed their hate and contempt by insulting and mocking Jesus. **Prophesy:** In Mk. and Lk. Jesus is blindfolded and then asked to tell who hit him; Matthew omits the blindfolding, so the demand to **prophesy** has no clear meaning. **You Christ:** Taunts his supposedly false claim to Messiahship and his inability to show the power expected in the Christ.

With vss. 69-75 cf. Mk. xiv. 66-72; Lk. xxii. 56-62; Jn. xviii. 15-18, 25-27. This section connects with vs. 58. While Jesus was examined in the high priest's palace, **Peter** sat in **the courtyard** around which the house was built; from the courtyard a **gateway** (vs. 71) opened on the street. A **servant girl** of the palace, convinced by his dress, his furtive manner, his voice (cf. vs. 73), or the word of someone who had been in Gethsemane, directly charged that he had been **with Jesus the Galilean** (this title was derogatory in her use; cf. vs. 71). **You also:** Does **also** mean 'as well as' Judas? Or 'another disciple' (Jn. xviii. 15)? Or does it mean: you, who brazenly come in here? Peter had hoped to escape identification. In fear and panic he first denies knowing what she means; then flinching from the hostile looks, he withdraws into the covered **gateway,** where perhaps it was darker and he was near the street if he chose to flee. In Matt. **another servant girl,** probably on duty at the gate, tells the men standing near that Peter had been with **Jesus the Nazorean** (a title not used since ii. 23; same as 'Nazarene'?). Now Peter denies knowing Jesus. But soon men standing in the gateway, perhaps guards or members of the crowd that arrested Jesus, menacingly insisted that he really belonged to Jesus' followers. Here first a reason is given; his **speech** shows he is a Galilean, so he must be a follower of the Galilean Jesus. With repeated curses and oaths he denies that he even knows Jesus. **A cock crowed:** This reminds Peter that Jesus had foreseen his inability to withstand threatening hostility. Filled with dismay and sorrow, he flees from the palace and weeps in bitter agony.

Note two things: (1) Peter was not a weakling. In the Synoptic Gospels, he alone of the Twelve had the courage to follow the arresting party to the courtyard of Caiaphas. Plainly he wanted to stay loyal to his Master. When danger caused his courage to fail, he had already shown more courage than the other disciples. (Even if, as Jn. xviii. 15 indicates, 'another disciple' accompanied him, Peter was the braver; that other disciple was known and assured of some protection in that house; Peter had no such special privilege there.) (2) Whatever Peter did in the next two days, he did not surrender to helpless remorse. When Jesus appeared to his disciples after the resurrection, Peter was with them. He had found his way back to his friends.

CHAPTER XXVII

xxvii. 1-31. JESUS CONDEMNED BY PILATE

When morning came all the chief priests and the eldeis 1 of the people took counsel against Jesus to put him to death. And they bound him, led him away, and delivered 2 him to Pilate the governor.

Then Judas, who had betrayed him, saw that he was 3 condemned, and he repented and returned the thirty silver coins to the chief priests and elders, saying, 'I 4 sinned in betraying innocent blood'. But they said, 'What is that to us? You will answer for that.' And throwing the 5 silver coins into the temple building, he departed, and went away and hung himself. The chief priests picked up 6 the coins and said, 'It is not permitted to put them into the temple treasury, since they are blood money'. So 7 after taking counsel they bought the Potter's Field with them, as a burial place for strangers. For this reason that 8 field has been called Blood Field to this day. Then was 9 fulfilled what was spoken through Jeremiah the prophet, who said, 'And they took the thirty silver coins, the price

for the man whose price was set, on whom some of the
10 sons of Israel set a price, and they paid them for the
potter's field, as the Lord commanded me'.

11 Now Jesus stood before the governor, and the governor
asked him, saying, 'Are you the King of the Jews?' Jesus
12 said, 'You say so'. And when he was accused by the chief
13 priests and elders he made no answer. Then Pilate said
to him, 'Do you not hear how many charges they bring
14 against you?' But he gave him no answer, not even one
word, so that the governor marvelled greatly.

15 At the festival the governor was accustomed to release
16 to the crowd one prisoner whom they chose. They had
17 then a notable prisoner named Barabbas. So when they
were assembled Pilate said to them, 'Whom do you wish
me to release to you, Barabbas or Jesus who is called
18 Christ?' For he knew that they had handed him over be-
19 cause of envy. As he was sitting on the judge's bench his
wife sent to him, saying, 'Have nothing to do with that
righteous man, for I have suffered much in a dream
today because of him'.

20 Now the chief priests and the elders persuaded the
21 crowds to ask for Barabbas and put Jesus to death. The
governor answered and said to them, 'Which of the two
do you wish me to release to you?' They said, 'Barabbas'.
22 Pilate said to them, 'What then shall I do with Jesus who
is called Christ?' They all said, 'Let him be crucified'.
23 He said, 'But what evil has he done?' But they kept up an
24 incessant shout, saying, 'Let him be crucified'. So when
Pilate saw that he was accomplishing nothing but that
rather a disturbance was in the making, he took water and
washed his hands in the presence of the crowd, saying,
25 'I am innocent of this blood; you will answer for it'. And
all the people answered and said, 'Let his blood be on us
26 and on our children'. Then he released Barabbas to them,
but Jesus he flogged and handed over to be crucified.

27 Then the soldiers of the governor took Jesus into the
praetorium and gathered the entire cohort around him.
28 And they stripped him and put a scarlet cloak on him,
29 and weaving a crown of thorns they put it on his head and

a staff in his right hand, and they kneeled before him and
mocked him, saying, 'Hail, King of the Jews!' And spit- 30
ting on him they took the staff and repeatedly struck him
on the head. And when they had mocked him, they 31
stripped the cloak from him and put his garments on
him, and led him away to crucify him.

With vss. 1 f. cf. Mk. xv. 1; Lk. xxii. 66; xxiii. 1; Jn. xviii.
28-32. Lk. places the entire trial after daybreak. Matt. and Mk.
report a hearing at night to formulate the charge and find
proper witnesses, and record only the fact of a second meeting.
In Jn. Jesus is questioned by Annas, held by Caiaphas until
morning, and then sent to Pilate. Probably the Sanhedrin met
both at night and at daybreak, and more happened at the second
meeting than Matt. reports. Only the purpose of the consulta-
tion, to effect the execution of Jesus (cf. xxvi. 59), is noted.

Their plan ready, the Sanhedrin delivered Jesus to Pontius
Pilate, Roman **governor** of Judea and Samaria (A.D. 26–36).
He now faces a problem strange to him, but he fails not for lack
of understanding but because he is callous with human life and
cynical in dealing with a man innocent of political crime.

Vss. 3-10 occur only in Matt. In Acts i. 18 f. Judas buys a
field with his money; a fall there kills him. 'Matthew' implies
that **Judas** was near the room in the temple area where
the Sanhedrin held their morning meeting. When Jesus was
led away bound to Pilate, Judas, seeing that Jesus had been
condemned, **repented** (changed his mind, $\mu\epsilon\tau\alpha\mu\epsilon\lambda\eta\theta\epsilon\acute{\iota}\varsigma$) in
anguish and remorse. He feels no such loyalty as to go and ask
Jesus for forgiveness, but he cannot justify his act or live with
himself. He has the tainted money given him by the Sanhedrin
to betray Jesus (xxvi. 15). As the Sanhedrin leave to ask Pilate
to execute Jesus, Judas brings the money back to them and
admits his sin. **Innocent blood:** He foresees Jesus' death, testi-
fies that it is undeserved, and confesses his share of guilt for it.

The callous Sanhedrin members have used Judas for the help
they needed. Now they grimly drop him; his guilt or fate, they
say, is his affair. He hopes that to get rid of the money will
relieve his burning sense of guilt. He throws it into the temple.
Since $\nu\alpha\acute{o}\varsigma$ generally refers to the main sanctuary rather than

the entire temple area, this hardly means that he dropped the coins in an offering box in the Court of the Women; the word 'throw' and Judas' obvious desperation seem to imply that he went into the Court of Israel, near the altar of burnt-offering, and threw the coins westward into the door of the main **temple building** (a difficult feat, to say the least). Then, in the grip of hopeless remorse, he went away and committed suicide by hanging.

The **chief priests** think it improper to put money paid to effect a man's death into the usual **temple treasury** (as κορβανᾶν means here). The sentence breathes irony; these men, so careful to keep rules about acceptable temple gifts, but callous about their tool's remorse or their part in the execution of Israel's Messiah! So as not to defile the temple's sanctity or violate the Law, they buy a **field** near Jerusalem, known as the **Potter's Field,** and make it a **burial place for strangers** who die while in Jerusalem on pilgrimage or for business. When Matt. was written, this field was also called **Blood Field.** 'Matthew' says that the connection with the blood money paid Judas was the reason the field received this name (reference to the death of Judas is excluded, since in Matt. Judas dies by hanging—no blood was shed in that suicide—and vs. 6 connects the thought of blood with Jesus' death). **To this day:** The date of writing of Matt., a few decades after the purchase of the field. The words give no help in dating the Gospel; they would fit a date as early as the sixties or as late as the nineties.

In this purchase 'Matthew' sees another fulfilment of prophecy, but the passage is not from **Jeremiah.** It is basically Zech. xi. 13 (xxvi. 15 uses Zech. xi. 12), with reminiscences of Jer. xviii. 1 ff.; xxxii. 6-9. The resulting composite passage means: The chief priests took the **thirty silver coins,** the **price** that they, as **some of the sons of Israel,** had **set** on Jesus and **paid** Judas (there is irony in this low price set on their rightful Messiah), and they used them to buy the **Potter's Field, as the Lord** God had **commanded** Jeremiah. The fulfilment of O.T. prophecy assured the Church that a divine purpose was at work in the dark events that marked the end of Jesus' earthly life.

With vss. 11-14 cf. Mk. xv. 2-5; Lk. xxiii. 2-5; Jn. xviii. 33-38 (but Jn. differs greatly). Vs. 11 connects with vs. 2. It does not directly state what charge the Sanhedrin made against Jesus, but Pilate's question implies that the charge of blasphemy (xxvi. 65), which the Roman **governor** would not consider his affair, had been re-phrased to make political and military aspects, which Jesus had set aside, stand out in his Messianic claim. Thus Jesus, claiming to be **the King of the Jews,** was liable to execution as a rebel against Rome. (Cf. Lk. xxiii. 2.) **You say so:** I could truthfully use the title, but you give it a meaning I cannot accept, so I cannot give you a clear Yes. The Sanhedrin members present kept presenting charges against Jesus, but their content is not given; it is only said that Jesus did not dignify them by a reply, even when Pilate tried to arouse Jesus to defend himself. This silence might have prejudiced the governor against him; it might have seemed an attempt to conceal guilt. But Pilate sensed the partisan hostility of the Jewish leaders (vs. 18) and noted their failure to prove the charges (vs. 23). He **marvelled** at Jesus' poise and lack of fear, and began to look for a way to release Jesus without openly shaming the Jewish leaders, whose co-operation he needed in his administration.

Jesus kept silent before the Sanhedrin except when asked the crucial question which would make clear his claim (xxvi. 64). He refused to defend himself against the charge of fomenting revolt against Rome. Why? Not simply to fulfil Isa. liii. 7, though the Church made that point, but also because fraud marked the charges made before both the Sanhedrin and Pilate. Violent argument would not show the baselessness of the accusations. He had made his appeal to the people and to their leaders; they had rejected it. He could no longer get a clear hearing for his real message. And he would not obscure the sin of condemning him by conceding that the charges were solid enough to need refutation.

With vss. 15-26 cf. Mk. xv. 6-15; Lk. xxiii. 17-25; Jn. xviii. 38 to xix. 16. Only in Matt. does Pilate's wife send a message and Pilate wash his hands. **Pilate,** though puzzled, saw no reason to condemn Jesus. Justice dictated prompt release of Jesus, but rather than offend the Jewish leaders by doing that, he tried to create a demand for the release. The Gospels give our earliest witness for the custom of releasing a **prisoner** at the Passover festival, but the custom was known elsewhere, and is credible here. To let the crowd choose the prisoner they wanted was intended to pacify the Jews at a time of national enthusiasm in crowded Jerusalem. The indefinite **they** (vs. 16) must mean the Romans, for Pilate can and does release **Barabbas** (vs. 26). Why he was so well known is not said; probably as a bandit who caused trouble for the Romans; his criminal career had a patriotic aspect and appeal. In the name **Barabbas** Christians perhaps saw a word play (of which Pilate would be unaware); it is an Aramaic word transliterated into Greek, and means 'son of the father'. The Jews choose between the real Son of the Father and the outwardly glamorous but really unimportant son of an unnamed human father. The word-play would be almost certain if the prisoner's name was Jesus Barabbas (as some good ancient textual authorities read). To whom does Pilate offer the choice? Only the Sanhedrin (vss. 12, 18)? Vss. 15, 20 show that crowds are present and the question seems addressed to them too. **Called Christ:** Pilate may mention this as a reason why they should choose Jesus.

In the story the message from **his wife** keeps Pilate occupied while the leaders persuade the crowd (vs. 20). Pilate's wife, who has come with him to Jerusalem from Caesarea, the governor's usual residence, takes a **dream** as a premonition that this prisoner can bring trouble to her and Pilate; she wants Pilate to **have nothing to do** with him, that is, release him. Had Pilate's household heard of Jesus' claims? Did she have a troubled dream and then, hearing of the prisoner, connect it with him? What she heard led her to call him a **righteous man.** This adjective **righteous** was important to 'Matthew' (cf. vss. 4, 23, 24). Jesus was innocent; everyone involved in his arrest and conviction was guilty of sin.

During this interruption, the Sanhedrin had persuaded **the crowds** to choose **Barabbas** and get Jesus condemned. What arguments they used is not said (Barabbas a loyal Jew? Jesus' teaching contrary to the Law? Jesus guilty of blasphemous claims?), but they blocked Pilate's plan to release Jesus by popular demand. The crowds ask for Barabbas; it is their privilege to choose (vs. 15); this settles the question (vs. 26). But it leaves Pilate worse off than before; he knows Jesus is not guilty. Desperate, he asks the crowd what to do with Jesus. **Called**

Christ: As in vs. 17, probably not sarcastic: 'this so-called Christ', but an attempt to stir Jewish nationalist interest in Jesus. But the crowd are tools of the Jewish leaders' purpose. (This controlled crowd was but a small fraction of the people in Jerusalem at the time.) They repeat the slogan taught them: **Let him be crucified.** Pilate's protest that Jesus has done no evil arouses still further the captive mob's sense of righteousness and wisdom; it repeats its slogan and shows signs of getting out of hand. Pilate, by failure to face facts and announce a just decision, has been pushed step by step into the disgraceful position of being controlled by unreasoning mob anger manipulated by leaders who know what they want.

Helpless and without moral courage, Pilate tries the last desperate measure of a guilty man who knows he is doing wrong; he tries to put the blame on others. By a symbolic ritual and in words he declares he is **innocent** of the blood about to be shed. Is symbolic washing done to carry his point to Jews who do not speak Greek (as Pilate did)? **You will answer:** Cf. vs. 4. They accept the responsibility, and any guilt involved, for themselves and their **children** (cf. Deut. v. 9, 29). By saying that **all** said this and by using λαός, the word for the chosen **people** as contrasted with the Gentiles, Matt. emphasizes the terrible responsibility the Jews took in demanding Jesus' execution. It is true that privilege brings responsibility, but few Jews shared in this decision, forgiveness was open even to them (Acts iii. 17), and later generations must not be blamed for what they do not approve; and Pilate by pretence of innocence cannot evade his responsibility.

When the crowd took the blame, Pilate's last feeble defence was gone. He **released Barabbas,** had Jesus scourged (a preliminary of crucifixion), and delivered him to a military detachment for crucifixion.

With vss. 27-31 cf. Mk. xv. 16-20. Pilate had handed Jesus over to his (Roman) **soldiers** to be crucified (vs. 26). They took him from the open-air place of judgment (vs. 19) into the **praetorium,** which was Pilate's residence while in Jerusalem and also a barracks for his soldiers. This praetorium was probably the fortress just inside the west gate of Jerusalem, but may have been the so-called Tower of Antonia, at the north-west corner of the temple area. **The entire cohort** (normally 600 soldiers, but perhaps not so many in this instance) indulged in some rough humour at the prisoner's expense. They knew he had been condemned for plotting to become king of the Jews (vs. 11), a title they understood in terms of earthly kingship This pitiful weakling seemed to them a ludicrous pretender. To ridicule his claim they decked him out as a king. A **scarlet** soldier's **cloak** was used to imitate the royal robe; they quickly wove a victor's wreath or **crown,** such as a triumphant king might wear, but made of thorny branches to make a painful joke of his claim; a **staff,** made perhaps of some reed plant, substituted for a royal sceptre. Then, in mock submission and homage, they **kneeled** and said in hollow pretence, **Hail, King of the Jews!** Soon they abandoned the pretence of homage, spat on Jesus, and with the staff **repeatedly** (ἔτυπτον, imperfect tense) **struck him on the head.** After this short interlude they put his clothes back on him for the walk to the place of crucifixion, and a small detachment **led him away** to execute Pilate's sentence.

What did Jesus think while all this took place? We are not told. He was silent, as he had been before the Sanhedrin and Pilate. But to 'Matthew' the story had a deeper meaning. It not only revealed how callous men can be, but in irony said to Christians something that the soldiers never suspected. To these soldiers the idea that this weakling Jesus could rightly be called a king was only a huge joke. Pilate himself, in asking Jesus about his claim (vs. 11), may have had the same scepticism, better concealed; he will publicly ridicule the claim in the title put on the cross (vs. 37). But to 'Matthew' and the Church that title told the truth; Jesus was the rightful King of Israel. He was of royal descent, the son of David (i. 1), and born to be King of the Jews (ii. 2). The Gospel presents the mocking as the unwitting expression by callous men of the truth for which believers thank God.

xxvii. 32-66. THE CRUCIFIXION AND BURIAL

32 As they went out they came upon a man of Cyrene named Simon. Him they pressed into service to carry his cross.

And when they came to a place called Golgotha (which 33
means Place of a Skull), they gave him a drink of wine 34
mixed with gall; but when he had tasted it, he refused to
drink it. After crucifying him they divided his garments 35
among themselves, casting lots; then, sitting down, they 36
kept watch over him there. And above his head they 37
placed in writing the charge against him, 'This is Jesus
the King of the Jews'.

Then two bandits were crucified with him, one on his 38
right and one on his left. The passers-by reviled him, 39
shaking their heads and saying, 'You who can destroy the 40
temple and build it in three days, save yourself, if you are
the Son of God, and come down from the cross'. Likewise 41
the chief priests also, with the scribes and elders, mocked
him and said, 'Others he saved; himself he cannot save. 42
He is king of Israel! Let him come down now from the
cross and we will believe in him. He has put his trust in 43
God; let him deliver him now if he wants him; for he
said, "I am the Son of God".' The bandits also who had 44
been crucified with him kept reviling him in the same
way.

From the sixth hour darkness came over all the land 45
until the ninth hour. About the ninth hour Jesus cried out 46
in a loud voice, saying, 'Eli, Eli, lema sabachthani', that
is, 'My God, my God, why hast thou deserted me?' Some 47
of those standing there, when they heard it, said, 'This
man is calling Elijah'. And at once one of them ran and 48
picked up a sponge and filling it with sour wine and putting it on a staff gave him a drink. But the others said, 'Let 49
us see whether Elijah comes to save him'. When Jesus had 50
cried out again in a loud voice, he gave up his spirit. And 51
behold, the curtain of the temple was torn in two from top
to bottom, and the earth was shaken, and the rocks were
split, and the tombs were opened and many bodies of the 52
saints who had fallen asleep were raised; and going forth 53
from the tombs after his rising they went into the holy
city and appeared to many. The centurion and the men 54
with him who were keeping watch over Jesus, when they
saw the earthquake and what was happening, were greatly

frightened, saying, 'This man was truly God's Son'.

55 Present there and observing from a distance were many women who had followed Jesus from Galilee and 56 ministered to him, among whom was Mary of Magdala, and Mary the mother of James and Joseph, and the mother of the sons of Zebedee.

57 Late in the afternoon there came a rich man of Arimathea, named Joseph, who also had become a disciple of 58 Jesus; he went to Pilate and asked for the body of Jesus. 59 Then Pilate commanded that it be given him. And Joseph 60 took the body and wrapped it in a clean linen cloth, and placed it in his new tomb which he had hewn in solid rock, and he rolled a large stone to the door of the tomb 61 and departed. Mary of Magdala and the other Mary were there, sitting opposite the grave.

62 On the next day, which followed the day of preparation, 63 the chief priests and the Pharisees met with Pilate, saying, 'Lord, we have remembered that that deceiver said 64 while still alive, "After three days I will rise". So command that the grave be securely guarded until the third day, lest his disciples come and steal him and tell the people, "He has risen from the dead", and the last de- 65 ception will be worse than the first.' Pilate said to them, 'Take a guard; go and make it as secure as you know 66 how'. So they went and made the grave secure, sealing the stone with the help of the guard.

With vss. 32-44 cf. Mk. xv. 21-32; Lk. xxiii. 26-43; Jn. xix. 17-27. Jesus was expected by custom to carry his cross; probably the actual custom was for the condemned criminal to carry the cross bar on which his arms would be stretched out. But weakened by agony of spirit more than by physical strain, he proved unable to carry it once the procession left the praetorium and started for Golgotha. The soldiers impressed into service (v. 41) a man passing by, a Cyrenian named **Simon** (naming him implies he became a Christian; Mk. xv. 21 implies his two sons also became Christians; cf. Rom. xvi. 13; on Cyrenians in the early Greek-speaking Church cf. Acts vi. 9; xiii. 1).

The Aramaic place-name was **Golgotha, Place of a Skull,**

so called because a burial had been discovered there or, more likely, because in shape the hillock resembled a skull. The traditional location, in the present Church of the Holy Sepulchre, may then have been outside of, but very close to, the north wall of Jerusalem. The quite ancient tradition may be correct, but has one unlikely feature; it places the spot just outside the wall; the wall, instead of enclosing the hillock, runs just beside it on the east and south, and thus leaves just outside the walls a hillock from which enemies could operate against the city's defenders.

Wine mixed with gall: (cf. Ps. lxix. 21): Given as a narcotic to deaden the pain of crucifixion. Did the women of Jerusalem, as other ancient tradition suggests, provide it? The soldiers offered Jesus the drink. He **tasted it,** realized that it contained the drug, and **refused to drink** more, preferring to remain conscious.

The central act, the crucifixion, is told in two Greek words, with no elaboration to stir the emotions; restraint actually heightens the impression. The soldiers, having done their job, **divided his garments,** as executioners were permitted to do (Jesus was stripped of all garments but one before crucifixion), and in a callous gamble that to Christians recalled Ps. xxii. 18, they cast **lots** to avoid a dispute as to who should have the best. Then they had only to wait and keep **watch** to see that no one rescued the condemned criminal.

A placard, probably prepared in the praetorium and stating **the charge** against Jesus, was placed over his head on the upright beam of the cross. The charge meant that Jesus had planned to revolt against Rome and set up an independent kingdom in Palestine. On the irony of this, see comment on vss. 27-31.

The **two bandits,** like Barabbas, may have combined hostility to Rome with robbery and plunder. Pilate uses the occasion to have them executed with Jesus, who thus was 'numbered with the transgressors' (Isa. liii. 12).

Three groups taunt Jesus as he hangs on the cross in lingering pain. (1) **The passers-by.** Cf. Ps. xxii. 7. They are not ignorant outsiders; they know and repeat the charge against Jesus (xxvi. 61). They taunt him to use his alleged divine power to save himself, and challenge his claim, cautiously expressed to the high priest (xxvi. 63 f.), and reflected elsewhere (iv. 3, 6; xvi. 16), to be **the Son of God.** They think that only weakness and helplessness can explain his suffering; they do not know the divine necessity of the cross. (2) The Sanhedrin. They too think that crucifixion proves helplessness and fraudulent claim. Though he has **saved others** (from sickness, demons, and death), he cannot **save himself.** They assume that he would promptly save himself if he could. His willing acceptance of suffering to further in death the purpose for which he had lived is an idea they cannot grasp. To them **King of Israel** and **Son of God** are preposterous claims, obviously discredited by crucifixion. Ps. xxii, used throughout this passage, appears again; its vs. 8 is used to clinch the taunt that crucifixion shows God's rejection. (3) The crucified **bandits.** They echo the taunts already reported. But while opponents show their spiritual blindness, the point that God is doing his saving work through the suffering of his Son is made by brilliant irony and effective indirect suggestion.

With vss. 45-56 cf. Mk. xv. 33-41; Lk. xxiii. 44-49; Jn. xix. 25-30. The **darkness** was from noon to 3 P.M. This does not mean that Jesus was crucified at noon, for the period of taunting (vss. 39-44) followed the crucifixion and preceded the darkness. **The land:** Here probably means **the land** of Palestine rather than all the 'earth'. This darkness was not due to an eclipse, which could not occur at Passover time. It is considered a supernatural portent, not only of Jesus' death but also of God's judgment on the sin so well illustrated in vss. 39-44. In this dark hour God may seem to forsake his Son and even Jesus must struggle with this suspicion (vs. 46), but God is alert and active to defeat men's evil plots.

The cry of Jesus comes at the end of the period of darkness. Is it hinted that at the cry the darkness begins to lift and the note of despair receives an answer? The words of the cry are the first words of Ps. xxii. 1. The text in Matt. varies, leaving it uncertain whether Jesus is thought to speak in Hebrew or Aramaic. We must avoid two easy explanations of Jesus' words. On one translation he expresses not despair but confidence: 'My God, my God, for this I was kept' (that is, I clearly know that I was kept for this moment, to die to fulfil the word of God). But Ps. xxii. 1

does not express confidence. Another view holds that when
Jesus quoted this verse he was really thinking of all the confident lines in later verses. But this ignores his inner struggle and
human inability to see the full meaning of his physical torture
and anguish of spirit. Yet even in this clouded moment he can
still say, **My God;** God must have an answer, and in anguish
and baffled spirit Jesus asks what it is. His humanity and limited
understanding show clearly as he feels left alone yet not finally
abandoned by God.

Some bystanders, whether soldiers or, more likely, Jews who
knew about Elijah, thought he was **calling Elijah** for help. One
man, apparently not because he understood the cry but out of
sympathy, held a **sponge** soaked with **sour wine** up to the lips
of the suffering man (cf. xxv. 35), the one reported expression
of human kindness in the last hours of Jesus' life (cf. vs. 34).
But the crowd discourages this act of sympathy; they want to see
whether the challenges of vss. 40, 42 will be answered. But
Elijah does not come; with another **loud** cry, indicative of
anguish of body and spirit, Jesus expires. To all but the eye of
faith he is a defeated, discredited pretender.

But note three indications of a different answer.

(1) Vss. 51-53: The rending of the **curtain in the temple,**
either the curtain before the Holy of Holies (cf. Heb. ix. 8; x.
20), or the one at the entrance to the Holy Place. The latter,
which could be seen by looking through the porchway of the
building, may be meant here if a visible rending is in mind; only
a specially chosen priest (cf. Lk. i. 9) could go into the Holy
Place and see the curtain before the Holy of Holies. The point
of this story is that by his death Jesus has opened a new access
to God for his people. With this sign goes a portent of nature:
an earthquake that split rocks in two. Dead saints, honoured
dead of Jewish tradition, rose; the earthquake **opened** their
tombs and they could emerge. But they did emerge and appear
only after Jesus had risen; the story infers that Christ's death
opens the tombs and gives life to the dead (cf. Jn. vi. 25-29). Is
the phrase **after his rising** intended to preserve the place of
Jesus as the first born from the dead (Col. i. 18; Rev. i. 5)? This
puzzling story may originally have been a figurative teaching,
but 'Matthew' takes it as a real event.

(2) Vs. 54: The fearful tribute of the soldiers (Mk. and Lk. tell only of the centurion). They see divine power active in the nature portents and declare in terror that **This man was truly God's Son.** They would not mean by these words what 'Matthew' would mean, but he sees in them an expression of faith which Christians can hear with deeper understanding.

(3) Vss. 55 f.: The many women standing at a distance. Silent, watching in mute sorrow, love, and faith, they witness what happens (Simon, vs. 32; Joseph, vs. 57; and the centurion, if he became a believer, are other possible sources for such stories). Later they can tell others what they have seen. They ministered to Jesus in Galilee (Lk. viii. 3), and then came loyally with him to Jerusalem. **Magdala:** A city on the west coast of the Sea of Galilee. **Mary the mother of James and Joseph:** Hardly the mother of Jesus and of his four brothers (xiii. 55); she would hardly have been mentioned second, without reference to her relationship to Jesus. This is rather 'the other Mary' (vs. 61; xxviii. 1). **The mother of the sons of Zebedee:** Ambitious for her sons (xx. 20 f.), but loyal to Jesus. These women can stand unmolested where the disciples if present would have met with hate and mistreatment from hostile Jews.

With vss. 57-61 cf. Mk. xv. 42-47; Lk. xxiii. 50-56; Jn. xix. 38-42. Jesus died shortly after 3 P.M. on Friday (vss. 46, 50). The Sabbath would begin at sundown; before it came and all work ceased, the body should be buried. Moreover, Deut. xxi. 23 forbade leaving the body of an executed criminal to hang there overnight. **A rich man** took action; cf. Isa. liii. 9, which Christians certainly recalled when telling the story. **Arimathea:** A little over twenty miles north-west of Jerusalem. But **Joseph** had moved to Jerusalem, for he had a **new tomb** there which he had **hewn in** the **solid rock,** probably just north of the city. As a man of wealth and standing, Joseph could act to bury Jesus. At the risk of incurring Pilate's hostility, he **asked for the body,** and obtained it; ancient rulers sometimes gave the body of an executed criminal to friends for burial. The adjective **clean** suggests the respect and reverence with which he performed the burial. When the body had been placed in the tomb, no doubt on the rock shelf already hewn out for that purpose,

Joseph rolled the **large,** heavy, flat circular **stone** into place; it
rolled out of a prepared groove or slot on one side and covered
the entrance. Perhaps his servants helped him, but there is no
hint that any leading disciples were present (cf. Jn. xix. 39).

The two Marys of vs. 56 (and xxviii. 1) are still watching;
later they can tell of the burial. Apparently the mother of the
sons of Zebedee and the other women (vs. 55) had left.

Vss. 62-66 is one of four passages (cf. xxvii. 19, 24 f.; xxviii.
11-15) found only in Matt. and dealing with Pilate's relation to
Jesus. The story implies that the grave was later found empty
and that Jewish leaders started the story of the stolen body to
discredit the resurrection witness of the Church.

The day of preparation: A name for Friday, on which preparations for the Sabbath were made. Even on the Sabbath, the
Sanhedrin, clearly at their initiative, meet with Pilate. They
have heard that Jesus promised to rise **after three days** (previously Matt. has said 'on the third day'; cf. vs. 64: **until the
third day;** resurrection on the third day is meant in both
phrases). **That deceiver:** His disciples, they think, also lack
integrity. So they want the grave guarded until **after three
days,** to prevent the disciples from stealing Jesus' body and
spreading the false rumour that he has risen from the dead. **The
last deception:** A false rumour of resurrection. **The first:**
Apparently the false claim to Messiahship and Sonship.

Take a guard: The Greek $\check{\epsilon}\chi\epsilon\tau\epsilon$ can mean: 'You have' a
guard. But the Jewish leaders seem to have no police authority
at the grave; they want a guard of Roman soldiers, which Pilate
puts at their disposal. **Sealing the stone:** The unbroken seal
would show that no one could have entered the tomb. The guard
was also to remain on duty until the three days had passed
(cf. xxvii. 64; xxviii. 11).

The story may be doubted, not because it reports Jewish
action on the Sabbath (the leaders spent most of the Passover
night in machinations against Jesus), but because the leaders
speak freely of the promised resurrection. Jesus never spoke of
this publicly; unless Judas had reported his promise, or xxvi. 61
was understood, as in Jn. ii. 21, to apply to his resurrection, they
would not have known of it. The apologetic value of the story,
however, is clear. It prepared for the story of the empty grave

and so supported the resurrection witness. And it indicates that one fact was common to Jews and disciples in later debates: On the third day the body of Jesus was found not to be in the tomb.

CHAPTER XXVIII

xxviii. 1-15. THE RESURRECTION FACT

1 After the Sabbath, as day dawned on the first day of the week, Mary of Magdala and the other Mary came to see 2 the grave. And behold, a great earthquake occurred; for an angel of the Lord descended from heaven, and ap-3 proached and rolled away the stone and sat upon it. His appearance was like lightning and his garment white as 4 snow. The guards shook for fear of him and became like 5 dead men. The angel answered and said to the women, 'Do not you be afraid, for I know that you are looking for 6 Jesus the crucified one. He is not here; for he has risen, 7 as he said. Come! See the place where he lay. And go quickly and tell his disciples, "He has risen from the dead, and behold, he precedes you to Galilee; there you 8 will see him". Behold, I have told you.' And they departed quickly from the tomb with fear and great joy, and ran to 9 report to his disciples. And behold, Jesus met them, saying, 'Hail!' And they came to him, took hold of his feet, and 10 worshipped him. Then Jesus said to them, 'Do not be afraid; go and tell my brothers to depart to Galilee, and there they will see me'.

11   As they were going, behold, some of the guard went into the city and reported to the chief priests all that had 12 happened. And when they had assembled with the elders and formed a plan, they gave the soldiers large sums 13 of money, saying, 'Tell people: "His disciples came by 14 night and stole him while we were sleeping". And if this reaches the ear of the governor, we will pacify him and

keep you out of trouble.' So they took money and did as 15
they had been instructed. And this report has been circulated among Jews to this day.

With vss. 1-10 cf. Mk. xvi. 1-8; Lk. xxiv. 1-11; Jn. xx. 1-18.
These Gospels have no parallels to vss. 2-4, 9 f., and differ in
other respects. **After the Sabbath:** ὀψέ may mean 'Late on' the
Sabbath, but it sometimes means **after,** which fits here, for only
after the Sabbath ended at sundown on Saturday could the women
properly go to the grave. How long they waited after the Sabbath ended is indicated by the following phrase, **as day dawned**
on Sunday. Has 'Matthew' shortened a tradition (cf. Mk.) in
which the women bought spices after sunset on Saturday, and
went to the grave at dawn on Sunday? But Matt. has no word
of spices. The two women go only **to see the grave.** They had
seen Jesus' death and burial (xxvii. 56, 61); they are now to
become witnesses also of Jesus' resurrection.

The **earthquake** does not explain how the grave was opened;
a strong, visible **angel from heaven** did that. It indicates
rather, as in xxvii. 51, the significance of the event; God was
actively working through the angel. The **stone** was **rolled
away,** not that Jesus might emerge from the grave—it is implied that he had already risen—but to let the women enter and
see that Jesus' body was not there. They had seen him placed
in the tomb; now, it is implied, they entered and saw that it was
empty. In Matt. the grave was not opened until they came, so
no one could have removed his body by stealth. He must have
risen and left before the tomb was opened.

The angel's **white garment** indicates purity and his dazzling
brightness the presence and working of divine power. **Fear**
seizes the Roman soldiers on guard. In the Bible fear is a many-
sided word. Here it is blind, paralysing terror, which the angel
and Jesus tell the women not to have (vss. 5, 10). But the true
worshipper has a wholesome, inevitable fear, a reverent awe in
the presence of God or his messengers; this the women have
(vs. 8); and such fear does not paralyse the believer but may be
combined with joy at God's majesty and work. **Do not you be
afraid: You** is emphatic; you women must not feel blind terror
as the soldiers do. The angel's coming brings no threat to the

women. They have come to see the grave, drawn there by sorrow, love, and, perhaps, inarticulate hope. For their loyalty and persistent love they hear first the news of the resurrection. **As he said:** Contains a light reproach, in view of xii. 40; xvi. 21; xvii. 23; xx. 19; xxvi. 32; but the tone is reassuring, and they are invited to **see the** burial **place** and be fully convinced that what Jesus promised has really occurred. Then they must hurry to **tell** the Eleven the glad news and give them a special message: Jesus will go on ahead to Galilee; they will see him there (xxvi. 32). This assumes that the disciples are still in Jerusalem; since only the Sabbath has intervened since Jesus was buried, they have had no opportunity to leave. **Behold, I have told you:** Seems addressed to the women; the angel has fulfilled his mission. The women, convinced that Jesus has risen, hurry off to inform the disciples.

Behold occurs four times in vss. 1-10, to mark the importance and striking character of the events. At the fourth use the risen Jesus meets the women (only in Matt.). Since Jesus only echoes the angel's words, is this a later form of an angelic appearance? Jesus greets them. They recognize him instantly, approach him, and grasp his feet to cling to him (cf. Jn. xx. 17); they worship him, for they sense that the risen Christ is the risen Lord with power and authority (vs. 18). He reassures them and gives them the message to the disciples already received from the angel. **My brothers:** Though risen, he still is bound with them in ties of brotherhood; in the resurrection his humanity has been taken up into a new and glorified life in which his sympathy and power will find wider and more effective expression.

The modern student has many questions about the N.T. resurrection narratives. He cannot combine them all in one consistent scheme and make them convincing to modern men. But there are two problems here. One is the varied and unscientific witness of the sources. One angel (or man) or two? Did a visible angel push a huge stone out of the way? Did Jesus rise with the same physical body he had when he died (there is evidence that the early Church usually did not think this)? In the excitement and inexpressible enthusiasm of the first days after the resurrection faith seized the shaken group of disciples, they were not

capable of cold analysis and control of the evidence. The other
problem goes deeper. What kind of a world is this? If it is an
impersonal machine, if reality is limited to what man can grasp
and state, then the resurrection makes no sense. It seems possible only to men with vivid faith in the living God, who works
with power to fulfil his holy and gracious purpose. This faith
the interpreter of the Gospel must have to know what these
early witnesses were saying. With its help the central message
of the resurrection becomes convincing, and only in this
message does the rise and power of the early Church find
explanation.

Vss. 11-15 (only in Matt.) connect with xxvii. 62-66 and
xxviii. 4. The soldiers, recovering from paralysing terror at the
sight of the angel, had to report the opening of the tomb. They
did so promptly; some of their group entered the city at
the time the hastening women did. Though they seem to be
Roman soldiers, Pilate had put them at the disposal of the
chief priests and Pharisees (xxvii. 62, 65), so they **reported
to the chief priests.** They assembled the entire Sanhedrin.
It decided to spread the report that while the soldiers on
duty slept (the penalty for this was death), the disciples of
Jesus had stolen his body. 'Matthew' understands that sub-
stantial payments of money, and promises to keep Pilate from
punitive action if he heard the story, induced the soldiers to
do as told.

To this day: Shows why this section was inserted. The Jews
were attacking the resurrection story as a deliberate deception;
Jesus died, and stayed dead, but the disciples stole his body and
then announced his resurrection. There was Christian contact
with Judaism when Matt. was written, and vigorous debate was
going on between the two groups; the Jews could not deny the
story of the empty tomb; they explained it as a fraud; and
'Matthew' countered with this story of the bribing of the guard.
The weakness in this story is, first, that it assumes that the
Jewish leaders had advance notice of the resurrection, and
second, that in it the guard consented to the circulation of a
story which made them liable to the death penalty. The solid
fact that emerges is that the tomb was empty; the transformed
attitude of the disciples was connected with that fact; to this

situation no theory does justice which limits the resurrection to psychological recovery by the disciples or a purely spiritual survival by Jesus.

xxviii. 16-20. JESUS COMMANDS A WORLD MISSION

16 **Now the eleven disciples went to Galilee, to the moun-**
17 **tain where Jesus had directed them, and when they saw**
him they fell before him in worship, but some doubted.
18 **And Jesus came near and spoke to them, saying, 'All**
authority has been given to me in heaven and on earth.
19 **Go therefore and make disciples of all nations, baptizing**
them in the name of the Father and of the Son and of the
20 **Holy Spirit, teaching them to observe all that I have com-**
manded you; and behold, I will be with you all the days
to the end of the age.'

Only Matt. definitely reports that the risen Jesus first appeared to the Eleven in Galilee. Mk. xiv. 28; xvi. 7 clearly imply that he did, and if xvi. 8 was not Mark's original conclusion, Mk. must have reported some such appearance as Matt. gives. In Lk. and Jn. the Eleven first saw the risen Jesus in Jerusalem. 1 Cor. xv. 4-7 gives no clear help. Its reference to the third day supports the tradition of the empty tomb, and mention of a first appearance to Peter may indicate a Jerusalem tradition. Had the disciples rallied and waited in Jerusalem (Lk. xxiv. 49; Acts i. 4), there would have been no place for the Galilean appearance. Probably the Galilean appearance came first for the Eleven, and later, when the Church assembled in Jerusalem and further appearances occurred there, the northward journey from Jerusalem to Galilee and the return to Jerusalem seemed negligible and were dropped. **The Eleven:** Judas was gone (xxvii. 5). **The mountain:** Not mentioned in xxvi. 32; xxviii. 7, 10, but the words here imply that one had been specified. The Greek may mean: 'the mountain where Jesus had given them commands' in the Sermon on the Mount (v. 1), but probably means: 'the mountain to which Jesus had told them to go'. As they arrived they saw him there (vs. 7), recognized him, and **fell prostrate before him in worship.** At least most of the Eleven did. Does οἱ δέ mean that 'others' besides the Eleven were present, and doubted whether this was really the risen Jesus? No; it means that **some** of the Eleven did not at once recognize him. This hints that there was some mysterious change in the appearance of the risen Jesus.

Jesus **came near**—in reverence they had not tried to approach too close—and gave his final instructions and promise. He has full **authority** to claim their lifelong active service. The authority embodied in his words (vii. 29), mighty deeds (viii. 8 f.), and forgiveness of sins (ix. 6) was recognized during his ministry, and he had asserted sweeping authority in xi. 27. But now he claims more complete authority. This authority (1) rests upon his ministry, death, and resurrection; (2) is universal, extending over all people and all of God's creatures in heaven; and so (3) excludes any rival lord. Cf. Dan. vii. 13 f.; Phil. ii. 9-11.

With such complete and universal authority, the Risen One can properly give the instructions in vss. 19 f.; many manuscripts omit οὖν **(therefore),** probably wrongly, but in any case the meaning is that Jesus has full right to say what follows. **Go:** The mission to Israel (x. 5 f.; cf. xv. 24) must now become a world-wide mission. **Make disciples:** Teach them, win them to obedient faith, make them active members of the larger group of disciples.

What ministries do the Eleven (and other preachers) owe to those won to faith? Vss. 19 f. name two:

1. Baptism. Unless *Didache* vii. 1 dates from the first century, which seems doubtful, this passage in Matt. is the only first-century occurrence of this trinitarian baptismal formula. Baptism 'in the name of Jesus' is common in Acts; the added reference to the Father and the Holy Spirit is surprising. But John the Baptist promised that the Christ would give the Spirit (iii. 11); this verse attests that the trinitarian formula is not alien to the work of Jesus or the mind of 'Matthew', though the complete lack of other evidence for the use of this formula in the Apostolic Church raises a serious question whether Jesus explicitly commanded its regular use. (For other N.T. passages

where Father, Son, and Holy Spirit are mentioned together, see
1 Cor. xii. 4-6; 2 Cor. xiii. 14, the most striking example; and
1 Pet. i. 2.

Baptism **in the name of** means baptism which (1) clearly
names Father, Son, and Holy Spirit; (2) confesses the full right
of Father, Son, and Holy Spirit to worship and loyalty; (3)
gratefully acknowledges the gracious blessings given by the
Father through the Son by the working of the Holy Spirit; and
(4) pledges obedience to Father, Son, and Holy Spirit. The
formula is not a denial of monotheism; it recognizes that God
has opened the way to faith and salvation by the historical work
of the Son carried forward by the Holy Spirit.

2. The other ministry of the disciples is continued **teaching.**
Converts won to faith and baptized are to be taught **to observe
all** that Jesus has taught. The purpose of this continuous Christian education is to effect real obedience to Christ. Here we see
why this Gospel has emphasized so much the teaching of Jesus.

The Gospel ends with a promise. The risen Christ will be
with the disciples wherever they go every day of their work until
the end comes and the perfect eternal Kingdom is established.
His resurrection has set him free to be present, not visibly but
really, with all his loyal people everywhere. This Gospel includes
the assurance of his exaltation to the Father and the promise of
his coming at the end to complete the divine purpose. But
though exalted, he is no absentee Lord; his presence, authority,
and power are with his people and especially with his witnesses,
and that presence will be the source of their success.

The Eleven did not undertake systematic evangelistic work
among all nations; in Acts it is the Hellenistic Jewish Christians,
and especially Paul, who carry on that work (cf. Gal. ii. 8). The
Eleven tried first to win their own people. They did not reject
the world mission (they acknowledged Paul as the legitimate
interpreter of Christ), but carried the gospel 'to the Jews first'.
The world mission had its basis in Jesus' expectation and
message, but 'Matthew' sums up here the final meaning rather
than the literal words of the teaching and ministry of Christ.

INDEX

This Index lists all passages of the Bible and other ancient sources to which the Introduction and Commentary refer, except that, in indexing the Commentary, references to verses in the passage of Matt. which is under discussion are not included. For example, in dealing with xiv. 1-12, the reference to pp. 167 f. (in heavy type) will show that these pages give the translation of this passage and that the Commentary on it follows, beginning on p. 168, but the reference on that page to vs. 2 is not listed in the Index, since the reader interested in vs. 2 will know where to look for the basic commentary on that verse and its context.

OLD TESTAMENT

INDEX

GOSPEL ACCORDING TO ST. MATTHEW

INDEX

INDEX

INDEX

JEWISH WRITINGS

EARLY CHRISTIAN WRITINGS